מבוא למסורה הטברנית
INTRODUCTION TO THE TIBERIAN MASORAH

THE SOCIETY OF BIBLICAL LITERATURE
MASORETIC STUDIES

edited by
Harry M. Orlinsky

Number 5

מבוא למסורה הטברנית
INTRODUCTION TO THE TIBERIAN MASORAH

by
Israel Yeivin

SCHOLARS PRESS

מבוא למסורה הטברנית

INTRODUCTION TO THE TIBERIAN MASORAH

by

Israel Yeivin

translated and edited by

E. J. Revell

Published by

SCHOLARS PRESS

for

The Society of Biblical Literature

and

The International Organization for Masoretic Studies

מבוא למסורה הטברנית
INTRODUCTION TO THE TIBERIAN MASORAH

by

Israel Yeivin

translated and edited by

E. J. Revell

Library of Congress Cataloging in Publication Data
Yeivin, Israel.
Introduction to the Tiberian Masorah.

(Masoretic studies ; no. 5 ISSN 0145-2746)
Translation of Mavo la-masorah ha-tavranit.
Bibliography: p.
Includes index.
1. Masorah. 2. Hebrew language—Accents and accentuation. I. Title. II. Series.
BS718.Y4413 221.4′4 79-24755
ISBN 0-89130-373-1
ISBN 0-89130-374-X (pbk.)

TRANSLATOR'S PREFACE

The study of the text of the Hebrew Bible in the first half of this century was almost exclusively concerned with the attempt to reconstruct a form of that text which might have existed prior to the production of the Greek translation. The Masorah was widely considered to result from an academic recension or reconstruction of the tradition made long after the end of the Talmudic period. Even those with less extreme views generally regarded it as without significant roots in the past, and hence of no interest to the "scientific" student of the Hebrew text.

Early materials discovered at Qumran and elsewhere have shown that the view of the history of the biblical text which gave rise to such ideas was oversimplified, and there is a growing appreciation of the fact that the Masoretes did not revise, but preserved a tradition which had developed over a very long period. Even now, however, it is still widely considered more valuable for the serious student of the Hebrew Bible to study Greek, or Akkadian, or any Semitic language, than to learn anything about the manuscripts imperfectly reproduced in the edition which he studies, and if such a student should look for an up to date and comprehensive introduction to the Masorah, he would find it only in Hebrew.

The mere existence of such a gap in the English literature on the Hebrew Bible is sufficient reason for undertaking a translation of Israel Yeivin's excellent *Introduction to the Tiberian Masorah*. In addition, however, it is hoped that this book, by demonstrating the early origin of some strands of the masoretic tradition, and the complexity of its development, will lead increasing numbers to realize that the study of the history of the Masoretic Text is a necessary part of research into its antecedents.

Dr. Yeivin has very kindly allowed me to include my own opinion in one or two cases where it differed from his, and I have added a few explanatory notes and an index. Otherwise the translation follows the Hebrew original, and the same paragraph numbering is used. Dr. Yeivin very kindly read over the first draught, and also proofread the final typescript, preventing many errors on both occasions. Prof. H. M. Orlinsky has also suggested many corrections and improvements. I am most grateful to both scholars for their help. I am indebted to various others for suggestions and assistance, but particularly to Dagnija Karklins, who knows no Hebrew, but nevertheless undertook the final typing. The clarity and accuracy of her work deserves the gratitude of every reader, as well as my own.

E. J. Revell

LIST OF ABBREVIATIONS

1. General

bA	Ben Asher
BHK	*Biblia Hebraica*...ed. R. Kittel...P. Kahle. Third and later editions (1937 and later).
BHS	*Biblia Hebraica Stuttgartensia*...ed. K. Elliger et W. Rudolph...masoram elaboravit G. E. Weil, Stuttgart, 1969 on.
bN	Ben Naftali
LXX	The Greek translation of the Hebrew Bible (Septuagint).
Mm	Masorah magna (see #126-130)
Mp	Masorah parva (see #111-125)
MS(S)	Manuscript(s)
RV	The Revised version of the Authorized English Translation of the Bible.
TB	Talmud Babli
TY	Talmud Yerushalmi

2. Sigla of MSS

A	The Aleppo MS (see #26)
B	British Museum MS Or. 4445 (see #31)
C	The Cairo Codex of the Prophets (see #32)
L	Leningrad MS B19a (see #30)
L^1-L^{21}	Other MSS from Leningrad (see #35)
N	New York, Jewish Theological Seminary MS 232 (see #53)
P	Leningrad MS B3, a codex of the Prophets with Babylonian vowel signs, dated 1228 S.E. = 916 C.E.
R	Karlsruhe MS #3. Codex Reuchlinianus of the Prophets, dated 1105-6. "Expanded Tiberian" pointing.
S	Jerusalem, National and University Library MS Heb 24° 5702, formerly MS Sassoon 507 (see #33)
S^1	MS Sassoon 1053 (see #34)
V	The Venice Bible edition of 1524-5 (see #60)

3. The Books of the Bible

Gen	Genesis	Nah	Nahum
Ex	Exodus	Hab	Habakkuk
Lev	Leviticus	Zeph	Zephaniah
Nu	Numbers	Hag	Haggai
Dt	Deuteronomy	Zech	Zechariah
Jos	Joshua	Mal	Malachi
Jud	Judges	Ps	Psalms
1S	1st Samuel	Prov	Proverbs
2S	2nd Samuel	Job	Job
1K	1st Kings	Song	Song of Songs
2K	2nd Kings	Rut	Ruth
Is	Isaiah	Lam	Lamentations
Jer	Jeremiah	Qoh	Ecclesiastes
Ez	Ezekiel	Est	Esther
Hos	Hosea	Dan	Daniel
Joel	Joel	Ezra	Ezra
Amos	Amos	Neh	Nehemiah
Ob	Obadiah	1C	1st Chronicles
Jon	Jonah	2C	2nd Chronicles
Mic	Micah		

Note on Transcription.

Common Hebrew words are given in standard anglicized spelling. Otherwise the Hebrew consonants are represented by ʾ (medial *alef* only) *b*, *g*, *d*, *h*, *w*, *z*, *ḥ*, *ṭ*, *y*, *k*, *l*, *m*, *n*, *s*, *ᶜ*, *p*, *ṣ*, *q*, *r*, *ś*, *š*, *t*. Vowels are represented by *u* (*shureq* or *qibbuṣ*), *o* (*ḥolem*), *ɔ* (*qameṣ*), *a* (*pataḥ*), *ɛ* (*segol*), *e* (*ṣere*), *i* (*ḥireq*), *ə* (*shewa*), *ɔ̆*, *ă*, *ɛ̆* (*ḥaṭef shewa*).

CONTENTS

INTRODUCTION

This book is intended as an introduction to the Masorah. The Hebrew words, מסורה, מסורת, have a variety of meanings; but in English, "Masorah" refers only to the system of notes and signs used to preserve the text of the Hebrew Bible, and the way it was written, from change. This is the main subject of this book. The scholars who developed and transmitted these notes and signs are called "Masoretes", and worked in the period 500-950 CE. They were also responsible for the vowel signs and accent signs found in many Biblical texts. Vowel signs were used in all forms of literature, and accents were used in Rabbinic literature, and sometimes in poetry, as well as in the Bible. Masoretic notes, however, are found only in texts of the Bible and in the Aramaic translation or Targum.

There were three schools of Masoretes, called the Tiberian, Palestinian, and Babylonian, which differed from each other in their methods of formulating notes and in the signs they used for vowels and accents. This book concentrates on the system of the Tiberian school, the best known of the three. Today this is the "received tradition" accepted by all Jewish communities, and even in early times it was accepted by most. Even within the Tiberian tradition itself we can distinguish a "standard tradition" (that represented by the received text of the Hebrew Bible), and non-standard traditions. MSS showing non-standard traditions differ from the received tradition in various ways. They may show differences because they were designed to be used not as "Model Codices" against which other texts could be corrected, but as private copies. Such texts often show signs of laziness and lack of care over the text and the vowel and accent signs. Some texts show no accent signs, no vowel signs, or no masoretic notes. In other texts the vowel signs may reflect the pronunciation customary in the scribe's community. Examples are texts which confuse *pataḥ* with *qameṣ*, or *ṣere* with *segol* (as in the Sefardic pronunciation), or *pataḥ* with *segol* or with vocal *shewa* (as in the Yemenite pronunciation). Manuscripts of this sort are of interest for the study of the pronunciation of different communities, but are beyond the scope of the present work.

Some manuscripts differing from the standard show an "expanded" Tiberian tradition of pointing (sometimes called the "Tibero-Palestinian" system). In MSS of this sort other letters are treated as *begad-kefat* and marked with *rafe* when preceded by a vowel or with (light) *dagesh* otherwise, and special signs are used to show whether *alef*, *waw*, and *yod* represent consonants or vowels; and the like. These expansions are intended to make the Tiberian system indicate more closely the pronunciation of particular groups. These texts also are of interest for the study of specific problems, but they, too, are outside the bounds of the present study, which concentrates on the standard Tiberian tradition. The book surveys the most important MSS which represent this standard tradition, and describes the "apparati" added to the letters of the Biblical text: the notes of the Masorah, the system of accents, and the use of *gaᶜya* (often called *metheg*). The vocalization signs and their history are beyond the concern of this study. However two features of pointing, *shewa* and *dagesh*, are included, since they are the subject of many masoretic comments.

The purpose of this survey of the standard Tiberian tradition is, from one point of view, to understand the Masorah in use today. That is, to read and understand the masoretic notes printed in the editions known as "Rabbinic Bibles" (מקראות גדולות), and in some others, such as BHK and BHS; and to understand the accents of the 21 Books and the system according to which *gaᶜya* is used. From another point of view an attempt is made to deal with the history of these features, and the history of the systems of notes and signs: that is, to provide a historical survey, as far as our knowledge permits, of the development of the Masorah and its signs, and to survey briefly the systems used in the most important MSS.

Besides the MSS, information provided by the manuscript fragments from the Cairo Geniza is also surveyed. These fragments, found in the Geniza of the synagogue of Fusṭāt ("Old Cairo") and now preserved in various libraries, are, in this work, treated separately from the Manuscripts which come from other sources. As a general rule, Manuscripts provide more text than Geniza fragments, (which generally consist of only a few pages), and in many cases the origin of the text can be determined. Some Geniza fragments are older, however. Our knowledge of some subjects comes from Manuscripts of others from Geniza fragments.

Cross references within this book are made to the numbered sections (as #32, #304). Quotations from the Bible are mostly taken from A, but L and V are also used. If a particular reading appears in only one or two MSS, they are identified by sigla before the verse reference (as L, Ruth 4:4).

This book was originally designed for use in a course on the Tiberian tradition taught by the author at the Hebrew University. Both the text of the book, and the bibliography provided, concentrate on the most basic materials. Some material has been added for the guidance of those interested in obtaining a deeper knowledge of the subject, but much material is omitted, and much literature not referred to. The material given is mostly derived from basic studies of the subject, such as Wickes' book on the accents of the 21 Books. Most of the material printed in the author's articles on the MSS of the Bible and on the Masorah (Yeivin, 1968b, 1968c) is included. The translation was made from a new edition of the text specially expanded and corrected by the author. Many of the errors corrected were pointed out to the author by his friends, or by readers, and he is most grateful to them for this help. Among them are N. Allony, Y. Ben David, M. Breuer, Shulammit Elizur, and M. Medan. The main additions are the paragraphs on *nesigah* (#307-310) and the appendix on *shewa* and *dagesh*.

PART I

MANUSCRIPTS OF THE BIBLE

LITERATURE

General

1. C.D. Ginsburg, *Introduction to the Massoretico-Critical Edition of the Hebrew Bible* (Ginsburg, 1897). A detailed survey of several dozen MSS, mostly from the British Museum, dating from the tenth century on. Ginsburg 1897a provides photographs of 15 of these MSS.

P. Kahle, *Masoreten des Westens I* (Kahle, 1927). Describes 14 Biblical MSS in the Leningrad Public Library dating from 930-1122, with a photograph of each.

P. Kahle, *The Cairo Geniza* (second edition, Kahle 1959). Describes the Cairo Geniza and its discovery, different traditions of Hebrew pointing, MSS ascribed to the ben Asher family, a number of printed editions of the Bible, etc.

P. Kahle, *Der hebräische Bibeltext seit Franz Delitzsch* (Kahle, 1961). Describes important MSS, C, A, L, and others, and discusses a number of the problems they present.

Articles in *Textus I* by I. ben-Zvi, M.H. Goshen-Gottstein, and D.S. Loewinger (Ben Zvi 1960, Goshen-Gottstein 1960, Loewinger 1960) demonstrate the connection of the Aleppo MS with Aharon ben Asher, and analyze some of its features.

I. Yeivin, Article in the אנציקלופדיה מקראית "Bible: Manuscripts of the Bible" (Yeivin, 1968b). A survey of MSS from the Tiberian school, with some from other schools.

I. Yeivin, כתר ארם-צובה (Yeivin, 1968) pp.357-375.

Describes a number of early MSS showing traditions related to that of A.

M.H. Goshen-Gottstein, "Biblical MSS in the U.S." (Goshen-Gottstein, 1962). Classifies and describes the most important Biblical MSS and Geniza fragments in the U.S.

Descriptions of Biblical MSS are also given in the catalogues of various libraries, especially those which have many of them, such as the British Museum, the Bodleian Library in Oxford, the library of the Jewish Theological Seminary in New York, and libraries in Parma (de Rossi collection), Paris, Cambridge, etc. The very important collection in the Saltikov-Schchedrin Library in Leningrad is only partly described in a catalogue (Harkavy-Strack 1975).

Facsimiles

2. Photographs of many Biblical MSS can be found in these catalogues, and in Birnbaum 1971. Photographs of several MSS appear in Ginsburg, 1897a, Kahle, 1927, and Yeivin, 1968, as indicated above. A complete facsimile reproduction of the Aleppo Codex (A) has been published by the Hebrew University Bible Project (Goshen-Gottstein, 1976), and facsimiles of L and C have been published by the Makor Press (Loewinger, 1970, 1971).

Scholarly Editions of the Bible based on MSS

3. S. Baer and F. Delitzsch, 1869-1895. (The complete text of the Prophets and Writings appeared, but only Genesis from the Torah). This text was prepared by Baer following his own system. It contains notes on textual variants in the MSS, variants between ben Asher and ben Naftali, etc., but they are not always trustworthy.

Kennicott, 1776, see #56.

J.B. de Rossi, 1784, see #56. De Rossi's work completes that of Kennicott. Both list variants from hundreds of MSS, but only variants in the letters of the text.

C.D. Ginsburg, 1908, 1926 (see #56). Lists variants in letters, and in vowel signs and accent signs, from 75 MSS and 19 early printed editions, but is not always trustworthy.

Printed Editions of the Bible

4. C. Rabin, Article in אנציקלופדיה מקראית "Bible: Printed Editions of the Bible" (Rabin, 1968). Gives a complete survey with Bibliography. Information can also be found in Ginsburg, 1897 (a detailed survey of 24 early editions of the Bible), Habermann, 1957, and Goldschmidt, 1950.

THE SCROLL AND THE CODEX

5. The scroll was the only accepted format for a Jewish book until the end of the Talmudic period (c. 600 CE). This was a strip of parchment, usually written on one side only, and rolled up. The codex form (the modern book form, made up of a number of separate sheets) does not seem to have been used until about 700 CE. As commonly occurs, the older form continued to be used for religious purposes, so the ancient scroll form continues in use in the Torah scrolls read in the synagogue today. Here also the text is preserved in its original form, without Masorah, accents, or vowel signs. (#7).

Today scrolls are used only for reading the Torah portions in the liturgy of the synagogue, books being used for ordinary reading, but before the codex form came into use no such distinction could be made. Only scrolls were in use, so some were used for liturgical purposes, and some were not.

As time went on, scholars began to add masoretic notes, and vowel and accent signs, to those scrolls which were not used for liturgical purposes, and we find fragments of such scrolls in the Geniza. However, the use of the scroll form for other than liturgical purposes decreased progressively as time went on.

The rules for the writing of Biblical texts are preserved in the Talmud, in the later tractate *Masseket Soferim* and in other later halakic works. These concern the material on which the text was written (leather or parchment), the form of the book, the letters, and so on. These rules were originally concerned with the writing of scrolls for liturgical use. Many of them were, however, applied to the writing of codices. Carefully written codices follow them quite closely; others less so.

The Scroll

6. The oldest known Hebrew scrolls are the "Dead Sea Scrolls" from the area of Qumran, among which are some Biblical scrolls. They show some of the conventions which became standard in later Biblical scrolls, for instance paragraph divisions, which are similar, in most cases, to the masoretic *petuḥot* and *setumot* (#74). However, it appears that, as a general rule, the conventions used in the writing of Biblical MSS did not differ from those used for other MSS. Fitzmyer, 1975, provides a good directory to information on the Dead Sea Scrolls.

7. Scrolls intended for liturgical use in the synagogue are called ספרי תורה, "books of Torah". Scrolls of this sort may contain the Torah itself, the five *megillot* (scrolls: The Song of Songs, Ruth, Lamentations, Ecclesiastes, and Esther--the scroll of Esther being particularly common) and *hafṭarot* (readings from the Prophets). Only the letters of the Hebrew text may be written in a Synagogue Scroll, with the exception of a few symbols specified in the Masorah, such as the dots on the ten words in the Torah (#79-80), and inverted *nun* (#81). Consequently there are no masoretic notes, accent signs, or vowel signs in Synagogue Scrolls. Examples are known in which a mark has been made at the end of a verse (*sof pasuq*, #208), or at the main division within it (*atnaḥ*, #213), by pressing a point into the parchment. This type of marking is not found before the thirteenth century. Probably it was assumed that only marks made in ink were forbidden in synagogue scrolls, while marks of this sort would not contravene the law. However, Strack informs us that in a few Synagogue Scrolls from Tschufut-Kale in the Crimea, which are now preserved in Leningrad, a dot or pair of dots is marked at the end of the verses.

8. The letters of Synagogue Scrolls are usually "crowned" with ornamental strokes called תגים *taggim* (#70). However, some scrolls which come from the East, dating from the eleventh century and later, have no *taggim* on their letters. These *taggim* are not generally used in codices, but a few codices are known in which *taggim* are used in addition to the accent and vowel signs.

9. As a rule no colophons (#15) are found in synagogue scrolls, or in other scrolls either. In the Harkavy-Strack catalogue of MSS in the Leningrad Library (Harkavy-Strack, 1875) some scrolls are mentioned with colophons giving very early dates, some even from the seventh century. It is generally supposed, however, that these dates were forged by Firkowitsch, and in fact no other Synagogue Scroll dating from before the eleventh century is preserved.

What has been said up to now applies to the typical manuscript of a synagogue scroll. Many fragments of scrolls are preserved in the Geniza. Some of these contain no vowel or accent signs, while in others such signs were added. It is difficult to know whether those scrolls which contain no signs were intended for liturgical use or not. Probably both types are represented. Most of these scrolls from the Geniza are represented only by small fragments, not even containing a complete *parashah*, from different parts of the Torah, or from the "Five Scrolls" or from *Hafṭara* scrolls. They have not yet been catalogued or studied.

Papyri

10. Only a very few Hebrew MSS written on papyrus are known. Most of those preserved contain *piyyuṭ* (liturgical poetry). The best known papyrus containing passages from the Hebrew Bible is that known as the "Nash Papyrus" (Birnbaum, 1971, No.151). This contains the Ten Commandments, and the beginning of the "*Shema*ᶜ" (Dt 6:4). This is not part of a Biblical MS, but is part of an order of prayers (*siddur*). It is dated between the second century BCE and the first century CE by most scholars. Fragments of Biblical books written on papyrus appear among the Dead Sea Scrolls from Qumran Cave six. The Books of Kings (second century BC) and Daniel (first century CE) are certainly identified (6Q4 and 6Q7, see Fitzmyer, 1975, p.21). Deuteronomy (6Q3) may also appear.

The Codex

11. The vast majority of manuscripts are codices. This work is concerned mainly with manuscripts provided with the masoretic "apparati": masoretic notes and vowel and accent signs. The system of vowel and accent signs called "Tiberian"

was accepted in most Jewish communities from about 1000 CE on, and is the only system in use today. For this reason it is no surprise that the number of manuscripts and Geniza fragments showing this system is immeasurably greater than the number of those written according to other systems, such as the Babylonian or Palestinian.

The Different Types of Tiberian MSS

12. Some MSS contain only the text of the Bible in Hebrew. Some contain the Hebrew text and a Targum in alternate verses. In most cases the Targum to the Torah used is that called "Onqelos", but some Geniza fragments show a Palestinian Targum with the Hebrew text of the Torah. Manuscripts of the Prophets containing the Hebrew text and a Targum in alternate verses are rare. Yemenite MSS often contain the text of the Torah with both Targum Onqelos and the Arabic translation of R. Saadya Ga'on, or the text of the Writings with Saadya's Arabic translation. Very late MSS may contain commentaries along with the Hebrew text.

Some MSS contain only the text of a translation. In some cases the first word of each Hebrew verse is given (a "lemma") and this is followed by the translation of the Hebrew verse; in other cases the translation alone is given, with no lemma to identify the Hebrew verses. Both the Targum Onqelos and the Arabic translation of R. Saadya Ga'on are presented in this way, as are Palestinian Targums. In the complete Palestinian Targum to the Torah recently identified by A. Díez-Macho (Targum Neofiti) each verse is identified by a lemma.

13. Older MSS, and Geniza fragments, usually contain only part of the Bible, such as the Torah, the Prophets, or the Writings. The oldest known MS which contains the whole Bible is A, and after it S^1 and L. From the twelfth century on, a great many MSS containing the whole Bible are found. At all periods, however, MSS containing smaller units--a part of a book or even a single *parashah* (#72) of the Torah--were produced.

14. Some Tiberian MSS found in the Cairo Geniza were

written in a form known as "*serugin*" ("shorthand", "brachygraphy"). In the oldest examples the first word of a verse is written in full, followed by a single letter from each of the other important words in the verse. The Tiberian vowel and accent signs are used, but in some MSS the Palestinian "o" sign is sometimes used to indicate *ḥolem*. Later examples represent each word in the verse, often by more than one letter, so that they end up by giving an almost complete text.

15. The majority of older texts and Geniza fragments are beautifully written and "complete" (that is, masoretic notes and vowel and accent signs were systematically added). They were written on parchment, with great care taken over the forms of the letters and over corrections, and they contain the Mm, Mp, and vowel and accent signs. They were written with two or three columns to a page. In most cases the letters were written by a specialist scribe (*sofer*), and a specialist in pointing (*naqdan*) or a masorete added the masoretic notes and the vowel and accent signs. In some cases a colophon was added--a note giving such information as the name of the scribe and the *naqdan*, the place where they lived, and the date when the MS was finished--very important information for students of manuscripts and their development. In some cases the colophon may contain the name of the owner of the book, the name of a congregation or synagogue to which the book was donated, the terms of the donation, and similar material--perhaps a blessing on anyone who reads the book and preserves it, and a curse on anyone who damages it or steals it. Not all MSS contained colophons, and where one did exist, it has not always been preserved. Some colophons are false, either because intentionally falsified--for instance by changing the original date to an earlier one, or because the MS was copied from a text which itself contained a colophon, and that colophon was copied unchanged. Some MSS contain several colophons, recording, for instance, changes in the ownership of the book.

16. Some MSS and Geniza fragments are less than "complete" in various ways. They may contain vowel and accent signs, but no masoretic notes, or they may contain only a small

selection of notes: perhaps on *qere* and *ketiv*, or on *ga^{c}ya*, *legarmeh*, or *paseq*, or on the *ḥillufim* of ben Asher and ben Naftali (#155). They may contain vowel signs but no accent signs, or accent signs but no vowel signs. Such MSS are generally less carefully written than complete ones. Some use many extra vowel letters, ignoring the masoretic spelling; some use vowel signs differently from the received tradition from ignorance, or to represent the local pronunciation; and such MSS show many textual variants. Such texts, known as "vulgar" texts, were meant for private use or for study. They are commonly written on paper. Most known examples come from the Geniza, where they are the most common type of Biblical text. They are generally of little importance.

17. The oldest known MSS come from the Near East: from Eretz Israel, Egypt, or elsewhere. Later texts are divided into Sefardic (Spanish),Ashkenazic (German or East European), Italian, Yemenite, etc. They differ from each other in material (parchment and ink), the form of the letters, and, to some extent in features of vowelling and accentuation. Spanish texts, for instance, tend to be very accurate, and to use *ga^{c}ya* sparingly. However a text produced in any one Jewish community would differ in some small details from those produced elsewhere.

THE STANDARD TIBERIAN TRADITION

18. The work of the Tiberian Masoretes, who studied and preserved the text of the Bible, began, it would seem, between 600 and 800, and reached its peak in the work of Aharon ben Asher (about 915). The work of individual Masoretes is still clearly reflected in MSS written up to about 1100, but increasingly faintly after that period. MSS are divided into two groups on this basis.

MSS written between 850 and 1100

19. Texts written between these dates show a tradition that is old, and generally not compiled from material of different origins. The earliest MSS in this group were produced within the "masoretic period", so that in them the systems of vowel and accent signs are not yet fully developed.

Such texts give some evidence of the way these systems were developed. In later MSS the systems of signs are fully developed, but may show the differences reflecting the opinions of different Tiberian Masoretes. The study of the systems in the older MSS allows a better understanding of some of the rules in ancient treatises on Masorah and grammar, such as the *ḥillufim* between ben Asher and ben Naftali (#155-157), the *Diqduqe ha-Teᶜamim* (#175), and the *Horayat ha-Qore* (#175), since their rules were based on texts of this type.

MSS written after 1100

20. These MSS are generally copies based on one or more older MSS. In most cases neither the text nor the masoretic additions are uniform, but reflect a mixture of different traditions. The influence of grammarians, and even of commentaries, can be recognized. Such MSS are of little interest for this work. Consequently our most important sources are the few dozen excellent MSS written before 1100 and preserved outside the Geniza. Some Geniza fragments are important, but they generally provide little material, and we are not forced to rely on them, as in the study of the Babylonian or Palestinian traditions.

Uniformity and Variation in Manuscripts Written before 1100

21. By about the middle of the tenth century, when the work of the last of the Masoretes was completed, the Tiberian tradition was, to all intents and purposes, fixed as regards words, letters, vowels, and accents. The last of the Masoretes themselves did not vary in matters of substance, but in minor details of vocalization or accentuation. The fully developed MSS preserved from that period, and Geniza fragments of the same type, reflect this fixed tradition closely; and the differences between individual MSS, which are numerous, are not differences of substance, but of insignificant detail. The differences between the traditions maintained by the various Tiberian Masoretes, such as ben Asher, ben Naftali, Pinḥas, Moshe Moḥeh (#151), are similarly of minor significance. Thus in spite of these differences in detail, the Tiberian masoretic tradition can be called homogeneous in contrast, for instance, with the Babylonian tradition, which differs considerably from it.

Differences in Individual Features

22. Variations between individual MSS of this group representing the standard tradition are of two types: differences in individual features, and differences in the system of pointing. Examples of differences in single features are the fact that a particular word may be written with a vowel letter in one MS, but without it in another; with the conjunction *waw* in one MS, but without it in another; here pointed with *pataḥ*, there with *qameṣ*; here with *gaᶜya*, there without it; here with a conjunctive accent, elsewhere with *maqqef*; and so on.

Differences in the System of Pointing

23. These differences mainly reflect the extent to which the *naqdan* attempted to indicate, in the pointing system, the minor details of the reading tradition, and the way in which he did it. Examples of such differences are:

(a) in vocalization. One MS may frequently use a *ḥaṭef shewa* with consonants other than the gutturals ʾ, *h*, *ḥ*, and ᶜ, (#388-391), while another uses it rarely. One may mark *qameṣ qaṭan* with ָ, while another uses ֳ. The dot called *mappiq* may be marked within the letter הּ, or below it ה̣. *Pataḥ* "furtive" may be marked under the letter, as רֵיחַ, or before it, as רֵיַח. One MS may mark *rafe* regularly, another only where it is necessary to avoid ambiguity. One may mark *rafe* only on the *begad-kefat* letters, another on other letters as well (#397). One MS may mark *dagesh* in words such as רַעְמָּה, וַיֶּאְסֹּר (#132, under דגש (3), also #414), or in a situation such as אֲגַם מַּיִם (#413), while another may not.

(b) Differences in the system of Accentuation. One MS may repeat the pospositive *pashṭa* sign on the stress syllable of all words with penultimate stress, while another may never repeat it, or only repeat it in certain cases (#239). One MS may repeat other prepositive or postpositive accent signs as well, while another may not do this, or only do it occasionally. One MS may mark *methiga-zaqef* after *pashṭa*, while another does not (#224). One may mark *maqqef* after a word with a conjunctive accent, while another may never do this (#293, 357).

(c) Differences in the marking of *gaᶜya* (very common). One MS may mark *gaʿya* in an open syllable only rarely, another frequently (#331). One MS may sometimes mark *gaʿya* twice in the same word, as וַיַּעֲמֹד, while another never marks it more than once in any word (#344). Some MSS use various types of "phonetic" *gaʿya* which are not used in others, and so on.

All of these variations--those in individual words and those in the system--are still within the boundaries of the standard Tiberian system. They have their source in minor differences between the individual Tiberian masoretes and their students, or in the attempts of later *naqdanim* to indicate accurately in writing the very smallest details of the reading tradition.

THE MOST IMPORTANT MSS

24. Aharon ben Asher (c. 915), the last of the masoretes, is considered the outstanding representative of the standard tradition. Many grammarians, and also Maimonides himself, relied on his Biblical tradition. Until recently it was thought that the text printed by Jacob ben Ḥayyim in Venice in 1524-5 (=V, see #139) was a good representative of the tradition of ben Asher. It has now been shown however, that although this edition is quite close to the original ben Asher tradition, it in fact represents a mixture of traditions derived from a few MSS written not long before the edition was printed, and consequently differs from the original ben Asher tradition in many minor details. These variations are not in matters of substance, so the edition is a good representative of the standard Tiberian tradition. Recently, however, scholars have concentrated their attention on the earlier MSS which are likely to represent the original ben Asher tradition more closely, and these are the main interest of this work.

25 Such MSS can sometimes be identified by colophons which indicate their relationship to the ben Asher tradition. Another indicator, and a very important one, is the *Sefer ha-Ḥillufim* which lists variants between ben Asher and ben Naftali (#155). If a particular MS generally follows the reading identified in the *Sefer ha-Ḥillufim* as that of ben Asher, in the hundreds of passages for which such variants are recorded, then it can be assumed that it represents the

tradition of ben Asher. The rules of the *Diqduqe ha-Teʿamim* (#175), a treatise ascribed to Aharon ben Asher, form another indicator. The extent to which an MS conforms to these rules is likely to indicate its closeness to the ben Asher tradition.

This study concentrates mainly on the ben Asher tradition. However, other MSS from the older period which follow a tradition differing from that of ben Asher, can be very important for the tracing of the history of the standard tradition, and for the identification of the various schools of pointing included within the Tiberian tradition.

The Aleppo MS (A)

26. This MS was written by the scribe Solomon ben Buyāʿa. According to a colophon written about 100 years after the MS was completed, Aharon ben Asher himself provided it with vowel points, accent signs, and masoretic notes. This colophon itself is now lost, but it was copied a number of times before its destruction (see *Textus* I, pp.13-15). Many scholars have cast doubt on the authenticity of the colophon, and have suggested that A was not the product of Aharon ben Asher at all. However, a number of tests show that this MS is closer to the ben Asher tradition than is any other MS known to us.

(i) Its text agrees with the ben Asher of the *Sefer ha-Ḥillufim*, against ben Naftali, in 94% of the cases--more than that of any other MS.

(ii) Where ben Asher and ben Naftali are recorded in the *Sefer ha-Ḥillufim* as agreeing against other scholars, A agrees with bA + bN in 90% of the cases.

(iii) The tradition of A conforms to the rules of the *Diqduqe ha-Teʿamim*.

(iv) The writing of the "Song of Moses" (Dt 32), and the marking of *petuḥot* and *setumot* (#74) in the part of the Torah still preserved, is close to that recorded by Maimonides from the Bible of ben Asher.

(v) A thorough study of the oldest MSS (A, L, B, S, S^1) and their Masorah, made recently by M. Breuer, (Breuer 1975), shows conclusively that A is superior to any other MS in spelling, in the writing of the songs in the Bible, and in its Masorah. Not only this, but A is the only one of these MSS in which the presentation of these features is almost everywhere flawless.

There are, indeed, a few differences between A and what is ascribed to ben Asher in other sources--mostly in a small proportion of the *ḥillufim*. These differences might result from errors in the *Sefer ha-Ḥillufim*, but even if we give them full value, there is no doubt that in its closeness to the tradition ascribed to ben Asher, and also in its accuracy and consistency, this MS must be considered superior to all other Tiberian MSS known to us. It is, therefore, the most important representative of the standard Tiberian tradition.

27. For a long time A was kept in Aleppo in Syria, where the leaders of the community would not permit anyone to study it, or photograph it for scholarly purposes. W. Wickes was able to publish a photograph of one page (Wickes, 1887, frontispiece). Jacob Sappir, who described it in the account of his travels, gained information about the spelling of some hundreds of words in it, as he relates in the periodical *Ha-Levanon* vol I, and in a short work entitled *Me'orot Natan* which is preserved in manuscript.

In 1948 riots against the Jews of Aleppo broke out. The Synagogue was set on fire, and the MS was thought to have perished. Much of it was, however, saved, and eventually brought to Israel. It is preserved today in Jerusalem in the library of the Ben-Zvi Institute. From an original total of about 380 pages, 294 are preserved, and these contain most of the Bible. However most of the Torah is missing. Gen 26:34-27:30 is preserved in the photograph of Wickes. Dt 4:38-6:3 is preserved in another photograph (*Textus* 5, 1966, pp.53-59). Dt 28:17 to the end of the book is preserved in the manuscript. The "Former Prophets" is preserved complete except for II Kings 14:21-18:13. The "Latter Prophets" is also complete save for Jeremiah 29:9-31:35, 32:2-4, 9-11, 15-18, 22-24, and in the Twelve "Minor" Prophets, Amos 8:13-Micah 5:1, Zeph 3:20-Zech 9:17. In the Writings, almost all of Chronicles is preserved (II Chron 35:7-36:19 is missing), as is most of Psalms (Ps 15:1-25:1 is lost). Job, Proverbs, Ruth, and Song of Songs 1:1-3:11 are also preserved. The end of the codex, which contained the rest of the Song of Songs, Qohelet,

Lamentations, Esther, Daniel, Ezra and Nehemiah, is missing, as are any colophons or masoretic notes there may have been at the beginning or end of the book.

28. The text of A is written in three columns (the three "poetical" books, Psalms, Proverbs, and Job in two). Vowel and accent signs are carefully and consistently added, and an early form of Mp and Mm is supplied. Some of the peculiarities of this text are: *Ḥaṭef shewa* is often used with letters other than the gutturals *ʾ*, *h*, *ḥ*, and *ʿ*. *Gaʿya* is rarely used in an open syllable. *Qere-ketiv* notes are somewhat fewer than in later MSS. The masoretic notes contain no reference to scholars or to variant readings (#151-155). Some sections of these notes use language similar to that of the *Diqduqe ha-Teʿamim*. The Mm contains only notes of the "elaborative" type (#126). The two-dot *sof pasuq* sign is not used at the end of most verses (see #208). The Aleppo Codex has been published in facsimile (Goshen-Gottstein 1976), and provides the text for the *Hebrew University Bible* (Goshen-Gottstein 1975).

29. A few Torah MSS written in the Yemen in the 15th and 16th centuries, some of which are in the British Museum (London), the Jewish Theological Seminary (New York), and in Israel, were written, according to their colophons, על תיקון הספר שהיה במצרים שהגיהו בן אשר "According to the Bible which was in Egypt which ben Asher corrected"--thus ostensibly according to A. However, comparison with the parts of the Torah preserved in A shows differences in details. Consequently it is thought that the purpose of these colophons is to point out that these texts represent the standard Tiberian tradition, and not that they were copied directly from A.

The Leningrad MS (L, Firkowitsch I. B 19a).

30. This is the MS showing the closest tradition to A. It was written in 1009, and copied and pointed according to an MS slightly different from A. According to a colophon, however, it was corrected לפי הספרים המדויקים של בן אשר "According to the most exact texts of ben Asher". Certainly many erasures are visible in it--mostly of *gaʿya*, but also of letters and

accents, and this could result from such correction. It is written in three columns (the poetical books in two), and contains the whole Bible, with masoretic lists at the end, and also sections from the *Diqduqe ha-Teᶜamim* (#175), *ḥillufim* between *Madinḥa'e* and *Maᶜarba'e* (#153), and other material. It is less exact than A in the writing of the Songs in the Torah, the marking of *petuḥot* and *setumot*, and the like, and often differs from A in the use of vowel letters. Its use of vowel and accent signs is very close to that of A. Among the few differences are: L uses *ḥaṭef shewa* with letters other than the gutturals ʾ, *h*, *ḥ*, and ᶜ, less than does A. L marks *gaᶜya* in an open syllable more frequently than does A (although some have been erased), but the principles according to which it is marked are similar to those of A. The Masorah of L often differs from that of A, and is evidently later. It gives more specific details than does that of A, such as the names of masoretic scholars and sources. The Masorah of L occasionally contradicts the text. L agrees with the ben Asher of the *Sefer ha-Ḥillufim* in 92% of the cases against ben Naftali, and in 90% where bA and bN agree against other Masoretes--almost as much as A.

L was used by Kahle as the basis for BHK, where the Mp is also printed. L was also used as the basis for BHS, where the Mp is printed by G.E. Weil (with additions intended to make it easier to use). Weil has also printed the Mm in a separate volume (Weil 1971). Dotan's careful edition of the Bible (Dotan, 1973a) is also based on the text of L. A facsimile of L has been published by the Makor Press (Loewinger 1970).

London, British Museum MS Or. 4445 (B)

31. This MS contains most of the Torah (Gen 39:20-Dt 1:33, excepting Nu 7:46-73, 9:12-18). It has no colophon, but appears to have been written about the same time as A (c. 925). Three columns. Agrees with bA of the *Sefer ha-Ḥillufim* in 80% of the cases, with bA + bN in 73%. Less carefully written than A and L, but the principles which govern its pointing are generally the same as those of A.

It contains Mp and Mm. The Mm is longer than that of A or L, and includes notes of the collative type (#129).

Ḥaṭef shewa is used with letters other than the gutturals, as in A. In a number of unimportant details it seems to represent a slightly less developed stage of the tradition than A. For instance *gaᶜya* is used less frequently in an open syllable, the repetition of *pashṭa* is less common than in A; and so on.

The Codex of the Prophets from the Qaraite Synagogue in Cairo (C)

32. Contains all the books of the Prophets. According to its colophon it was written in 896 by Mosheh ben Asher (the father of Aharon). Three columns. Text, vowel and accent signs, and Masorah are very carefully written--as carefully as A. The Mm is very short. It does sometimes mention masoretic scholars (mostly Moḥeh). Despite the relationship stated in the colophon, C differs from A in many details. It corresponds to the bA of the *Sefer ha-Ḥillufim* in 33% of the cases, but to bN in 64%. It points לְישְׂרָאֵל and similar cases according to the tradition of bN (not לְיִשְׂרָאֵל as bA, see #392-393). Where bA and bN agree, C agrees with them in 75% of the cases. This MS in fact corresponds more closely to what is known of ben Naftali than does any other, yet it is not a pure representative of the bN tradition. This is shown not only by the 33% of the *ḥillufim* in which it agrees with bA, but also by certain details in which it differs from the pointing ascribed to ben Naftali. For instance in יִשָּׂשכָר and בִּן־נוּן it follows bA, while bN points יִשְּׂשָׂכָר, בִּן־נּוּן.

Ḥaṭef shewa is used on letters other than the gutturals less frequently than in A. C shows some signs of a "fully developed" tradition. *Rafe* is used more frequently than in A (#397) and L. *Alef* representing a consonant is sometimes marked with *dagesh* (#395). *Gaᶜya* is frequently marked in an open syllable, and its use is near that of modern texts. *Methiga-zaqef* is marked even after a word bearing *pashṭa* (#224). *Munaḥ* is the only conjunctive used before *zarqa* and *legarmeh* (never *Merka*, as is required under some conditions, see #263).

In most of these "developed" features, C shows relationship to the MSS of the "expanded" Tiberian tradition (see introduction, p.2), but in most features it resembles A.

Because the MS was written by Mosheh father of Aharon ben Asher, it appears that the father's tradition differed in many details from his son's--it was, in fact, closer to that of ben Naftali, though not identical to it. A facsimile of C has been published by the Makor Press (Loewinger 1971).

Jerusalem, National and University Library, Heb. 24° 5702 (formerly MS Sassoon 507) (S)

33. Contains almost the whole Torah (from Gen 9:26 to the end, excepting Ex 18:1-23). Three columns. Probably from the tenth century. Written with great care. Agrees with the ben Asher of the *Sefer ha-Ḥillufim* in 52% of the cases, with bA + bN 76%. In some cases (though not always) it follows ben Naftali's tradition in the pointing of words such as בְּיִשְׂרָאֵל (#393).

This MS contains both Mp and Mm, including lists of the collative type. Vowel signs of the compound Babylonian pointing system are often used in the masoretic notes (however the pronunciation reflected is Tiberian, see #133).

Ḥaṭef shewa is scarcely used at all with letters other than the gutturals. The *rafe* sign is used even more than in C (#397). *Gaᶜya* is used in an open syllable more than in A and L, and almost as much as in C. "Phonetic *gaᶜya*" before a laryngeal (#354) is uncommon. *Methiga-zaqef* is not used at all (#224). The system of marking the servi of *zarqa* used in this MS differs from that of A. S shows a mixed tradition, since it shows a number of features characteristic of the "fully developed" tradition on the one hand, but also unusual features in the marking of some accents on the other.

MS Sassoon 1053 (S^1)

34. Contains the whole Bible, but a number of pages are wholly or partially missing. Three columns. Contains the Mp, but shows the Mm only on some of its pages. Ben Asher is mentioned in the Mm in a few places. Tenth century.

S^1 is less carefully written than the other MSS described. Signs such as the diacritical dot on ש, *dagesh*, *maqqef*, and *paseq* are often omitted. When two identical vowel signs should be written together, S^1 frequently shows only one, as in הַמֶּלֶךְ (Esther 2:1). As a general rule, simple *shewa* rather than *ḥaṭef segol* is used with *alef* (as אֱלֹהִים).

S[1] agrees with the bA of the *Sefer ha-Ḥillufim* in about 40% of the cases, and with bA + bN in about 60%. The pointing is less developed than that of A or L. *Gaᶜya* in an open syllable is marked less frequently than in A. The two-dot *sof-pasuq* sign is used at the end of most, but not all, of the verses.

OTHER MSS FROM LENINGRAD

35. The six MSS described above, which were all written before 1000, have been more or less completely studied. The majority of the other ancient MSS are now in the Leningrad Public Library, and have scarcely been studied at all. Most are found in the two Firkowitsch collections, which contain hundreds of Biblical MSS, some of which are very old. P. Kahle, who visited Leningrad and worked at the collections there, described 14 MSS with dated colophons (Kahle 1927, pp.56-77). Six of these were written before 1000. Other MSS from the same period are also preserved in Leningrad, but their colophons have not been preserved. Not all these MSS reflect the true bA tradition. Their importance lies in the fact that they are early, and so give evidence of the development of the Biblical tradition, since they undoubtedly derive from the masoretic scholars of Tiberias, the predecessors, contemporaries, or followers of Aharon ben Asher, whether they agreed with him in particular details or not. Photographs of a few of these MSS have been acquired by the Institute of Microfilms of Hebrew MSS at the National Library in Jerusalem. The following short descriptions are based on these photographs. (The MSS are numbered according to Kahle's list.)

Leningrad. Firkowitsch II.17 (L[1])

36. Contains most of the Torah, but a considerable proportion of its leaves are blurred or torn. Written in 930 by Solomon ben Buyāᶜa (who wrote the text of A). The pointing and Masorah were supplied by his brother Ephraim. A beautiful and carefully written MS, containing Mp and Mm. Shows rather a large number of *qere/ketiv* notes. Even though the same scribe wrote L[1] and A, they not only differ in various details of masoretic notes, and accent and vowel signs, which were the

work of different *naqdanim*, but they also differ in the marking of *petuḥot* and *setumot* and the method of writing out the songs, which were the work of the same scribe. Possibly the *naqdanim* were not only responsible for the work in their own field--the marking of vowel and accent signs--but also gave instructions to the scribe on the way the text was to be written out.

This MS does not show a definite tendency to agree either with the bA of the *Sefer ha-Ḥillufim*, or with the bN. *Gaʿya* is used in an open syllable a little more than in A, and about the same as in L. "Phonetic" *gaʿya* in the roots היה and חיה is used frequently.

Leningrad. Firkowitsch II.159 (L^2)

37. Four leaves only, containing Dt 31:10 to the end of the book. Written in 943. Differs greatly from A in the use of vowel letters, and shows various signs of lack of precision in the pointing. It also shows some features suggesting an early stage of the accent system. *Pashṭa* is never repeated (#239). *Methiga-zaqef* is not used. *Gaʿya* is rarely used on an open syllable. The use of *maqqef* is interesting (#293): on the one hand *maqqef* is often omitted from a word which has no accent (as וְאַל יָמֹת Dt 33:6), but on the other, *maqqef* may be used on a word which has a conjunctive accent--generally when the word has penultimate stress (as בְּטֶרֶם-אֲבִיאֶנּוּ Dt 31:21).

The pointing shows לִירְאָה (Dt 31:13) בִּישְׂרָאֵל (Dt 34:10) in the tradition of bN (#392). *Ḥaṭef shewa* is not used with letters other than the gutturals.

Leningrad. Firkowitsch II.10 (L^3)

38. Contains most of the Torah. Dedicated in 946. A very beautiful MS, but less carefully written than A and C, and inconsistent in some features of vocalization and accentuation.

Sometimes shows *ḥaṭef shewa* on letters other than the gutturals, but inconsistently. Interchanges *pataḥ* and *segol* in a few cases. Uses *gaʿya* in an open syllable more frequently than A, and nearly as much as L. Its system with respect to *gaʿya* in a closed syllable with a long vowel is somewhat different from that of A. *Methiga-zaqef* is used, but not consistently. The system of marking the first servus of *zarqa* is different from that of A.

Leningrad. Firkowitsch II.124 (L^4)

39. Contains some parts of the prophetic books. Written in 946 according to a colophon cited by Kahle. However it shows a number of features characteristic of MSS written about 1100, so it is difficult to be certain of its date.

This MS shows a number of signs of carelessness: scribal errors, inconsistency in the use of vowel and accent signs, and so on. On some pages there are many masoretic notes, but on others very few. Very few of the notes of the Mm are of the collative type.

Dagesh in *śin* is marked as ·שׂ. *Ḥatef shewa* is rarely used with letters other than the gutturals. L^4 agrees with the bN of the *Sefer ha-Ḥillufim* in somewhat more than half the cases. *Gaʿya* is used on open syllables about as much as in A, but less systematically. The *Pashṭa* sign (בׄ) is differentiated from *azla* (בׂ) in a way unknown from other MSS. *Methiga-zaqef* is used, but the system of marking it is not uniform.

Leningrad. Firkowitsch II.39 (L^5)

40. Contains most of the Former Prophets. Written in 989. A beautiful MS, carefully produced. Close to A in the system of marking vowel signs, accent signs, and *gaʿya*, even though it does not show a clear tendency to agree with either bA or bN of the *Sefer ha-Ḥillufim*. *Ḥaṭef shewa* is used only rarely with consonants other than the gutturals.

Leningrad. Firkowitsch II.115 (L^6)

41. Parts of the Writings. Written in 994. This MS is close to L both in date and in tradition. Shows a slight blurring of the distinction between *gaʿya* and *merka*, particularly in the three poetic books (as does L itself). *Ḥaṭef shewa* is used with consonants other than the gutturals, but not consistently.

(Kahle's #7 is the Leningrad MS Firkowitsch I.B19a, here L, described in #30).

Leningrad. Firkowitsch II.225 (L^8)

42. Nine leaves from the Latter Prophets belonging to two different MSS. One has a colophon, dated 1017, and the other

was probably written at about the same time. They show characteristics similar to L, but leaning somewhat towards C. The pointing of words like בישראל is corrected from the bN tradition to that of bA, and the MSS show many other corrections, especially of *ga^c ya*. *Ḥaṭef shewa* is used on consonants other than the gutturals. *Ga^c ya* is used on an open syllable more frequently than in A, but this has been erased in many cases.

Leningrad. Firkowitsch II.1283 (L^{10})

43. Part of the Latter Prophets. Bought in 1058. This MS was not carefully produced, and shows considerable inconsistency. *Ḥaṭef shewa* is not used with consonants other than the gutturals. The two dots of the *ḥaṭef shewa* are sometimes written inside the letter (as חֲמִישִׁי Jer 52:12), as in the expanded Tiberian pointing. *Dagesh* in *śin* is sometimes written to the left of the letter (as הֲיִשָּׂא Mal 1:9). *Ga^c ya* on an open syllable is seldom marked, as in A or even less frequently, and less systematically.

Leningrad. Firkowitsch II.25-26 (L^{11})

44. Part of the Prophets. Dedicated about 1036, but appears to have been written before that--perhaps about 950. The two volumes (#25 contains the Former Prophets, #26 the Latter) are very similar, but do not seem to belong to the same MS. The texts are beautiful and carefully produced, and are very similar to A (particularly #25). They are also very close to the bA of the *Sefer ha-Ḥillufim*. *Ḥaṭef shewa* is used with consonants other than gutturals as in A, and other features of the marking of *ga^c ya* and the accents are also similar to A.

Leningrad. Firkowtsch II.94 (L^{12})

45. About half of the Former Prophets and the Writings. Dedicated in 1100, but appears to have been written about a century earlier. A large MS, not very carefully produced, showing inconsistency in the use of vowel and accent signs, including a slight tendency to interchange *pataḥ* and *segol*. Shows the pointing עָשִׂיתְ, a form (with final *shewa*) not found in A and similar MSS. *Ḥaṭef shewa* is sometimes used with consonants other than gutturals. The marking of *ga^c ya* is also

inconsistent, especially in open syllables, and the same is true of *methiga-zaqef*.

Leningrad. Firkowitsch II.34 (L[13])

46. Most of the Writings. Bound in 1130, but probably written about 975. A beautiful and carefully produced MS, with short Mp and Mm. Agrees with the bN of the *Sefer ha-Ḥillufim* in a little more than half the cases. *Ḥaṭef shewa* is rarely used with consonants other than the gutturals. *Gaᶜya* is marked in an open syllable more or less as in L.

Both the two dots of the *sof-pasuq* sign and the accent *silluq* are marked at the end of each verse except in the three poetical books, where most verses end at the margin. Here the two dots are always marked, but *silluq* is marked only on words with penultimate stress (#208). *Methiga* is never used with *zaqef*.

Leningrad. Museum of the Peoples of Asia MS D62 (L[15])

47. Most of the Latter Prophets. According to a colophon (no longer preserved) it was written in 847, but may be 50 or 100 years later. The photograph available in Israel (a xerox print) is blurred, so it is difficult to read the pointing over most of it.

Short Mp and Mm, which uses some Babylonian terminology (#133). The notes of the Mp are sometimes put within the text--a characteristic of Babylonian MSS. The Mp also sometimes records a variant as "Babylonian". The text is similar to that of P.

Shows many signs of full development. *Pashṭa* and other accents are often repeated. *Ḥaṭef qameṣ* is sometimes used to indicate *qameṣ qaṭan*. The *rafe* sign is used frequently. Consonantal *alef* is sometimes marked with *dagesh*. The marking of the servi of *zarqa* is different from that of A.

Leningrad. Firkowitsch I.85 (L[16])

48. The Torah from Ex 29:37 to the end. Written about 950. A beautiful and carefully produced MS. *Ḥaṭef shewa* is not used with consonants other than the gutturals. Shows a slight tendency to agree with the bN of the *Sefer ha-Ḥillufim* lists. The marking of *gaᶜya* and the accents is very similar to

that of A.

Leningrad. Firkowitsch I.80 + I. B 13 (L[17])

49. Part of the Former Prophets, written about 975. A beautiful and carefully written MS. Shows some cases of *ḥaṭef shewa* with consonants other than the gutturals. Rarely marks *gaᶜya* in an open syllable. *Methiga* is not used with *zaqef*.

Leningrad. Firkowitsch I.59 (L[18])

50. About two-thirds of the Latter Prophets. Written about 1050. Differs greatly from the received tradition in the use of vowel letters. The forgeries of Firkowitsch can be recognized in a few places, as with בְּעִים (Is 11:15), וּבְצַעֵם (Amos 9:1), and so always שְׁתַּיִם, שְׁתֵּי, גָּזִית.

Contains Mp and Mm, including notes of the collative type. Interchanges *ṣere* and *segol*. *Alef* is sometimes pointed with simple *shewa* instead of *ḥaṭef segol* (as in S[1]). Often marks *gaᶜya* in open syllables, and may mark *gaᶜya* twice on the same word. Accentuation is similar to that of A. *Methiga* is sometimes used with *zaqef*, even after *pashṭa* (as in C).

Leningrad. Firkowitsch II.9 (L[20])

51. Most of the Latter Prophets. Written about 950. A very beautiful and carefully written MS. Occasional scribal errors. Vowel signs are sometimes omitted, but this is probably because the *naqdan* considered them unnecessary rather than through error. Contains Mp and Mm, including notes of the collative type. The Mp contains some notes on variants between *Madinḥaʾe* and *Maᶜarbaʾe* (#153), and the text was occasionally corrected from an "Eastern" reading to a "Western". *Ḥaṭef shewa* is rarely used with consonants other than the gutturals. The text generally agrees with the bA of the *Sefer ha-Ḥillufim*, but it has frequently been corrected by the addition or erasure of *gaᶜya*, etc.

The use of *gaᶜya* and the accents is similar to that of A. *Gaᶜya* is frequently marked in an open syllable in a word accented with *pashṭa*--even on the syllable immediately before the stress syllable (#329), as הָעִירוּ (Joel 4:9), פִּי-עֵץ (Jer 10:3). Sometimes *gaᶜya* is marked twice on the same word.

The two dots of the *sof-pasuq* sign are never used at

the end of the verses in this MS; only *silluq* is used (#208).

Leningrad. Firkowitsch II.B 13 R (L^{21})

52. About half of Chronicles and Psalms. Written about 950. Shows many scribal errors and signs of inconsistency in the use of vowel and accent signs and *gaᶜya*. *Ḥaṭef shewa* is scarcely ever used with consonants other than the gutturals. Shows no definite tendency to agree with either bA or bN of the *Sefer ha-Ḥillufim*. *Gaᶜya* is used in an open syllable as much as in L. The form of *galgal*, the servus of *pazer gadol*, is clearly a small *ṭet*, as in המשרתים (I Chron 28:1)--a form not known elsewhere.

OTHER EARLY MSS

New York. Jewish Theological Seminary MS 232 (= ENA 346)(N)

53. About half of the Latter Prophets. Written about 1000. Contains Mp and Mm, including notes of the collative type. Differs considerably from the standard tradition in the use of vowel letters. Sometimes interchanges *ṣere* and *segol*. As a general rule, *ḥaṭef shewa* is not used with consonants other than the gutturals.

Shows many signs of full development. *Dagesh* is sometimes used after a guttural with simple *shewa* (#414), as in יֶאְשְׁמוּ (Hos 10:2). *Gaᶜya* is often used on an open syllable, and is often marked twice on the same word. Accents are sometimes repeated on a word with penultimate stress.

Ann Arbor. University of Michigan MS

54. A Torah, written about 1050 with Mp and Mm. *Ḥaṭef shewa* is sometimes used with consonants other than the gutturals. *Gaᶜya* is frequently used on an open syllable, as is "phonetic" *gaᶜya* with the roots היה and חיה. Accents are sometimes repeated on words with penultimate stress.

Other MSS of Interest

55. *Cincinatti. Hebrew Union College MS HUC 1.* Torah with *hafṭarot*. Written about 1075.

Vatican MS 448 Torah. Written about 1100.

According to the description in Gottheil 1905 (pp. 609-655), there were a number of important Biblical MSS in Egypt. Nothing is now known of their location or condition.

Three small MSS, each containing a few dozen pages, were included in the Gaster collection, which is now in the British Museum. These are *British Museum MS Or. 9879*, (parts of the Writings from the tenth century), *MS Or. 9880*, (parts of Torah from the end of the tenth century), and *MS Or. 9881*, (parts of the Torah from the beginning of the eleventh century).

*Cambridge. Fitzwilliam Museum MS 364**. Former Prophets. Written about 1000 by more than one hand.

The oldest MSS at present in Israel are A, S^1, and Jerusalem, *National and University Library MS Heb 8° 2238*, containing the *parashah shelaḥ* (Nu 13-15). This is a small MS with Mp and Mm, written in 1106. (See Yalon, 1971, p.171-182.)

MSS WRITTEN AFTER 1100

56. Many MSS written in the twelfth century and after are preserved--more than 3,000 are known. In most of them the text tradition differs little from that of the earlier MSS, and the same is true of the pointing system, the accents and the use of *gaᶜya*. However, the tradition is less pure and less homogeneous, and shows evidence of the mixture of different sources.

Kennicott published an edition of the Bible with an apparatus of variant readings (only of letters, not of vowel or accent signs) taken from hundreds of MSS (Kennicott 1776). His work was complemented by de Rossi (de Rossi 1784). Both these authors give brief descriptions of the MSS they used. Most of them came from the libraries of Northern and Western Europe, and were written in the twelfth century or later. Some are carefully produced and fully developed. Others are less carefully produced and are full of scribal errors. C.D. Ginsburg produced an edition of the Bible with variant readings from 75 MSS and 19 early printed editions (Ginsburg 1908, 1926). In his *Introduction to the Massoretico-Critical Edition of the Hebrew Bible* (Ginsburg 1897) he gives a detailed description of the MSS he used. B, P, and R were among them. The others were from the twelfth century or later, mostly from the collection of the British Museum.

57. The apparatus in the BHK edition is not based on the study of many MSS. The ones mainly used were C and P, while

others were referred to only occasionally. The notes which refer to "Hebrew MSS" are based on the editions of Kennicott, de Rossi, and Ginsburg. Examples are:-

Is 1:3	עמי	ca 30 MSS ועמי	-- some 30 MSS read ועמי
Is 5:28	קַשְּׁתֹתָיו	mlt MSS 𝔅 שְּׁת	-- many MSS, and also V, read קַשְּׁתֹתָיו
Is 53:5	שְׁלוֹמֵנוּ	𝔅+pl MSS ־מֵינוּ	-- very many MSS, and also V, read שְׁלוֹמֵינוּ
Jer 14:14	לָכֶם	𝔅 et nonn MSS לָהֶם	-- a number of MSS, and also V, read לָהֶם
Jer 44:8	בְּמַעֲשֵׂי	ca 50 MSS ־שֵׂה	-- some 50 MSS read בְּמַעֲשֵׂה
Ez 7:5	אַחַת	ca 30 MSS Edd אַחַר	-- some 30 MSS and printed editions read אַחַר.

In the BHS edition the situation is much the same, but references to "MSS" are reduced (in most books) to "pc" - a few, 3-10 MSS; "nonn" - some, 11-20 MSS;"mlt" - many, more than 20 MSS; and the symbol ℭ is used to show that a reading is found in Geniza fragments.

THE CAIRO GENIZA

58. Thousands of pages from Bibles were found in the Cairo Geniza, some with Palestinian or Babylonian pointing, but the vast majority with Tiberian. In contrast to the MSS preserved in libraries, which are mostly complete, and contain either the whole Bible or standard divisions of it, the Geniza fragments provide us with part of a page, a whole page, or a few pages, and only rarely with any sizeable part of a book. Nevertheless their importance for the history of the text, the Masorah, and the vocalization and accentuation, is very great.

Some of these fragments may be older than the time of ben Asher, for the pointing and accentuation is incomplete, and differs, in some details from the standard. Some of them may be from the tenth century, the period when the ben Asher MSS were written. Many of them are later. Some pages come from beautiful and carefully produced MSS, written in two or three columns per page, with Mp and Mm in the margins, but such pages make up only a small proportion of the Geniza fragments. Most are fragments of "vulgar" texts, some without Masorah, without accents, with many extra vowel letters, and so on. One can estimate that the Geniza contains fragments of some 10,000 books containing some part or other of the Bible, showing different systems of masoretic notes, vowel signs, and accent signs, and written carefully or carelessly. They have not yet been classified or studied, but the production of a catalogue is progressing.

MSS written after 1100 contain, as a rule little of interest to the study of the standard tradition and its development, and for this reason this book is not concerned with them. They do, however, contain much of value to the study of the development of the tradition up to the time of printing, and also for the study of the pronunciation of Hebrew in different periods and localities.

PRINTED EDITIONS

59. In the sixteenth century, after the worst of the problems of printing Biblical Hebrew had been solved, printed Bibles replaced manuscript copies in Europe. Where there were no satisfactory presses, however, the hand copying of Biblical MSS continued much later. In the Yemen, for instance, it continued down to recent times.

The invention of printing made it much easier to maintain a uniform Biblical tradition, and the majority of printed editions differ very little from each other. They do not reflect the work of the individual scholars who created the standard tradition, but show the results of copying each edition from an earlier one. The best reading was chosen from the available sources without regard to its origin, resulting in a mixed text.

The Edition of Venice 1524-25 (V)

60. This edition, called the "Second Rabbinic Bible", is considered the "Received Edition". It contains Mp, Mm, vowel signs and accent signs, a form of the "*Masorah finalis*", and, in addition, the Aramaic translations and some commentaries. Its preparation required a great deal of work: classification of MSS, choice of masoretic notes, and the study and arrangement of them. The editor was Jacob ben Ḥayyim ben Adoniyahu. It appears that he used MSS from the twelfth century and later. The tradition presented in this edition--

both in the Masorah and in the vocalization and accentuation--was good, but it was not uniform. It contains many traces of much older features along with much later ones, that is, it represents the sort of mixed tradition described above. A facsimile of V has been published by the Makor Press (Goshen-Gottstein, 1972).

Most "Rabbinic Bibles" (מקראות גדולות) were copied from V. The Bible has been printed thousands of times in many countries, but the history of these editions is of no interest to the present subject.

Literature

Ginsburg, 1867a.

PART II

THE MASORAH

LITERATURE

General

61. The Masorah has been printed in the margins of most Rabbinic Bibles since the Venice edition of 1524-25. The Mp of L is printed in BHK and also (in a re-worked form) in BHS, where an index to the lists of the Mm is provided.

S. Frensdorff, *Die Massora Magna* (Frensdorff 1876) gives the notes of the Mm of V organised in a number of categories: Nouns and verbs, Names, Particles, Other notes. The notes are arranged alphabetically, with some explanatory comments.

C.D. Ginsburg, *The Massorah* (Ginsburg 1880). This work contains a great deal of material collected from different MSS. See below #140, 172.

S. Frensdorff, *Das Buch Ochlah W'ochlah* (Frensdorff 1864).

These three works are the basic tools for the study of the notes of the Masorah. The notes of the Mm of V are contained both in the work of Frensdorff and in that of Ginsburg. The latter also contains a large amount of material collected from manuscripts. Because of the large number of masoretic notes which Ginsburg collected, his work is likely to help in the decipherment of notes in other MSS, even those which Ginsburg did not himself examine. The work of Frensdorff is usually cited by book and page. In the first two volumes of Ginsburg's work--the major part of it--the lists are arranged alphabetically by word or subject, and the lists given under each letter of the alphabet are numbered. This system of reference is usually followed for these two volumes, but references to the third volume, containing additions, are by page number.

Description and Study of the Masorah

C.D. Ginsburg, *Introduction to the Massoretico-Critical Edition of the Hebrew Bible* (Ginsburg, 1897).

A. Sperber, "Problems of the Masora" (Sperber, 1942).

M.Z. Segal, in his מבוא המקרא, vol IV, pp.5-46 (Segal, 1960).

A.M. Habermann, "Bible and Concordance" (Habermann, 1957).

I. Yeivin, Article מסורה in אנציקלופדיה מקראית (Yeivin, 1968c). (Most of the information given there is included in this study).

A. Dotan, Article "Masorah" in *Encyclopaedia Judaica* (Dotan, 1974).

M. Breuer, כתר ארם צובה והנוסח המקובל של המקרא (Breuer, 1976).

Collections and Studies

62. The following are the most important collections of masoretic material, and studies of the Masorah.

Masseket Soferim (see #150)

Menaḥem ha-Me'iri, *Qiryat Sefer* 1-2 (see #161)

Me'ir ha-Levi Abulafia, *Masoret Siyag la-Torah* (see #160)

Menaḥem di Lonzano, *Or Torah* (see #162)

Eliahu ha-Levi, *Masoret ha-Masoret* (see #169)

Shelomo Yedidyah Norzi, *Minḥat Shay* (see #163)

THE MASORAH--ITS NAME AND PURPOSE

63. Masorah is the name used for the collected body of instructions used to preserve the traditional layout and text of the Bible unchanged. In the older sources the name is spelled in a variety of ways, such as מסורה, מוסרה or מסורת. It is clearly derived from the root MSR, but there is no agreement on the meaning or reference of the name. It is usual to connect it with the common meaning of the root, and to understand it as referring to the "transmission" of the tradition from one generation to another. However some connect it with another meaning of the root, and understand it as "sign". Recently it has been connected with the meaning "count" by Z. ben Ḥayyim. He argues that the form of the word is Aramaic מָסוֹרָ(ה) or Hebrew מוֹסֵרָ(ה), and that the masoretic scholars were given this name because they counted the letters,

words, and verses of the Bible (Ben Ḥayyim 1957).

64. The holiness of the Bible, and its importance in Jewish life, required that its form and text be carefully preserved, both for its own sake and because it was the basis for all the "Oral Law"--for even the minutest details of the text could be significant for the derivation of *halakah*. To achieve this preservation, scholars established general rules governing the method of writing out the Biblical text, and specific statements on the correct spelling of individual words where this might be uncertain. These instructions, which make up the Masorah, did, in fact, make possible the preservation of the Biblical text without significant change. It is true that the oldest manuscripts and the latest printed editions differ in many details; however these are not matters of substance, but minor points of spelling, such as מלא "plene" or חסר "defective", or details of vocalization or accentuation. Manuscripts of other Jewish literary works, such as the Mishnah, Midrash, or Talmuds, can be found which differ from the standard editions in almost every line; and these differences include addition or omission of words or phrases, and variations in wording or in sentence structure, as well as minor differences of spelling. Compared to these, the preservation of the Biblical text is virtually perfect, and this is due to the development of the masoretic instructions. The Masorah thus made possible the transmission of the Biblical text in unchanged form, so that it appears today almost exactly as it did in the time of the Masoretes.

65. The attempt to preserve the text of classic or holy works was also made in other cultures. For instance the classical Greek literature, especially poetry, was diligently studied by the grammarians and text critics whose work reached its peak in the schools of Alexandria in third and second centuries BCE. Their work, which was intended to fix the literary form of the works, consisted mainly in the comparison and evaluation of manuscripts, and the writing of marginal notes (*scholia*) on textual matters such as doublets, additions, omissions, doubtful passages, etc. This study, which led to the establishment of good text forms of the works studied,

corresponds to the initial stage of the development of the Masorah of the Hebrew Bible.

66. A closer parallel to the Jewish Masorah is found in the Syriac "Masorah" to the Old and New Testaments. Syriac "masoretic" manuscripts contain marginal notes on textual variants, on different features of words in the text, particularly on the pronunciation of both consonants and vowels, and on accentuation. Its main concern is thus to ensure that the text was read properly, and it was not designed to preserve the written text unchanged. However even its information on pronunciation is much less detailed than that of the Jewish Masorah. It is only descriptive. It does not reach the stage of enumeration (see #113) which is the outstanding characteristic of the fully developed stage of the Jewish Masorah.

THE WRITING OF THE BIBLICAL TEXT

67. Many details of the method of writing the Biblical text are already prescribed in the *halakah*. These include not only general rules, such as those on writing materials, the width of the margins, and the form of the script, but also rules on details, such as the special signs, the form of particular letters, etc. These matters form the subject of the הלכות ספר תורה *Hilkot sefer Torah* ("Rules for the Writing of Biblical Scrolls"), but they are also a part of the Masorah.

The rules for the writing of Bibles were first fixed for scrolls, since this was the accepted form for all books until the end of the Talmudic period (#5). Many rules are already enunciated in the Talmuds. These were collected in the מסכת סופרים *Masseket Soferim* "Tractate of the Scribes" which seems to date from the 9th century (#150). Many of the rules governing the writing of scrolls were transferred to the writing of codices. As a result the *Hilkot Sefer Torah* form part of the foundation of the Masorah.

The 'Hilkot Sefer Torah'

68. These rules (*halakot*) deal with the method of writing Biblical Scrolls, particularly on the following subjects: The writing materials, including the skin, the preparation of the

parchment, and the ink; who is permitted to write; the need to copy a written text rather than to write from memory; the dimensions of the scroll, including the size of the sheets of parchment and how they are to be joined together to form a scroll, the size of the columns, the necessity for rulings for lines and columns, the breadth of the lines, the spaces between columns and between lines, between words and between letters, the size of the script and the forms of the letters; rules for the correction of scribal errors; rules governing the writing of the holy names of God, which may not be erased; how to correct errors which might occur in them, and which names are to be considered holy. The rules also cover how the scroll is to be looked after and honoured, and what to do with a scroll which is torn or worn out, or in which letters or words have been rubbed out. They also detail how the Bible is to be read in the Synagogue, the number of readers, the sections to be read, and the days when they are to be read.

These separate *halakot* together form a tractate, or set of rules, most of which still continue to govern the writing of Synagogue Scrolls. As with other branches of the Talmudic *halakah*, this branch has undergone some development over the centuries. The *halakot* have been interpreted in the Rabbinic literature. They are included in the works of Maimonides and the *Shulḥan ᶜAruk*, and works have been written on the details of their theory and practice.

69. The *Hilkot Sefer Torah* were developed for the production of Synagogue Scrolls (#5, 7). No masoretic notes, or vowel or accent signs are marked in these, as such additions would render the scroll unfit for liturgical use. These notes and signs can only be written in texts made for secular use, and this was done from an early period both in scrolls and in codices intended for such use, as is shown by some early Geniza fragments. Such scrolls containing vowel and accent signs and masoretic notes, were still produced in conformity with most of the rules governing the production of Synagogue Scrolls, as were the early codices also. They are written on ruled parchment, and the spaces between the columns, lines, words, and letters, the size and form of the script, and the methods of correction, all conform to the rules for Synagogue

Scrolls. As time went on, however, special conventions governing the production of codices grew up, so that codices followed the rules for Synagogue scrolls less and less closely. Codices came to be written on paper, and eventually to be printed, so that the Synagogue Scroll and the Codex came to be two quite different categories.
Literature: Blau 1902.

'Taggim'

70. תגין, תגים *taggim* or *taggin* (crowns), are a form of decoration used in Synagogue Scrolls. They consist of slim strokes "crowning" the letters. They are also called זיונים *ziyyunim* or זיני *zayene* "armour". As a general rule they appear in the form of three small strokes, used on seven letters, which are usually listed in the mnemonic form שעטנ"ז ג"ץ. These ornaments are mentioned in the Talmud (TB *Menaḥot* 29b): "Rabba said: Seven letters require three *ziyyunim*, and these are שעטנ"ז ג"ץ." In masoretic treatises, and in a work known as the ספר תגים (Book of Taggim) it is noted that particular letters (in various places in the Torah) should have a different number of *taggim*, or that the *taggim* should take some special form. E.g. "There are seven *alefs* in the Torah which have seven *taggim*, and these are they...." As a general rule these unusual *taggim* are not marked in present day Synagogue Scrolls, but only those on the letters שעטנ"ז ג"ץ.

Taggim are generally used in Synagogue scrolls, although scrolls without *taggim* (mostly Oriental) are also found. As a general rule *taggim* are not marked in codices, although a few exceptions are known. The main requirements established in the *halakah* for the writing of Synagogue scrolls are described below. Most of these are also applied to the writing of Codices.
Literature: Goldberg, 1866.

The Order of the Biblical Books

71. The order of the Books in the Torah and the Former Prophets has been established from earliest times; however the order of the books in the Latter Prophets and the Writings is not fixed. The order customary today is that used in the first printed editions. In the Talmud (TB *Baba Bathra* 14b), however,

a different order is described: "The order of the Prophets is Joshua, Judges, Samuel, Kings, Jeremiah, Ezekiel, Isaiah, and the Twelve". The Latter Prophets are found in this order in many manuscripts, mostly Ashkenazic. In Oriental manuscripts such as A, L, C, however, and also in Sephardic and Italian MSS, the order is that customary today, with Isaiah before Jeremiah.

The same Talmudic passage states that "The order of the Writings is Ruth, Psalms, Job, Proverbs, Qohelet, Song of Songs, Lamentations, Daniel, Esther, Ezra, Chronicles." According to the *Sefer ha-Ḥillufim* (Lipschuetz, 1962, p.41) this was the Babylonian order, and a few Babylonian MSS are found which do follow this order, although they are fragmentary, and do not contain all the writings. In the same passage, the *Sefer ha-Ḥillufim* states that the order in use in Eretz Israel was "Chronicles, Psalms, Job, Proverbs, Ruth, Song of Songs, Qohelet, Lamentations, Esther, Daniel, Ezra", and this is the order found in the older MSS, such as A, L, S^1. The order customary today follows that used in Ashkenazic MSS and printed editions, in which Chronicles is placed at the end of the Writings, following the Talmudic order and that of Babylonia: with Proverbs before Job, and the order of the "Five Scrolls" (Song of Songs, Ruth, Lamentations, Ecclesiastes, and Esther) according to the order of the festivals on which they are read in the Synagogue.

In the Masorah and the manuscripts, Samuel, Kings, and Chronicles are each considered a single book, and so, too, Ezra and Nehemiah. They are not divided into two. In contrast, the Book of Psalms is divided into five "scrolls".

In the Torah, the space left between the books must be equivalent to four lines of writing. In the other parts of the Bible a space must be left between the different books, but its size is not fixed.

The Division into 'Sedarim' and 'Parashot'

72. The Torah is divided for the sabbath readings in the synagogue in two ways. The community of Eretz-Israel completed the reading of the Torah in three to three and a half years, so it was divided into 154 or 167 sections which are called סדרים *sedarim*. Different MSS show considerable variation in the number of *sedarim*. The beginning of each *seder* is shown in the

MSS by the sign ס in the margin, often with some ornamentation, as ס, ס etc. In Babylonia it was customary to complete the reading of the Torah in a single year, so it was divided into sections, which are called פרשות *parashot*. Each of these is given a title derived (as those of the books of the Torah) from the first few words. Thus, in Genesis, בְּרֵאשִׁית (1:1), נֹחַ (6:9), לֶךְ-לְךָ (12:1), וַיֵּרָא (18:1), and so on. Originally there were 53 *parashot*, but at a late period the *parashah* וַיֵּלֶךְ (Dt 31:1) was added, so that the number today is 54.

The beginning of each *parashah* is marked in manuscripts by the abbreviation פרשׁ in the margin, usually with some ornamentation added to make it conspicuous. In printed editions, the beginning of a *parashah* is indicated by a space, a heading, or some similar marker. Sometimes the threefold repetition פפפ or ססס is used, according to whether the *parashah* begins with a *petuḥah* or a *setumah* division (see #74).

73. The division into *parashot* continues in use, and provides the standard basis for the division of the Torah (and even for dating) throughout Rabbinical literature. *Parashot* are also marked in MSS from Eretz Israel--even the very early ones. The marking of *sedarim* was also continued long after the Babylonian custom became dominant in Israel, and the custom of reading the Torah over a three year period had ceased; and this division is found in most MSS, including Babylonian ones, up to the introduction of printing. In manuscripts the Books of the Prophets and writings are also divided into *sedarim*, but the significance of this division is uncertain. In many manuscripts a note at the end of each book, or at the end of the Torah, Prophets, and Writings, lists the number of *sedarim*, and identifies them.

The Division into Paragraphs and Verses

74. Paragraphs (based on content) called פסקות *pisqot* or פרשיות *parashiyyot*, are marked by spaces in the text. These spaces must occupy the width of at least three letters. They are of two types: the פתוחה *petuḥah* (open) in which the word starting the new paragraph must be written at the beginning of the line, (so that if enough space cannot be left on the last line of the old paragraph, a whole line must be left blank) and

the סתומה *setumah* (closed) in which the first word of the new paragraph is either written on the same line as the last of the old, or, if space is not available for this, it is written after an indentation on the next line. Thus

	Petuḥah	*Setumah*
(a) Paragraph ends at the	-----------	---------
beginning of a line	---	---- ---
	-----------	---------
(b) Paragraph ends at or near	-----------	---------
the end of a line	----------	--------

	-----------	---------

This method of marking paragraphs is that described by Maimonides. There are, however, other opinions on the correct method.

The Masorah mentions a third type of division, the פסקה סדורה *pisqa sedurah*, but it is not known what it was, or how it was marked. The categories of *pisqot*, their number, and the places where they were to be marked, is fixed by the Masorah, and in many MSS the number of *petuḥot* and *setumot* is listed at the end of each book. There are also MSS and Geniza fragments which contain lists of all the *petuḥot* and *setumot* like that published in Ginsburg 1897 (Appendix I pp. 977 ff). Maimonides gives a list of the *petuḥot* and *setumot* in the Torah according to a manuscript of ben Asher (possibly A) in the chapter *Hilkot Sefer Torah* in the second book of his *Mishneh Torah*. Early MSS content themselves with marking *pisqot* by leaving the appropriate space. In later MSS, and in many printed editions, the letter פ is added in the space to mark a *petuḥah*, or the letter ס to mark a *setumah*. The marking of these divisions is incorrect in many of the MSS and printed editions. Such errors render a Synagogue Scroll unfit for liturgical use according to the *halakah*, but this is not the case with codices, although the marking is customary in them.

The marking of *pisqot* is old. It is mentioned in the halakic midrashim (about 3rd cent. CE) "Why were the *pisqot* introduced? To give Moses time to reflect between each *parashah*, and between each subject." (*Sifra*, Leviticus 1:1, ed. Finkelstein p.6) "If a *petuḥah* is written instead of a *setumah*, or a *setumah* instead of a *petuḥah*, the scroll should be removed from liturgical use (*Sifre* in Deuteronomy, sect. 36).

A division between different subjects is marked by a space in the non-Biblical scrolls from the Dead Sea. The same method is used in the Biblical scrolls. In some of these, such as the complete Isaiah scroll ($1QIsa^{a}$) the divisions do not correspond closely to the received tradition, but in others, such as the scroll of the twelve prophets from Murabba^{c}at (Mur XII) the correspondence is very close. The *pisqot* seem also to have been marked in early (Jewish) MSS of the Greek translation, showing that they were already a well-established feature of the text before the turn of the era.
Literature: Perrot, 1969; Revell, 1971. For information on the Dead Sea Scrolls, see Fitzmyer, 1975.

75. The division into verses is later than that into *pisqot*. Nevertheless, it seems that the Bible was divided into verses in Talmudic times, since there are *halakot* which depend on this feature. Examples are the statement that in the synagogue one should read a single verse of the Torah, and then the Targum to it; or the *halakot* which fix the smallest extent of Torah or *hafṭarah* which is to be read. The Talmud records a few differences in the division of particular verses, in which the traditions of Babylonia and Eretz Israel disagreed. The verse is one of the basic textual units referred to in the masoretic literature of the post-Talmudic period, and in lists enumerating various features account is taken of the beginning, middle, or end of a verse, how many times a certain word occurs in a single verse, and so on. (See #132 under פסֹ).

Verse divisions are not marked in the Dead Sea Scrolls (save in some poetic sections, such as Dt. 32 and Ps. 119--again a feature preserved in some early Greek MSS). In a few early MSS a small circle is marked between verses, but in most MSS the end of a verse is marked by two dots, as is still customary. In some early MSS, such as A, B, S^{1}, these dots are not used consistently, and in others, such as L^{20}, the two-dot sign is not used at all (#208). In these cases the scribe marked only the *silluq* sign, considering it an adequate marker of the end of the verse.

Verse division does not always coincide with the earlier *pisqah* division, so that occasionally a *pisqah* division occurs within a verse, forming the so-called *pisqah be-emṣa^c pasuq*, on which there are comments in the Masorah.

Columns and Lines

76. In a synagogue scroll, care is taken to begin every column with some word beginning with *waw*, with the exception of six columns which must begin with particular words. These are בראשית (Gen 1:1), יהודה (Gen 49:8), הבאים (Ex 14:28) שמר (Ex 34:11), מה־טבו (Nu 24:5) and ואעידה (Dt 31:28) --although the masoretes were not fully agreed on some of them. This convention is not generally followed in codices. In A, the word ואעידה does stand at the beginning of a column. Since most of the Torah is not preserved in this MS, the practise in the case of the other words cannot be determined (however not all columns or pages begin with *waw*).

77. The "songs" in the Torah are also written in a fixed format, as is already noted in the Talmud (TB *Megillah* 16b). The "Song at the Sea" (Ex 15:1 ff) is written "Text over space and space over text", thus:

```
----   --------   ----
---------   ---------
----   --------   ----
---------   ---------
```

The "Song of Moses" *Ha'azinu* (Dt 32:1 ff) is written "space over space and text over text", thus:

```
---------    ---------
----------   ---------
-----        ---------
----------   ---------
```

In this way, the beginnings of all the lines of these songs are fixed, as are the beginnings of a few lines before and after them. Early Greek MSS show Dt 32 written in separate stichs (as does the Dead Sea Scroll fragment 4QDeut^q, although this is not a Biblical text), but the stichs are not arranged as in the received tradition. The early codices for the most part follow the conventions of the synagogue scrolls in the writing of the "songs" in the Torah.

The manner of writing the other songs in the Bible, and lists and so on, is less strictly fixed. Examples of these are the Song of David (2S 22), the list of the Kings of Canaan conquered by Joshua (Jos 12:9-24), the ten sons of Haman (Est 9:7-9), and the cities among which David divided the spoil (I Sam 30:27-30). Similarly, the rules for writing the three "poetical" books (Psalms, Proverbs, and Job) are less exact.

78. The most suitable length of the line (i.e. width of a column) was fixed as enough to write three words of ten letters each. TB *Menaḥot* 30a points out that line length depends on the number of columns on the sheet, for if they are few, the columns are broad, and if they are many, the columns are narrow. "The Rabbis have taught that one should use from three to eight columns per sheet. One should not use fewer than that, or more. The use of too many columns makes the text look like a legal document, and the use of too few obscures the contents (because the lines are too long to be read easily). The width of the column should be about enough to write לְמִשְׁפְּחוֹתֵיכֶם three times."

The Dotted Words

79. In fifteen places in the Bible (10 in the Torah, 4 in the Prophets, and 1 in the Writings) dots are marked above particular words. These dots have no connection with the vowel and accent signs. They are part of the "consonantal text", and so are written in Synagogue Scrolls as well as in codices. The Tanna'im mentioned these dots and interpreted them, and they are marked both in the Babylonian and in the Tiberian tradition. They Babylonian Masorah also mentions different dots on other words. In most such cases, however, there is no agreement on the placing of the dots even among the various schools representing the Babylonian tradition, so this is not merely a case of difference between Eastern and Western traditions.

In most cases the dots are marked above the letters--sometimes above all the letters in a word, and sometimes not. In one case dots are marked below the letters as well. The fifteen passages are:

			letter dotted
In the Torah	Gen 16:5	וּבֵינֶיׄהָ	*yod*
	Gen 18:9	אֵׄלָיׄוׄ	*alef yod waw*
	Gen 19:33	וּבְקוּׄמָהּ	*waw*
	Gen 33:4	וַׄיִּׄשָּׁׄקֵׄהוּׄ	all

	Gen 37:12	אֶת	both
	Nu 3:39	וְאַהֲרֹן	all
	Nu 9:10	רְחֹקָה	*he*
	Nu 21:30	אֲשֶׁר	*resh*
	Nu 29:15	וְעִשָּׂרוֹן	*waw*
	Dt 29:28	לָנוּ וּלְבָנֵינוּ עַד	all in two words, plus *ᶜayin*
In the Prophets	2S 19:20	יָצָא	all, but some read יָצָא
	Is 44:9	הֵמָּה	all
	Ez 41:20	הַהֵיכָל	all
	Ez 46:22	מְהֻקְצָעוֹת	all
In the Writings	Ps 27:13	לוּלֵא	all dotted above, and all but *waw* below.

80. Various suggestions about the functions of these dots have been made. The following are the most favoured explanations:

1) They indicate that the dotted letters should be erased. Dots are used for this purpose in early codices, and in the Dead Sea Scrolls, where the dot may be placed both above and below the letter to be erased, or only above it.

2) The dots indicate that the textual tradition was in doubt. This is suggested by the Rabbinic statement "Some say, 'why are the dots used?' Ezra said 'If Elijah should come and ask me why I accepted that reading, I can point out that I have dotted the letters in question (to show they are suspect), but if he should tell me that the reading is correct, I can remove the dots'" (*Avot de-Rabbi Nathan*, version A, 34, and elsewhere).

3) The dots relate to Midrashic commentary, as is suggested, for instance, by the comment on Gen 19:33 וַתַּשְׁקֶיןָ אֶת אֲבִיהֶן יַיִן...וְלֹא יָדַע בְּשִׁכְבָהּ וּבְקוּמָהּ "There is a dot on ובקומה since he did not indeed know of her lying down, but he did know of her rising". (*Bereshit Rabba* 51:8)

In a few of the cases it is indeed possible to argue that the dotted letter or word is superfluous, and in some of these cases it is not represented in one of the versions. Thus אשר (Nu 21:30) appears in the Samaritan Pentateuch as אש, and this was the word translated in the Septuagint. וישקהו (Gen 33:4) is not represented in the Septuagint. In other cases, however, there is no likelihood that the word is superfluous. In some of these cases, such as Dt 29:28, the suggestion that the dots refer to midrashic commentary would fit, but in others none of the three suggestions seems suitable, as is the case with Gen 37:12. Indeed, if any of these suggestions were true, one would expect to find dots on hundreds of words in the Bible on which the midrash comments, or where the textual tradition was uncertain. Furthermore, if this uncertainty were the reason for the dots, why were not the words in question treated as *qere* and *ketiv*? (#93). In most of the cases where a Rabbinic discussion of the dots is recorded, a midrashic explanation for their use is given, so it seems possible that even the Rabbis no longer knew the original meaning of these dots.

In the case of הֵמָּה (Is 44:9), 1QIsa[a] reads ועדיהמה (with המה written above) with the word which is dotted in the Masorah written above the line. Kutscher has argued that it was added by the scribe on the basis of another text.

Inverted 'nun'

81. In two places in the Bible, a symbol like an inverted *nun* is used--a total of nine times in all. In the sources this is referred to as נון מנוזרת *nun menuzzeret*, נקוד *naqud*, סימניות *simaniyyot*, שיפור *shippur* etc. In Nu 10:35-36 this sign is used at the beginning and end of the *pisqah* starting ויהי בנסע הארן. Thus it is stated in *Sifre* on Numbers (section 84) "The section ויהי בנסע הארן is *naqud* (dotted) before it and after it because this is not its place. The opinion of Rabbi is that it forms a book by itself." The second passage is Ps. 107:23-28 and 40, where the sign is used seven times. Printed editions and manuscripts--including Babylonian manuscripts--agree on the marking of this sign in the Torah, but not in the Psalms. Many Tiberian MSS do not mark inverted *nun* in Ps 107 at all, and where it is marked, it is not always put in the same place. Thus in L the sign is put at verses 21-26 and 40. In two Babylonian MSS which contain this passage inverted *nun* is not used.

Krauss and Liebermann explain the inverted *nun* as corresponding to a sign used by the Greek textual critics to indicate that a space should be left between two passages, or to mark passages included in the wrong place--exactly the two reasons for the use of inverted *nun* suggested in Sifre. These suggestions suit the passage in numbers, but it is difficult to see how they would apply to the Psalms verses, and no satisfactory explanation for their use here has yet been offered.

The inverted *nun* sign is similar in form to the Babylonian accent "half *ṭet*" which represents a major disjunctive accent. In a few Geniza fragments signs like these are used at the ends of sentences. Possibly the form of these signs was influenced by the *simaniyyot*.

Literature: Butin, 1906; Liebermann, 1962, pp.38-46.

Letters with unusual forms

82. The Masorah lists certain letters in the Bible which must be written in an unusual form. Many such letters are mentioned in the Talmud and Midrash. Despite this, there is less agreement among MSS and masoretic lists in this category than in the others discussed. The marking of such letters is, however, customary in codices as in synagogue scrolls.

83. <u>"Suspended" Letters</u>. Four letters in the Bible are called תלויות, "suspended", and are written above the normal line. They are מְנַשֶּׁה (Jud 18:30), מִיַּעַר (Ps 80:14), רְשָׁעִים and מֵרְשָׁעִים (Job 38:13, 15). All masoretic MSS agree in marking them. The *nun* of *Menasseh* could be seen as a correction of משה (Moses) to מנשה to avoid using the name of Moses in connection with descendants of his who became idol priests. The *ᶜayin* of מיער may have been raised to mark it as the middle letter of the Book of Psalms (a position already noted in TB *Qiddushin* 30a). There is no obvious reason for the two other suspended letters. They may have originated in a correction by which the *ᶜayin*, accidentally omitted, was added above the line. This is a form of correction common in the Dead Sea Scrolls, and particularly common with *ᶜayin*.

84. <u>Large Letters</u>. The Masorah lists a few dozen words in which one letter is written larger than the others. It is sometimes possible to suggest a reason for this, such as:-

1) A large letter stands at the beginning of a book (Genesis, Proverbs, Chronicles) or at the beginning of a new section (as סוף דבר Qoh 12:13).

2) It draws attention to some significant point, as גָּחוֹן (Lev 11:42) וְהִתְגַּלָּח (Lev 13:33) which mark the half-way point in the Torah in letters and in words, or הַ־לַיהוה (Dt 32:6) where the *he* is written as a separate word.
3) It is a warning that reading must be precise, as in שְׁמַע יִשְׂרָאֵל ה' אֱלֹהֵינוּ ה' אֶחָד (Dt 6:4).
In most cases, however, there is no obvious reason for the large letter, as in וּבְהַעֲטִיף (Gen 30:42) וַיַּשְׁלִכֵם (Dt 29:27) מִשְׁפָּטָן (Nu 27:5) וַיַּהַס (Nu 13:30).

85. Small Letters. These are less common than large letters. The Masorah mentions three cases of small *nun* אֹרֶן (Is 44:14) וּנְבוּשַׁזְבָּן (Jer 39:13) וְנִרְגָּן (Prov 16:28). Other small letters are found, e.g. in וַיִּקְרָא (Lev 1:1) תֶּשִׁי (Dt 32:18) בְּהִבָּרְאָם (Gen 2:4) קַצְתִּי (Gen 27:46).
The marking of large and small letters is not uniform in the MSS. A and L use very few, and in fact use the ordinary forms for most of the letters mentioned in the Masorah as large or small. In fact L shows only 3 large letters שמע, אחד and משפטן, and three small (the cases of small *nun*).

86. Other Unusual Letter Forms. Various other letters with special forms are mentioned in the Masorah, such as וי״ו קטועה the broken *waw* in שלום (Nu 25:12). This is mentioned in TB *Qiddushin* 66b, but nevertheless in old MSS, such as L, this *waw* appears in the usual form. The *qof* in בְּקָמֵיהֶם (Ex 32:25) and הַפְּקֻדִים (Nu 7:2) is mentioned in the Masorah as "*qof* joined and without *taggim*". In the early MSS the vertical stroke of *qof* is usually joined to the horizontal, so it is possible that these letters are only unique in respect of the *taggim*. Other similar notes also seem to refer only to *taggim*, as פ׳ לפופה "rolled up *pe*", אותיות עקומות "curved letters" and so on, and it seems that such forms were only used in a few MSS. פ The "rolled up *pe*", for instance, is much used in Yemenite MSS.
Literature: Albrecht, 1921; Faur, 1967.

Sacred Names

87. Because it was a duty to write the name of God with extra concentration, and particularly because of the special

rules about the correction and erasure of letters in the name, it was necessary for the Masoretes to indicate whether words such as אֵל or אֱלֹהִים were sacred or not--that is, whether or not they referred to the God of Israel. Rules were drawn up, and detailed lists produced, which indicated whether such names were sacred or not in all the cases in which there might be doubt. E.g. in Gen 3:5 "*Elohim* knows that on the day you eat of it your eyes will be opened and you will be like *Elohim*". The first name is sacred, the second is not (*Masseket Soferim* 4:5). In a few Tiberian MSS the notes of the Mp in the margins indicate whether the name is sacred or not in each such case. In the Babylonian tradition the sign for *rafe* was marked on the word if it was sacred (אלהים) and the sign for *dagesh* if it was not (אלהים). There was even a discussion over whether it was permitted to erase personal names and other words which contained groups of letters which could represent a divine name, as הַלְלוּיָה, יְהוּדָה. In addition to this particular problem, the Masorah lists all the places where the name of God occurs in a particular form (e.g. אֲדֹנָי - 134 times) or in a particular combination (e.g. הָאָדוֹן ° יְהוָה ° צְבָאוֹת - 5 times).

THE PRESERVATION OF THE TEXTUAL TRADITION: SPECIAL FEATURES

88. The work of the Masoretes directed towards maintaining the textual tradition can be divided into two classes:- (1) The noting of individual phenomena in the writing of the text, and (2) the preservation of the Biblical text in general. Traditions concerned with individual peculiarities in scribal requirements have been described above. Other traditions, described below, are concerned with the form of individual words or phrases.

תקוני סופרים *'Tiqqune Soferim'* Corrections by the Scribes

89. The Masorah, and also Talmudic sources (*Mechilta, Sifre, Tanḥuma, Shemot Rabba*) use the term כינה הכתוב "The text substitutes (one word for another)" or תקוני סופרים "Corrections by the Scribes" (or "by Ezra", or "by the men of the Great Synagogue") to describe some passages showing unexpected wording which was evidently understood as representing a change intended to avoid expressions which might seem disrespectful to God. In most cases what is said to have

been changed is a letter representing a pronoun, as in

Jer 2:11 וְעַמִּי הֵמִיר כְּבוֹדוֹ בְּלוֹא יוֹעִיל

כְּבוֹדִי היה אלא שֶׁכִּינה הכתוב

"It used to read 'My (i.e. God's) glory', but the text substitutes (its)".

Nu 11:15 וְאַל אֶרְאֶה בְּרָעָתִי

בְּרָעָתְךָ היה אלא שֶׁכִּינה הכתוב

"It used to read 'Your (i.e. God's) wretchedness' but the text substitutes (my)".

Occasionally a greater change is suggested as in Job 32:3

וַיַּרְשִׁיעוּ אֶת אִיּוֹב

וודין כלפי למעלה אלא שכינה הכתוב

"This certainly referred to God, but the text substitutes (Job)".

So also Gen 18:22

וְאַבְרָהָם עוֹדֶנּוּ עֹמֵד לִפְנֵי יְהוָה

וה' עוֹדֶנּוּ עוֹמֵד היה ...

"It used to read 'God was still standing', but the text substitutes (Abraham)"; or, as it is put in *Bereshit Rabba* 49:7

אמר ר' סימון תקון סופרים הוא זה שהשכינה היתה ממתנת לאברהם

"This is a *tiqqun soferim*. God was waiting for Abraham."

18 *tiqqune soferim* are listed in the Masorah. Some, but not all, of these are mentioned in Talmudic sources. In many Biblical MSS, the Mp notes at each case מן י"ח תקון סופרים "One of the 18 *tiqqune soferim*", but in others, such as A, the *tiqqune soferim* are not mentioned.

Some of the sages of the Talmudic period held the opinion that a single letter could be removed from the Torah in order to prevent "profanation of the name of God", and these attributed the supposed corrections to the scribes. Others, who held that no man was free to change any letter of the Torah used the term "The text substitutes"--that is, the supposed substitution was already made in the original text, and there is no question of change by a scribe (so Liebermann). Two similar opinions are held today. Some argue that the original text showed the received reading, and the list of *tiqqunim* represents midrashic interpretation, not text history. Others believe that these corrections were indeed made by the scribes, and they ascribe the same origin to other corrections, not mentioned in the Masorah, which were also intended to avoid profanation of the name of God, such as the use of the root BRK with reference to God as a substitute for some offensive term (e.g. in Job 2:9).

90. The known manuscripts and printed editions of the Bible, and also the versions, for the most part represent the received text where these *tiqqune soferim* are supposed to have occurred. However, the versions do sometimes show a reading corresponding to what is said, in the lists of *tiqqune soferim*, to be the original, uncorrected text (e.g. the LXX in 1S 3:13, Job 7:20), but this could possibly result from a free or interpretative translation of the received reading (as the RSV with BRK in Job 2:9). The tradition states of Hab 1:12

אֱלֹהַי קְדֹשִׁי לֹא נָמוּת

לֹא תָמוּת היה אלא שכינה הכתוב

"It used to read 'you will not die' but the text substitutes (we)". The text is not preserved in 1QpHab, but the comment on it reads

פשר הדבר אשר לוא יכלה אל את עמו ביד הגוים

"The meaning is that God will not destroy His people by the hand of foreign nations", which suggests the same reading as the received text.

Literature: Liebermann, 1962, pp.28-37; McKane, 1974.

'ᶜIṭṭur Soferim', 'Miqra Soferim'

91. These two terms are mentioned (in TB *Nedarim* 37b) as "*Halakah* of Moses from Sinai". The name *ᶜiṭṭur soferim* is given to a list of five places in the Bible in most of which the conjunction *waw* is expected but is not used, as in אַחַר תַּעֲבֹרוּ (Gen 18:5). It is suggested that the scribes removed the conjunction. There are a great many places in the Bible in which the conjunction *waw* might have been added to a word, and a great many in which the MSS differ in using or not using *waw*, and it is not clear what would make these five cases unique. Again, if the scribes had wished to delete a *waw* which was written in the text, why did they not use the *qere/ketiv* system? A possible answer to this is that the *qere/ketiv* system was used where the form to be read differed from that written, but the written text was not to be changed, but with

the *ʿiṭṭure soferim*, as with the *tiqqune soferim* (#89), the original text really was changed. There is, however, really no evidence either for or against this suggestion.

92. Under the title *miqra soferim* the Talmud lists the words ארץ, שמים, and מצרים, with no explanation. The Ge'onim suggested that the term referred to the change in the pronunciation of these words in pause. It is also suggested that the reference might be to the use of these words with the "*he* directional" (אַרְצָה etc.), but there is really no evidence to support any theory about this term either.

'Qere/Ketiv' Situations: Marking the Text

93. The words *ketiv* and *qere* are Aramaic passive participles meaning "(what is) written" and "(what is) read". They refer to cases in which the letters of the traditional text (*ketiv*) suggest some word other than that traditionally read (*qere*).

In some early MSS *qere/ketiv* situations are not marked at all. In others, mostly with Palestinian pointing, two dots (..) are marked in the margin beside the line in which the *ketiv* form occurs. Sometimes the *ketiv* form in the text is marked with a dot, but this is not consistent, and may not be original.

In many early MSS a sign like a large final *nun* ן is used in the margin opposite the line in which the *ketiv* form occurs, with no further note. This sign is found in MSS with Tiberian, Palestinian, or Babylonian pointing, and continues in use up to the twelfth century. Kahle explained it as an abbreviation for קריין ("What are read"), but the use of the last letter (especially *nun*) to represent a word would be astonishing. In the prolegomena to BHK the equation ן = נסחא "variant" is suggested, but this also seems unsatisfactory. In a masoretic note listing the words marked with a dot in the Babylonian tradition, it is said

אליין מלייא באורייתא דכתיבן לבר מן דפא ןׄ ומנקדין מירום
מילתא או מירום אחא ואינון זיטימא ומחלוקת ופליגין עליהון

(Ginsburg, 1880, III, p.278) "These are the words in the Torah where ןׄ is written beside the column, and a dot is marked above a word or letter. That word or letter is uncertain, and there are different opinions on it". Possibly this *nun*-like sign derived from a *zayin* representing זיטימא "uncertain"--and indeed the sign has a short *zayin*-like form in some Palestinian MSS. It is also possible, however, that this sign does not represent any word, but is just a sign which happens to look like a letter.

In a few MSS in which this *nun*-like sign, or the two dot sign, is used to draw attention to the *ketiv* form, a single letter characterizing the *qere* form is marked beside it, as in Jer 18:22, text שיחה° margin ן̇ו. I.e., *ketiv* שיחה *qere* שׁוּחָה. In later MSS the whole *qere* form may be written beside the sign, and identified as the *qere* form by ק̇ etc., thus text שיחה°, margin ן̇ שוחה ק̇, or, in the Babylonian MS Ec 2 at Ps 22:24, text יגורו° margin ן̇ וגורו קרו. Where this *nun*-like sign is not used, the usual method of marking *qere/ketiv* situations in Babylonian MSS is that found in Ec 1 at Prov 20:4, text כת ישאל°, margin ושאל כ ק. In Tiberian texts the circle (the typical indicator of masoretic notes) is used above the *ketiv* form in the text, with the *qere* form in the margin identified by ק̇, קר̇, or קרי, as Jer 50:44, text אֲרִוֺצֵם, margin אריצם ק̇. In later MSS the whole of the *qere* form is given in this way, but in earlier ones it is often represented only be the letter(s) in which it differs from the *ketiv*. Thus in Jer 18:22 on שִׂיחָה the margin of C has ן̇וק̇; that of L שוחה ק̇, and in Jer 34:11 on וַיִּכְבִּישׁוּם the margin of C has ן̇ יתי̇ י̇ "superfluous *yod*" while L has ויכבשום ק̇.

94. A variety of terms may be used in *qere/ketiv* situations, as is shown by the following examples. (For the meaning of the abbreviations used, see #132, and on *qere wela ketiv* and *ketiv wela qere* see #102).

Gen 8:17 text	הַוְֺצֵא
margin	היצא ק̇
Dt 33:2 text	אֵשְׁדָּת°
A margin	כת̇ מלה חדה וקרי תרת̇ מלין
"written as one word, read as two"	
L margin	אש דת ק̇
1K 6:16 text	מִיַּרְכְּוּתֵי

A margin	יתיר ו̇
"superfluous *waw*"	
L margin	מירכתי ק̇
Masoretic fragment	ל̇ ק̇ ו̇
"*waw* is not read"	
1K 6:21 text	בְּרַתּ֯יקוֹת
A margin	ו̇ קרי
L margin	ברתוקות ק̇
1K 7:23 text	וְקָוה֯
A, L	וקו ק̇
Masoretic fragment	ל̇ ק̇ ה̇
"*he* is not read"	

In fully developed MSS *qere/ketiv* notes do not stand out from the other masoretic notes. In less developed (or less complete) MSS, early or late, only a selection of notes from the Masorah may be given (as in most printed editions), and in these the *qere/ketiv* notes, which are essential to the traditional reading, are marked, and tend to stand out from the few other masoretic notes added.

Notes giving the *qere*, like other notes discussed in this section, are not written in Synagogue Scrolls, as is remarked in Adler, 1897, p.35. "With reference to *ketiv* and *qere* notes given in codices, in Synagogue Scrolls, only the *ketiv* form is given. The *qere* form is not given, because it is part of the reading tradition, not part of the written text."

95. Manuscripts do not all agree on the places where *qere/ketiv* notes are given. The majority usually give such notes where the *qere* form differs greatly from the *ketiv*, but where the difference is slight, many MSS fail to give the notes. Thus some MSS, like S, annotate all cases where the 3ms pronoun is written with *he*, as אָהֳלֹ֯ה -- אהלו ק̇, but most MSS give no notes on such forms. Some MSS even mark forms like קָו -- קיו ק̇, and חַסְתָו (Song 2:11)--הסתיו ק̇. Others annotate cases such as תַּעֲשֶׂ֯ינָה as יתיר י̇ "superfluous *yod*" and so on, but most MSS do not give notes on such cases. In some MSS cases of unusual plene or defective spellings are treated as *qere/ketiv* situations, but others mark them simply as מלא or חסר. For example:

Is 56:10	צֹ֯פָו

L margin	צפיר ק̇
A margin "unique and defective"	ל̇ וחס
Jer 32:35	הַחֲטִי
L margin	החטיא ק̇
A margin "two spellings lacking *alef*"	ב̇ חס א̇
Jer 19:15, 39:16	מֵבִי
L margin	מביא ק̇
A margin "spelled 9 times without *alef*"	ט̇ חס̇ א̇
Is 26:20	יַעֲבָור-
L margin	יעבר ק̇ יתיר ו̇
A margin "seven cases plene"	ז̇ מל
Prov. 22:14	יִפָּול-
L margin	יפל ק̇
A margin "occurs twice, once defective and once plene".	ב̇ חד חס וחד מל̇
Ps. 34:10	יִראוּ
L margin "spelled with superfluous *alef*"	יתיר א̇
A margin "occurs three times"	ג̇

Because of differences of this sort, the number of *qere/ketiv* notes differs considerably in different MSS and scholarly estimates. The smallest of these is about 800, but a manuscript like L in fact contains fewer notes than this. The highest estimate might be as high as 1500.

96. Most of the differences recorded in the name of the *Madinḥa'e* (Easterners) and *Ma^{c}arba'e* (Westerners) (#153) are matters of *qere/ketiv*. In some cases the *Ma^{c}arba'e* require a *qere/ketiv* note in some particular place, and their *qere* is the *ketiv* of the *Madinḥa'e*, or vice-versa. In the standard list, the *Madinḥa'e* and *Ma^{c}arba'e* differ in some 10% of the *qere/ketiv* situations in the Prophets and Writings, but in fact the proportion of disagreement in this feature between the known Babylonian and Tiberian MSS is much greater.

'Qere/Ketiv' Situations: Pointing the 'qere' Form

97. In printed editions the general rule is that the *ketiv* form in the text is pointed with the vowels belonging to the *qere*, while the *qere* form in the margin is not pointed (and

so BHK, BHS). This is also the most common method in MSS from all periods. However in some MSS, mostly Babylonian, the *qere* form is also pointed. MSS from different schools show slight differences in the method of pointing the *ketiv* form in the text. For example in ותראנה (1S 14:27, *qere* וַתָּאֹרְנָה) some MSS point the *ketiv* וַתָּרְאֹנָה, showing the vowels in the order in which they appear in the *qere* form; while some point it וַתָּרְאֹנָה, showing the vowel signs on the letters on which they occur in the *qere* form, and others point it וַתָּראֹנָה, combining the two principles.

Some printed editions point the *qere* form only, leaving the *ketiv* without vowel signs, but this system is not found in the manuscripts.

Categories of Qere/Ketiv notes

98. 1) Euphemisms. In 16 cases in the Bible, the *qere* form presents a euphemism, replacing an unpleasant word, as in Is 13:16 *ketiv* תִּשָּׁגַלְנָה, *qere* תִּשָּׁכַבְנָה; 1S 5:9 *k.* עְפֹלִים *q.* טְחוֹרִים. The Talmud (TB *Megilla* 25b) remarks on these "Wherever the text is written indelicately, we read it delicately".

99. 2) Unusual plene or defective writings. Where the word might be difficult to recognize, an unusual plene or defective writing may be treated as a *ketiv*, with the regular spelling given as the *qere*, as כִּקְסוֹם- (Ez 21:28) כִּקְסָם-ק. For further examples see #95. As noted there, not all MSS mark such cases as *qere/ketiv* situations. Many such cases are listed in *Okhlah we-Okhlah* (#143). E.g. List #103

מ"ח מלין נסבין א' במצעא תיבות' ולא קרין

"48 words spelled with a medial *alef* which is not read, as תֹאסִפוּן (Ex 5:7) etc." Also list #104

י"ב מלין דכתבין א' בסוף תיבות' ולא קרין

"12 words spelled with a final *alef* which is not read, as אָבוּא (Is 28:12) etc." Also list #128

נ"ו מלין חסר י' במצע' תיבות' וכל חד לי' דכו' חסר

"56 words with *yod* lacking within the word, (but read), each of which is a unique form", as צַוָּארָו (Gen 33:4) etc."

100. 3) "Correcting" archaic or dialectal forms which are not normal Biblical spellings. For example

אַתְּי (2K 4:16, 23, etc.) *qere* אַתְּ
לָכִי (2K 4:2) *qere* לָךְ and similar forms, cf. *Okhlah* list #127

מ"ג מלין כתבן י' בסוף תיבות' ולא קרין

"43 words written with final *yod* which is not read".
נִשְׁבְּרָה (1K 22:49) *qere* נִשְׁבְּרוּ, cf. *Okhlah* list #113

י"ד מלין כתיב ה' בסוף תיבות' וקרין ו'

"14 words written with final *he* but read with *waw*".
צָרְופָה (Ps 26:2) *qere* צָרְפָה, דוֹיֵג (1S 22:18, 22) *qere* דוֹאֵג, and many others.

101. 4) <u>Other Categories</u>. The other categories of *qere/ketiv* can be seen as the result of different types of scribal error (which would affect the text but not the reading tradition) although this is not the only possible explanation.
i) Metathesis. וַיִּקָּלֲהוּ (2S 20:14) *qere* וַיִּקָּהֲלוּ. Cf. *Okhlah* list #91

ס"ב מלין דכתבן מוקדם מאוחר

"62 words showing metathesis of letters".
ii) difference in word division. וּמִתַּחְתָּה לְשָׁכוֹת (Ez 42:9) *qere* וּמִתַּחַת הַלְּשָׁכוֹת. Cf. *Okhlah* list #101

ג' מלין תיבות' קמייתא נסבא מן תנינא

"3 pairs of words in which letters of the second are added to the first." Also list #102

וחלוף ב' מלין תנינא נסבא מן קמיית'

"And the reverse: two words in which letters of the first are added to the second." Also list #99

ט"ו דכתבן תיב' חדא וקרין תרין מלין

"15 cases of one written word read as two." Also list #100

וחלוף ח' כתבין תרין מלין וקרין מל' חדא

"And the reverse: 8 cases where two written words are read as one."
iii) Omission of a letter. (In some cases this could result from haplography). וָאַרְבֶּ (Jos 24:3) *qere* וָאַרְבֶּה. Cf. *Okhlah* list #111

כ"ט מלין חסר ה' בסוף תיבות' וקרין

"29 words lacking final *he* which is read".
אֵינָם (Lam 5:7) *qere* וְאֵינָם. Cf. *Okhlah* list #117

י"ב מלין חסר ו' בריש תיבות' וקרי'

"12 words lacking initial *waw* which is read".
iv) Addition of letters. וירֶה (Jer 5:24) *qere* יוֹרֶה. Cf. *Okhlah* list #118

י"א כתב' ו' בריש תיבות' ולא קרין

"11 words with initial *waw* which is not read".

וְקוה (1K 7:23) *qere* וְקו. Cf. *Okhlah* list #112

כ' מלין כתב' ה' בסוף תיבות' ולא קרין

"20 words written with final *he* which is not read". Also list #120

י"א מלין כתב' ו' בסוף תיבו' ולא קרי'

"11 words written with final *waw* which is not read".

v) Replacement of one letter by another of similar form.

יפְצְחוּ (Is 49:13) *qere* ופִצְחוּ. Cf. *Okhlah* list #134

כ"ב מלין כתיבין י' בריש תיבות' וקרין ו'

"22 words spelled with initial *yod*, but read with initial *waw*". Also list #135

וחלוף י' כתבן ו' בריש תיבות' וקרין י'

"And the reverse: 10 words spelled with initial *waw*, but read with *yod*". In the same way *waw* and *yod* interchange within the word (*Okhlah* lists #80-81, 138-148) and at the end of the word (lists #136-7). Other letters are also interchanged, as are inflected forms of nouns and verbs, and even whole words, as בְּרֹכב (2K 19:23) *qere* בְּרֹב, הָעִיר (2K 20:4) *qere* חָצֵר. Many forms in this category could be seen as resulting from variations in dialect or reading tradition, as שְׁבִית (Ez 16:53 and elsewhere) *qere* שְׁבוּת, יְעִיאֵל (1C 9:35 and elsewhere) *qere* יְעוּאֵל, הַיְּהוּדִיים (Est 8:1 and elsewhere) *qere* הַיְּהוּדִים, נַעֲרָ (Gen 24:14 and elsewhere) *qere* נַעֲרָה.

102. 5) *'Qere we-la Ketiv'* and *'Ketiv we-la Qere'*: The Masorah lists ten cases in which a word is to be read although it is not represented in the consonantal text in any way, and eight places where letters appear in the consonantal text, but no word is read. (See *Okhlah* lists #97-98). This category is mentioned in the Talmud (TB *Nedarim* 37b) as "*Halakah* of Moses from Sinai", but only seven and five (respectively) of the cases are listed.

103. 6) Perpetual *'Qere'*. In the case of some words, the form traditionally read is always different from that suggested by the letters. This class is related to *qere/ketiv*, but is not marked as such. The leading example is the tetragrammaton, יהוה, which is pointed יְהוָה or יְהֹוָה to indicate the *qere* אֲדֹנָי

or יְהוִה or יְהֹוִה to indicate the *qere* אֱלֹהִים. The Talmud (TB *Pesaḥim* 50a) remarks on this

לא כשם שאני נכתב אני נקרא נכתב אני ביו"ד ה"א
ונקרא אני באל"ף דל"ת

"I am not read as I am written, I am written with *yod he*, but read with *alef dalet*". It is possible that the writing of the Divine Name in Hebrew characters in some Greek MSS, and its writing in Old Hebrew characters (or with four dots) in some of the Qumran Scrolls, was similarly intended to guard the sanctity of the name of God. Other cases of perpetual *qere* are ירושלם read יְרוּשָׁלַיִם (the regular spelling in non-Biblical texts), הוא representing the 3fs pronoun read הִיא, and יששכר, read (according to the ben Asher pointing) יִשָּׂכָר.

The Date of the 'Qere/Ketiv' Readings

104. Categories 1 and 5 of *qere/ketiv*, and also the perpetual *qere* of the divine name, are mentioned in the Talmud, and must consequently be very old. In contrast, many of the notes in category 2 are based on the vowel signs, and result from the fact that the spelling was not consistent with the pointed form. They must, then, be later than the invention and establishment of the vowel signs, that is, no earlier than the eighth century.* The lack of agreement between the MSS in the marking of notes in this category is also evidence of their late date. However even though many *qere/ketiv* notes were not fixed until after the introduction of vowel signs, the Masoretes only introduced such notes where there was a conflict between the text and the reading tradition. They did not use them where only vowel or accent signs were involved (as Eliahu ha-Levi clearly demonstrated). Thus *qere/ketiv* notes are not used, for instance, where *pataḥ* is used instead of expected *qameṣ*, or one accent instead of another, or to note unusual stress position, or unusual use of *dagesh* or *rafe*, *śin* or *shin*, etc.

---

* It could however be argued that many notes of this type are, in fact, a way of indicating the pronunciation of a word where the spelling is ambiguous or misleading, and thus must have been introduced before the introduction of the vowel signs, by which they were rendered redundant. (E.J.R.)

The other categories of *qere/ketiv* must have been introduced after the earliest (1, 5, and 6), but before the late category 2. It is clear, then, that the system of *qere/ketiv* notes was already established in the Talmudic period, and indeed the literature of this period contains occasional references to notes in categories other than 1, 5, and 6. It cannot, however, be assumed that the whole *qere/ketiv* system was established in this period, and in fact the system continued to develop until the end of the Masoretic period.

Examples of 'Qere/Ketiv' notes from Talmudic Literature

105. (In all these cases the *qere/ketiv* situation is marked in the received text.)

2K 20:4, וַיְהִי יְשַׁעְיָהוּ לֹא יָצָא הָעִיר הַתִּיכֹנָה

TB ^{c}*Erubin* 26a"העיר is written, but we read חָצֵר"

TY *Sanhedrin* 10, fol.28c. "העיר is written"

Hag 1:8 וְאֶרְצֶה בּוֹ וְאֶכָּבְדָ

TB *Yoma* 21b "וְאֶרְצֶה בּוֹ וְאֶכבד is written, but we read וְאֶכָּבְדָה"

Lev 23:13 וְנִסְכֹּה יַיִן רְבִיעִית הַהִין

Menaḥot 89b "The text says וְנִסְכּוֹ יַיִן רְבִיעִית הַהִין.

R. El^{c}azar said 'ונסכה is written, but we read וְנִסְכּוֹ'".

1S 2:9 רַגְלֵי חֲסִידָו יִשְׁמֹר

TB *Yoma* 38b "חֲסִידָיו (pious ones) is plural in meaning.

R. Naḥman bar Yiṣḥaq says 'חסידו is written' (which would normally indicate the singular ".

Ez 1:8 וִידֵו אָדָם מִתַּחַת כַּנְפֵיהֶם

TB *Pesaḥim* 119a "What does וִידֵי אָדָם mean? וידו (as if singular) is written".

2S 16:23 כַּאֲשֶׁר יִשְׁאַל בִּדְבַר הָאֱלֹהִים

TY *Sanhedrin* 10b "Where the Bible says 'and the counsel of Aḥitophel which he counselled in those days was as if a man had enquired of the word of God' אִישׁ (a man) is read but not written. The scriptures could not use the term 'man' of him".

2K 5:9 וַיָּבֹא נַעֲמָן בְּסוּסָו וּבְרִכְבּוֹ

TY *Sanhedrin* 10, fol.29a "When Naaman commander of the army of the King of Aram came to Elisha, he came to him 'with his horses (בְּסוּסָיו) and his chariots'. R. Johanan says בסוסו is written (as if singular).

2S 21:4 אֵין לָי כֶּסֶף וְזָהָב

TY *Sanhedrin* 6:9, fol.23d. "Where the Bible says 'We have no silver or gold' אֵין לִי 'I do not have' is written (but אֵין לָנוּ 'we do not have' is read).

Gen 8:17 כָּל הַחַיָּה אֲשֶׁר אִתְּךָ... הַוְצֵא אִתָּךְ

Bereshit Rabba 34:8 "R. Yudan says 'הוצא is written, but it is read הַיְצֵא"

Prov 23:31 כִּי יִתֵּן בַּכִּיס עֵינוֹ

Wayyiqra Rabba 12:1 "בכיס is written (but בַּכּוֹס is read)".

106. The LXX translation sometimes follows the *ketiv* and sometimes the *qere*, with no decided preference. There is, similarly, no decided tendency to present either the *ketiv* or the *qere* form in the Dead Sea Scrolls. In the three cases in Isaiah in which the *qere* form presents a euphemism, 1QIsa[a] shows the *qere* in ת[שכ]בנה (Is 13:16 תשגלנה), but the *ketiv* in חריהמה and שיניהמה (Is 36:12 *qere* צוֹאָתָם and מֵימֵי רַגְלֵיהֶם).

The Origin of 'Qere/Ketiv'

107. Various suggestions on the origin of the *qere/ketiv* situations have been made, but none provides a satisfactory explanation for all examples. Some have suggested that *qere* represents an arbitrary correction, noted in the margin by the Masoretes. There are, however, examples (admittedly rare) in which the *qere* is more difficult to understand than the reading suggested by the *ketiv*, as הוצא (Gen 8:17) read הַיְצֵא not הוֹצֵא, and מגדיל (2S 22:51) read מִגְדּוֹל not מַגְדִּיל. Others suggest that the *ketiv* represents the reading of some form of model manuscript, while the *qere* represents a variant reading from some other MS(S), or that two or three model MSS were used to determine the authoritative text, and that the *ketiv* represents the reading of the preferred text, or of the majority, while the *qere* gives the alternative or minority reading. Another suggestion is that the *qere* readings are simply corrections suggested by the Masoretes on the basis of some manuscript. All that is clear, however, is that the wording of the reading tradition is not, at these points, represented by the letters of the received text. Suggestions on the origin of the phenomenon are all speculative.

'Al Tiqre'

108. One of the methods of interpretation used by the

Rabbis is known as אל תקרי *al tiqre* "do not read", since it was based on a slight change (often only of vowels) in the traditional reading, and was introduced by ...אל תקרא... אלא "Do not read (the received text) but (some similar alternative)". E.g. "Do not read חָרוּת (Ex 32:16) but חֵרוּת (Mishnah *Avot* 6:2). This is superficially similar to the *qere/ketiv* of the Masoretes, but in fact is not connected with it. The *al tiqre* reading is a deliberate change in the received tradition--a sort of a pun--made solely as the basis for a homily. It does not derive either from written tradition or from a reading tradition, but from midrashic interpretation. There is no question of any real change in the received tradition.

Literature: Gordis, 1937; Orlinsky, 1940, 1960.

'Sevirin'

109. The Masorah frequently notes a reading different from the written text not as a *qere*, but as סבירין "*sevirin*", abbreviated סביׄ, also noted as סבירין ומטעין, or מטעׄ. The MSS and Masoretic lists do not agree on the number of such notes. L shows 71, while V shows some 200, and many more could be collected from other texts and lists. *Sevirin* are not always clearly distinguished from *qere/ketiv* notes on the one hand, or textual variants on the other, so that one MS may give a reading as a *sevir*, while another gives it as a *qere*. The corresponding term in the Babylonian Masorah is דחזי or משתבשין (מישׁ).

The term *sevir* marks readings that avoid some difficulty in the received text. E.g.

Jer 48:45 (Mp of L) אֵשׁ יָצָא מֵחֶשְׁבּוֹן--גׄ סבׄר יָצְאָה

"(One of) 3 cases where יָצְאָה is wrongly suggested for יָצָא" (אֵשׁ is normally feminine).

Nu 33:8 וַיִּסְעוּ מִפְּנֵי הַחִירֹת --גׄ מטעׄ

"(One of) 3 cases where מִפִּי is wrongly suggested for מִפְּנֵי" (cf. פִּי הַחִירֹת Ex 14:2, 9).

2C 13:3 גִּבּוֹר חַיִל--גׄ סברין גִּבּוֹרֵי

"(One of) 3 cases where גִּבּוֹרֵי is wrongly suggested".

Similarly ה' סבירין כַּאֲשֶׁר וקרינן אֲשֶׁר

"כַּאֲשֶׁר is wrongly suggested in five cases where we read אֲשֶׁר",

and the reverse כַּאֲשֶׁר י' סבירין אֲשֶׁר

"אֲשֶׁר is wrongly suggested in ten cases where we read כַּאֲשֶׁר"

So also וַיָּבוֹא -- ח' סבירין לשון רבים

"וַיָּבוֹא (singular) -- eight times the plural is wrongly suggested."

ד' סבירין וּבְנֵי וקרין וּבֶן וד' סבירין וּבֶן וקרין וּבְנֵי

"וּבְנֵי is wrongly suggested in four cases where וּבֶן is read, and וּבֶן is wrongly suggested in four cases where וּבְנֵי is read."

וּבְכָל -- ה' דמטעין בהון דסבירין בְּכָל

"In five cases where וּבְכָל is written people err and suggest בְּכָל".

אֱלֹהֵיכֶם -- ב' דמטעין בענין וסבירין אֱלֹהֵיהֶם

"In two cases in this section where אֱלֹהֵיכֶם is written people err and suggest אֱלֹהֵיהֶם (Examples taken from Frensdorff, 1876, pp.369-373).

Examples from the Babylonian Masorah are

1C 2:48 פִּלֶגֶשׁ כָּלֵב מַעֲכָה יָלַד -- יָלַד דחזי לה יָלְדָה

"יָלְדָה is wrongly suggested for יָלַד" (a feminine verb form is expected, as the subject is פִּילֶגֶשׁ).

Prov 31:6 לאובד

The Babylonian pointing shows the article, the Tiberian לְאוֹבֵד does not.

The note *sevirin* does not show that the consonantal text does not indicate the form to be read, or that the text is in any way in doubt. It presents a reading which seems to avoid a difficulty in the text, but the purpose is to warn that this reading is not correct. It is thus given as a support for the received reading. There is no basis for the common suggestion that the *sevirin* notes are a way of correcting the received text.

110. There are different opinions on the source of the alternative readings against which the *sevirin* notes warn, and on the reason why these notes are given in some places where error is likely, but not in others. One possibility is that they are a warning against suggestions by readers; another that they are used as a necessary warning where people commonly did introduce erroneous readings, or where such readings were found in inferior texts. Another possibility is that the *sevirin* readings represent ancient alternative traditions--and it is true that in some cases *sevirin* readings are supported by the

ancient versions. It is also true, however, that a translation is in many cases almost forced to avoid difficulties found in the original text, so it is not surprising that in doing this they often coincide with the *sevirin*. As with other such questions, there is not enough evidence to permit any definite statement on the source of the *sevirin*.

Literature: Reach, 1895.

THE PRESERVATION OF THE TEXTUAL TRADITION: THE TEXT AS A WHOLE

(i) The 'Masorah Parva' (Mp)

111. The purpose of the Masoretes was not merely to preserve those unusual features of the textual tradition discussed above, but to preserve the whole text, that is to say every letter of every word, and also--after the introduction of the vowel and accent signs--each one of these signs as well. For this purpose a range of terms and techniques was developed and used in the masoretic notes on the text. These notes were presented in a highly abbreviated form, with the words often represented only by their initial letters. These notes were written in the margin to the right or left of the line of text containing the word to which they referred. This is known as the מָסוֹרָה קְטַנָּה, latinized as *Masorah parva* (Mp) the "small Masorah". The word in the text to which the note refers is marked with a small circle--the characteristic masoretic signal. When a note refers to more than one word, the circle is marked between them. If the note contains more than one word, they are written one below the other.

column of text (Is 56:7)	margin
וַהֲבִיאוֹתִים אֶל־הַר קָדְשִׁי	ד׳[1] יו׳[2] וכל אל הר הכרמל
וְשִׂמַּחְתִּים בְּבֵית ° תְּפִלָּתִי	ב׳[3] ל׳[4]
עוֹלֹתֵיהֶם וְזִבְחֵיהֶם לְרָצוֹן	ב׳[5] כת כן

1) This spelling (וַהֲבִיאוֹתִים) occurs four times.

2) The combination אֶל הַר occurs 16 times, and, in addition, always in the phrase אֶל הַר הַכַּרְמֶל

3) This spelling (וְשִׂמַּחְתִּים) occurs twice.

4) The combination בְּבֵית תְּפִלָּתִי is unique.

5) The word עוֹלֹתֵי... occurs twice with this spelling (the other case is in Dt 12:11).

The order of the notes from right to left is the same as that of the words in the text. Thus note 1), ד׳, refers to

וַהֲבִיאוֹתִים, and note 2), יֹו וכל אֶל הַר הַכַּרְמֶל, refers to the combination אֶל־הַר. Similarly, note 3), בׄ, refers to וְשִׂמַּחְתִּים, and note 4), לׄ, refers to the combination בְּבֵית תְּפִלָּתִי.

112. A note placed in the margin between two columns could refer to either column, and in order to determine where it does apply, one must assign the notes in the corresponding lines in both columns to their respective words. For example

Col II (Dt 28:28-29) Col I (Dt 28:20)

לֵבָב׃ וְהָיִיתָ מְמַשֵּׁשׁ בַּצָּהֳרַיִם לׄ לׄ אֶת־הַמְּהוּמָה וְאֶת־הַמִּגְעֶרֶת רבׄת

Note (1), "Occurs twice, here and with רבת (Ez 22:5)" refers to the word המהומה, note (2), "unique", refers to the word המגערת in the column to the right of the note, while note (3), "unique" refers to the word ממשש in the column to the left.

113. The Masorah does not annotate every word in the Bible, but only those in which errors are likely to be made, particularly those which may be spelled either חָסֵר "defective" --without a vowel letter, or מָלֵא "plene"--with a vowel letter. Words which appear with or without the conjunction *waw*, or with or without some other particle, are also common subjects of notes. As a rule the need for a note was judged on the basis of factual comparison--i.e. on the basis of the fact that a word actually was spelled defective in some cases and plene in others, or that a word actually did have prefixed *waw* in some cases but not in others. Theoretical considerations--i.e. the fact that a word could be spelled in different ways--are not unsually the source of notes. For this reason the Masorah does not usually present simply a description of the spelling of the word (as "plene" or "defective"), but adds, at the same time, enumeration; that is, it gives the accepted number of occurrences of that particular spelling, as יִפּוֹל (Amos 9:9) זׄ מל "seven times spelled plene". If the form in that spelling is unique in the Bible, the masoretic note is לׄ, abbreviated from לֵית "There is no other (case of the same spelling)". E.g. וְלִמְשֹׁל (Gen 1:18) לׄ. I.e. the word וְלִמְשֹׁל occurs only here, although לִמְשֹׁל without the conjunctive *waw* does occur elsewhere. This לׄ is the most common masoretic note. Occasionally it is noted that the spelling of a word is always the same. The term

here is כול "All (cases have the same spelling)". E.g. פְּרֻכִים (Ex 36:8) כל אורייי חסר וי"ו "All cases in the Torah are written defective (without *waw*").

114. The basis of the Masorah in practical observation can also be seen in the fact that a note on some particular word or combination of words is often followed by information on a similar form or combination, introduced by וחד "One (other case)", or some other term. E.g.

Dt 32:39 וַאֲחַיֶּה -- ל̇ וחד אֲנִי אֲחַיֶּה

"Unique (with this spelling), but אֲחַיֶּה (אֲנִי) does occur once".

Lev 4:35 יוּסַר -- ל̇ וחד בַּיּוֹם הַהוּא יוּשַׁר

"Unique (with this spelling), but יוּשַׁר does occur once" (Is 26:1). Similar information is introduced by ושאר "The rest, the other cases", as

2C 31:17 וּלְמָעְלָה -- ב̇ ושאר וָמָעְלָה

"Twice (with this spelling), elsewhere ומעלה occurs" (without the prefixed ל).

1C 8:6 אֵחוּד -- ל̇ ושאר קריי אֵהוּד

"Unique, elsewhere in the Bible אֵהוּד is used" (with *he*, not *ḥet*). וכל also occurs in similar contexts, as

Dt 16:18 מִשְׁפַּט°צֶדֶק -- ל̇ וכל קרייה צֶדֶק וּמִשׁ

"This combination is unique, in all other cases in the Bible the order is צֶדֶק וּמִשְׁפָּט" (reversed).

Nu 34:3 צִן -- כל צִין חסר וכל סִין מלי

"צִן is always spelled defective (without *yod*), but סִין always plene (with *yod*)." (In this note, as often, the vowel letter is added to "צין" for the convenience of the reader, as this was considered more important in such cases than consistency with the Biblical spelling).

Lev 14:10 וְכַבְשָׂה -- כל קריי כַּבְשָׂה וכל שְׁמוּאֵל כִּבְשָׂה

Literally "All the Bible has כַּבְשָׂה (with *pataḥ*, as here), but all of Samuel has כִּבְשָׂה (with *ḥireq*) ", or, as we would put it, "The *kaf* is always pointed with *pataḥ* in all cases but those in the Books of Samuel, where it always has *ḥireq*."

115. In enumerating variant spellings, if one spelling is regularly used in some unit (such as a book), the Masorah treats this unit independently, and merely enumerates the variant spellings in the other parts of the Bible. This may be

done even where there is some inconsistency within the unit. The term used is וכל followed by the name of the unit. The unit may be a Book, as

Hos 1:4 מַמְלְכוּת -- בׄ וכל יהושע

" This spelling occurs twice, and always in Joshua", or, as we would put it "This word is always spelled this way in the Book of Joshua, and also in two cases in other Books."

Nu 22:39 חֲצוֹת -- בׄ חסׄ וכל ירמׄ בׄ מׄ דׄ

"This word is spelled *ḥaser* (with no *waw* after the *ḥet*) in all cases but four in the Book of Jeremiah, and twice in other Books".

The unit may also be some recognized section of the Bible (see #116), as

Nu 36:1 רָאשֵׁי°הָאָבוֹת -- בׄ וכל כתיבׄ דכותׄ בׄ מׄ זׄ

"This combination (with the definite article) is always used in the Writings with the exception of seven cases, and is found twice elsewhere in the Bible".

Sometimes the unit is a combination of words, as

Nu 28:10 שַׁבַּת -- דׄ וכל שַׁבַּת שַׁבָּתוֹן דכותׄ

"The *bet* always has *pataḥ* in the combination שַׁבַּת שַׁבָּתוֹן and also has that vowel (and not *qameṣ*) in four other cases".

Nu 24:23 יִחְיֶה -- יחׄ וכל חָיוֹ יִחְיֶה דכותׄ

"This form (and not יהיה) occurs in all cases of the combination חָיוֹ יִחְיֶה, and also in 18 other cases".

Sometimes the unit is a semantic one, as

Dt 1:21 רֵשׁ -- בׄ וכל מסכינות דכותׄ

"This vocalization occurs in two cases (meaning possession, with *ṣere*), but referring to poverty it is always vocalized this way."

Jos 6:26 יַצִּיב -- לׄ וכל לשון ארמית

"Unique outside (the parts of the Bible written in) the Aramaic language." (This last note illustrates the fact that the basic concern of the Masorah is the letters of the text; letters representing different parts of speech, or even words from different languages, are frequently treated by the Masorah as the same "word", which is, of course, correct where a word is defined as a group of letters.)

Sometimes the unit is provided by the accentuation, as

Nu 22:18 אֱלֹהָי -- חׄ וכל אתנחׄ וסופׄ פסוק דכותׄ בׄ מׄ בׄ

"This word always has *qameṣ* (under the *he*) with the accents *atnaḥ* and *sof pasuq*, save for two cases (where it has *pataḥ*), and it has *qameṣ* in 8 other cases also."

Position in the verse may also define a unit, as

Dt 4:46 וּבְנֵי °יִשְׂרָאֵל -- הׄ וכל ראשׁ פסוׄ דכותׄ

"This combination is always spelled this way (with prefixed *waw*) at the beginning of a verse, and in 15 other cases as well."

116. Where a masoretic note refers to the whole Bible, this may not be indicated, or it may be shown by בקׄ (בקרייה "In the reading מקרא"). Where the note refers to part of the Bible only, this is indicated as follows:-

"In the Torah" בתוׄ (בתורה) באורׄ (באורייתא)
"In the Prophets" בנבׄ (בנביאים)
"In the Writings" בכתוׄ (בכתובים)
"In the Book" בסיפׄ (בסיפרא)
"In the Context", בעינׄ (בעינײנא)
or "In passages dealing with the same subject" as
1S 19:1 יוֹנָתָן -- לׄ בעינׄ
"Unique in the Context"--i.e. in the rest of the passages on David and Jonathan, the name is spelled יְהוֹנָתָן with *he*."

The Masoretes developed a wide range of technical terms for the various features which they needed to note, such as letters, accent and vowel signs, stress position, *dagesh* and *rafe*, the names of the Books of the Bible, and so on. A few of these terms, which seem to have originated in the period of the Mishnah (before 200 CE) are Hebrew. Examples are פתוחה *petuḥah*, סתומה *setumah*, נקוד *naqud*. In general, however, the language of the Masorah is Aramaic. An alphabetical list of the common masoretic terms is given in #132 below. The subjects with which the Masorah is mainly concerned are discussed in the following paragraphs.

The Most Common Subjects of Masoretic Notes

117. 1) The Letters of the Word. The majority of the masoretic notes deal with spelling which is plene (with a vowel letter) or defective (without one). Such a note may deal with the spelling of a unique word, such as

Nu 15:33 הַמְּצְאִים -- לׄ וחסׄ

"Unique, and written without *waw*". It may deal with words found a number of times, as

Gen 10:21 הַגָּדוֹל -- חׄ מלׄ בתוׄ

"Occurs eight times plene (with *waw*) in the Torah."

Gen 30:38 בְּבֹאָן -- בׄ חד חסׄ וחד מלׄ

"Occurs twice, once defective (without *waw*), once plene".

Gen 5:16 שְׁלֹשִׁים -- כל קריׄ חסׄ בׄ מׄ דׄ

"Always spelled defective (without *waw*) in the Bible save in four cases".

The note may also mention the correct spelling of similar words, to prevent confusion, as

1K 22:8 יְמְלָה -- דׄ בׄ כתבׄ הי ובׄ כתׄ א

"Occurs four times, twice spelled with (final) *he*, and twice with *alef*."

Ps 71:3 מָעוֹן -- דׄ בנוןׄ

"Spelled four times with final *nun*" (as distinct from the more common מָעוֹז spelled with *zayin* which is similar in shape, at the end).

118. 2) Combinations of Words. Notes of this sort deal with combinations of words in which confusion would be easy, as

Gen 1:2 וְרוּחַ°אֱלֹהִים -- בׄ

"Twice". I.e. this combination occurs twice only in the Bible. It is to be distinguished from similar combinations such as רוּחַ אֱלֹהִים or רוּחַ יְהוָה.

Rut 4:9 לְכִלְיוֹן°וּמַחְלוֹן -- לׄ וכל קריׄ חלוף

"Unique (in this order), elsewhere the order of the names is reversed".

Nu 1:1 וַיְדַבֵּר°יְהוָה אֶל°מֹשֶׁה -- י בתורׄ

"This combination occurs ten times in the Torah."

Jer 26:12 אֶת°כָּל°הַדְּבָרִים -- יׄגׄ חסׄ הָאֵלֶּה

"This combination occurs 13 times without הָאֵלֶּה at the end."

Other notes deal with cases where the same words are repeated in different orders, as

Dt 11:1 וְחֻקֹּתָיו וּמִשְׁפָּטָיו וּמִצְוֹתָיו -- קׄ פׄ צׄ

but Dt 8:11 מִצְוֹתָיו וּמִשְׁפָּטָיו וְחֻקֹּתָיו -- צׄ פׄ קׄ

where the three letters of the note represent the three words in their differing order. So also

Nu 36:11 מַחְלָה תִרְצָה וְחָגְלָה וּמִלְכָּה וְנֹעָה -- סימנׄ מׄ תׄ וׄ וׄ וׄ

the letters of the mnemonic note (סימן #126) indicate the order of the first two names, and the fact that the others have the conjunction *waw* prefixed. In Nu 27:1, the names occur in a different order, and with a different combination of conjunctions. The note there is

מַחְלָה נֹעָה וְחָגְלָה וּמִלְכָּה וְתִרְצָה indicating סימ מ נ ו ו ו

In Jos 17:3 the note is מוחמו, indicating

מַחְלָה וְנֹעָה חָגְלָה מִלְכָּה וְתִרְצָה

The order of the names in the various lists of the nations of Canaan is recorded in a similar way, for instance

Ex 23:23 הָאֱמֹרִי וְהַחִתִּי וְהַפְּרִזִּי וְהַכְּנַעֲנִי וְהַחִוִּי וְהַיְבוּסִי -- מחפכוס

1K 9:20 הָאֱמֹרִי הַחִתִּי הַפְּרִזִּי הַחִוִּי וְהַיְבוּסִי -- מחפוס

Ex 33:2 הַכְּנַעֲנִי הָאֱמֹרִי וְהַחִתִּי וְהַפְּרִזִּי הַחִוִּי וְהַיְבוּסִי -- כמחפוס

119. 3) <u>Particles</u>. A noun or verb may be used in combination with different particles and these particles may be used with or without prefixed *waw*. Variations in the use of such elements was common as is shown by the known MSS, and for this reason the Masorah is particularly careful in noting the correct reading. For example

Ez 17:18 וְכָל°אֵלֶּה -- ל̇ ושארא כָּל אֵלֶּה

"Unique. Elsewhere כָּל אֵלֶּה" (without the *waw*).

Nu 4:26 וְעַל°הַמִּזְבֵּחַ -- ב̇

"Twice" (to distinguish these cases from וְאֶל הַמִּזְבֵּחַ which occurs three times).

Gen 3:16 אֶל°הָאִשָּׁה -- ל̇ ראש פסוק

"Unique at the beginning of a verse" (although common within a verse).

Ex 25:20 עַל הַכַּפֹּרֶת וּפְנֵיהֶם אִישׁ אֶל אָחִיו אֶל הַכַּפֹּרֶת יִהְיוּ פְּנֵי הַכְּרֻבִים
-- יד̇ פסו̇ עַל אֶל אֶל

"There are 14 verses containing the prepositions עַל אֶל אֶל (in that order and without conjunctions).

Gen 11:26 וַיּוֹלֶד אֶת אַבְרָם אֶת נָחוֹר וְאֶת הָרָן -- יב̇ אֶת אֶת וְאֶת

"There are 12 verses containing the combination "אֶת אֶת וְאֶת

Ps 72:11 כָל־מְלָכִים כָּל־גּוֹיִם

-- י̇ פסוקין בקריה אית בהון כל כל וחד מלה ביניה̇

"10 verses in the Bible have כָּל כָּל with one word between them".

120. 4) <u>Vocalization</u>. The Masorah notes the occurrence of similar words with different vocalization, as

Gen 40:7 בַּמִּשְׁמַר -- גֿ

"Three times with *pataḥ*" (in contrast to בְּמִשְׁמָר)

Job 23:11 אָט -- לֿ

"No other case with *qameṣ*" (but אַט does occur).

Nu 7:61 לְמִנְחָה -- כול רפי בֿ מֿ בֿ דגש

"Always *rafe*, i.e. without the definite article, see #132 under רפֿ (2), except for two cases which have *dagesh* (i.e. לַמִּנְחָה)."

Dt 7:23 וְהָמָם -- בֿ חד קמצ וחד פתח

"2 cases, one with *qameṣ* and one with *pataḥ* (וְהָמַם Is 28:28)."

Nu 32:42 לָה -- גֿ לא מפק הֿ

"3 cases with no *mappiq* in the *he*"

Ps 16:1 שָׁמְרֵנִי -- לֿ געי

"No other case with *gaᶜya*."

The Masorah may also note cases of pausal vocalisation in contextual situations, and the opposite, as

Prov 14:28 עָם -- יֿוֿ וכל זקפֿ ואתנֿ וסופֿ פסוקֿ דכותֿ

"Always with *qameṣ* when the accent is *zaqef*, *athaḥ*, or *sof pasuq*, and in 16 other cases as well".

Rut 4:18 פָּרֶץ -- לֿ זקף קמצ

"There is no other case with *qameṣ* when the accent is *zaqef*".

121. 5) <u>The Accents</u>. The Masorah notes words in which the accent position varies, as

Job 10:15 אַלְלַי -- לֿ בטע וחד אַלְלַי

"Unique with the accent in this position, but there is one case of אַלְלַי".

Ps 90:13 שׁוּבָה -- הֿ בטע

"There are five cases with the accent (on the final syllable)" (In four cases the stress in penultimate).

The Masorah also notes words or word groups which have some particular accentuation, as

Jer 42:2 וַיֹּאמְרוּ -- זֿ בטע

"7 times with the accent (*gershayim*).

Jer 4:3 כִּי־כֹה -- זֿ בטע בסיפֿ

"7 times with *maqqef-legarmeh* in this book".

Rare accents or rare combinations are also noted, as

Rut 1:10 וַתֹּאמַרְנָה־לָּהּ -- חֿ בטע

"This accentuation (*mayela-atnaḥ*, #216) occurs 8 times".

Lev 8:23 וַיִּשְׁחָט -- זֿ בטע מרע

"The accent *marᶜim* (*shalshelet*) occurs in 7 cases".

Song 3:5 עַד שֶׁתֶּחְפָּץ -- יׄא בטע
"עַד (or וְעַד) has a conjunctive accent (and not *maqqef*) before *silluq* in 11 cases".

122. 6) Unique Usage. The Masorah also notes words which are rare or unique from the point of view of syntax or meaning, as Ps 16:2 אָמַרְתְּ לַיהוָה -- לׄ לשׁ זכר
"Unique as a masculine form (but used elsewhere as a feminine)".
Ps 61:8 מַן יִנְצְרוּהוּ -- לׄ לשון קדש
"Unique in the Holy Tongue" (I.e. Hebrew, but it does occur in Biblical Aramaic).
Jud 19:13 לְךָ -- גׄ חסׄ בהליכה
"In 3 cases this defective spelling (not לְכָה) is derived from הלך 'walk' (and is not a preposition with the 2ms suffix)".
Gen 26:33 שִׁבְעָה -- לׄ שם באר
"Unique as the name of a well" (but used as a number elsewhere).
Gen 26:4 הָאֵל -- חׄ לשון חל
"This form is not a divine name (see #87) in 8 cases" (=הָאֵלֶּה).
Nu 34:23 אֵפֹד -- לׄ שם אנש
"Unique as a man's name" (elsewhere denotes a cult object).
Jos 15:42 וְעָשָׁן -- הׄ שם קריה
"5 times the name of a city" (and not denoting "smoke").
Gen 8:11 עֲלֵה -- וׄ באטרופי
"6 times with the meaning 'leaf'" (and not the imperative עלה).

123. 7) Variants in Parallel Passages. Words or word groups which appear in different places in different forms, or with different accentuation, may also be noted in the Masorah, as Jos 23:16 וַאֲבַדְתֶּם מְהֵרָה -- יׄ״א זוגין
"11 pairs". The note indicates that this phrase is one of 11 pairs of phrases which occur once with the accent *zaqef* and once with *revia* (cf. וַאֲבַדְתֶּם מְהֵרָה Dt 11:17).
Notes of this type are especially common where parallel passages occur, as in 2K 18-20 and Is 36-39, 2S 22 and Ps 18, the lists of returning exiles in Ezra and Nehemiah, etc. For example 2K 19:29 סָחִישׁ -- לׄ ישעיה שָׁחִיס
"Unique. (The parallel passage in) Isaiah has שָׁחִיס".
Is 37:9 עַל°תִּרְהָקָה -- לׄ דמלכים אֶל תִּרְהָקָה
"Unique. (The parallel passage in) Kings has אֶל - תִּרְהָקָה".
Is 37:14 וַיִּקְרָאֵהוּ -- מלכים וַיִּקְרָאֵם

"(The parallel passage in) Kings has וַיִּקְרָאֻם".

124. 8) Other Opinions. The Masorah occasionally notes the opinions of particular authorities on some feature of the tradition. These authorities are: *Madinḥa'e* and *Maᶜarba'e*, Tiberias, specific texts called מחזורא רובא *Maḥzora Rabba*, מוגה *Muggah*, הללי *Hilleli*, זנבוקי *Zanbuqi*, etc., or individual scholars such as Pinḥas, Moḥeh, ben Asher, ben Naftali. Occasionally such variant traditions are noted simply as מחלפ̇(ין) or פלוג̇(תא) "There is a different opinion".

125. 9) Counting. The Masoretes did not restrict the use of enumeration to their notes on the different characteristics of words. They also counted verses and other features of the Biblical text. The Masorah notes the number of *sedarim* (#72), of verses, of words, and of letters in the whole Bible, in individual books, in the פרשיות (#72) of the Torah, and so on. The middle word and the middle letter of Books, of the Torah, and of the whole Bible are also noted. This activity is noted in the Talmud--indeed it is said of the "Scribes" (סופרים from ספר meaning both "write" and "count") that they got this name "because they used to count (היו סופרים) all the letters of the Torah, for they noted that the *waw* of גָּחוֹן (Lev 11:42) was the middle letter of the Torah, דָּרֹשׁ דָּרַשׁ (Lev 10:16) were the middle words, וְהִתְגַּלָּח began the middle verse (Lev 13:33), the *ᶜayin* of יַעַר (Ps 80:14) was the middle letter of the Psalms, and וְהוּא רַחוּם יְכַפֵּר עָוֹן began the middle verse (Ps 78:38)". In the same way they counted the number of verses in the Books of the Torah, Psalms, and Chronicles (TB *Qiddushin* 30a). Much of the information given there is different from that given in our Masorah, but the efforts of scholars to explain these differences are so far unsuccessful.

The poem beginning אֹהֶל מְכוֹן פְּנִינָי, ascribed to R. Saadya Ga'on (d. 942) makes use of early masoretic information, and gives the number of occurrences of each letter in the Bible, including the final letters כמנפ"ץ.

The Masoretes counted verses from different viewpoints: verses containing only three words (the shortest)--and the opposite, the longest verse. Further examples are

Nu 29:33 ב̇ פסוק בתורה כל סוף מליהון מ̇

"(One of) two verses in the Torah of which all the words end in *mem*" (also Gen 32:15).

Lev 13:9 יֺאֺ פסֺ רישהון נו"ן וסופיהון נו"ן

"(One of) 11 verses beginning and ending with *nun*".

2K 6:32 כֺוֺ פסוקֺ אית בהון אלף בית

"26 verses containing all the letters of the alphabet". Similarly verses in which all the words include *shin* (Nu 26:24, Song 1:1) are noted. Words are occasionally treated in a similar way, as

Est 9:3 וְהָאֲחַשְׁדַּרְפְּנִים -- גֺ מלין בקרֺ דמיין

"(One of) three words in the Bible which are similar (in that they contain 11 letters)".

THE PRESERVATION OF THE TEXTUAL TRADITION: THE TEXT AS A WHOLE

(ii) The Masorah Magna (Mm)

The Elaborative Masorah magna

126. The basic function of the מָסוֹרָה גְּדוֹלָה, latinized as *Masorah magna* (Mm) is to give the details of the information summarized in the notes of the Mp. The Mp simply notes the number of cases in which a particular spelling occurs in the Bible. The lists of the Mm provide references to the individual passages in which the words in question occur. Notes of this sort, which list the occurrences of a word or a combination of words are called מסורה מפרטת "Elaborative Masorah".

The notes of the Mp must be written in a limited space, and so do not, as a rule, include references. Occasionally--usually where the word in question appears in no more than two places--the marginal notes of the Mp do give a reference (סימן) to passages other than the one commented on. E.g.

Dt 29:19 יֶעְשַׁן -- בֺ אַפְּךָ

"Occurs twice, (here and) יֶעְשַׁן אַפְּךָ (Ps 74:1)".

The note בֺ רַבַּת in #112 is another example.

Occasionally the Mp mentions cases similar to the one discussed, but a clear reference is not usually given, as

2C 6:26 בְּהֵעָצֵר הַשָּׁמַיִם -- לֺ וחד בְּהֵעָצֵר שָׁמַיִם

"Unique, but there is one case of בְּהֵעָצֵר שָׁמַיִם" (without the article, 1K 8:35).

However such references in the notes of the Mp are exceptions.

In most cases lists of references could not be included with the notes of the Mp in the small amount of space available in the margins beside the columns. If the side margins were unusually wide, such lists of references might be written in them, but usually these lists, which form the Mm, were placed in the upper and lower margins of the page. In most early MSS this occupies two or three lines at the top and bottom of the page, but some texts show much more--even as much as ten lines.

The numbering of chapters and verses was a very late introduction into Biblical texts, consequently verses can only be identified by quoting a word or two from the immediate context. These "identifying quotes" are known as the סימן *siman* "sign", i.e. "reference". In the earlier MSS these סימנים are short--usually one word only, and seem to be adapted for oral learning and teaching. In late codices, however, the סימנים are longer, so that the verse they represent is more easily identified. For example

Ez 27:7 אֱלִישָׁה

C has	L has	V has	
אֱלִישָׁה ג̇ וסימנהון	אֱלִישָׁה ג̇	אֱלִישָׁה ג̇ בקריאה וסי'	
מִבְּנֵי יָוָן	וּבְנֵי יָוָן אֱלִישָׁה וְתַרְשִׁישׁ	וּבְנֵי יָוָן אֱלִישָׁה וְתַרְשִׁישׁ	Gen 10:4
וּבְנֵי יָוָן	וחביר̇	וחברו דד"ה	1C 1:7
מֵאִיֵּי	מֵאִיֵּי אֱלִישָׁה הָיָה	מֵאִיֵּי אֱלִישָׁה הָיָה מְכַסֵּךְ	Ez 27:7

Ez 28:2 גָּבַהּ

C has	L has	V has	
גָּבַהּ ה̇ וסימנהון	גָּבַהּ ה̇	גָּבַהּ ה' בקריאה וסימ'	
בְּיָפְיֶךָ	לִבְּךָ בְּיָפְיֶךָ	גָּבַהּ לִבְּךָ בְּיָפְיֶךָ	Ez 28:17
לִנְגִיד	אֱמֹר לִנְגִיד צֹר	אֱמֹר לִנְגִיד צֹר	Ez 28:2
כִּגְמוּל	וְלֹא כִגְמֻל עָלָיו	וְלֹא כִּגְמוּל עָלָיו הֵשִׁיב דחזקיהו דדברי הימים	2C 32:25
שִׁיר	שִׁיר הַמַּעֲלוֹת יְהוָה לֹא גָבַהּ	לֹא גָבַהּ לִבִּי וְלֹא רָמוּ עֵינַי	Ps 131:1
וּכְחֶזְקָתוֹ	וּכְחֶזְקָתוֹ	וּכְחֶזְקָתוֹ גָּבַהּ לִבּוֹ דדברי הימים	2C 26:16

Is 52:13 וחד וְגָבַהּ יָרוּ׳ וְנִשָּׂא וְגָבַהּ   וחד יָרוּם וְנִשָּׂא וְגָבַהּ

(The five references are given in the order in which they occur in C, to facilitate comparison. L gives them in the same order, save that 2C 26:16 precedes Ps 131:1. In V the order is Ez 28:2, 28:17, 2C 26:16, 32:25, Ps 131:1).

127. Occasionally the Masorah compounds, from the סימנים, a mnemonic representing all the cases identified in the Mm. A mnemonic of this sort is also called סימן. It is generally in Aramaic, and forms a meaningful sentence which it would be easy to remember. For example

1K 3:11 הָבִין

"הָבִין Occurs 5 times with *qameṣ* — הָבִין ה׳ וקמצין
at 1K 3:11 — וסי׳ יַעַן אֲשֶׁר שָׁאַלְתָּ
Is 56:11 — וְהַכְּלָבִים עַזֵּי נֶפֶשׁ
Is 28:19 — מִדֵּי עָבְרוֹ יִקַּח (וְהָיָה רַק זְוָעָה)
Prov 14:8 — חָכְמַת עָרוּם הָבִין
Ps 32:9 — אַל תִּהְיוּ כְּסוּס כְּפֶרֶד
Their *siman* in Aramaic is — וסי׳ בלשון תרגום
'Dogs were asking wisdom from horses'." — הוון כלביא שאלין חכמתא לסוסיא

(For another example see #132, דגש (2), the note on Ps 10:8.) In some MSS an Aramaic sentence of this sort is the only form of reference given, as is the case in the note on הבין at 1K 3:11 in C.

Mnemonic *simanim* of other types are also common in the Masorah. They are used particularly where it is necessary to remember the differences between parallel passages, and they occasionally reflect the sharpness of their authors' wit, as

Jer 10:25 וְעַל מִשְׁפָּחוֹת אֲשֶׁר בְּשִׁמְךָ לֹא קָרָאוּ

The parallel passage in Ps 79:6 reads וְעַל מַמְלָכוֹת

The Mm of L remarks

ירמיה וְעַל מִשְׁפָּחוֹת תהלים וְעַל מַמְלָכוֹת
וסימנהון כִּי הִנְנִי קוֹרֵא לְכָל מִשְׁפְּחוֹת מַמְלְכוֹת

"Jeremiah reads מִשְׁפָּחוֹת, Psalms מַמְלָכוֹת, their *siman* is Jer 1:15 (where the two words occur in the same order).

Another example occurs in the Mm of L at Jer 52:15

מלכים וּמִדַּלַּת ירמיהו וּמִדַּלּוֹת
וסימנה׳ מלכיא מסכינותא יחידיה ירמיה מסכינותה סגיאה

"Kings (2K 25:12) reads *middallat*, Jeremiah (52:15) *middallot*. Their *siman* is "Kings solitary/singular poverty, Jeremiah much/ plural poverty".
Similarly on דְּמֵי טָהֳרָה (Lev 12:4, 5 with no *mappiq* in the final *he*) and יְמֵי טָהֳרָהּ (Lev 12:4, 6, with *mappiq*), the Mm of V notes

דמים מכוסים ימים מגולים

"With דְּמֵי (the *he* is) hidden (i.e. not pronounced), with יְמֵי, revealed (pronounced)." In the *Minḥat Shay* (#163) this phenomenon is presented as follows: וסימנך יהודה
"The *siman* is *Yehudah*--and the explanation is that the *he* following the *yod* is consonantal, that following the *dalet* is not. In the same way the final *he* of טָהֳרָהּ following יְמֵי (beginning with *yod*) is consonantal while that of טָהֳרָה following דמי (beginning with *dalet*) is not".

The Mm gives details of the information summarized in all the notes of the Mp which deal with letters, or vowel or accent signs. It presents lists of variants between parallel passages, lists of verses which resemble each other in some characteristic, and so on.

128. The Mm sometimes not only gives the details of the information summarised in the Mp, but also notes other forms of the same word, or similar words, as in the Mm of C on Is 55:8

מַחְשְׁבוֹתַי ל̇ מל̇ מַחְשְׁבוֹתֵיכֶם ב̇ מל̇

כִּי לֹא מַחְשְׁבוֹתַי הֵן יָדַעְתִּי מִמַּחְשְׁבֹתֵיכֶם ל̇ וחס̇ ו̇

"מַחְשְׁבוֹתַי plene (with *waw*) is unique here. מַחְשְׁבוֹתֵיכֶם occurs twice plene (Is 55:8, Job 21:27), and מִמַּחְשְׁבֹתֵיכֶם is unique, and is defective (without *waw* Is 55:9)."
The Masorah refers to a group of similar words of this type as בלישנא, as in the Mp of L on Is 11:10
"Two cases defective (without *waw*)" ב̇ חס̇ -- מְנֻחָתוֹ, on which the Mm comments ד̇ חס̇ בלישנא
"This and similar words have defective spelling in four cases", and lists the two cases of מְנֻחָתוֹ, and also מְנֻחָה and לִמְנֻחָה.
Notes of this sort are also given on features of vocalization and accentuation. Thus in the Mm of S on Gen 50:23, (on בִּרְכֵּי)

כל לשון בִּרְכֵּי בִּרְכַּי הַבִּרְכַּיִם דג̇ בר מן ב̇ רפי

"בִּרְכֵּי, בִּרְכַּי, etc., always have *dagesh* (in the *kaf*) save for two cases where it is *rafe*."
Similarly, the Mm of S on Lev 20:14,

כל תיבותה דסמיכה להִיא או להוּא אית בה טעם אריך
כגון נִדָּה הִיא זִמָּה הִיא טָמֵא הוּא... כלם לעולם

"Any word immediately preceding הִיא or הוּא has a "long" accent (i.e. an independent accent as opposed to *maqqef*), as נִדָּה הִיא, etc. ... all of them, always."

Similarly rules of this sort are given for particles used with a particular noun or verb, as in the Mm of Jer 50:35

כל לשון חֶרֶב חַרְבּוֹ אֶל קרי בר מן ה֗ עַל

"The word חֶרֶב, חַרְבּוֹ, etc., is always used with אֶל, save for five cases where עַל occurs".

Also at Jer 50:42

כל לשון סוּסִים סוּסָיו הַסּוּסִים עַל בר מן ב֗ אֶל

"סוּסִים etc., is always used with עַל, save for two cases where אֶל occurs".

The Collative Masorah magna

129. Lists of the elaborative type, giving the occurrences of a single word or combination of words, are the most common type of note in the Mm. In many MSS, the Mm also contains lists of another type, called מסורה מצרפת "Collative Masorah". These collative notes list words which are different, but which share some common characteristic. Lists of words against which the Mp has the note ל֗ "unique" are particularly common. Various characteristics are used as the basis for the compilation of such lists.

Sometimes the words are arranged one by one, and the list gives individual words which have some characteristic in common. They may end in the same sound, as in B on Ex 38:4

אָלֹה ל֗ אִישׁוֹ ל֗ בָּזֹה ל֗ בְּחִירוֹ ל֗... אלפ֗ בית֗ כל חד וחד ל֗ כות֗

"An alphabetical list of words (ending in "o") of which each occurs only once. Similar lists are

B on Lev 6:21 וּמֹרַק ל֗ וְשֻׁרַק ל֗ וּפֹרַק ל֗ ...

B on Lev 11:34 יֵאָפֶה ל֗ כות֗ יִבְלֶה ל֗ כות֗ יִגְעֶה ל֗ כות֗ ...

Other lists are based on similarity in vocalization, as B on Lev 15:3

אָט ל֗ בָּל ל֗ גָּב ל֗... אלין אלפבית כל חד וחד מן ב֗ אות֗

"An alphabetical list of words, each of which has only two letters, (is pointed with *qameṣ*, and occurs only once)".

Another basis is similarity of grammatical form, as S on Lev 19:20 נֶחֱרֶפֶת נֶחֱרֶבֶת נֶאֱמֶנֶת הַנֶּאֱכֶלֶת לית כות֗

"These four forms are unique".

Similarity of accentuation also forms a basis, as S on Gen 36:16

אַלּוּף־קֹ֣רַח וַיִּקְח֤וּ־אֶ֫בֶן וַיִּשְׁלַח־שָׁ֫מָּה חֲרַשְׁתֶּם־רֶ֫שַׁע דמיין בטעמׄ

"Four unique phrases with the same accentuation".

Similar combinations of words are also listed, as

B on Nu 28:4 הַכֶּבֶשׂ אֶחָד ל̇ וְנָשִׂיא אֶחָד ל̇ וְעֵד אֶחָד ל̇...

"Some unique combinations ending in אֶחָד"

Other lists give words with similar forms (but not necessarily from the same root), as B on Ex 3:10

וְהוֹצֵא ל̇ וָאֵצֵא ל̇ כְּמוֹצֵא ל̇ הֲתֹצִיא ל̇...

Also B on Lev 23:39

בְּאָסְפְּכֶם ל̇ וְהָאסַפְסֻף ל̇ אָסְפָּה ל̇ אֶסָּפֶה ל̇ דָסְפָה ל̇ כְּסוּפוֹת ל̇...

Sometimes the words in these lists are arranged in pairs, and the two words in each pair differ from each other only in one feature. This can be a letter, as

B on Ex 40:32 כֹּהֵן ל̇ וְכֹהֵן ל̇ כֻּפַּר ל̇ וְכֻפַּר ל̇...

(pairs of unique words one of which does, and one does not, have prefixed *waw*), or B on Ex 9:4

וְהִפְלָה ל̇ כתב ה וְהִפְלָא ל̇ כתב א יִתְרָה ל̇ כתב ה יִתְרָא ל̇ כתב א...

(pairs of unique words of which one has final *he*, the other final *alef*),

The difference can be a feature of pointing, as

B on Lev 2:14 גֶּרֶשׂ ל̇ גֶּרֶשׁ ל̇ הִשְׂבִּיעַנִי ל̇ הִשְׁבִּיעַנִי ל̇...

listing pairs of unique words of which one has *sin*, the other *shin*, or

B on Ex 39:21 וַיִּרְכְּסוּ ל̇ וְיִרְכְּסוּ ל̇ וַיֵּצְאוּ ל̇ וְיֵצְאוּ ל̇...

listing pairs of unique words with *waw* pointed with *shewa* or *pataḥ*, or B on Lev 18:23

לְרִבְעָהּ ל̇ מפק הי לְרִבְעָה ל̇ לא מפק הי וּשְׂעָרָהּ ל̇ מפק הי
וּשְׂעָרָה ל̇ לא מפק הי...

giving pairs where the final *he* has or has not *mappiq*.

Similarly word groups which differ in one word are listed, as B on Ex 39:17

עַל קְצוֹת ל̇ אֶל קְצוֹת ל̇ עַל רִבקה ל̇ אֶל רִבְקָה ל̇

giving words which occur once with עַל and once with אֶל, or B on Ex 9:8

פִּיחַ כִּבְשָׁן ל̇ פִּיחַ הַכִּבְשָׁן ל̇ פְּרִי בֶטֶן ל̇ פְּרִי הַבָּטֶן ל̇

where the group occurs once with, and once without the article.

Occasionally this type of Masorah lists individual words which occur two or more times in the Bible.

Lists of this collative type do not occur in all Tiberian MSS. None are found in A or L. A few occur in C, and many in B and S. They are rare in late MSS, but there are a few in V.

Masorah at the Beginning and End of Books

130. In many MSS masoretic lists are given at the beginning or the end of Books. In early MSS those found in this position mostly give the authors of the books, the number of years in the period covered by each book, lists of variants between *Madinḥa'e* and *Maᶜarba'e* (#153), or between bA and bN (#155), variants between parallel passages, sections from the *Diqduqe ha-Ṭeᶜamim* (#175), etc. In Yemenite MSS the treatise known as *Maḥberet ha-Tījān* (#175) is sometimes given, either in the long (Hebrew) form, or the short (Arabic) form. In late MSS, grammatical treatises are sometimes given along with masoretic material, and these include books such as the *Miklol* of R. David Qimḥi, or the *Darke ha-Niqqud weha-Neginot* of R. Moshe ha-Naqdan.

The Masorah at the end of V, called מערכת--Latinized *Masorah finalis*, which contains masoretic lists in alphabetical order, is not found in manuscripts, but is an innovation by Jacob ben Ḥayyim, the editor of V (#139). He collected in it long lists from the Mm for which he did not have room in the appropriate places. These lists are mostly of the elaborative type, but a few belong to the collative category.

MASORETIC TERMINOLOGY AND ITS USE

131. In each of the early MSS, the terms of the Masorah are still uniform, the product of one school at one period. In later MSS, and in editions such as V, terms deriving from different schools and different periods are used, indicating the diverse origin of the masoretic notes. For instance the vowel sign ֵ may be called צירי "*ṣere*", or קמץ קטן "small *qameṣ*", or שתי נקודות "two dots". The Torah is sometimes called תוׄ(רה) (Hebrew) and sometimes אוׄר(ייתא) (Aramaic). Variant opinions may be referred to as פלוגׄ(תא), or as מחלפׄ(ים), etc.

A list of masoretic terms is found in the BHK and BHS

Index siglorum et abbreviationum masorae parvae. The term is generally given in abbreviated form, in full, and in Latin translation. A comprehensive list of terms, with explanation and examples, is given in Frensdorff 1876. In his introduction to his edition of *Ochlah W'ochlah*, Frensdorff gives a list of abbreviations of terms with a translation into German. Eliahu ha-Levi, one of the renaissance students of the Masorah, gives a list of masoretic terms with an explanation of them in his *Masoret ha-Masoret* (#169). See also Hyvernat, 1902.

In #132 a list of the most common terms and abbreviations found in the Masorah is given, with examples of their use. This list is based on that of Frensdorff and other sources, and is arranged alphabetically, ignoring prefixed particles. I.e. בטעׄ is given under ט for טעם etc. It should be noted that abbreviations were not standardized, so that the same word may be represented in several different ways. The abbreviations most commonly used for each word are given, and will serve as a guide to others which may occur. Letters or vowel or accent signs may be represented by the name spelled out in full (or abbreviated) or by the sign, thus מם or מׄ "*mem*" ב̸ָׄ or ב קמץ "twice with *qameṣ*" etc. Cross references are given to occurences of a term under different entries by means of the abbreviation used as a heading for the entry, and the reference to the verse in the comment on which the term occurs. This is not done for very common terms, and, indeed, a few very obvious terms are not listed at all.

132. *List of Masoretic Terms*

One — אׄ - אחד

Gen 47:19 — תֵּשָׁם -- בׄ אָ' ואַ'

"Occurs twice, once with *qameṣ* and once with *pataḥ*".

1, 2, 3, 4... — אׄ בׄ גׄ דׄ...

The numbers continue with יׄ 10, כׄ 20, לׄ 30, etc., up to קׄ 100, רׄ 200, שׄ 300, תׄ 400. Higher numbers are produced by combination, e.g. תׄשׄ 700. These are used to indicate the number of times some feature occurs, as

Is 41:28 — וּמֵאֵלֶּה -- גׄ

"Occurs three times"

Is 11:12 — וְנָשָׂא -- לו֗
"Occurs 16 times"

Alphabet — א"ב

1) All the letters of the alphabet

Jer 22:3 — כ"ו פסוקין אית בהון א"ב
"(One of) 26 verses in which all the letters of the alphabet occur".

Ex 16:16 — אית ביה אלף בי
"Contains all the letters of the alphabet".

2) A list of words given in alphabetical order

Lev 23:27 — יוֹם הַכִּפֻּרִים -- ל֗ ומשמש א"ב חד נסיב ה"א וחד לא נסיב ה"א
"A unique combination, included in an alphabetical list of pairs of unique combinations of which one has, and one has not *he* (the definite article prefixed to the second word)".

Jud 5:8 — לָחֶם -- ל' מלרע ומשמש א"ב
"Unique with final stress position, and is included in alphabetical list (of pairs of unique words of which one has final and one penultimate stress)".

1S 19:20 — עַל מַלְאֲכֵי -- ל' וא' אֶל מַלְאֲכֵי ומשמש א"ב
"Unique, but אֶל מַלְאֲכֵי also occurs once. Included in an alphabetical list (of words found once with עַל and once with אֶל)".
(For other examples see #144).

3) Alphabet -- a name for Ps 119, which is also called אלפא ביתא רבא "The Great Alphabet" and תמניא אפי "The Eightfold".

Dt 33:10 — וְתוֹרָתְךָ -- ב֗ וכל אלפ֗ בית֗ דכות֗
"This form occurs only twice outside Ps 119".

Use of the Tetragrammaton — אדכ֗ - אדכרא (=הזכרה)

Dt 31:3 — ג֗ פסו֗ ראש֗ וסופ֗ אדכ֗
"(One of) 3 verses which begin and end with the tetragrammaton".

Is 63:9 — וּמַלְאַךְ -- ב֗ פת֗ וּמַלְאַךְ פָּנָיו וּמַלְאַךְ הַבְּרִית וכל דסמיך לאדכרה כות֗
"*Pataḥ* is used under the *alef* in this form--here and

Mal 3:1--and also in all cases where the word is followed by the tetragrammaton".

(In) the Torah (ב)אורייתא - או֗, אור֗, אורי֗, באו֗, באור֗

Nu 4:33 עֲבֹדַת -- כל אורי֗ חס֗

"Always defective in the Torah".

Cf. ת֗(ורה)

They אינון (=הם)

1C 27:4 דּוֹדַי -- ב֗ ואינון ב֗ ליש֗

"Occurs in two cases, and they have different meanings".

2C 1:14 וַיַּנִּיחֵם -- ב֗ ואינון בחד סיפ֗

"Occurs in two cases, and they are both in one book".

There is/are אית (=יש)

Dt 32:39 י֗ג֗ פסוק֗ אית בהון וְאֵין וְאֵין

"(One of) 13 verses in which ... וְאֵין...וְאֵין occurs".

Within (a verse, word, etc.) אמצ֗, באמ֗ - (ב)אמצע

(See also מצ֗ ,מציעתא=)

This is contrasted with ראש פסוק (the beginning) and סוף פסוק (the end of the verse) and can refer to any word which is not first or last in the verse.

Is 48:16 וְרוּחוֹ -- ג֗ חד ר"פ וחד ס"פ וחד מצע' פסוק

"Occurs 3 times, once at the beginning, once at the end, and once within the verse".

Jos 13:21 וְכֹל עָרֵי הַמִּישֹׁר וְכָל מַמְלְכוּת סִיחוֹן -- י' פסוק' ראש' וכל ואמצ' וכל

"(One of) ten verses having וכל both at the beginning and within the verse".

Gen 4:7 וְאִם°לֹא -- י֗ו֗ מצ֗ פסו֗

This combination occurs 16 times within a verse".

This term may also refer to a letter within a word, as

Joel 2:6 פָּארוּר -- ג' והוא מן מלין דנסבין א' במצעו' תיבותא ולא קריין

"Occurs three times--and is one of the words spelled with non-consonantal medial *alef*".

The three 'poetical' books אמ"ת - אִיּוֹב, מִשְׁלֵי, תְּהִלִּים

Torah, Prophets, and Writings   אנ"ך - אורייתא, נביי, כתיבי

This term is used when a word occurs once in each of the three sections, but became a term for the whole Bible.

Dt 32:2   לְקְחִי -- ג' וסימן יַעֲרֹף כַּמָּטָר, וַתֹּאמֶר זַךְ לִקְחִי, לִי פַּת לֶחֶם אנ"ך

"Occurs three times, Dt 32:2, Job 11:4, and 1K 17:11 -- once in each section of the Bible".

Man's name   אנש, בר נש, שום בר נש, שום גברא

This term is usually used when the same word can represent a man's name or a common noun.

1C 4:11   מְחִיר -- ל שום אנש

"Unique as a man's name".

Gen 22:24   תַּחַשׁ -- ל שם אנש

"Unique as a man's name"

Woman's name   אנת - אנתתא or אתת - אתתא

Used in the same way as אנש.

1C 8:9   חֹדֶשׁ -- ל שום אתת

"Unique as a woman's name".

2S 17:20   מִיכַל -- ל וכל שם אנת דכות

"Unique (as a common noun). Elsewhere this form is a woman's name".

Atnaḥ and *Sof Pasuq*   אס"ף, אתנ וסופ פסו

These are the two major pausal accents (*sof pasuq* is sometimes called *silluq*) with which pausal forms usually occur.

Gen 49:7   עָז -- ב קמצ וכל אתנ וסופ פסו כות

"This word always has *qameṣ* with *atnaḥ* and *sof pasuq*, and *qameṣ* occurs in two other cases as well".

Nu 11:11   לְעַבְדֶּךָ -- ז וכל אתנ וסופ פסוק דכות ב מ א

"This (pausal) vocalization occurs in 7 cases as well as all cases with *atnaḥ* and *sof pasuq* with one exception (Ps 119:65)".

One verse serves as a mnemonic   אפ"ס - אחד פסוק סימן

This term is used after a list of similar phrases with different wording to introduce a mnemonic giving a key to the difference.

Gen 22:17

אֶת שַׁעַר אֹיְבָיו -- קדמה שַׁעַר אֹיְבָיו תנינ׳ שַׁעַר שֹׂנְאָיו

ואפ"ס עַל אֹיְבֶיךָ וְעַל שֹׂנְאֶיךָ אֲשֶׁר רְדָפוּךָ

"The first instance (Gen 22:17) reads אֹיְבָיו (enemies), and the second (Gen 24:60) שֹׂנְאָיו (haters). Dt 30:7 "Against your <u>enemies</u> and your <u>haters</u> who pursue you" serves as a mnemonic."

Gen 24:23, 25 קדמי׳ לָלִין תנינ׳ לָלוּן ואפ"ס הֲלִילוּ

"The first case (Gen 24:23) has לָלִין, and the second (24:25) לָלוּן, and the word הֲלִילוּ (with *lamed yod* followed by *lamed waw*) serves as a mnemonic".

The Aramaic Language (of Daniel and Ezra) ארמׄ - ארמית

1C 11:31 אִיתַי -- ל׳ וכל לשון ארמית כותׄ

"Unique in Hebrew, but used in Aramaic".

Jud 7:23 וּמִן כָּל -- בׄ וכל ארמׄ דכותׄ

"Twice (in Hebrew), but this form of the phrase (with *nun* not assimilated) is always used in the Aramaic section".

Letters אתא, אתין (=אותיות)

1S 20:29 עַל כֵּן לֹא בָא אֶל שֻׁלְחַן -- הׄ פסוק

דאית בהון חמש מלין מן בׄ אתין

"(One of) five verses which contain five (consecutive) words of two letters each".

The Accent *Atnaḥ* אתנׄ, אתנחׄ - אתנחתא

See אס"פ, and also פתׄ Gen 34:25.

See אנתׄ אתחׄ

Except for one (2, 3, etc.) בׄ מׄ אׄ, במ"א - בר מן אׄ (בׄ, גׄ...)

Gen 44:25 שִׁבוּ -- כל אוריית חסׄ בׄ מׄ גׄ מלׄ

"Always defective in the Torah, with three exceptions which are plene."

Dt 31:29 יְדֵיכֶם -- ל׳ בתוׄ וכל קרי׳ דכותׄ בׄ מׄ אׄ

"Unique in the Torah (elsewhere only יְדְכֶם occurs), but this spelling (יְדֵיכֶם) always occurs elsewhere, with one exception (יְדְכֶם 2C 29:31)".

See also דגש Jud 1:8, Lev 19:15, דכׄ Ex 6:6, וידבר Lev 7:38, חטף 1C 29:18, etc.

In them — בהון

For examples see סמֹ Gen 35:17, פסוֹ Nu 7:20.

In it — ביה

Between them — ביניהֹ

The Book of Genesis — ברא֒ - בראשית

See אנש, also שם Jer 22:16. — בר נש

After (it)--the last — בתר֒, דבתר֒ - בתרא, (ד)בתריה

Lev 14:37   שְׁקַעֲרוּרֹת -- לי וחסר ו' בתרא

"Unique, and lacking the last *waw*"

1S 18:5   וְגַם בְּעֵינֵי עַבְדֵי שָׁאוּל: -- כֹּאֹ פסוק

וגם ובתר֒ תלת מלין

"(One of) 21 verses containing וגם with three words after it". Also מצֹ Ex 10:1, נסיב 1C 22:16, סֹי (3) Lev 17:11.

A man's name (cf. אנש) — גבר, גברא

1C 25:28   לְהוֹתִיר -- לֹ שום גבר

"Unique as a man's name".

With *ga*^{c}*ya/metheg* (#311) — געי֒ - געיא, גיעיה, בגעֹ

Is 65:8   הַשְׁחִית -- לֹ וגעיא

"Unique and has *ga*^{c}*ya*".

Zech 9:2   חָכְמָה -- לֹ געיא

"Unique with *ga*^{c}*ya*".

2C 34:4   וַיְנַתְּצוּ -- לא געי֒

"Without *ga*^{c}*ya*".

See also חטף, and also the last example under מתאֹ.

A secondary accent, or *ga*^{c}*ya* — גרש, גריש

Ps 78:17   לַמְרוֹת -- לֹ גריש

"Unique with *ga*^{c}*ya*".

כל מלה דבקריה דאית בה גרשה ותברא

אית ביניהין שוא בלבד כמות וְהַמַּיִם גָּבְרוּ

"In all the Bible, if a word has both *tevir* and a secondary accent, they are separated only by *shewa*, as in וְהַמַּיִם גָּבְרוּ (Gen 7:19)". (From the Mm of A giving the rules for *merka* and *tevir* on one word. See #253).

The Book of Chronicles — דׄ הׄי, דׄ ימׄ, ד"ה -- דברי הימים

See #126, references to 1C 1:7, 2C 26:16, 32:25, in V.

Dagesh — דגש, דיגׄ - דיגשא

1) as used in modern grammars

Is 31:4 — לְצְבֹּא -- לׄ דגש

"Unique with *dagesh*"

Dt 6:2 — מְצַוֶּךָ -- בׄ חד רפי וחד דגש

"Occurs twice, once with (the *kaf*) *rafe*, and once with *dagesh*".

Jud 1:8 — שִׁלְּחוּ בָאֵשׁ -- ד׳ דגשין בקריאה וסי׳...
וכל דסמיכי לאֵשׁ דכוו׳ דגשים במ"א רפי
וסי׳ שִׁלְחוּ בָאֵשׁ מִקְדָּשֶׁךָ ומטעים ביה

"(One of) four cases in the Bible in which the *lamed* of שִׁלְּחוּ has *dagesh*. The references are .... All cases where the word is followed by אֵשׁ (בָּאֵשׁ etc.) similarly have *dagesh* with one exception (Ps 74:7) in which (the *lamed*) is *rafe*--some make mistakes here."

2) with the preposition ל, כ, ב, *dagesh* indicates vocalization with the definite article (thus usually with *pataḥ*) as opposed to *rafe* indicating vocalization without it (thus usually with *shewa*), and similarly with the conjunction *dagesh* indicates the vocalization of *waw* "consecutive", *rafe* that of *waw* "simple".

1C 6:48 — בַּגּוֹרָל -- וׄ דגשׁ

"6 times with *dagesh*" (i.e. with the article).

Lev 19:15 — בַּמִּשְׁפָּט -- חׄ דגשׁ וכל איוב דכותׄ בׄ מׄ אׄ

"8 times with *dagesh* (the article), and also all cases in Job but one".

Ps 10:8 — בַּמִּסְתָּרִים -- ג׳ דגשים וסי׳ אִם יִסָּתֵר אִישׁ,
בַּמִּסְתָּרִים יַהֲרֹג נָקִי, לִירוֹת בַּמִּסְתָּרִים תָּם,
וסי׳ בלשון תרגום גברא קטיל שלימא

"3 times with *dagesh* (the article). The references are Jer 23:24, Ps 10:8, 64:5. Its mnemonic in Aramaic is "The man is killed, the upright." Also ח"כ, Lev 11:3

3) a guttural pointed with a simple *shewa* may be referred to as "dageshed" in contrast to pointing with a *ḥaṭef shewa* which is *rafe*.

2C 33:19 — וּמַעְלוֹ -- לׄ ומעלו מחלפין בדגשׁ

"Unique, but there is a variant opinion on the *dagesh*"

(i.e. some hold that the word should not have a simple *shewa*, but a *ḥaṭef*) (See #414).

This דֵּין

Ex 6:6 סִבְלֹת -- ב' חד חסר וחד מלי' דין חסר

"2 cases, one defective and one plene--this one is defective".

1C 5:10 הַהַגְרִאִים -- ג ב מל ודין חס

"3 cases, 2 plene (with *yod* after the *resh*) and this one is defective (without it)".

Also חֹבֹ 1C 9:44, מל Ex 28:20.

Like it/them דכ, דכו, דכות - דכותיה, דכותהון

Ex 6:6 בִּזְרוֹעַ -- ג מל בת וכל נבי וכתיב דכות ב מ ג

"3 times plene in the Torah, and is always spelled that way in the Prophets and Writings, with three exceptions".

See כל Nu 29:11, 29:8, Dt 33:6, נקי Gen 24:40, שטה Prov 1:1, Dt 14:24, etc.

"Incomplete" דלוג

Most common in the lists of *Okhlah we-Okhlah*, as the following (#7)

א"ב מן חד וחד חד ד' וחד ר' דלוג ולית דכו'

An alphabetic list of pairs of unique words of which one is spelled with *dalet*, the other with *resh*--but incomplete (i.e. all letters of the alphabet are not represented).

The letter *dalet* דלת

2C 2:17 לְהַעֲבִיד -- ל דלת והשאר לְהַעֲבִיר ריש

"Unique with *dalet*, other (similar) words are spelled לְהַעֲבִיר with *resh*".

Similar (words, phrases, etc.) דמיין (=דומים)

1C 6:13 וַשְׁנִי -- ג מילין דמיין וַשְׁנִי וַנְיָה וַיְזָתָא

"(One of) 3 similar words ... (each of which is a personal name beginning with *waw* with *pataḥ* which occurs only once)."

Gen 31:53 אֱלֹהֵי אַבְרָהָם וֵאלֹהֵי נָחוֹר יִשְׁפְּטוּ בֵינֵינוּ

אֱלֹהֵי אֲבִיהֶם -- ג פסוק דמיין

"(One of) 3 passages similar (in containing the same word 3 times, the second case with prefixed *waw*, and the first and third without it)".

Gen 8:19 ד֗ פסוק֗ דמיין דאית בהון כל כל וכל כל

"(One of) four verses similar in containing four cases of כל, the third with prefixed *waw*, and the rest without it".

Also the last example under מתא֗, קרחי **Ex 18:21**, קר֗ל Est 9:3.

These הלין (=אלה)

The name of an authoritative Biblical MS often mentioned in notes in the margins of MSS. Nothing is known of its date or origin (see #152). הללי

The letter *waw* וא

The Book of Numbers (more commonly במדבר), from its first word. וידבר

Lev 7:38 בְּמִדְבַּר°סִינָ֑י -- ל֗ וכל וידבר דכות֗ ב֗ מ֗ ב֗

"Unique in the Bible, save for the Book of Numbers, where the phrase always appears this way (with prefixed preposition *bet*) with two exceptions (Nu 10:12, 33:16, which have prefixed *mem*)".

Pairs (of words or phrases united by some feature) זוגין

Ex 5:17 נִזְבְּחָה°לַיהוָֽה -- חד מן ה' זוגין מתחלפין קדמאה אלהים תני' יְהוָה וסי' וַיֹּאמֶר אֱלֹהִים אֶל נֹחַ וַיֹּאמֶר יהוה לְנֹחַ...

"(A member of) one of five pairs of phrases differing in that the first contains אֱלֹהִים and the second the tetragrammaton".

Job 30:12 פִּרְחַח -- ל֗ וחד פִּרְחָה ואינון חד מן ט"ו זוגין חד ח' וחד ה' ולית להון זוגא

"Unique, but פִּרְחָה occurs once (Nu 8:4)--and these form one of 15 pairs of words of which one is spelled with *het*, the other with *he*, and both are unique forms".

Also מלע֗ (1) Gen 19:20, מלע֗ (2) Lev 13:10

Masculine (gender) זכר

Nu 11:15 אַתְּ עֹשֶׂה -- גֹ בלשׁ זכר
"אַתְּ occurs three times as a 2ms pronoun".

Small (letter, see #85) זעיר, זעירא
Gen 23:2 וְלִבְכֹּתָהּ -- כף זעירי
"Written with a small *kaf*".

The accent *zaqef* זק, זקפ - זקף, זקפא
Usually mentioned in connection with pausal forms, which most commonly occur with *atnaḥ* and *silluq*, but may occur with *zaqef* (and other accents).
Dt 28:67 תִּפְחָד -- לֹ זקף קמֹ
"Unique with *qameṣ* (i.e. in pausal form) when accented with *zaqef*."
Gen 44:10, 17 עָבֶד -- בֹ זק קמֹ
"Occurs twice with *qameṣ* (i.e. in pausal form), when accented with *zaqef*."

The accent *zarqa* זרק - זרקא
Dt 31:7 וֶאֱמָץ -- יֹטֹ קמֹ סמיך לזרק
Spelled with *qameṣ* (i.e. a pausal form) in 19 cases (with the disjunctive accent) following *zarqa*". (i.e. with *segolta*, which is often indicated in this way rather than by its own name).

Its companion (word/phrase etc.) חבֹ, חבי, וחבֹ - (ו)חברו
Used in lists of verse references to indicate the second of two similar or identical passages.
1C 9:44 בְּכֹרוֹ -- בֹ דין וחבֹ
"Occurs twice, here and in the similar passage (1C 8:38)".
1C 13:9 שָׁמְטוּ -- בֹ וחביל דשמֹ
"Occurs twice, here and in the similar passage in Samuel (2S 6:6)".
Ex 20:2 הוֹצֵאתִיךָ -- גֹ׳ מלאים וסי׳ מֵאוּר כַּשְׂדִּים, אָנֹכִי יְהוָה אֱלֹהֶיךָ, וחברו דמ"ת
"Plene three times in the Bible, Gen 15:7, here (Ex 20:2) and the similar passage in Deuteronomy (Dt 5:6)".
Gen 1:11 לְמִינוֹ -- די באורי׳ וסימן תַּדְשֵׁא הָאָרֶץ אֵת כָּל עֹרֵב לְמִינוֹ וחבירו דמשנה תורה אֶת הָאַרְנֶבֶת לְמִינוֹ
"4 cases in the Bible: Gen 1:11, Lev 11:15 and the

similar passage in Deuteronomy (14:14), and Lev 11:22".
Also #126, reference to 1C 1:7 in L and V.

One, once (=אחד) חד

Lev 10:5 וַיִּשָּׂאֻם -- ב̇ חד חס̇ וחד מל̇
"Occurs twice in the Bible, once defective, and once plene".

Dt 8:7 וּבָהָר -- ב̇ חד ראש פסוק̇ וחד סוף פסוק̇
"Occurs twice in the Bible, once at the beginning of a verse, and once at the end".

Nu 11:11 אֶת מַשָּׂא -- ל̇ וחד וְאֶת מַשָּׂא נַפְשָׁם
"This phrase is unique, but וְאֶת מַשָּׂא occurs once (Ez 24:25)".

Okhlah list 71 א"ב מן חד וחד ו' בריש תיב' וקמ' ולית
"An alphabetical list of unique words, each of which has prefixed *waw* with *qameṣ*".

Ordinary, not sacred (see #87) חול

Gen 19:25 הֶעָרִים הָאֵל -- ח' בלישׁ' חול
"(One of) 8 cases in which הָאֵל is not a sacred word (i.e. it is a demonstrative equivalent to הָאֵלֶּה, not אֵל "God").

Without *gaᶜya* (see געי) חטף

This is mostly used to indicate that a vowel is short.

2C 6:42 זָכְרָה -- ל̇ חטף בסיפ̇
"The only form in this book without *gaᶜya*" (i.e. it has short *qameṣ*, and so is a long form imperative, not 3fs perfect).

Dt 33:17 רִבְבוֹת -- חטף
"Without *gaᶜya* (after the *hireq*).

1C 29:18 שָׁמְרָה זֹּאת -- ל̇ חטף וכל תלים דכות̇ ב̇ מ̇ ב̇
"Unique without *gaᶜya* except in the Psalms, where it is always like this except in two cases". The word חטף here does not refer to the *shewa* under the *shin* (which is a way of distinguishing the *qameṣ* as short, not long) but to the fact that the *qameṣ* is to be read as short, without the lengthening represented by *gaᶜya* (see #315, 326). I.e. the form is again imperative, not perfect.

Variation (a difference in form, word order, etc. cf. פלג, מחל). חלוף, חילופׄ, חילוף

Dan 1:5 שָׁנִים שָׁלוֹשׁ -- לׄ וכל קריׄ חלוף

"Unique. In the other cases (where these two words occur) in the Bible, the order is reversed, שָׁלוֹשׁ שָׁנִים.

"Defective" spelling חסׄ, חסיׄ, חסירׄ, חׄ - חסר

Generally used if a word is spelled without a *yod* or *waw* which occurs in other forms.

Ex 24:6 בָּאַגָּנֹת -- לׄ וחסׄ

"Unique and defective (spelled without *waw* before the *taw*).

Gen 24:47 וָאָשִׂם -- הׄ חסׄ

"Five times defective (without *yod* before the *mem*).

The word חסר may also refer to *alef* or *he*.

Dt 28:57 הַיּוֹצֵת -- לׄ חסׄ אׄ

The spelling without *alef* is unique.

Ex 40:8 וְנָתַתָּ -- כׄטׄ חסׄ

"29 times defective" (not וְנָתַתָּה).

Nu 23:13 לְךָ -- גׄ חסׄ בליש

"3 times defective with the sense of 'walk'".

(Usually לְכָה).

Jer 33:6 וְלֹא יָדְעוּ כִּי רְפָאתִים מלׄ
וְאֵין בָּקָר בָּרְפָתִים כתב חסׄ אלף

"(Here) and in Hos 11:3 spelled plene (with *alef*), but בָּרְפָתִים (Hab 3:17) is spelled without the *alef*". (Mm of S[1]).

Doubly defective, lacking two possible vowel letters חסׄ דחסׄ

Gen 24:13 לִצְאֹת -- לׄי חסׄי דחסׄי

"Unique with doubly defective spelling (lacking both *waws*)."

Ex 21:22 בִּפְלִלִים -- גׄי בליׄי בׄי חסר יׄי קדמא ואׄי חסׄי דחסׄי

"This and similar words occur three times: twice lacking the first *yod* (between the *lameds*) and once doubly defective (with no *yod* before the *mem* either)".

(With the) accent טעׄ, טעם, בטעׄ, בטעם, בטעמא

1) Refers to the position of the accent sign, i.e. the position of the main word stress.

Dt 32:27 רָ֫מָה -- ג בטע בריש

"(One of) three cases with the accent on the *resh*"

2S 20:10 שָׁנָה לוֹ -- ל בטע

"Unique with this accent position"

Ex 40:4 וְהַעֲלִיתָ -- ל וטעם בתיו

"Unique spelling, and the accent sign is on the *taw*".

Nu 10:36 שׁוּבָה -- ה בטע

"(One of) five cases with the accent in this position". Also ל Nu 30:3.

2) Having some particular accentuation

2S 19:26 וַיְהִי -- כ בטע ראש פסו

"(One of) 20 cases where this word, with this accent (*tevir*), is the first in the verse."

Ez 36:7 לָכֵן -- כב בטע בסיפ

"(One of) 22 cases of this word with this accent (*revia*) in Ezekiel."

Ex 8:1 וַיֹּאמֶר יהוה -- ה בטע בסיפ

"(One of) 5 cases of this combination in Exodus with this accentuation (*munaḥ-zarqa*)".

Nu 10:36 רִבְבוֹת -- ל בטע

"Unique with this accentuation" (i.e. with *gaʿya*).

Ezra 9:4 כֹּל חָרֵד -- יא בטע דסמיכ

"(One of) 11 cases of these two accents together". (I.e. *yetiv* and not *mehuppak* before *pashṭa*. See #249). Also סיפ Gen 43:21, עינ Lev 13:56, רא פס Jos 9:12.

3) The word is also used for an independent accent as opposed to *maqqef*, as

Gen 38:17 עַד שָׁלְחֶךָ -- יא בטע

"(One of) 11 cases with this accentuation". (I.e. with a conjunctive accent, and not *maqqef*, on עַד).

Unusual (words or word combinations) יחיד, מיחד, מיוחד - יחידאין, מיחדין

Qoh 9:6 גַּם אַהֲבָתָם גַּם שִׂנְאָתָם גַּם קִנְאָתָם כְּבָר אָבָדָה

--יב יחיד דרא פסו אית בהון מן ג ג מלין קרחי

"(One of) 12 verses unusual in that they contain 3 identical words without prefixed *waw* (of which the first is the first in the verse)".

Ex 26:7 לְאֹהֶל עַל הַמִּשְׁכָּן -- ה מיחדין

"(One of) 5 unusual cases of לְאֹהֶל". (It does not have מוֹעֵד after it).

Gen 19:37 עַד־הַיּוֹם -- ט מיחדין

"(One of) 9 unusual cases of this phrase". (It is not followed by הַזֶּה.)

Superfluous (letter etc.) יתי׳ - יתיר

This is one of the terms used in *qere/ketiv* situations (#94).

Here כה (=כאן)

1S 13:19 ז׳ פסוקין שבעה מכה ושבעה מכה ומציעי׳ כת׳

"(One of) 7 verses with 7 words at the beginning and seven at the end, and between them a word on which there is a *qere/ketiv* note".

See דכ׳ כות׳, כוותהון

Written (spelled etc.) in this way (cf. כת׳) כ״כ, כת׳ כן, כן כתיב

Gen 36:9 תֹּלְדוֹת -- ג׳ כת׳ כן

"(One of) 3 cases spelled in this way". (With *waw* after the *daleth* but not after the *taw*).

Gen 25:16 נְשִׂיאִם -- ד׳ כ״כ בתו׳

"(One of) four cases in the Torah spelled this way". (With *yod* after the *shin* but not after the *alef*).

Ex 2:10 מְשִׁיתִהוּ -- ל׳ וכ״כ

"Unique spelled this way". (With *yod* after the *shin* but not after the *taw*).

All (examples, places, etc.) כ׳ל, כ״ל, כול

1) Used generally

Gen 26:20 וַיָּרִיבוּ -- כ״ל מ״ל

"All examples are written plene (cf. מ׳ל Ex 27:7)

Gen 5:7 וּשְׁמֹנֶה -- כל אורייתי׳ חסר

"All examples in the Torah are defective (lacking *waw* after the *mem*).

1K 2:40 מִגַּת -- כל לישׁ׳ פתחין

"All examples of this word have *pataḥ* (and never *qameṣ* as would be expected in this case with the accent *silluq*)".

2C 33:9 לַעֲשׂוֹת רָע -- כל עשייה רע פתח ב׳ מ׳ ז׳

"In all cases of the combination עשׂה + רע the *resh* has *pataḥ*, save for seven in which it has *qameṣ*". Also מל Ex 27:7, דמל מל Gen 26:28.

2) "All examples in" in the statements of usage in particular unites of text (see #115).

Nu 29:11 חַטָּאת -- ז וכל תרי עשׂ דכות בׄ מׄ אׄ

"(One of) seven cases of this spelling--and all the cases but one in the Twelve Prophets are also spelled this way", or

"This word is always spelled this way in the Twelve Prophets with one exception, and this is one of seven cases of this spelling in the rest of the Bible".

Nu 29:8 רֵיחַ נִיחֹחַ -- חׄ וכל אִשֵּׁה רֵיחַ נִיחֹחַ דכותהון

"(One of) eight cases of this combination--apart from the cases of אִשֵּׁה רֵיחַ נִיחֹחַ".

Dt 32:2 כִּשְׂעִירִם -- לׄ וכול ליש כן כתׄ בר מן בׄ מל

"This spelling is unique, but all similar forms are spelled the same way (with *yod* only after the *ᶜayin*) except for two, which are plene (with *yod* after the *resh* as well)".

Dt 33:6 יְחִי -- בׄ וכל יְחִי הַמֶּלֶךְ דכותׄ

"(One of) two cases of this word--apart from the cases of יְחִי הַמֶּלֶךְ".

Written (cf. כ"כ) כתׄ - כתיב, כתוב

Dt 28:60 מַדְוֵה -- בׄ חד כתׄ הׄ וחד כתׄ יׄ

"Occurs twice, once written with *he* and once written with *yod*".

Gen 20:6 מֵחֲטוֹ -- גׄ חד כתׄ טא וחד כתׄ טו וחד כתׄ טוא

"Occurs three times, once written מֵחֲטֹא, once מֵחֲטוֹ, and once מֵחֲטוֹא".

Gen 3:7 עֲלֵה -- בׄ כתׄ הׄ

"(One of) two cases spelled with final *he* (as opposed to עֲלֵי)".

2S 1:22 נָשׂוֹג -- לׄ כתׄ שׂ

"The writing with *sin* is unique".

1K 18:40 וַיּוֹרִדֵם -- לׄ וכתׄ כן

"Unique, and is written this way (with *waw* as a vowel letter, but no *yod* after the *resh*)".

1S 22:2 נֹשֶׂא -- ג̇ וחס̇ וכת̇ א̇

"(One of) three cases spelled defective, and written with final *alef*".

Also ל̇ Is 16:6

The same term is commonly used in *qere/ketiv* notes (#94), as

1S 6:17 טְחֹרֵי -- ב̇ כת̇ וקר̇

"One of two cases where the word is both written and pronounced in this way". (Usually it is written עפל etc., and pronounced טחר, as 1S 6:4).

The Writings--the third division of the Bible כת̇, כתו̇ - כתיביא, כתובים

Qoh 3:5 לִרְחֹק -- ד̇ חס̇ בכתיב̇

"(One of) four defective spellings in the writings".

Also נב̇ Ex 6:6.

Unique ל̇, לי - לית, ליתא

This term is often used alone of words or phrases

Gen 27:20 הִקְרָה -- ל̇

"Unique (word)".

Gen 21:14 וְאֶת°הַיֶּלֶד -- ל̇

"Unique (phrase)".

It may also be combined with some note on the spelling.

Jer 26:19 נַפְשׁוֹתֵינוּ -- ל̇ מל̇

"Unique spelled plene" (elsewhere defective).

Jer 24:1 וַיְבִאֵם -- ל̇ חס̇

"Unique spelled defective". (Elsewhere plene).

Jer 24:1 מוּעָדִים -- ל̇ ומל̇

"Unique and spelled plene" (and not found elsewhere).

Jer 16:6 יִתְגֹּדַד -- ל̇ וחס̇

"Unique and spelled defective (and not found elsewhere)".

The translations above give the correct meaning of these notes, but the two types of note, ל̇ חס̇ "Occurs elsewhere, but this is the only defective spelling" and ל̇ וחס̇ "This is the only case of this word. Note that it is defective" are used indiscriminately in some MSS, and in V.

ל̇ is also used with other modifications

Is 16:6 גֵּא -- ל̇ כת̇ א̇

"Unique spelled with *alef*".

Gen 20:16 — לְאָחִיךָ -- לׄ בסיפׄ

"Unique in this book".

Dt 20:9 — צְבָאוֹת -- לׄ בתורׄ

"Unique in the Torah".

Dt 28:54 — הָאִישׁ -- לׄ ראש פסוׄ

"Unique at the beginning of a verse".

Nu 30:3 — הִשָּׁבַע -- לׄ בטעׄ

"Unique with this accent position".

It may also be used in notes on vocalisation.

Gen 34:26 — וַיֵּצְאוּ -- לׄ

"Unique with *pataḥ*" (*waw* consecutive).

Gen 27:8 — מְצַוָּה -- לׄ

"Unique with *qameṣ*" (in a feminine form).

Nu 8:7 — הַזֵּה -- לׄ

"Unique with *ṣere*" (imperative)

Ex 13:17 — נָחָם -- לׄ

"Unique with two *qameṣ* signs".

Additional information is sometimes supplied.

Gen 40:14 — זְכַרְתַּנִי -- לׄ וחד וּזְכַרְתַּנִי

"Unique, but וּזְכַרְתַּנִי (with prefixed *waw*) occurs once".

Ex 27:21 — לַפָּרֹכֶת -- לׄי וחד לְפָרֹכֶת

"Unique, but לְפָרֹכֶת (without the definite article) occurs once".

The accent *legarmeh* (#277) — לגׄ, לגרׄ, לגרמׄ - לגרמיה

This term is commonly used in MSS with "expanded" Tiberian pointing to distinguish *legarmeh* from the combination *munah* + *paseq* which is identical in form (see #280 and cf פסקׄ). It is rarely used in standard Tiberian MSS, but does appear, as

Dan 3:2 (L) — לְמִכְנַשׁ -- לגרמׄ

"*Legarmeh* (not *munaḥ* + *paseq*)".

(Literally "tongue") — ליש׳, בליש׳, בלישנא (=לשון)

1) Designates a group of similar forms (see #128).

Ez 32:1 — בִּשְׁנֵי עָשָׂר -- וׄ בלישנא

"This combination (with שְׁנֵי not שְׁנַיִם) occurs six times in this and similar forms (e.g. לִשְׁנֵי עָשָׂר etc.)"

Is 54:2 — וִירִיעוֹת -- הׄ מ״ל בלישנא

"Written five times plene in this and similar forms (e.g. יְרִיעוֹת, פִּירִיעוֹת, הַיְרִיעוֹת etc.)".

Dt 31:21 ב֗ חס ה בלשנ וְהָיָה פִּי תִמְצָאן, וּמְצֶאן, מְנוּחָה

"(One of) two similar forms spelled without final *he*: תִּמְצֶאן, (Dt 31:21) and וּמְצֶאן, (Rut 1:9).

Also כ֗ל (1) 1K 2:40, מל֗ Ex 16:19, רפ֗ (3) Ps 62:9.

2) Meaning

2.a Usually used when a form has an unusual meaning.

Is 10:29 לָנוּ -- ל֗ לשון לינה

"Unique with the meaning "pass the night". (I.e. from the root לון, not the preposition ל + the 1cpl suffix).

1C 21:3 יוֹסֵף -- ל֗ מל֗ בלש֗ חוספ֗

"Unique spelled plene in the sense of 'addition' (and not a personal name)".

1S 28:16 עָרֶךָ -- ח֗ לשון שנאה

"(One of) 8 cases of this word with the sense of 'hating' (not 'city')".

Job 40:30 כְּנַעֲנִים -- ג֗ לשון תגרייא

"(One of) three cases of this word meaning 'merchant' (and not the name of the people)".

1S 18:15 וַיָּגָר -- ב' לשון דחילו' וַיָּגָר מוֹאָב

"(One of) two cases of this form meaning 'fear' (here and) Nu 22:3".

Also חס֗ Nu 23:13, שם Jer 22:16, Jos 15:43.

2.b This term is sometimes used with words which have several meanings.

Gen 46:21 וָרֹאשׁ -- ב֗ בחו֗ ליש֗

"This word occurs twice, and in two different meanings, as a personal name and as a common noun."

Ex 1:15 שִׁפְרָה -- ב֗ בחרי לישני

"Occurs twice, in two different meanings (personal name and common noun)".

Dt 29:21 חִלָּה -- ב֗ בחו֗ לשנין אֲשֶׁר חִלָּה יְהוָה בָּהּ וּכְהָצֵר לוֹ חִלָּה

"Occurs twice with two meanings: 'sickness' (Dt 29:21), and 'entreaty' (1C 33:12)".

Also אינון 2C 27:4.

The word occurs, in an extension of this sense, as a common part of standard grammatical terminology, as in

לשון זכר/נקבה (masculine/feminine gender), לשון רבים (plural number), etc., see under רבים, קדש, חול, זכר.

3) Language
2S 24:10 סָפַר-- ל̇ בלש̇ קודש
"Unique in the 'Holy Tongue' (Hebrew) (but occurs in Biblical Aramaic)".
Also ארמ̇ 1C 11:31, דגש (2) Ps 10:8, תרג̇ Dan 2:10.

The accent *merka* מארכ̇ - מארכא, מאריכין
This term is also used to indicate any conjunctive accent as opposed to *maqqef*.
Neh 6:18 בֶּן בֶּרֶכְיָה -- ו̇ מארכ̇ בטע̇
"Occurs six times with (long) accent (and not *maqqef*)". (See #305).
Nu 34:14 כִּי לָקְחוּ -- ה̇ מאריכין בריש פסוקי
"Occurs five times with a (long) accent (and not *maqqef*) at the beginning of a verse".

The Scroll of Esther מגל̇ - מגלה

The *Madinḥa'e* "Easterners" מדנ̇, מדנח̇, למד̇, למדנ̇ - (ל)מדנחאי
Refers to the Babylonian Masoretes, as opposed to the *Maᶜarba'e* "Westerners" of Eretz Israel and Syria. (See #153).
Dan 9:9 לַאדֹנָי -- למד̇ ליהוה כת̇
"The Eastern tradition writes ליהוה here".
Dan 9:7 כַּיּוֹם -- למדנ̇ כהיום
"The Eastern tradition writes *he* in this word".
2C 20:10 (in L, A has בב(ו)אם) בְּבֹאָם -- למדנ̇ חס̇
"Defective in the Eastern tradition".
2K 25:1 בִּשְׁנַת -- בשנה כתיב למדנחאי
"The Eastern tradition has בשנה as *ketiv*.
1S 1:3 וּפִנְחָס -- למערבאי חסי̇ למדנחאי מלי̇
"The Western tradition writes this word defective, the Eastern plene".

A meticulously written or corrected text or texts מוג̇, ספ̇ מוג̇ - ספר מוגה
(see #152)
Qoh 9:15 מִסְכֵּן חָכָם - ל̇ ובספ̇ מוגה

"The combination is unique, and occurs thus in a correct text (and not וְחָכָם)".

1S 23:4 (in V) קְעִילָה - בקצת ספרים ח' ובספי מוג' מ"ל

"Some texts write this word defective, but in a correct text it is plene (with *yod*).

Doubled, repeated מוכפ - מוכפל

See פסק Gen 22:11.

A Variant (tradition etc., cf. מחל, מחלפ - מחלפין (פלג; חילופ

Dan 7:12 זְמַן -- זמָן מחלפ

"There is a variant tradition using *qameṣ* here".

2C 12:13 הִשָּׁבַע -- וּשַׁבַע־ מחלפ

"There is a variant tradition using *maqqef* not *azlah*" (see #282).

Ex 30:23 וְקִנְּמָן־ -- ל מחלפ

"Unique (with this vocalization) but there is a variant tradition (ben Naftali וְקִנְּמֹן־)".

Also דגש (3) 2C 33:19.

They err, mistakes are made. מטע, מטעין, דמטע

1) Used where similar words or phrases might erroneously be interchanged or conflated.

Lev 17:11,14 ב פסוק מטע כִּי נֶפֶשׁ הַבָּשָׂר בַּדָּם הִוא
כִּי נֶפֶשׁ כָּל בָּשָׂר דָּמוֹ בְנַפְשׁוֹ הוּא

"Mistakes are made (confusing) these two passages".

Lev 23:12 וַעֲשִׂיתֶם-- י"א זוגין מטע'

"(One of) 11 pairs (of identical words with different accents) in which mistakes are made". (Cf. וַעֲשִׂיתֶם in verse 19).

2) Used in notes of the *sevirin* category (#109)--i.e. cases where another reading might seem better, but is incorrect.

Ex 17:2 וַיָּרֶב הָעָם עִם מֹשֶׁה וַיֹּאמְרוּ תְּנוּ לָנוּ מַיִם
-- מטעים ביה תנה

"It might seem that תְּנָה should be read, not תְּנוּ, but this is wrong".

Gen 45:25 וַיָּבֹאוּ אֶרֶץ כְּנַעַן -- ה דמט

"(One of) five cases where the reading אַרְצָה instead of אֶרֶץ before כְּנַעַן seems better, but is wrong".

2C 29:15 כְּמִצְוַת -- כַּף־ ומטע

"With prefixed *kaf*--*bet* might seem better, but is wrong".

מיחד, מיוחד — See יחיד

מל, מ"ל - מלא — "Plene" spelling

This usually refers to the use of *waw* or *yod*.

Gen 24:3 יוֹשֵׁב -- ג מל בסיפ

"Spelled plene (with *waw*) three times in this book"

Gen 40:6 אֲלֵיהֶם -- יז מל בתור

"Spelled plene (with *yod*) seventeen times in the Torah".

Ex 16:19 יוֹתֵר -- ז׳ בלישי מ"ל

"Spelled plene (with *waw*) seven times in this and similar forms".

Ex 27:7 וְהוּבָא -- כולי מ"ל

"Always plene (with *waw*)".

Ex 28:20 בְּמִלּוּאֹתָם -- ב׳ חד מ"ל וחד חסר דין מ"ל

"Occurs twice, once plene, and once defective. This case is plene".

The term is also used of other vowel letters

Gen 27:7 וַאֲבָרֶכְכָה -- ל מל וחד חס

"Unique spelled plene (with final *he*), but occurs once defective."

Gen 31:14 וַתֹּאמַרְנָה -- ל מל בתו

"Unique spelled plene (with final *he*) in the Torah".

מל דמל, מ"ל דמ"ל - מלא דמלא — Doubly plene, spelled with two vowel letters.

Gen 26:28 בֵּינֵינוּ -- כ"ל מ"ל דמ"ל במ"א

"Always spelled with two vowel letters (both *yod*) save for one case".

מלה, מלין — Word, Words -- used in various contexts

1C 7:10 וַאֲחִישָׁחַר -- לי ומלה חדה

"Unique, and written as one word (not two)".

1K 8:38 כָּל תְּפִלָּה כָל תְּחִנָּה -- י פסוק כל כל ומלה ביניה

"(One of) ten verses in which the word כל occurs twice with one word between the two cases".

Ex 2:3 וַתַּחְמְרָה -- חד מן י"ח מלין דלא מפקי ה׳ בסוף

תיבותא ומטעים

"One of 18 words ending in *he* with no *mappiq*, where *mappiq* may seem to be needed, but this is wrong". Also מפֿ Ex 6:24, מחאֿ Ez 21:32, and the last example there.

"*Mille^cel*" (above) and "*millera^c*" (below) מלעֿ - מלעיל, מלרֿ - מלרע

These terms are used to distinguish contrasting possibilities of vocalisation much as are דגש and רפה.

1) Referring to stress position (as in modern grammars). *Mille^cel* designates stress which is "above", i.e. closer to the beginning of the word--penultimate, while *millera^c* designates stress which is "below", i.e. closer to the end of the word--final.

1S 17:33 אַתָּ֫ה -- כֿו מלעל

"(One of) 26 cases of this word with penultimate stress (but with *pataḥ*, not *qameṣ*)".

Jos 2:3 הוֹצִיאִי -- ל̇ לשון נקבה ומלעֿ

"Unique in feminine gender (2fs imperative, not infinitive with a suffix). It has penultimate stress." (Stress position is not usually indicated by the sign for this accent (*telisha gedolah*), but in L the sign is repeated on this word to do this. See #270).

1K 21:5 סָרָ֫ה -- ל̇ מלרע

"Unique with final stress".

Gen 19:20 אִמָּלְטָ֫ה -- חד מן י״ב זוגין חד מלרע וחד מלעיל

"One of 12 pairs of words which occur once with final and once with penultimate stress". (*Okhlạh* list #51). Also מצ' Ex 10:1.

2) With reference to vowel quality, to distinguish words which are homographs but not homophones. (i) With the prepositions ב, כ, ל or conjunctive *waw* (as with דגש and רפה).

Lev 13:10 בַּשְּׂאֵת -- חד מן י״א זוגין חד מלרע וחד מלעיל נסבין ב' בריי' תיבותא

"One of 11 pairs of words with prefixed *bet* which is "below" in one case (having *shewa*, or *ḥireq* derived from *shewa*) but "above" in the other (having *pataḥ*, or some other pointing of the article)".

א"ב מן חד וחד לא' בריש תיבות' ולית מלעיל דלוג

וסימ' לָאֲנָשִׁים (Gen 19:8) לַבָּתִּים (Jos 7:14)

"An incomplete alphabetical list of single words with prefixed *lamed* which is unique pointed as the article". *Okhlah* list #26.

וחלופם א"ב מן חד וחד מלרע לא' בריש תיב'

וסימ' לְאֵפוֹד (Jud 8:27) לִבְקָרִים (Job 7:18)

"And the reverse: an alphabetical list of single words with prefixed *lamed* pointed with *shewa* or *ḥireq*". *Okhlah* list #27

3) To distinguish homographs (ii) other situations. In these cases *milleᶜel* "above" indicates that the characteristic or distinctive vowel of the word is nearer the top of the list of vowels in conventional order *shureq/qibbuṣ*, *ḥolem*, *qameṣ*, *pataḥ*, *segol*, *ṣere*, *ḥireq*, in contrast to *milleraᶜ* " below" which indicates that it is nearer the bottom.

Gen 22:22 — יִדְלָף -- בׄ חד מלרע וחד מלעיל וסי'

וְאֶת פִּלְדָּשׁ וְאֵת יִדְלָף מלרע וּבְשִׁפְלוּת יָדַיִם יִדְלֹף מלעיל

"Occurs twice: once with a "lower" vowel (יִדְלָף Gen 22:22) and once with an "upper" vowel (יִדְלֹף Qoh 10:18)".

Gen 37:25 — אֹרְחַת-- לי חד מלעיל דְּדָנִים

"Unique (with the 'lower' vowel *pataḥ*), but occurs in one case with an 'upper' vowel (אֹרְחוֹת Is 21:13).

א"ב מן חד וחד חד מלעיל וחד מלרע דלוג ולית דכותי'

וסי'... בְּמֹעַל בְּמַעַל

"An incomplete alphabetical list of pairs of unique words which occur once with an 'upper' vowel and once with a 'lower'."

בְּמֹעַל (Neh 8:6, 'upper') בְּמַעַל (Jos 22:22, 'lower') etc. *Okhlah* list #5.

On meanings (2) and (3) see S. Morag, אנציקלופדיה מקראית 5, 837-840, and A. Dotan, *Masoretic Studies I* (1974), p. 21-34.

מנוגן — See נגן

מנה - מנהון (=מהם) — Of/from them

Ex 12:3 — הַפָּרוּ -- ד' ג' מנהון ר"פ

"Occurs in four cases. Three of them begin a verse".

Is 57:11 וּמֵעֹלָם -- ג חד מנה חס

"Occurs three times, one of which is defective".

Gen 30:14 וַיָּבֵא -- נא יח מנה בתור

"Occurs in 51 cases, 18 of them are in the Torah".

Also נקׄ 2C 29:1, סׄל Dt 14:11.

Masorah finalis. Refers to lists of Mm at the end of V. (#139). מס׳ רבתא

The *Ma^carba'e* "Westerners" מעׄ, מערׄ, למעׄ - מערבאי

Refers to the Masoretes of Eretz Israel and Syria as opposed to the Easterners or Babylonians. See מדנחאי

Dan 11:30 קוֹדֶשׁ -- לׄ מלׄ למעׄ

"Unique with plene spelling according to the tradition of the Westerners".

Est 8:7 אֲחַשְׁוֵרֹשׁ -- דׄ חסׄ למעׄ

"The western tradition writes this word defective in four cases."

1C 29:21 אֵילִים -- למערׄ חסׄ יׄ קדמׄ

"The western tradition spells this without the first *yod*".

They pronounce, is pronounced מפׄ, מפיק - מפקין

This term generally refers to the pronunciation of final *he*.

Nu 32:42 לָהּ -- גׄ לא מפקׄ הׄ

"(One of) three cases in which the *he* is not pronounced (and therefore has no *mappiq* in it)".

Also מלה Ex 2:3, שטה Dt 33:27.

The term is also used of *alef* with consonantal value.

Ex 6:24 וַאֲבִיאָסָף -- י״ז מלין מן חד וחד מפקין אלף

"(One of) 17 different words in each of which *alef* is pronounced". (Cf. אֶבְיָסָף with no *alef* after the *yod*).

The term is also used of *waw* and *yod* with consonantal value.

2K 17:15 עֵדְוֹתָיו -- ה׳ מפקין ו״ו

"(One of) five cases with the *waw* pronounced". (Cf. עֵדוֹתָיו)

Within (a word, verse, etc.) מצ׳ - מציעא

See אמצע above. In addition to the uses shown there, this term may refer to the middle one of a set of examples, as

Ex 10:1 — שִׁתִי -- ג׳ ב׳ חס׳ וא׳ מ״ל וסי׳... מציעת׳ מל׳ וקדמא טעמא מלרע וב׳ בתראי מלעיל

"This word occurs three times, twice defective and once plene. The cases are Ex 10:1, Is 16:3, and Jer 31:21. The middle one (Is 16:3) is plene. They also differ in accent position. In the first it is final, in the other two penultimate".

Also כה 1S 13:19.

מ״ת - משנה תורה — The book of Deuteronomy (cf. Dt 17:18)

See חב֯ Ex 20:2, Gen 1:11.

מתא֯ - מתאמין — Similar, the same

Ez 21:32 — עַוָּה עַוָּה עַוָּה -- ב֯ מן תלת מלין מתאמין

"(One of) two cases where the same word is used three times".

Gen 46:2 — יַעֲקֹב יַעֲקֹב -- ד֯ שמוא֯ מתא֯

"(One of) four cases where the same name is repeated".

כל מלה דבקרייה דאית בה תריין מתאמין דמיין אן קדם להון געי רבא או געי זעירא פתחין בפמה...

"Where two identical letters occur in any word in the Bible, if they are preceded by greater or lesser *ga*^{c}*ya*, *shewa* between them is pronounced as *pataḥ* (is vocal)..." (The beginning of the rules on *shewa* under the first of two identical letters, from the Mm of A. See #385).

מתח֯, מתחל֯, מתחלפין — See חילוף above

נ״א - נוסחא אחרינא, נוסח אחר — Variant text or tradition

נב֯, נב֯י, נביא֯, נביי, בנב֯, בנב֯י, בנביאי — (In the) Prophets (the 2nd division of the Bible).

Is 28:24 — לִזְרֹעַ -- ג֯ חס֯ בנב֯

"(One of) three cases of defective spelling in the prophets".

Ex 6:6 — בִּזְרוֹעַ -- ג֯ מל֯ בת֯ וכל נב֯י וכתיב֯ דכות֯ ב֯ מ֯ ג֯

"(One of) three cases of plene spelling in the Torah, but all cases in the Prophets and Writings are spelled this way but 3".

"Make music" (*pi^cel*). Forms from this root refer to the musical value of the accents. See קמׄ Lev 1:5. נגן

According to the tradition of Neharde^ca — נהׄ, נהרׄ, לנׄ - לנהרדעי
(One of the great scholarly academies of Babylonia. Cf. סוׄ .)

With, including, added. נסיב
1C 5:23 — וּשְׂנִיר -- לׄ נסיב וָא
"Unique with prefixed *waw*".
Ex 5:7 — תֹאספוּן -- חד מן מ"ח מלין נסבין אלף באמצע תיבותא ולא קריין
"One of 48 words with *alef* included in the middle of the word but not pronounced".
1C 22:16 — לַזָּהָב לַכֶּסֶף וְלַנְּחֹשֶׁת וְלַבַּרְזֶל -- דׄ יחידׄ אית בהון דׄ מילין בׄ קדמׄ לא נסבין ווי ובׄ בתרׄ נסבׄ וויי
"(One of) four unique four-word phrases in which the first two words do not have prefixed *waw*, but the second two do have prefixed *waw*".
Also קדׄ Gen 17:24, etc.

Feminine gender — נקבׄ, נקיבה, נקיבות
Nu 36:6 — בְּעֵינֵיהֶם -- לׄ בנקיבות
"Unique with feminine gender". (Referring to the suffix which here has the daughters of Ṣelofḥad as antecedent.)
2C 29:1 — אֲבִיָּה -- יחׄ בׄ מנהון בנקׄ
"Occurs 18 times, two of which are feminine (a woman's name)".
Gen 24:40 — אִתָּךְ -- הׄ וכל יחזקׄ ונקבׄ כותׄ
"Occurs five times (as את + 2ms pronominal suffix in pausal form)--and in addition all cases of this combination in Ezekiel, and all cases where the suffix is feminine, are pointed this way".
Also מלעׄ Jos 2:3

Dots, dotted — נקדׄ, מנקדין
1) The dots on the letters in the consonantal text (see #79), as
Gen 16:5 — וּבֵינֶיׄךָ -- יׄ נקדׄ בתורׄ
"(One of the) ten dotted words in the Torah".

2) In the names of the vowel signs "two dots" (*ṣere*) and "three dots" (*segol*), as

1C 15:1 — וַיֶּט־ -- בׄ מנוקדין בתלת

"(One of) two cases pointed with three dots".

Marks the beginning of a *seder* (see #72) — ס

ס״א - ספרין אחריין, ספרים אחרים — Other books

Ex 23:15 — כִּי־בוֹ -- ס״א

"In other books this combination is accented "כִּי בוֹ".

סבׄ, סיבׄ, סברׄ, סבירׄ, סבירין — *Sevirin* (see #109)

1K 22:43 — בְּכָל דֶּרֶךְ אָסָא אָבִיו לֹא סָר מִמֶּנּוּ -- הׄ סבריׄ ממנה

"(One of) five cases where מִמֶּנָּה is wrongly suggested for מִמֶּנּוּ".

2C 21:6 — הָיְתָה לּוֹ אִשָּׁה -- גׄ סיבׄ לאשה

"(One of) three cases where it is wrongly suggested that לְאִשָּׁה should be read instead of אִשָּׁה".

Dan 8:9 — יָצָא קֶרֶן אַחַת -- גׄ סיבׄ יצאה

"(One of) three cases where יָצְאָה is wrongly suggested for יָצָא".

Lam 3:14 — הָיִיתִי שְּׂחֹק לְכָל עַמִּי -- גׄ סברׄ עמים וקרׄ עַמִּי

"(One of) three cases where עַמִּים is wrongly suggested, but עַמִּי is (correctly) read".

2C 21:2 — יְהוֹשָׁפָט מֶלֶךְ יִשְׂרָאֵל -- גׄ סבריׄ יהודה וקריׄ יִשְׂרָאֵל

"(One of) three cases where יְהוּדָה is wrongly suggested, but יִשְׂרָאֵל is (correctly) read".

Nu 13:22 — וַיַּעֲלוּ בַנֶּגֶב וַיָּבֹא -- חׄ סברׄ לשון רבים

"(One of) 8 cases where it is wrongly suggested that a plural form be used instead of a singular".

סׄ פׄ, ס״פ, סופׄ פסׄ, סופׄ פסוקׄ — *Sof pasuq*, the end of a verse

Gen 39:1 — שָׁמָּה -- יחׄ סופׄ פסוקׄ

"(One of) 18 cases occuring at the end of a verse".

Gen 24:29 — וּלְרִבְקָה -- בׄ חד ראׄ פסׄ וחד סופׄ פסוקׄ

"Occurs twice, once at the beginning of a verse, and once at the end of a verse".

Also אמצע Is 48:16, חד Dt 8:7, and cf. רׄ פׄ.

This term is also used as the name of the last accent in the verse (*sof pasuq* = *silluq*), see אס״פ.

According to the tradition of Sura סו֯, סור֯, סוראי, לס֯, לסור֯
(One of the great scholarly academies of Babylonia.
Cf. נה֯).

"Their signs" ס֯, סימ֯, וס֯, וסימ֯
1) Denotes phrases quoted as references to the verse in which the forms discussed occur. See #126.

וַיִּטַּע -- ג' וסי' גַּן בְּעֵדֶן מִקֶּדֶם, וַיָּחֶל נֹחַ, וַיִּטַּע אֶשֶׁל
Gen 9:20
"Occurs three times. References are Gen 2:8, Gen 9:20, Gen 21:33".

In the Mm of V, the note וסימן נמסר "The references are given" is used frequently where the references for the complete list of occurrences of some phenomenon are given elsewhere in the text.

Dt 14:11 טְהֹרָה -- ה' ב' מנהון מלא וסימן נמסר בסדר נח
"Occurs five times, of which two are spelled plene. The references are given in (the note on the case in) seder Noaḥ (Gen 7:2)".

In notes of this sort סימן may be used with the additional sense of "section, chapter".

Lev 22:7 וּבָא -- י"ז ר"פ נמסר בישעיה
סי' נט גבי פסוק וּבָא לְצִיּוֹן גּוֹאֵל
"Occurs 17 times at the beginning of a verse. The references are given in Isaiah Chapter 59 (in the note) on the verse beginning וּבָא לְצִיּוֹן גּוֹאֵל (59:20)".

2) Refers to an Aramaic mnemonic phrase composed from the Hebrew Simanim (see #127)

Gen 40:17 מַאֲכַל וּמַאֲכַל ד' פתחין וסי' וּבַסַּל הָעֶלְיוֹן,
וּמַאֲכַל שֻׁלְחָנוֹ וּמוֹשַׁב עֲבָדָיו, וחברו, וְנַפְשׁוֹ מַאֲכַל תַּאֲוָה,
וסי' בלשון ארמית סלא דנפשיה פתורא דחבריה
"The words מַאֲכַל and וּמַאֲכַל occur four times with *pataḥ*. The references are Gen 40:17, 1K 10:5, 2C 9:4, Job 33:20. The Aramaic phrase 'the basket of himself, the table of his friend' (a translation of key words from the Hebrew references) serves as a mnemonic".

Gen 18:7 וָטוֹב -- ה' קמ' וסי' וְהַנַּעַר שְׁמוּאֵל, וְלוֹ הָיָה בֵן
וּשְׁמוֹ שָׁאוּל, וְאֶל הַבָּקָר רָץ, וַיִּמְצָאוּ מִרְעֶה שָׁמֵן וָטוֹב,

הוּסַפְתָּ חָכְמָה וָטוֹב, וסי' שמואל טליא בחירא רהט ואשכח חוכמא

"This word occurs five times with *qameṣ*--Gen 18:7, 1S 2:26, 1S 9:2, 1C 4:40, 1K 10:7. The following Aramaic phrase, ('Samuel, a chosen youth, ran and found wisdom',) serves as a mnemonic".

3) Indicates a mnemonic recalling the differences between two similar passages.

Lev 15:26 כָּל־הַמִּשְׁכָּב -- קדמא דזָב ברביע דזָבָה בשני גרשין וסימן אִשָּׁה גְרוּשָׁה

"The first (of the two occurrences of this phrase) which is said of a man with a flux (Lev 15:4) has the accent *revia*, (the second) that referring to a woman (Lev 15:26) has the accent *geresh*. The phrase אִשָּׁה גְרוּשָׁה "A woman divorced/gereshed" (= Lev 21:7) serves as a mnemonic.

Lev 17:11, 14 כִּי נֶפֶשׁ הַבָּשָׂר בַּדָּם הִוא, כִּי הַדָּם הוּא בַּנֶּפֶשׁ יְכַפֵּר, כִּי נֶפֶשׁ כָּל בָּשָׂר דָּמוֹ בְנַפְשׁוֹ הוּא, כִּי נֶפֶשׁ כָּל בָּשָׂר דָּמוֹ הִוא -- קדמ' ובתרא' היא וב' מצי' הוא וסי' נְקֵבָה תְּסוֹבֵב גָּבֶר

"The first and last case of הוא are to be pronounced הִיא.

The two in between are to be pronounced הוּא. The clause נְקֵבָה תְּסוֹבֵב גָּבֶר (Jer 31:22) 'woman surrounds man' serves as a mnemonic".

4) This term is also used of mnemonics referring to lists of nouns, as

Jer 24:9 לְחֶרְפָּה וּלְמָשָׁל לִשְׁנִינָה וְלִקְלָלָה -- חמש"ק סימן

Jer 44:12 לְאָלָה לְשַׁמָּה וְלִקְלָלָה וּלְחֶרְפָּה -- אשקף סימן

A key letter from each of the four nouns is used to make up a nonsense word which serves as a mnemonic. (See also #118).

In this book סיפ, בס, בסי, בסיפ, בסיפר - בסיפרא

Nu 28:6 בְּהַר סִינַי -- ב בס

"Occurs twice in this book".

Jer 14:12 עֹלָה -- ל חס בסיפ

"Unique spelled defective in this book".

Gen 43:21 וַיְהִי -- ה בטע בסיפ

"(One of) five cases with this accent (*gershayim*) in this book".

Close, closely preceding or following — סמ, סמי, דסמי - סמיך, דסמיכי

Generally used of combinations of words.

Ex 28:2 — בִּגְדֵי°קֹדֶשׁ -- ג' דסמיך

"These words occur three times together".

Gen 1:2 — תֹהוּ°וָבֹהוּ -- ב דסמיכי

"This phrase occurs twice".

The term is also used of words used together, one following the other, as

Gen 35:17 — כִּי גַם זֶה לָךְ בֵּן -- ו' פסי' דאית בהון ה' מלין דסמי' מן ב' ב' אותיות

"(One of) five verses containing five words together each of which has two letters".

2C 25:24 — עֹבֵד°אֱדוֹם -- ל מל דסמי לעבד

"The word אֱדוֹם is written plene, only here among the cases where it follows "עֹבֵד".

Ex 32:23 — מֶה הָיָה -- כד וכל דסמיך לע ולח ב מ ה

"The pronoun מה has *segol* in 24 cases, and in addition it has this pointing in all cases where it is followed by *ʿayin* or *ḥet*, with five exceptions".

Also זרק Dt 31:7, טע (2) Ezra 9:4, רפ (1) Jer 1:16.

Context, section — ענ, בענ - בענינא

Neh 2:15 — שֹׁבֵר -- ב ובחד ענין

"Occurs twice in the Bible, both in the same context".

Ex 21:3 — בְּגַפּוֹ -- ג' ובענין

"Occurs three times, all in the same context."

Lev 13:56 — וְאִם -- ב בטע בענ

"Occurs twice with the accent *zarqa* in this section (also Lev 13:53)".

Nu 1:38 — אֲבֹתָם -- כל עינינ חס

"In the section on the census, (Numbers 2) this word is always spelled defective".

Division, difference (cf. חילופ, מחל) — פלג, פלגי, פיל, פולג, פלוגתא

Gen 39:19 — וַיְהִי°כִשְׁמֹעַ -- פלוגתא דגש

"There is a difference of opinion over (whether the *kaf* should have) *dagesh* (or no)".

Ezra 4:8 אִגְּרָה -- כת̇ כן ופולג̇

"Spelled (correctly) thus, although there is a difference of opinion (some spell it אגרא)".

Gen 40:8 תֲלוֹא -- י"ג מ"ל באורי ואי פלוגתי

"(Written) plene in 13 cases in the Torah, but there is a difference of opinion over one of them (some spell it defective)".

Jer 22:13 בְּלֹא־צֶדֶק -- בֶלֹא־צֶדֶק פלוג

"There is disagreement over the pointing of בְלא--some mark $ga^{c}ya$ (see #333)."

Ez 1:19 וּבְהִנָּשֵׂא -- פלג̇ וּבְהִנָּשֵׂא

"There is disagreement over the pointing--some do not use $ga^{c}ya$ under the *waw*". (See #324)

Someone, a certain person פלוני

1K 12:26 וַיֹּאמֶר יָרָבְעָם בְּלִבּוֹ -- ג̇ ויאמר פלוני בלבו

"(One of) three verses with the wording וַיֹּאמֶר + someone's name + בְּלִבּוֹ".

(In) the verse פס̇ פסו̇, פסוק̇, בפס̇, בפסו̇, בפסוק

Sometimes refers to a single verse, as

Ex 21:6 וְהִגִּישׁוֹ -- ב̇ בפסוק

"There are two occurrences in the Bible, both in the same verse".

Ex 21:25 פְּוִיָּה -- ב̇ בפס̇

"There are two occurrences in the Bible, both in the same verse".

Also קרחי̇ 1C 23:29.

The term may refer to a number of verses grouped for various reasons, as

Gen 49:18 לִישׁוּעָתְךָ קִוִּיתִי יְהוָה -- יד̇ פסוק

"(One of) 14 verses (composed of three words only)".

Lev 1:2 מִן הַבְּהֵמָה מִן הַבָּקָר וּמִן הַצֹּאן -- ב̇ פסוק̇ מן מן ומן

"(One of) two verses in which the combination ...מִן ... מִן ... וּמִן occurs".

Gen 18:25 י"ד פסו' לְךָ לָךְ

"(One of) 14 verses containing both לְךָ and לָךְ".

2K 4:10 י' פסוק' שָׁם שָׁמָּה

"(One of) 10 verses containing both שָׁם and שָׁמָּה".

Nu 7:20 כב̇ פסו̇ דלי̇ בהון לא ו̇ ולא יוד

"(One of) 22 verses which contain neither *waw* nor *yod*".

2K 14:12 ז' פסוקי מן ז' מלין כל מלה אית בהון יוד
"(One of) 7 verses containing 7 words each of which contains *yod*".
Also סמי֯ Gen 35:17 etc., קרחי֯ Ex 18:21, and cf. ר֯ פ֯, ס֯ פ֯.

The sign *paseq* (#283) פס֯, פסק֯

This note occurs constantly in MSS with "expanded" Tiberian pointing, and is sometimes seen in standard Tiberian MSS as well. It is used to distinguish *paseq* from *legarmeh*. (See #280 and cf. לג֯)

Is 42:5 (L) הָאֵ֣ל׀ יְהוָ֗ה -- פ֯ס֯ק֯
"(The stroke represents) *paseq* (not *legarmeh*)".

1C 17:22 יִשְׂרָאֵ֣ל׀ לְךָ֛ -- פס֯י
"*Paseq* (is used after יִשְׂרָאֵל)."

Gen 22:11 אַבְרָהָ֣ם׀ אַבְרָהָ֑ם -- ג' שמו' מוכפ' ופס'
"(One of) three cases where a name is repeated, and *paseq* is used after the first case".

1C 28:1 וּמִקְנֶה֩ -- ה֯ תלש֯ פסק֯
"(One of) 8 cases where the accent *telisha* (*qeṭannah*) is used with *paseq*".

See #75 פסקא בא"פ - פסקא באמצע פסוק

(In the) *parashah*, section (#72) פרש֯, בפרש֯, בפרשה

Lev 13:28 וְטִהֲרוֹ -- ד֯ בפרש֯
"Occurs four times in this *parashah*".
The abbreviation פרש֯ in the margin--generally decorated in some way--marks the beginning of a *parashah* in the Torah.

The vowel (sign) *pataḥ* פת֯, פתח, פתחין

1) refers to the vowel *pataḥ*, or the sign for it.

Ex 1:22 הַבַּת -- ד֯ פת֯
"(One of) four cases pointed with *pataḥ* (not הַבָּת Ez 45:11)".

Gen 19:2 וְרַחֲצוּ -- ב֯
"(One of) two cases pointed with *pataḥ* (not וְרָחֲצוּ)".

2S 13:4 דַּל -- יב֯
"(One of) 12 cases pointed with *pataḥ* (not דָּל)".

Dt 7:23 וְהָמָם -- ב֯ חד קמצ֯ וחד פת֯
"Occurs twice, once with *qameṣ* and once with *pataḥ* (וְהָמַם)

2S 7:29 וִיבֹרַךְ -- ד׳ בָּ ובַ

"Occurs four times, two with *qameṣ*, and two with *pataḥ*".

Also ס׳ (2) Gen 40:17.

2) The term may refer to the vowel *segol* (also called *pataḥ qaṭan*).

Ex 36:19 מִכְסֶה -- ב׳ פתחין

"(One of) two cases with *pataḥ* (not מִכְסֵה)".

Gen 34:25 בֶּטַח -- חד מן פתחי׳ באתנח׳ דספר׳

"One of the words in this book which have *pataḥ* (or *segol*) with *atnaḥ* (i.e. which does not change form in pausal position)".

Also קמׄ Lev 13;58, Lev 1:5, Dt 14:7.

3) the name *pataḥ* may also refer to the pronunciation of vocal *shewa*.

See the last example under מתאׄ.

(The) first קד׳, קדמׄ - קדמאה

Lev 5:2 או נֶפֶשׁ -- קדמא רביע תנין פזר

"(This phrase occurs twice) the first case with the accent *revia*, the second with the accent *pazer* (Lev 5:4)".

בְּהִמֹּלוֹ בְּשַׂר -- ג׳ זוגין קדמאי׳ לא נסב אֶת תנין נסב אֶת

Gen 17:24

"(One of) three pairs of phrases, of which the first occurrence does not include אֶת, while the second does (בְּהִמֹּלוֹ אֵת בְּשַׂר Gen 17:25)".

Jer 34:19 הַסָּרִסִים -- ב׳ חסר י׳ קדמא

"(One of) two cases lacking the first *yod*".

Also מעׄ 1C 29:21, מצׄ Ex 10:1, נסיב 1C 22:16, etc.

Holy קדש, לשון קדש

1) The "holy tongue" (Hebrew as opposed to Aramaic)

Dan 4:30 כְּצִפְּרִין -- לשון הקודש בקמץ

"In Hebrew the *pe* would be pointed with (*ḥaṭef*) *qameṣ*".

2) Sacred, distinguishing names referring to God from others, (#87).

Ps 86:14 אֱלֹהִים זֵדִים קָמוּ עָלַי -- קודש אלא שהקורא צריך שיהיה מפסיק בקריאתו

"Sacred (אֱלֹהִים refers to the God of Israel), but the

reader must pause in his reading (so that זֵדִים will not appear as an adjectival modifier of אֱלֹהִים--cf. the *paseq*)". *Masseket Soferim* 4:24.

With the vowel (sign) *qameṣ* — קמׄ, קמצ

1) Refers to the vowel *qameṣ*, or the sign for it.

Lev 17:4 — שָׁפָךְ -- בׄ קמצ

"(One of) two cases with *qameṣ* (not שָׁפַךְ)".

Nu 2:33 — הָתְפָּקְדוּ -- דׄ

"(One of) four cases with *qameṣ* (under the *he*)".

2K 3:26 — חָזַק -- הׄ

"(One of) five cases with *qameṣ* and *pataḥ* (not חָזָק)".

Nu 3:47 — תִּקָּח -- בׄ זקׄ קמׄ

"Occurs twice with *qameṣ* (i.e. in pausal form) and the accent *zaqef*".

2) This term may also refer to *ṣere* (also called *qameṣ qaṭan*), as

Lev 13:58 — הָעֵרֶב -- כו״ל קמץ וכל רמשא פתחין

"Always pointed with *qameṣ* (i.e. *ṣere*), however with the meaning "evening" it has *pataḥ* (i.e. *segol* הָעֶרֶב).

Lev 1:5 — בֵּן -- כל בן המנוגן בקמץ במ״ז פתחין

"Whenever בֵּן has an accent (as opposed to *maqqef*) it has *qameṣ* (i.e. *ṣere*), except for seven cases where it has *pataḥ* (i.e. *segol*)".

Dt 14:7 — מַעֲלֵה -- כלהון קמץ במ״ח פתחין

"Always pointed with *qameṣ* (i.e. *ṣere*) save for eight cases which have *pataḥ* (i.e. *segol*, מַעֲלֶה)".

Also סׄ (2) Gen 18:7 etc.

"Bald"--i.e. without prefixed *waw* — קרחי

1C 23:29 — לְמִנְחָה -- קרחא בפסוק

"Written without prefixed *waw* in this verse".

Ex 18:21 — שָׂרֵי אֲלָפִים שָׂרֵי מֵאוֹת שָׂרֵי חֲמִשִּׁים וְשָׂרֵי עֲשָׂרֹת
-- ד׳ פסוקים אית בהון ד׳ מלין דמיין קדמאה ותניינא
ותליתא קרחי ורביעי׳ נסיב וי״ו

"(One of) four verses in which the same word occurs four times, the first three cases without prefixed *waw*, and the fourth with it".

Also יחידׄ Qoh 9:6.

Qere (see #94) ק̇, קר̇, קרי

(In) the whole Bible קר̇, בק̇, בקר̇, בקר̇י, בקריה - בקריאה

(As opposed to Torah, Prophets, Writings, This Book, etc.)

Is 37:29 וּמִתְגִּי -- ב̇ בקריה

"Occurs twice in the Bible".

Is 40:13 תִּכֵּן -- ג̇ בק̇

"Occurs three times in the Bible".

Ex 6:24 אַסִּיר -- כל קריה מל̇ ב̇ מ̇ א̇

"Always written plene in the Bible with one exception".

Ez 36:23 הַמְחֻלָּל -- ל̇י וכל קרי̇י המהולל

"Unique. Elsewhere in the Bible this word always appears with *he* הַמְהֻלָּל".

Ex 29:18 אִשֶּׁה°לַיהוָה°הוּא -- ל̇ וכל קריה אִשֶּׁה הוּא לַיהוָה

"Unique combination. Elsewhere in the Bible the words occur in the order אִשֶּׁה הוּא לַיהוָה".

Jos 12:9 יְרִיחוֹ -- כל קרי̇י יריחו כת̇ ב̇ מ̇ א̇

"Always spelled יְרִיחוֹ in the Bible with one exception יְרִיחֹה 1K 16:34)".

Est 9:3 וְהָאֲחַשְׁדַּרְפְּנִים -- ג̇ מלין בקר̇ דמיין

"(One of) three words in the Bible similar (in that they have eleven letters)".

Also ב̇ מ̇ א̇ Dt 31:29, גרש last example, דגש (1) Jud 1:8, and the last example under מתא̇.

Place name קריה, קרתא

Jos 15:42 וְעָשָׁן -- ה̇ שם קריה

"(One of) five cases where this word is a place name (and not the noun 'smoke')".

Also שם Jos 15:43.

The beginning of a verse ר̇ פ̇, רא̇ פס̇ - ראש פסוק

Gen 36:2 עֵשָׂו -- ל̇ ראש פסוק

"Unique at the beginning of a verse".

Dt 28:54 הָאִישׁ -- ל̇ ר̇ פ̇

"Unique at the beginning of a verse".

Gen 33:3 וְהוּא -- ל̇ג ראש פסו̇ ג̇ מנה̇ בתור̇

"Occurs 33 times at the beginning of a verse. Three of these cases are in the Torah".

Jos 9:12 זֶהוּ -- ג׳ ראש פסֹ בטעֹ

"(One of) three cases where this word occurs with the accent *legarmeh* at the beginning of a verse".

Gen 9:3 כָּל רֶמֶשׂ... אֶת־כֹּל -- י׳ פסוק׳ ריש וסוף

"(One of) ten verses beginning and ending with the same word".

Also טעֹ (2) 2S 19:26, יחידֹ Qoh 9:6, לֹ Dt 28:54, מארכֹ Nu 34:14, סיֹ Lev 22:7, שטה Dt 14:24, and cf. ס"פ.

Great, large רבי, רבתֹ, רבתי = רב

Gen 30:42 וּבְהַעֲטִיף --ף רבי מאותיו׳ גדולות

"(Written with) a large final *pe*, one of the large letters" (in the Torah, #84).

Nu 27:5 מִשְׁפָּטָן -- לֹ נון רבֹ

"There is no other case of a large *nun*".

Plural רבים, לשון רבים

See סבֹ Nu 13:22.

The letter *resh* (see דלת) ריש

Rafe (i.e. without *dagesh*, cf. דגש) רפֹ - רפי, רפה

1) *Rafe* as used in modern grammars, the opposite of *dagesh* (1), as Ex 1:19 חָיוֹת -- לי רפי

"Unique with the *yod rafe* (not חַיּוֹת)".

Job 15:5 עֲרוּמִים -- ב׳ רפי׳

וסימ׳ וְתִבְחַר לְשׁוֹן עֲרוּמִים, מֵפֵר מַחְשְׁבוֹת עֲרוּמִים, וב׳ דגשי׳
וסימני׳ וַיִּהְיוּ שְׁנֵיהֶם עֲרוּמִּים הָאָדָם, וּבִגְדֵי עֲרוּמִּים תַּפְשִׁיט
וסימ׳ ערטלאין דגשי׳ חכימין רפין

"This word occurs twice with (the *mem*) *rafe*--Job 5:12, 15:5, and twice with *dagesh* (in the *mem*)--Gen 2:25, Job 22:6. The Aramaic clause "The naked have *dagesh* and the wise *rafe*" (i.e. with *dagesh* the word means 'naked', with *rafe* 'wise') serves as a mnemonic".

Jer 1:16 וְדִבַּרְתִּי מִשְׁפָּטַי אוֹתָם -- ט׳ דסמיך לדבור רפין

"In nine cases the *taw* of אתם is *rafe* when following (or joined with) the idea of speaking". (i.e. אֹתָם not אִתָּם)

2) Refers to the prefixed prepositions ל ,כ ,ב when not pointed as the definite article, or to *waw* when not pointed with *pataḥ*

or *qameṣ* as "consecutive" (the opposite of *dagesh* 2).

Gen 23:9 וְיִתֶּן־-- י"ג ר"פ

"(One of) 13 cases (with *waw*) *rafe* (i.e. not וַיִּתֶּן־)".

Ex 5:21 וְיִשְׁפֹּט-- לׄ רפי

"Unique *rafe*". (I.e. elsewhere וַיִּשְׁפֹּט).

Dan 8:12 וְתַשְׁלֵךְ-- לׄ רפׄ וגׄ דגשׁ

"Unique *rafe*, but there are three cases with *dagesh* (i.e. וַתַּשְׁלֵךְ)".

Lev 15:24 וּתְהִי -- יׄדׄ רפי

"(One of) 14 cases *rafe* (not וַתְּהִי).

Nu 7:13 לְמִנְחָה -- כל קריׄ רפי בׄ מׄ בׄ דגש

"Always *rafe* in the Bible save for two cases which have *dagesh* (i.e. לַמִּנְחָה)".

Dt 29:11 בִּבְרִית -- גׄ רפׄ

"(One of) three cases *rafe* (i.e. not בַּבְּרִית)".

3) A word containing a guttural pointed with a composite *shewa* (or a full vowel) instead of simple *shewa* may also be called *rafe* (opposite of *dagesh* 3. See #414).

Ps 62:9 מַחֲסֶה -- ט' רפין בליש' בקריא'...
וכל אֶחֱסֶה דכוו' רפין במ"א וּבְצֵל כְּנָפֶיךָ אֶחְסֶה

"This and similar forms occur nine times *rafe* (with composite *shewa* under the *ḥet*) in the Bible. Similarly אֶחֱסֶה is *rafe* (has composite *shewa* under the *ḥet*) in all cases but one (אֶחְסֶה Ps 57:2)".

Ex 1:11 רַעַמְסֵס -- לׄ רפי

"Unique *rafe* (other cases רַעְמְסֵס)".

Gen 14:20 מַעֲשֵׂר -- ג' רפים וסי'... וכל המעשר דכו'

"(One of) three cases *rafe* (not מַעְשֵׂר) and all cases of הַמַּעֲשֵׂר are pointed that way".

The rest, the others שאׄ, שארׄ - שארא

Lev 11:13 שֶׁקֶץ°הֵם -- ג' ושארא שֶׁקֶץ הוּא

"This phrase occurs three times. In other cases the text reads שֶׁקֶץ הוּא ".

Dt 4:5 בָּאִים°שָׁמָּה°לְרִשְׁתָּהּ -- בׄ ושארׄ עֹבְרִים שָׁמָּה לְרִשְׁתָּהּ

"This phrase occurs twice. In other cases the text reads עֹבְרִים שָׁמָּה לְרִשְׁתָּהּ".

Also דלת 2C 2:17.

List שטה, שיטה

Dt 33:27 — מְעֹנָה -- שטה מן י״א חד מפיק וחד לא מפיק
"(Belongs in) a list of eleven pairs of words of which one has *mappiq* in the final *he*, and the other does not."

Prov 1:1 — שטה כל חד וחד לי׳ דכותי׳
וכל מלה אחרי מן לישנ׳ דכו׳
וסימ׳ אֻמְנָם וַיֹּאמֶר יְהוָה אֶל אַבְרָהָם לָמָּה זֶּה וכל הַאֻמְנָם דכו׳
"A list of words each of which is itself unique, although similar forms occur with the same spelling. E.g. אֻמְנָם (Gen 18:13) is unique (with *qibbuṣ* under the *alef*), but all cases of הַאֻמְנָם have this pointing".

Dt 14:24 — וְכִי יִרְבֶּה -- ח׳ ר״פ בסיפ׳
והוא חד מן שטה מן חד חד משמש וְכִי ולית דכוותא
"(One of) 8 cases of וְכִי at the beginning of a verse in this book, and the two words together belong in a list of unique phrases which begin with וְכִי".

The following (word, verse, etc.) — שלא֯, שלאח֯ - שלאחריו
The Mm of L[20] at Is 44:11 חֲבֵרָיו ד֯ ג֯ כת֯ חֲבֵרָו ודין דהכא
מל֯ וסימנ֯ הֵן כָּל חֲבֵרָיו קח לְךָ עֵץ אֶחָד ב֯ בו ושלא֯
"חֲבֵרָיו occurs 4 times, of which 3 are written חברו. This (Is 44:11) is the case written plene (with *yod*). The references are Is 44:11, Ez 37:16 where it occurs twice, and the one after it (Ez 37:19).

(Personal) name(s) — שם, שום, שמא, שמו׳, שמוא׳
1C 7:18 — אִישְׁהוֹד -- ל֯ וחד שמא כת֯ וקר֯
"This form is unique, and is written and read as one name".

Jer 22:16 — דָּן -- ג׳ לישן דין וכל שום בר נש דכו׳
"(One of) three cases with the meaning of 'judging'. The personal name (of the tribe and its ancestor) is always spelled this way as well."

Jos 15:43 — וְיִפְתָּח -- ג׳ ב׳ קמץ וא׳ פתח
וסי׳ וְיִפְתָּח וְאַשְׁנָה, וְיִפְתָּח הַגִּלְעָדִי, וְיִפְתַּח שְׂפָתָיו עִמָּךְ
חד שום קרתא, חד שום גברא, חד לישן פתיחא
"Occurs three times, twice with *qameṣ* and once with *pataḥ* (וְיִפְתַּח). The references are Jos 15:43, Jud 11:1, Job 11:5. In one case it is the name of a city, in one the name of a man, and in one (a verb) meaning 'open'". See also אנש, אנתתא, אשה, גברא, קריה etc.

The book(s) of Samuel — שמו׳, שמוא׳ - שמואל

(In) the Torah (cf. או׳) — ת׳, תו׳, תור׳, בת׳, בתו׳, בתור׳ - בתורה

Lev 5:16 — יוֹסֵף -- ל׳ מל׳ בתור׳

"Unique in the Torah spelled plene".

Gen 49:14 — חֲמֹר -- ד׳ חס׳ בת׳

"(One of) four cases spelled defective in the Torah".

Also ל׳ Dt 20:9, מל׳ Gen 40:6, 31:14, נב׳ Ex 6:6.

Word (cf. מלה) — תיב׳, תיבו׳, תיבות׳ - תיבותא

1K 18:10 — יַמְצָאֶכָּה -- כ׳ מלין כת׳ הי בסוף תיבות׳

"(One of) 20 (unique) words with *he* as the last letter".

(Used in many other examples).

Second — תינ׳, תנ׳ -- תנין, תניינא

Ex 23:11 — וְהַשְּׁבִיעִת -- ל׳ וחס׳ י׳ תנין

"Unique and is spelled without the second *yod*".

Also קד׳ Lev 5:2, Gen 17:24.

The book Leviticus — ת"כ - תורת כהנים

Lev 11:3 — בַּבְּהֵמָה -- ו׳ דגשים וסי׳ בָּעוֹף בַּבְּהֵמָה דנח,

מַעֲלַת גֵּרָה בַּבְּהֵמָה דתורת כהנים, וחברו דמשנה תורה...

"(One of) six cases with *dagesh* (i.e. the prefixed *bet* is pointed with the article). The references are Gen 9:10 (in the *parashah* Noaḥ), Lev 11:3, the similar case in Dt 14:6, etc.".

The Book of Psalms — תלים, תלין = תהלים

See אנ"ך — תנ"ך

Two, second — תר׳, תרי׳ - תרין

Lev 23:21 — מוֹשְׁבֹתֵיכֶם -- ח׳ מלין בתרי טעמי

"(One of) eight cases in which these two accents (*merka* and *tifḥa*) are used on the same word". (#233).

The book of the twelve (minor) prophets — תר׳ עש׳, תרי עשר

For examples see כל׳ (2) Nu 29:11.

See ליש׳ — תרי לישני

The language of the Targum, Aramaic — תרג׳ - תרגום, לשון תרגום

Dan 2:10 — יוּכַל -- ל׳ בלש׳ תרג׳

"Unique in (Biblical) Aramaic (but found in the Hebrew text)".

Babylonian Terminology and Pointing in the Tiberian Masorah

133. In some early Tiberian MSS, the Masorah is clearly Tiberian, but is occasionally pointed with Babylonian vowel signs. This occurs, for instance, in A and S, and a great many other early MSS and Geniza fragments. It is unlikely that this is evidence of the influence of the Babylonian Masorah. It is probable that the use of such signs was in some way fashionable, or that the Babylonian signs are used simply because there is more space available for vowel signs above the words than below them. In any case these Babylonian signs represent Tiberian, not Babylonian pronunciation. E.g. in S, Mm to Nu 8, יעבֹר is equivalent to Tiberian יֵעָבֵר. The standard Babylonian vowelling would be יעבֹר (= יֵעָבַר). Mm to Dt 7, מפנה = Tib מָפנה. The Babylonian pointing would be מפנה = Tib מֵפֵנה. Mm to Ex 22, כרע = Tib כרֵעַ. The Babylonian pointing does not mark *pataḥ* "furtive".

Babylonian terminology is occasionally used in many early Tiberian MSS. A, B, and S, provide examples. E.g.

Gen 30:40 (Mp of S) עַל צֹאן לָבָן -- ד׳ דחזי להון עִם

"(One of) four cases in which עִם is wrongly suggested (for עַל)". דחזי is the Babylonian equivalent of Tiberian סביר.

Gen 14:6 (Mp of S) אֵיל פָּארָן -- שלמ׳ במתואתא

"Plene spelling (with *yod*) is used where אֵיל is a place name. These terms are the Babylonian equivalent for מלא בשום קריה.

Babylonian terms also occur occasionally in L, as Mm on

Job 1:3 ראשיה דאיוב וסיפיה אתונות שלמ׳ דשלמ׳

"At the beginning and end of the book of Job אתונות is written doubly plene (with two *waws*)".

There are also many Babylonian MSS which show a Tiberian Masorah. P is an example of this. Manuscripts of this sort generally show strong Tiberian influence on the text tradition and vocalisation as well, whereas there is no sign of such influence on genuinely early Babylonian MSS.

For a study of the Babylonian vocalization see Yeivin, 1968a, 1973, and for a list of Babylonian MSS, including those of the Babylonian Masorah, see Díez Merino 1975.

The Masorah to Targum Onqelos

134. When the Scriptures were read in the Synagogue, the Targum Onqelos was read immediately after the Torah, and so gained a certain sanctity. Consequently it was also provided with a Masorah, since its liturgical importance required that it also be preserved unchanged. In a few MSS, the notes of this Masorah are written in the margins beside the text, and a few lists from it are also preserved in MSS. The Masorah to this targum is found either with Babylonian or with Tiberian pointing, but there are various indications that this Masorah was originally produced in Babylonia. When the Masorah was copied into Tiberian MSS which included this targum, the Babylonian pointing was evidently changed to Tiberian.

135. The Masorah to the Targum Onqelos is not mainly concerned with the spelling of words and the number of times they occur, as is the Biblical Masorah, although there are some notes of this sort, as

Gen 27:1 כל אוריתא סיב בר מן א̇ כד סַב יצחק

"סיב is used throughout the Torah save for (this) one case of סַב".

Gen 24 איתָאָה לפלניא י̇א ב̇א... ושא̇ר לות פלניא

The verb אתא is found in combination with ל 11 times in the Torah. Elsewhere it is used with לות".

Lev 18:5 בחיי עלמא ב̇ באור̇ יְחִי רְאוּבֵן ודין

"בחיי עלמא is used twice in the Torah: Dt 33:6 and Lev 18:5".

The major concern of the Masorah to Targum Onqelos, however, is the way the Hebrew is translated, and the majority of the notes refer to cases where one Hebrew word is translated by more than one Aramaic equivalent. These equivalents may be words from different roots, different words from the same root, or the same word with different particles added, etc. Targum Onqelos gives a remarkably faithful translation of the Hebrew, generally word for word, but naturally there is some variation in the translation of the same word used in different contexts. The term used in notes of this sort is דמתרגמינן, abbreviated דמ̇, דמתרג̇, דמיתרג̇, תרג̇ as

כִּי דמתרג̇ לא ב' באי' כִּי אִישׁ הָרַגְתִּי, כִּי חַרְבְּךָ

"Hebrew כִּי is represented by Aramaic לא in two cases in the

Torah: Gen 4:23 and Ex 20:25".

אֱלֹהִים דמתרג רב ב֗ באורי֗ וְאַתָּה תִּהְיֶה, רְאֵה נְתַתִּיךָ

"אֱלֹהִים is translated רב twice in the Torah: Ex 4:16, 7:1."

בּוֹ דמתרג בַּהּ ב֗ באור֗ וְקָרָא בוֹ, וְהִתְעַמֶּר־בּוֹ

"בּוֹ is translated בַּהּ twice in the Torah, Dt 17:19 and 24:7".

The Masorah to the Targum uses a good deal of terminology parallel to that on the Biblical text. For instance מטעין or משתבשין, the equivalent of סביר֗ (#109). E.g.

יתהון דמשתבשין בהון ג' באורי' סֹלֶת חִטִּים, וַיְשַׁבֵּר אוֹתָם, וַיִּקְרָא אֶתְהֶן חַוֹּת

"There are three cases in the Torah where the Targum gives יתהון, but error is likely (because the feminine form, יתהין, might be expected) Ex 29:2, 32:19, Nu 32:41". Other notes refer to differences between the scholars of the two great academies, Sura and Neharde^{c}a. These may refer to words, as

Lev 27:8 עַל פִּי לנהרד֗ על פום לסור֗ על מימר

"For עַל פִּי the Targum gives על פום according to the Nehardeans, but על מימר according to the Surans".

Similar notes refer to differences in pointing, as

Nu 11:7 בְּדוֹלְחָא לנ֗ בְּדוּלְחָא לס֗

The *waw* in בדולחא is pointed as *ḥolem* according to the Nehardeans, *shureq* according to the Surans".

Nu 10:32 וְהָיָה הַטּוֹב טוּבא לנ֗ טָבָא לס֗

"הַטּוֹב is here translated טובא by the Nehardeans, טבא by the Surans".

Sura and Neharde^{c}a are the only schools mentioned in the Masorah to the Targum, whether it occurs in a Babylonian or Tiberian MS. This is one of the indications of the Babylonian origin of this Masorah.

The Masorah to Targum Onqelos was published on the basis of Tiberian MSS in Berliner, 1877, and in Landauer, 1896. Some Geniza fragments contain lists from the Masorah to Targum Onqelos, some with Tiberian and some with Babylonian pointing.

MASORETIC TREATISES

The Masorah in the Margins of Manuscripts

136. Since it was forbidden to add any sort of sign to Torah scrolls, it can be assumed that the notes of the Masorah were at first transmitted orally, or were collected in treatises

by themselves before they were introduced into the margins of Biblical texts. Among the earliest Biblical fragments preserved in the Geniza--those written in scroll form--there are some which have no signs or notes at all added to the consonantal text, and there are some which show some vowel and accent signs, but few or no masoretic notes. Examples are the fragments of scrolls with Palestinian pointing which appear to have been written in the eighth or ninth century. It seems likely, then, that the practice of writing masoretic notes in the margins of MSS is later than that of adding vowel and accent signs.

Eventually, however, the Masoretes, who received the masoretic tradition from their teachers, or who possessed various lists of masoretic notes, began to write the notes of the Masorah--either Mp or Mm--in the margins of their codices. As a general rule, in carefully produced texts, a scribe would write the letters of the Biblical text, while a Masorete would add the vowel and accent signs and the masoretic notes. The work of writing these was called מָסוֹר or מַסֵּר. The Masorete was also responsible for the correctness of the textual tradition. If the scribe had copied a certain word in one form, and the Masorete found from his notes that the word should be written in another form, he would erase and correct it.

The Masoretes transmitted their tradition one to another, each generation adding to the material it had received from the last, until the margins of the text were filled with notes on a large number of words in which errors of spelling might easily be made. They worked with reverent devotion to analyze and record all significant details of the textual tradition so as to fix the traditional form of the text, and maintain it unchanged. However they did not all reach the same conclusion on all points, so that, in the course of time, "schools" which held different opinions were formed. We do not, however, know the reason for the differences between these schools. Presumably they received their traditions from different sources, or used different compilations of masoretic lists, etc. In any case it seems probably that there never was a single uniform Masorah at any period. The available evidence only shows us different manuscripts containing masoretic notes, many of which are the same, but some of which differ from, or even contradict each other. Even MSS which derive from the same school do not present identical Mp and Mm.

137. The early "Model Codices" were each the work of an individual Masorete representing a single school. When one of these was recopied, the copyist would often add masoretic notes from other sources. Through this process, the Masorah of a manuscript soon ceased to be a homogeneous description of the particular textual tradition which the manuscript contained, and became a heterogeneous collection of textual notes, not directly related to any particular tradition. This phenomenon can be recognized in variations in the terminology of the notes, in repetition, and also in cases where the text conflicts with the Masorah. The only model codices of the Masoretes which have been preserved for us are A, the work of Aharon ben Asher, the last of the Masoretes, (#26) and C, the work of his father, Mosheh ben Asher (#32). The other early MSS known to us, such as the tenth century MSS B, L, S, S[1], already show such evidence of mixed traditions. This evidence consists in the use, within a single MS, of synonymous terms from different origins, such as שם אנש and שום גבר, לשון ארמית and לשון תרג', בחו̇ר and באו̇ר. Repetitions occur as in the Mp of L at Is 26:20 הַלְחִיךְ -- יתיר י̇ דלחך ק̇ "superfluous *yod*" and "the *qere* is הֲלָתְךָ" are different ways of saying the same thing (see #94). Some masoretic notes conflict with the text. Sometimes a note on one verse conflicts with the text in another, as in L where the Mp at Ps 64:5 notes לִירוֹת -- ב̇ חד חס̇. "This word occurs twice --once spelled defective", but the text in the other case (Ps 11:2) also shows a plene spelling. In other cases a note may even conflict with the text it refers to, as in L at 2K 10:5, where נַמְלִיךְ in the text, spelled plene, is annotated ל̇ וחס̇ "Unique with defective spelling". According to A and C this note is correct. In these MSS the word is written without the *yod*, but the textual tradition of L is different.

138. Despite occasional irregularities of this sort, the Masorah corresponds closely to the text in MSS from the early period and up to the twelfth or thirteenth century, and the text in these MSS is fixed according to the Masorah. In the

later MSS, however, the scribe who wrote the text, and the one who added the pointing, simply reproduced the text of the MS from which they were copying, and the masoretic notes were copied in in the same way, without any check to ensure that they did not conflict with the text. In this way the Masorah lost the function for which it was created, and came to be little more than an ornament to the text. In some MSS, indeed, the notes of the Masorah were formed into various geometric patterns, and, later on, even into patterns formed of plants, animals, etc. In this form their function was clearly mainly decorative, for they are very difficult to read.

This outline refers to the development of complete masoretic texts, containing both Mp and Mm. In all periods, however, from the earliest up to the introduction of printing, texts were produced with vowel and accent signs, but with few or no masoretic notes. This is typical of MSS with Palestinian and Babylonian pointing, and there are many examples with Tiberian pointing also. We also find MSS which contain only scattered notes, sometimes restricted to a particular category. Some contain only *qere/ketiv* notes. Some note regularly the distinction between *legarmeh* and *paseq*, some have notes on *ga*^{c}*ya* (mainly *shewa-ga*^{c}*ya*), or on variant traditions, and so on.

The Masorah in Printed Editions

139. When Jacob ben Ḥayyim prepared his edition of the Bible (V, Venice 1524-25) he attempted to produce a strictly correct text, and he realized the value of the Masorah for this purpose. Since the Masorah in most of the MSS of his period was merely ornamental, he searched for early MSS and masoretic compilations. He collected and compared the notes from these, and attempted to establish his correct text on this basis. In his edition, the Mp was printed in the margin beside the text, the Mm under it, and the "*Masorah finalis*" containing lists of both the Elaborative and the Collative type, was printed in a separate compilation at the end of the Bible.

The work of Jacob ben Ḥayyim rescued the Masorah from its debased state, and restored it to its original function--the establishment and preservation of the textual tradition. However Jacob ben Ḥayyim did not have access to the actual MSS of the masoretic scholars, nor even texts from their period or close to it (9th to 11th centuries). He had to use texts produced close to his own time, which contained a mixture of notes from various schools and MSS. Consequently, despite all his work in comparing and analyzing the material he collected, he did not produce much real improvement, but presented an immense collection of masoretic notes with much less homogeneity than was found in any of the MSS he had used.

Jacob ben Ḥayyim's edition, the first printing of the Masorah, was accepted as a sort of codification of it. Most of the *Miqra'ot Gedolot* ("Rabbinic Bibles") printed from his time to our own have copied his Masorah, and the treatises on the Masorah are based on it. In 1876, S. Frensdorff published an index to the Mm in this edition. He arranged it in alphabetical order according to subjects, and added a detailed commentary. (He did not, however, copy the wording exactly, or give complete references).

140. Another collection of masoretic material is to be found in C.D. Ginsburg's *The Massorah* (Ginsburg 1880). Ginsburg collected masoretic notes from dozens of manuscripts from different periods and countries. He arranged these notes alphabetically by subject. He even included whole treatises--various forms of the "*Diqduqe ha-Ṭeᶜamim*", of the lists of *ḥillufim* between ben Asher and ben Naftali, and between the *Madinḥa'e* and *Maᶜarba'e*, the *Sefer Taggim*, an old form of the Babylonian Masorah on the Torah, the *Ḥeleq ha-Diqduq* of R. Yaḥya Saliḥ (from the Yemen, #164), and more. This immense collection contains much of great value to students of the Masorah, but it is much worse than the collection of Jacob ben Ḥayyim in the way it mixes material from different sources.

141. Later editions of the Bible (apart from "Rabbinic Bibles") generally present only selected notes from the Masorah: mainly *qere/ketiv*, *sevirin*, notes on unique vocalisation and accentuation, etc. BHK, which printed the text and Mp of L, was a significant innovation. This edition is important because it presents the text and Masorah from a single manuscript, and not a text with a collection of notes from different manuscripts. It is particularly important that

the manuscript chosen was an early one, as its Masorah reflects the situation a long time before V. It is also true, however that L is not the product of a masoretic scholar, but is removed a generation or two from the Masoretes, and its Masorah is not entirely homogeneous. The new Stuttgart edition, BHS, now completed, also presents the Mp of L, edited by G.E. Weil in a form somewhat different from that found in the manuscript. Weil has published the lists of the Mm in a separate volume, and intends also to publish a volume of commentary.

The Masorah in Independent Treatises

142. Before the discovery of the Cairo Genizah, the Masorah was scarcely known in any form other than that found in the margins of MSS, but in the Genizah, many fragments of independent masoretic lists of different types were found. In general these were separate leaves, or fragments of leaves--fragments of treatises which contained the Masorah of single books or of larger sections of the Bible.

Some of these contained lists of the notes of the Mp following the order of the Biblical text, as (Cambridge, TS NS 287:21. Masorah to Hos 10: 6-11).

לְמֶלֶךְ כֿטֿ: בָּשְׁנָה לֿ: יִקָּח גָֿ: נִדְמֶה לֿ: כְּקֶצֶף לֿ: וְנִשְׁמְדוּ
כֿוֹ פסוֹ מפקין אלפביתה: כַּסּוּנוּ לֿ: נִפְלוּ לֿ: עַלְוָה גֿ:
וְאֶסֳּרֵם לֿ: חֲטָאתָ לֿ: בְּאַוָּתִי לֿ: וְאֻסְּפוּ בֿ: עֹינֹתָם כתֿ עוֹנ קֿ
ולֿ כוֹ: וְאֶפְרַיִם הֿ וכל מְנַשֶּׁה וְאֶפְרַיִם כוֹ: מְלֻמָּדָה בֿ: אֹהַבְתִּי
לֿ: לָדוּשׁ לֿ: טוּב יֿטֿ: יְשַׂדֶּד גֿ:

Some such lists contain only Mm, as Cambridge TS D1:1 on Judges.

בִּשְׂחוֹק (Jud 16:27) בֿ שִׁמְשׁוֹן גַּם בִּשְׂחוֹק יִכְאַב: לַיָּמִים (17:10)
הֿ וְעֶרֶךְ וּבְגַלְּחוֹ הֲיַעֲמֹד וּבָאתִי עַל כֵּן: מַכְלִים (18:7) בֿ וְאֵין
מַכְלִים דָּבָר בָּאָרֶץ וישקיט וְאֵין מַכְלִים: וַיַּסֵּבּוּ (18:23) גֿ
פְּנֵיהֶם מִמִּשְׁכַּן אֶת אֲרוֹן:

Most of these lists, however, contain both Mp and Mm, as Cambridge TS D1:72. (Masorah to Mica 5:5-6:3)

בִּפְתָחֶיהָ לֿ. וְהִצִּיל גֿ גָּנוֹן עֵינֵינוּ מֵאַשּׁוּר. וְהָיָה זֿ בטֿ בסֿ.
כְּטַל בֿ חֶרְמוֹן. לִבְנֵי אָדָם לֿ בסֿ. תָּרֹם לֿ וחסֿ. מַרְכְּבֹתֶיךָ בֿ.
יָדֶיךָ הֿ מלֿ בנבֿ תֶּחֱזַקְנָה אֲצִילוֹת תִּשְׁתַּחֲוֶה הַמַּכּוֹת תֶּרֶף. וְתִשְׁמַעְנָה
לֿ. וְהָאֵתָנִים מוֹסְדֵי למעֿ לבני מזרח במוֹסרות שלהם מֹסְדֵי חסֿ.
מַה יָּעַץ בָּלָק כתֿ ולמעֿ אין להם בזה מאומה כמות קריין כך הם

כתובים. יְתֻוּבָּח לׄ. הֶלְאֵתִיךָ לׄ.

Not only are there many lists of the complete Masorah, as these examples, but also there are lists covering particular subjects, such as *qere/ketiv*, *petuḥot* and *setumot*, unique letter forms, dotted letters, differences between parallel passages, the *ḥillufim* between ben Asher and ben Naftali, between the *Madinḥa'e* and the *maᶜarba'e*, and so on. Some lists contain mixtures between Palestinian and Tiberian, or Babylonian and Tiberian Masorah.

Just as the marginal Masorah is not identical in different Biblical MSS, so that one MS will show notes which do not appear in another, so in these masoretic lists one list contains notes not found in another, although of course a considerable proportion of the notes is common to the different lists and to different Biblical MSS.

'Okhlah we-Okhlah'

143. The largest independent masoretic compilation is that known as *Okhlah we-Okhlah*, and this was the only such compilation known before the discovery of the Genizah. This compilation contains some 400 masoretic lists, long or short, mostly from the collative MM (#129). The first of these lists is an alphabetic list of pairs of unique words, of which one has prefixed *waw* while the second does not. The first of the pairs in this list provides the title "*Okhlah we-Okhlah*". Many similar lists are found in the margins of Biblical MSS, but this list is longer, and contains hundreds of pairs. It is followed by many other lists of different types from the collative Masorah, such as lists of single words which share some common feature of spelling or vocalization; lists of pairs of words which differ from each other in one letter, or in one vowel sign, or in accentuation, or in meaning; or lists of verses which resemble each other in the number of words, or in the use and arrangement of particles, and so on. Examples are given in the following paragraph.

144. The following selection of titles of the lists in *Okhlah we-Okhlah* will give some idea of the subjects treated.

List 2 א"ב מן חד וחד חד אֶל וחד עַל וליח דסמי' וסימניהון ...

An alphabetical list of pairs of unique phrases, of which one begins with אֶל and the other with עַל, as אֶל אֵם (Ez 21:26) עַל אֵם (Jer 15:8).

א"ב מן חד וחד חד כ"ף וחד בי"ת דלוג ולי' דכותהון וסימניהון ...
List 4

An incomplete alphabetical list of pairs of unique words, of which one has prefixed *kaf*, and the other prefixed *bet*, as כְּאִיּוֹב (Job 34:7), בְּאִיּוֹב (Job 32:2).

List 13 א"ב מן תרין א' וחד וא' וסי' ...

An alphabetical list of words which occur twice without prefixed *waw*, and once with it, as אֵרָאֶה (Lev 16:2, 1K 18:15), וְאֵרָאֶה (Ps 42:3).

List 18 א"ב מן חד חד ומ' ברי' תיבותי' ולי' דכותהון וסי'

An alphabetical list of unique words beginning -ומ, as וּמֵאָז (Ex 5:23), וּמֵאֹתוֹת (Jer 10:2).

List 21 א"ב מן חד וחד קמץ ולי' וסימניהון

An alphabetical list of unique words pointed with *qameṣ*, as אַרְפַּכְשָׁד (Gen 11:11), אֶתְוַדָּע (Nu 12:6).

List 26 א"ב מן חד וחד לאי בריש תיבותי' ולית מלעיל דלוג וסימ'

An incomplete alphabetical list of unique words beginning with *lamed* pointed with the definite article, as לָאֲנָשִׁים (Gen 19:8), לָאֱלֹהִים (Ex 22:19).

List 33 א"ב מן חד וחד ו' בסוף תיבותי' ולי' וסימ'

An alphabetical list of unique words ending with *waw* (or the vowel "o") as אִישׁוֹ (1K 20:20), אָלֹה (Hos 4:2).

List 44 י"א זוגין מן חד וחד חד מפיק ה' וחד לא מפיק ה'
וכל חד לי' וסימניהון

A list of 11 pairs of unique words with final *he* one of which is marked with *mappiq* while the other is not, as מִכְרָהּ (Prov 31:10), מִכְרָה (Gen 25:31).

כ' זוגין מן חד וחד חד מלרי' וחד מלעיל וא' בריש תיב' ולי' וסי'
List 47

A list of 20 pairs of unique words beginning -וא, one of which is "*milleʿel*" (the *waw* is pointed with *pataḥ* or *qameṣ* as *waw* consecutive) and one of which is *milleraʿ* (pointed as *waw* simple), as וַאֲבָרְכֵהוּ (Is 51:2), וָאֲבָרְכֵהוּ (Gen 27:33).

List 58 א"ב מן ב' ב' ותרויהון בחד פסו' דלו' וסי'

An incomplete alphabetical list of words which occur only twice in the Bible, both times in the same verse, as אֲרָחוֹת

(Jud 5:6), אָרוּם (Ps 46:11).

List 72 א"ב מן ב' ב' מותאמים וכל חד וחד לי' דסמיי' דלוג וסי'

An incomplete alphabetical list of unique phrases composed of two identical words, as אַבְשָׁלוֹם אַבְשָׁלוֹם (2S 19:5), אֱכוֹל אֱכוֹל (Ez 3:1).

A group of some 80 lists in this compilation forms a unique collection classifying *qere/ketiv* notes from different viewpoints (see #98), as

List 112 כ' מלין כתב' ה' בסוף תיבות' ולא קרין וסי'

A list of 20 words spelled with final *he* which is not read, as וָאֵרֶאה (Jos 7:21) etc.

List 162 י"א מלין לא כתבן ת' וקרין וסי'

A list of 11 words in which *taw* is not written, but is read, as אַמֹּה (2K 25:17).

List 91 ס"ב מלין דכתבן מוקדם מאוחר וסימן

A list of 62 words in which there is metathesis of letters, as הָולֹךְ (Jos 6:13), הָאֹהֶל (1K 7:45).

List 101 ג' מלין תיבות' קמייתא נסבא מן תנינא וסי'

A list of three cases in which the final letter of one word is to be read as the first of the next, as הָיִיתָה מוֹצִיא (2S 5:2).

List 127 מ"ג מלין כתבן י' בסוף תיבות' ולא קרין וסי'

A list of 43 words spelled with final *yod* which is not read, as הַיֹּשַׁבְתִּי (Ez 27:3).

A further collection of lists in this compilation covers various features of the Masorah, such as large letters, small letters, suspended letters, dotted words, inverted *nun*, *tiqqune soferim*, *iṭṭure soferim*, various types of variant readings, and so on.

145. The material in this collection contains some very old lists, as some of the lists of *qere/ketiv*, dotted words, *tiqqune soferim*, etc. On the other hand it also contains lists dealing with features of vocalization and accentuation which are not earlier than the eighth or ninth century. It seems probable that the *Okhlah we-Okhlah* was compiled in the ninth century. The variations in the meanings of several terms used in it show that the lists were gathered from different sources, and from different periods. For instance the terms *millera*ᶜ and *mille*ᶜ*el* are used to refer to accent position,

or to the presence or absence of the definite article, or to different vowel qualities (see #132 under מלע̇).

The *Okhlah we-Okhlah* was already known in the tenth to eleventh centuries, and in many cases references to המסרה הגדלה appear to refer to this compilation. R. David Qimḥi was the first to refer to a work under the name "*Okhlah we-Okhlah*", and the same name is used by Eliahu ha-Levi, but it is not certain whether this was the same compilation as the one we know by that name, or another containing many of the same lists. Jacob ben Ḥayyim included many lists from it in the *Masorah finalis* of V. After this, the compilation was forgotten until an edition of it was published by S. Frensdorff in 1864. He based this on a manuscript preserved in Paris, to which he added notes and an index. In the meantime, H. Hupfeldt had discovered, in Halle, another MS which was more precise, and included more lists than the Paris MS. The Spanish scholar, F. Díaz Esteban has published an edition based on this MS, and on Genizah fragments, some of which have Palestinian or early Tiberian pointing. (Díaz Esteban, 1975).

THE HISTORY OF THE MASORAH

146. The Masorah consists of a mass of data collected over a long period by many scholars. It includes the work of different schools and individuals, with different opinions, but in general only the information itself was considered important, and its origin is not recorded. Despite recent discoveries of very ancient Biblical texts and masoretic fragments, we still do not have information which shows clearly who produced the Masorah and how it was done. The outline of its development can only be sketched on the basis of vague hints, and with much speculation.

It appears that the first to work on masoretic matters were the *soferim*--the pupils of Ezra the Scribe in the early second temple period. Their work extended into the period of the Talmud (300-600 CE). After this the period of the Masoretes began, and their work continued until the final establishment of the received Tiberian tradition, including its vocalisation and accentuation, in the tenth century. To some extent the work of clarifying the textual tradition, and preserving it according to the tradition of the Masorah, has continued up to our time.

The Masorah in the Talmudic Literature

147. In the Talmudic period, the rules for writing the Biblical text in general, and for the writing of particular passages (see #67 ff.) were established. This is also true for a considerable proportion of the traditions on the unusual features of the text, among them the *tiqqune soferim*, the dotted words, inverted *nun*, and early categories of *qere/ketiv*. The Talmudic literature includes interpretations based on various details of the textual tradition, such as the presence of conjunctive *waw* or a preposition, plene or defective spelling, and so on. Since such features formed a basis for the establishment of *halakah*, it must be assumed that there was already general agreement on the spelling of the consonantal text.

The foundations of the Masorah were thus already well established in this period. מסורות *Masorot* (traditions?) are mentioned in TB *Nedarim* 37b (on Neh 8:8), where "So that they understood the reading" is interpreted "This refers to the text divisions (פיסוק טעמים, possibly the basis of the accentuation), but some say it refers to the מסורות". In addition various activities related to the realm of the Masorah are mentioned. "The early scholars were called '*soferim*' because they used to count (היו סופרים) all the words of the Torah". "They were thoroughly versed in the defective and plene readings, but we are not". (TB *Qiddushin*, 30a).

148. Some Talmudic comments refer to features of the text in the same way as does the Masorah, and seem to be a prototype of characteristic masoretic notes. E.g. "אב (father) always precedes אם (mother) in the Biblical text. You might therefore think that honouring the father was more important than honouring the mother. However the text says "Each must revere his mother and his father" (Lev 19:3), showing that both are equal (Mishnah *Keritot* 6:9). Compare the note in the Mp of L on Lev 19:3 אִמּוֹ וְאָבִיו -- ל̇ וכל קריה אָבִיו וְאִמּוֹ
"The phrase is unique. Elsewhere אָבִיו וְאִמּוֹ appears".

"How does this praisegiving (2C 20:21) differ from all the praisegivings in the Torah? In the Torah the phrasing is always הודו לַיהוָה כִּי טוֹב כִּי לְעוֹלָם חַסְדּוֹ
but here it says הודו לַיהוָה כִּי לְעוֹלָם חַסְדּוֹ
(*Mekilta de-R. Yishmaᶜel*, *Beshallaḥ*. ed. Horowitz-Rabin, p.118).

Compare the Mp of L on 2C 20:21 ג֯ חס֯ כִּי טוֹב
"כִּי טוֹב is missing (from this phrase) in three cases".
Note also the Mm of V here, and Frensdorff, *Masorah Magna*, p.76 note 1. The Mekilta and the Masorah note the same phenomenon. The unique feature of the Masorah is that it adds the number of cases involved, (#113), noting that there are in all three cases where כִּי טוֹב is not used in this context.

Talmudic literature also contains many interpretations of different Biblical verses which recall the observations of the Masorah. These are based on the forms of words, usually in connection with plene or defective spelling, the addition of conjunctive *waw*, and similar details, and may even include a statement on the number of occurrences--that is to say observations on similar cases. Examples are

כל תּ֯לְד֯ת שנאמרו בתו' חסרין בר מן תריין, אֵלֶּה תּוֹלְדוֹת פָּרֶץ והדין
"All cases of תּ֯לְד֯ת in the Torah (here meaning the whole Bible) are spelled defective except two: Ruth 4:18 and this one (Gen 2:4)". (*Bereshit Rabba* 12:6)

דאמ' ר' יוחנן כל צַדִּיקִים שנ' בסדום צַדִּיקִם כת'
"R. Yoḥanan notes that whenever צַדִּיקִים is used in connection with the men of Sodom it is spelled defectively". (*Bereshit Rabba* 49:9).

בכולם כת' קָרְבָּנוֹ ובו כת' וְקָרְבָּנוֹ, בכולם כת' עַתֻּדִים חסר
ובו כת' עַתּוּדִים
"In all other cases the spelling is קָרְבָּנוֹ but in this case (Nu 7:13) וְקָרְבָּנוֹ. In all other cases the spelling is עַתֻּדִים, defective, but in this case (Nu 7:17) עַתּוּדִים (plene). (*Sifre Zuṭa* on Nu 7:11, ed. Horowitz, p.252).

ר' אחא בשם ר' חננא בכל ספר מלאכי כת' ייי צְבָאוֹת וכן כת' אֱלֹהֵי
יִשְׂ' כביכול לא ייחד שמו על הגירושין אלא אֱלֹהֵי יִשְׂ' בלבד
"R. Aḥa said in the name of R. Ḥanina, 'Throughout the book of Maleachi יהוה צְבָאוֹת is written, but here, with reference to divorce (Mal 2:16) אֱלֹהֵי יִשְׂרָאֵל, as if to show that His name has

no bearing on divorce but as the name God of Israel only". (*Bereshit Rabba* 18:5).

ר' יהודה בן בתירא אומר נאמר בשני וְנִסְכֵּיהֶם ונאמר בששי וּנְסָכֶיהָ
ונאמר בשביעי כְּמִשְׁפָּטָם הרי מ"ם יו"ד מ"ם הרי כאן מים מכאן
רמז לניסוך המים מן התורה

R. Juda ben Bethera said "Of the second day of the feast Scripture says וְנִסְכֵּיהֶם (Nu 29:19), and of the sixth day וּנְסָכֶיהָ (Nu 29:31, and not וְנִסְכָּהּ as of other days - Nu 29:16, 22 etc. I.e. the *mem* of וְנִסְכֵּיהֶם and the *yod* of וּנְסָכֶיהָ are special additions). Of the seventh day Scripture says כְּמִשְׁפָּטָם (Nu 29:33, not כַּמִּשְׁפָּט as elsewhere - Nu 29:18, 21, etc. I.e. the final *mem* is also an addition).
Here you have the letters מ י ם forming the word "water". And here you have an allusion, in the Torah to the libation of water". (TB *Taᶜanit* 2b)
Compare the Mm of V on Nu 29:19 (referring to ונסכיהם)

ל' רמז לנסוך המים וסימן בו"ז מים

"Unique. Allusion to the libation of water. The reference is 267 (the description of the 2nd, 6th, and 7th, days provide the letters) מ י ם (water).
Also the Mp of L on Nu 29:33 כְּמִשְׁפָּטָם -- סימׄ בׄוׄזׄמׄיׄםׄ
See also *Okhlah* list #293.

As shown in some of the examples given above, terminology characteristic of the Masorah is also used in Talmudic literature. Other examples are:

TY *Shabbat* 9:2 (f. 12a). מלא, חסר

אישתאלת לר' חונא ספרא דסדרא ואמ' זֵרוּעֶיהָ מלא

"R. Ḥunna the scribe of the congregation was asked, and he said that זֵרוּעֶיהָ (Is 61:11) is written plene".

(*Bereshit Rabba* 68:3) אנ"ך

ר' פינחס בשם ר' אבהוא בתורה ובנביאים ובכתובים מצינו שאין
זיווגו שלאיש הזה אלא מן הקב"ה. בתורה - וַיַּעַן לָבָן וּבְתוּאֵל
וַיֹּאמְרוּ וגו', בנביאים - וְאָבִיו וְאִמּוֹ לֹא יָדְעוּ כִּי מֵיי' וגו',
בכתובים - בַּיִת וָהוֹן וגו'

R. Pinḥas said in the name of R. Abbahu "We can see from the Torah, Prophets, and Writings that marriages are made in heaven : in the Torah from Gen 24:50 "Laban and Bethuel replied 'This word has come from God...'", in the Prophets from Judges 14:4 "His father and mother didn't realize that this was from God" and in the Writings from Prov 19:14 "A prudent wife is from God"."

(*Wayyiqra Rabba* 15:2) חברו

אמר ר' סימון שני פסוקין נתנבא (בארה) ולא היה בהן כדי ספר
וניטפלו בישעיה ואלו הן - וְכִי יֹאמְרוּ אֲלֵיכֶם, וחבירו

"R. Simon said 'Two *pesuqin* (i.e. verses) did Beeri speak as a prophet, and because they were not sufficient to form a book, they were included in the book of Isaiah. They were "When they shall say unto you..." (Is 8:19) and the companion verse (Is 8:20).

(*Bereshit Rabba* 74:16) חול

אֱלֹהֵי אַבְרָהָם וֵאלֹהֵי נָחוֹר יִשְׁפְּטוּ בֵינֵינוּ, אֱלֹהֵי אַבְרָהָם קודש,
אֱלֹהֵי נָחוֹר חול, אֱלֹהֵי אֲבִיהֶם משמש קודש וחול

"In Gen 31:53 אֱלֹהֵי in 'The God of Abraham' is sacred (referring to the God of Israel), but in 'The God of Naḥor' it is not. In 'The God of their father' it may be either sacred (if it refers to the father of Abraham) or profane".

On the masoretic work of the Amora R. Naḥman bar Yiṣḥaq see Levin, 1911.

Even though it is clear that the work of the Masoretes began in the talmudic period, there is no evidence of the existence of any sort of apparatus of masoretic notes at this time. It can, therefore, be assumed that the Masorah in its narrow sense, the Mp and Mm which preserve the textual tradition and fix the details of it, did not exist in this period. It can also be assumed that, in this period, there were no scholars who specialized in matters of textual tradition, and it seems likely that the scholars whose names are attached to statements on such matters investigated this area only as part of their work in the *halakah* as a whole.

149. It can also be noted that the Talmudic statements on masoretic phenomena do not always agree with the tradition of the received text, and occasionally conflict with it. For instance in *Wayyiqra Rabba*, a midrash compiled before the close of the Talmudic period, it is said
צוּר יְלָדְךָ תֶּשִׁי - התשתם כוחו שליוצר, יוד זעיר ולית בקריא כוותיה
(*Wayyiqra Rabba* 23:13, ed. Margoliouth, p.548, cf. *Bemidbar Rabba* 9:1). This midrash states that תֶּשִׁי in Dt 32:18 has a

small *yod*, and bases a homily on this fact. Not only this, but the text states in characteristic masoretic terminology that this small *yod* is unique (i.e. it includes enumeration, see #113). In all early MSS, however, such as *A* and *L*, this *yod* is written normally, not small, in clear contradiction of the midrashic statement.

In a number of cases in the Talmud it is indicated that Psalms 1 and 2 form a single psalm. Three observations on this are preserved in TB *Berakot* 9b-10a, and a fourth in TB *Megilla* 17b. In TY *Shabbat* 16 (p.15c) it is said "The number of Psalms is 147, corresponding to the Years of the patriarch Jacob". This number also appears to assume that Ps 1-2 form a single psalm. However in the Masorah, e.g. that of L, in the *Sefer ha-Ḥillufim*, etc., the number of psalms is given as 149 (with 114-115 considered as a single psalm), and not 147, and Psalms 1-2 are treated as separate psalms. Here, then, the Talmud gives different information from the Masorah. (See also *Minḥat Shay* on the end of the Book of Psalms).

Contradictions between statements in the Talmudic literature and in the Masorah are listed in *Sefer Mishpaḥat Soferim* by Shemuel Rosenfeldt, (Rosenfeldt, 1883). He argues that in such cases of disagreement the Talmudic statement, not the Masorah, should be followed.

'Masseket Soferim'

150. Two ancient treatises are concerned with the rules for the writing of the Biblical text and the Masorah. The מסכת ספר תורה *Masseket Sefer Torah* is early, short, and treats the rules in the narrow sense. מסכת סופרים *Masseket Soferim* is later--evidently compiled in the ninth century--and includes the material in the *Masseket Sefer Torah* as well as a lot more. In its first five chapters the rules for writing the Torah scroll are given. In chapters six to nine, other features are treated: inverted *nun* , large and small letters, the dotted words, lists of various categories of *qere/ketiv* situations, and variants between Ps 18 and 2S 22, and between Is 36-39 and 2K 18-20. This last section is real Masorah, and resembles the lists in *Okhlah we-Okhlah*. Most of the phenomena treated in *Masseket Soferim* are already mentioned in the Talmud, but the

enumeration of them, and the arrangement of them in lists, began after the period of the Talmud, and this represents the beginning of the work of the Masoretes.

The Masoretes

151. Eliahu ha-Levi says in his "third introduction" to his book *Masoret ha-Masoret* "There were hundreds and thousands of Masoretes, generation after generation over a long period, neither the beginning nor the end of which is known". The same is true for us today. We know absolutely nothing about the scholars who performed the immense labour of which the masoretic notes are the fruit. The notes of the Masorah preserve the names of a few scholars, but these are only from the latest generations. Nearly all those scholars who are mentioned by name, are mentioned because they held particular opinions on details of vocalization or accentuation, and so cannot have lived before the eighth century. We also have lists of the Masoretes of Tiberias, but in most cases we know no more than their names. One such list is the "Chain of ben Asher", which lists seven generations of Masoretes, the last of which is the famous Aharon ben Asher. The first name in the list is that of "R. Asher ha-Zaqen ha-Gadol", who must have worked at the end of the eighth century. A note on the pronunciation of שְׁתַּיִם also gives the names of a number of Masoretes: Abraham ben Rīqāṭ, and Rīqāṭ his father, Abraham ben Parāt, etc. It seems likely that all of these lived after the vocalization and accentuation had been fixed.

In various notes in the margins of MSS, or in independent lists, variant readings are preserved in the names of different authorities, most commonly בעלי טבריה "The Scholars of Tiberias", or simply טבריה "Tiberias", מחזורא רבה/רובה "The *Maḥzora Rabba* or *Rubba*, משה (בן) מוחה Mosheh (ben) Moḥeh, חביב בן פיפים Ḥabib ben Pipim, פינחס ראש הישיבה Pinḥas the head of the Yeshiva, or simply Pinḥas (possibly the poet Pinḥas ha-Cohen, some of whose poems have been found in the Cairo Genizah) and משה גמ(זוז) Moshe Gamzuz.

These names appear, in scattered notes here and there in Biblical texts, as authorities for the vocalization or accentuation of individual words. These traditions give no evidence of any definite characteristics of the views of any of these scholars. In the *Diqduqe ha-Ṭeʿamim* (Dotan, 1967, chapter 20) a list is given in the name of R. Pinḥas which contains words in which a composite *shewa* and not a simple *shewa* is to be read with a non-guttural letter. The Mm of L, in reference to Prov 3:13, gives different methods of accentuation in the name of the *Maḥzora Rubba*, the Scholars of Tiberias, and ben Asher. In the Cambridge Geniza fragment TS 18A:1, the Mp notes on Job 8:3

יְעַוֵּת צֶדֶק -- ר׳ משה מוה׳ ור׳ משה גמז׳ יְעַוֵּת־צֶדֶק ר׳ פינ׳ יְעַוֵּת

"R. Mosheh Moḥeh and R. Mosheh Gamzuz read a *maqqef* on יְעַוֵּת. R. Pinḥas reads *merka*". The same opinions are given in the names of ben Naftali and ben Asher in the *Sefer ha-Ḥillufim*.

In the *Sefer ha-Ḥillufim*, it is recorded that bA read יִשָּׂשכָר, bN יִשְׂשָׂכָר, and Mosheh Moḥeh יִשְׂשָׂכָר. On מֶרְקָחִים (Song 5:13), a note on the margin of a manuscript (recorded in *Diqduqe ha-Ṭeʿamim*, Baer-Strack 1879, p.84) states that Pinḥas and Ḥabib b. Pipim read מֶרְקָחִים, but the *Maḥzora Rubba* reads מֶרְקַחִים. (The *Sefer ha-Ḥillufim* notes that bA and bN agree in the use of *qameṣ* on this word.) The various similar notes all deal with small details of vocalisation or accentuation. It seems likely that all the scholars mentioned were among the last of the Masoretes, who had received the basic teaching of the Masorah on matters of writing and spelling from their teachers, and only disagreed in a few small details of the reading tradition.

152. Among authoritative texts the name מוגה *muggah*, "corrected" or ספרי מוגהי *sifre muggahe* "corrected codices" is often mentioned, but seems to refer not to a specific text, but to any sort of carefully corrected text.

In late MSS the names of various other texts are given: Hilleli, Yeriḥo, Sinai, Zanbuqi, Yerushalmi, Aspami, and others. These are no doubt texts which were well known and renowned in their day for their accuracy and their authoritative Masorah, but we know nothing about them today. The readings presented on their authority cover various matters of spelling, vocalisation or accentuation. Just as the scholars listed above were among the Masoretes who established the correct reading (mainly in matters of vocalization and accentuation) on the basis of the traditions they held, so these names represent highly valued texts on the authority of which certain readings were transmitted. A large number of readings of this sort,are given in Ginsburg, 1880 (e.g. vol.I, pp.599 ff.).

Variants between 'Madinḥa'e' and 'Maᶜarba'e'

153. The Talmud mentions some differences between the scholars of Babylonia and Eretz Israel in the division of verses in certain passages, or in the order of the books. The study of Biblical texts with Babylonian pointing has shown that the Babylonian tradition differed from the Tiberian in many points of spelling, vocalization, accentuation, and Masorah.

A list copied at the end of some Bibles (as in L), or in separate treatises, gives about 250 differences between "Easterners" (מדׄ) and "Westerners" (מעׄ). This list is uniform in all sources, and gives variants only in the Prophets and Writings, not in the Torah. The variants listed are variants in the letters of the text, notin vocalization or accentuation. They include variations in spelling, as יְהוֹרָם/יוֹרָם (2K 8:16), variations in the use of particles, as אֶל אַבְנֵי/עַל אַבְנֵי (Is 14:19), and, (the most common type) variations in *qere/ketiv* situations, as

Job 17:10 הבֹאו לׄמעׄ -- יבאו כׄתׄ ובאו קרי לׄמדׄ

"The Western tradition has הבֹאו, in the Eastern tradition יבאו is written, ובאו is read."

Lam 4:17 עוֹדֵינָה כׄתׄ נוּ קרי לׄמעׄ עודינו כתיב וקרי לׄמדׄ

"In the Western tradition עודינה is written, עודינו is read, but in the Eastern tradition עודינו is both written and read".

Further examples of *Madinḥa'e/Maᶜarba'e* variations, taken from the Ezekiel section of the list at the end of L, are given below.

Ez 27:31 לׄמעׄ וְהִקְרִיחוּ אֵלַיִךְ קָרְחָה כׄ לׄמדׄ והקריחו אליך קרחא כׄ אׄ

"Westerners write קָרְחָה, Easterners write קרחא with *alef*".

Ez 29:4 לׄמעׄ וְנָתַתִּי חַחִים כׄתׄ וקׄרׄ לׄמדׄ ונתתי חחיים כׄתׄ חחים קׄ

"Westerners have חַחִים as *ketiv* and *qere*, Easterners have חחיים *ketiv*, חחים *qere*".

Ez 27:6 לׄמעׄ מֵאִיֵּי כִּתִּים כׄ כִּתִּיִּים קׄ לׄמדׄ כתים כׄתׄ וקׄרׄ

"Westerners have כִּתִּים *ketiv*, כִּתִּיִּים *qere*, Easterners כתים *ketiv* and *qere*".

Ez 31:11 למע֗ וְאֶתְּנֵהוּ בְּיַד אֵל חס֗ י למד֗ ביד איל גוים שלמ֗

"Westerners have אֵל defective, Easterners איל plene". (שלמ֗ is the Babylonian term corresponding to Tiberian מלא plene).

Ez 37:24 למע֗ וְעַבְדִּי דָוִד מֶלֶךְ ע֗ חס֗ למד֗ ועבדי דויד מל֗

"Westerners have דוד defective, Easterners דויד plene".

Ez 42:8 למע֗ וְהִנֵּה עַל פְּנֵי הַהֵיכָל למד֗ אל פני ההיכל

"Westerners read עַל in this phrase, Easterners אֶל".

Ez 43:20 למע֗ וְנָתַתָּה עַל אַרְבַּע ק֗ למד֗ אל ארבע קרנתיו

"Westerners read עַל in this phrase, Easterners אֶל".

Ez 43:26 למע֗ שִׁבְעַת יָמ֗ יְכַפְּרוּ כת֗ וק֗ למד֗ וכפרו כת֗ יכפרו קרי

"Westerners have יכפרו as *ketiv* and *qere*, Easterners have וכפרו as *ketiv*, יכפרו as *qere*".

Ez 44:3 למע֗ אֶת הַנָּשִׂיא לֶאֱכָל חס֗ למד֗ לאכול לחם מל֗

"Westerners read לֶאֱכָל defective, Easterners read לאכול plene".

Besides this standard list of variants, the Masorah notes many other places in which there were variants between the *Madinḥa'e* and *Ma^carba'e*. Even in L, where the standard list is given at the end of the Bible, the Masorah notes a few variants in addition to those in the list. These additional notes include a number of variants in method--such as the fact that the Easterners read a group of letters as one word in many places where the Westerners read it as two, such as the names תּוּבַל־קַיִן, בֵּית־אֵל etc. Also preserved are lists of words on which the Easterners, but not the Westerners, marked dots (see #79).

154. The manuscripts known to us, whether Tiberian or Babylonian, do not agree in all respects with these lists of variants. Tiberian MSS show some readings ascribed to the *Madinḥa'e*, (e.g. L shows the "Eastern" reading in Ez 29:4, 31:11, and 44:3 in the examples above), and Babylonian MSS show reading ascribed to the *Ma^carba'e*. Apart from this, the two groups of MSS show a great many other places in which the Babylonian tradition differed from the Tiberian. We have no idea when the standard list of *Madinḥa'e/Ma^carba'e* variants was compiled, nor on what sources it was based. Eliahu ha-Levi concludes, from the fact that the list does not deal with features of vocalization and accentuation, that it was compiled before the vowel signs were standardized in the text. This is

possible, but it is not a necessary conclusion, since the compilers could well have restricted themselves to differences in the consonantal text because of the well-known differences between the Tiberian and Babylonian systems of vocalization and accentuation.

Literature: Ginsburg, 1899.

Variants between ben Asher and ben Naftali

155. Aharon ben Asher and Mosheh ben Naftali (who lived in the first half of the tenth century) are considered as the last of the Masoretes, and the tradition of ben Asher is considered to be the received tradition. The earlier Masoretes who are mentioned by name (#151) are only mentioned rarely, but ben Asher and ben Naftali are often mentioned, and their different opinions in the vocalization and accentuation of certain words are frequently noted in the margins of manuscripts, or in lists copied at the beginning or end of Bibles, or circulated separately. Many of these lists are full of errors, and contain additions and omissions, and even ascribe to bA or bN opinions which they did not hold. The most correct form of the list is that edited by *Misha'el ben ᶜUzziel*, who appears to have lived close to the time of these scholars. His original work, known as the *Kitāb al-Khilaf*, was in Arabic. The Hebrew form of it is known as *Sefer ha-Ḥillufim*, the "Book of Variants". This treatise is found in a number of MSS and Genizah fragments, and an edition of it was recently published by L. Lipschuetz (Lipshuetz 1962, 1965). Even in this edition, a few statements are not fully clear, but it nevertheless presents the variants in a trustworthy form.

156. According to this list, bA and bN disagreed in a few general matters, and on 867 specific passages in the Bible, while they agreed in 406 other passages where their joint opinion was contrary to that of other unnamed Masoretes. The following examples of bA/bN variants are taken from the *Sefer ha-Ḥillufim* on Genesis (Lipschuetz, 1962, p.ז).

פרשׁ וְאֵלֶּה תּוֹלְדוֹת יִצְחָק תֿלתֿהֿ אסדאר כאמלה. וְאֵלֶּה תּוֹלְדֹת יִצְחָק
אֹ, וַיְהִי כִּי זָקֵן בֹ, וְיִתֶּן־לְךָ הָאֱלֹהִים גֹ. ועדד פואסיקהא
מאיהֿ וסתהֿ קוֹ יואזיה יהללאל ופיהא מן אלכֿלף סבעהֿ כלמאת

Genesis	נפתלי	בן אשר	
25:22	וַיִּֽתְרוצצו הבנים בקרבה	וַיִּתְרֹצְצוּ הַבָּנִים בְּקִרְבָּהּ	1
25:32	ולָֽמה־זה לי בכורה בגעיה	וְלָמָּה־זֶּה לִּי בְּכוֹרָה	2
26:22	כִּֽי עתה הרחיב בשופר	כִּי־עַתָּ֗ה הִרְחִיב במקף	3
26:27	וַֽתשלחוני מאתכם בגעיה	שְׂנֵאתֶם אֹתִי וַתְּשַׁלְּחוּנִי	4
27:13	קִֽלְלתך בני אך שמע	עָלַי קִלְלָתְךָ בְּנִי	5
27:27	וַֽיברכהו ויאמר ראה	רֵיחַ בְּגָדָיו וַֽיְבָרְכֵהוּ	6
27:40	ועַֽל־חרבך תחיה	וְעַל חַרְבְּךָ תִחְיֶה	7

27:6 ואלתי ליס בכלף כלמתין והי וְרִבְקָה אָמְרָה אֶל־יַֽעֲקֹב

27:41 וְאַהַרְגָה אֶת־יַֽעֲקֹב אָחִי

The *parashah* (#72) וְאֵלֶּה תּוֹלְדֹת יִצְחָק (Gen 25:19 ff.) contains three complete *sedarim* (#72); 1) וְאֵלֶּה תּוֹלְדֹת יִצְחָק (Gen 25:19ff), 2) וַיְהִי כִּי זָקֵן (Gen 27:1 ff), 3) וְיִתֶּן־לְךָ הָאֱלֹהִים (Gen 27:28 ff). It has 106 verses, the "parallel" (word representing a number) for which is יהללאל (the numerical value of the letters of which, 10 + 5 + 30 + 30 + 1 + 30 adds up to 106). There are seven *ḥillufim* in it. These are ... (the forms indicated by the vowel signs and accents in the list above). There are also two cases where there is no *ḥilluf* (i.e. where bA and bN agree against some other authority), and these are אֶל־יַֽעֲקֹב (Gen 27:6) and אֶת־יַֽעֲקֹב (Gen 27:41).

The subject of the first variant is the use of *gaᶜya* in a closed syllable in a form which is "not fully regular". The word has a conjunctive accent (see #322.4). The second variant is concerned with *gaᶜya* in a closed syllable in the middle of a word pointed with a "long" vowel (see #337). The third concerns the use of *maqqef* (#301). The fourth, fifth, and sixth, concern the use of *gaᶜya* in a closed syllable in a form which is "not fully regular" (#322.1, 3, 4). The seventh and also the two cases of agreement concern the use of *gaᶜya* in a closed syllable in a word of "regular" form which has a conjunctive accent (#320).

These variants are matters of minor detail in the accent system. In a few places, however, variants in spelling are recorded, e.g. עַד or וְעַד in Jer 7:25, or in division of words, e.g. עַל־מוּת or עַלְמוּת in Ps 48:15. The lists also give a number of variants in vocalization, e.g. bA points לְיִשְׂרָאֵל, לִירְאַת, etc., while bN points לְיִשְׂרָאֵל, לִירְאַת etc. (#392), and they differ in the pointing of יששכר (#151). Variants in the use of *dagesh* and *rafe* are also noted, as וַיְהִי כִּשְׁמֹעַ/וַיְהִי כֿשְׁמֹעַ (Jos 9:1), (see #401.5), or לִצְפּוּנָיו/לִצְפֿוּנָיו (Job 20:26). Variations in vowel quality are noted, as שְׁפׇךְ־/שְׁפׇךְ־עֲלֵיהֶם (Ps 69:25), יֻלַּד/יֻלָּד (Gen 41:50), and also variation in the use of simple or composite *shewa*, for instance in certain forms form the roots אכל and גרש (#379, 380) and others. There are some eighty variants in the use of *maqqef*, as וּבְנֵי/וּבְנֵי־דָן (Gen 46:23), וַיַּעַזְבוּ/וַיַּעַזְבוּ־שָׁם (2S 5:21, 1C 14:12). There are also about 200 cases of variation or agreement in the use of particular accents (usually conjunctives), most of which occur in the three "Poetical" books. The remainder of the variants concern the use of *ga^{c}ya*: particularly *ga^{c}ya* in a closed syllable, and *shewa-ga^{c}ya* (#319ff, 333ff).

In a few of these variants, such as the pointing of לישראל, and in some categories of the use of *ga^{c}ya*, bA and bN follow different systems, but in the majority of the variants no system can be seen, so that these variants simply represent different traditions accepted by the two scholars.

157. Among the many manuscripts considered to represent the school of ben Asher, A, which appears to have had the vowel signs, accent signs, and masoretic notes added by Aharon ben Asher himself, agrees with the ben Asher of the *Sefer ha-Ḥillufim* in nearly all cases (#26), and L agrees almost as closely (#30). These MSS also agree closely with the statements of the *Diqduqe ha-Ṭe^{c}amim*, which is ascribed to Aharon ben Asher, and of which he probably did compile at least a part (see #175). The closest MS to the ben Naftali of the *Sefer ha-Ḥillufim* is C, which agrees in nearly two thirds of the cases (#32), but this was the product of Moshe ben Asher, and so can hardly be taken as a genuine representative of the school of ben Naftali.

Paul Kahle put forward the opinion that manuscripts pointed with the "expanded" Tiberian pointing, also called "Tibero-Palestinian", and, following Kahle's theory, "(Pseudo) ben Naftali" derived, in fact, from the school of ben Naftali. However, although these MSS do show some of the characteristics ascribed to bN, the resemblance is not very close, and this view cannot be accepted. We have to conclude, then, that no MS

genuinely representing the school of ben Naftali is known.
Literature: Lipschuetz, 1962, 1964, 1965 (edition of the *Sefer ha-Ḥillufim*) and Pérez-Castro and Azcárraga, 1968, (a review of this edition). Also Ben David, 1957, Goshen-Gottstein, 1963, Pérez-Castro, 1955.

WORK ON THE MASORAH

(i) The Continuation of Masoretic Work and the Collection of Masoretic Materials

158. The age of bA and bN can be seen as the end of the masoretic period. Various types of work on the Masorah have been carried on between that time and ours: the collection of notes and arrangement of them according to various viewpoints; the continuation of the masoretic work in various ways, such as the establishment of the textual tradition of the Bible on the basis of the Masorah, or of manuscripts; the study and interpretation of the Masorah, and so on.

The masoretic scholars who lived after the time of bA and bN were concerned with the establishment of the text not through oral teaching, but through the masoretic notes in the margins of MSS or in independent treatises, and through the use of carefully corrected MSS. In addition, both during and after the masoretic period, there was a tendency to elaborate the system of vowel and accent signs. This elaboration is characteristic of MSS of the "expanded" Tiberian tradition such as R. The intention was to distinguish phenomena--such as short and long *qameṣ*, or the different types of *shofar* (#220)--which were marked by the same sign in the standard pointing. Some such phenomena were no doubt distinguished only in certain communities, but not in the standard Tiberian reading tradition. In any case such elaboration remained peripheral, and had little influence on the received tradition. In later periods the opinions of grammarians also helped to maintain the textual tradition. Hebrew grammar is based on Biblical Hebrew, so it is not surprising that grammarians have in all periods attempted to clarify the tradition at many points, and that they relied on the Masorah and on carefully corrected texts to do this. This is true, for instance, of Ibn Janāḥ, Abraham ibn Ezra, and especially of R. David Qimḥi. Biblical commentators also, such as Rashi, often refer to the Masorah.

Many scholars have worked over the years to compile the Masorah and to establish the textual tradition--some were Naqdanim (specialists in adding vowel and accent signs to the consonantal text) or grammarians, and worked out of professional interest. Others were Biblical or Talmudic scholars who worked on the Masorah in addition to their other interests. The following are those who made the greatest contribution.

Yequti'el ben Yehudah ha-Naqdan

159. *Yequti'el ha-Naqdan* (יהב"י) possibly lived in the last half of the twelfth century. His book *ᶜEyn ha-Qore* contains a grammatical introduction and notes on the whole Torah, and also Esther and Lamentations. The notes do not deal with matters of spelling, but only with vowel signs, accent signs, and *gaᶜya*. The author based his work on six Spanish MSS, and on grammatical and masoretic treatises such as *Horayat ha-Qore* (see #175), the work of Yehudah Ḥayyūj, ibn Janāḥ, and ibn Parḥon. Wolf Heidenheim edited *ᶜEyn ha-Qore* on the Torah with part of the introduction in his *Me'or ᶜEynayim* (Rödelheim 1818-1821). He published the notes on Esther there in 1825. Y. F. Gumpertz published the "*Shaᶜar ha-Methigot*" (section on the *metheg/gaᶜya*) from the introduction to this book with an introduction and notes as "Yequtiel ha-Naqdan's Treatise on the Metheg" (Gumpertz, 1958). Recently A. Eldar has published the *Shaᶜar Noaḥ ha-Tevot* (the rules on the position of the word stress, Eldar, 1976).

Me'ir ben Ṭodros ha-Levi Abulafia

160. *Me'ir ha-Levi Abulafia* (הרמ"ה, lived about 1180-1244). Author of the treatise *Masoret Siyag la-Torah*, which has appeared in many editions, and is considered one of the classical treatises on the Masorah. It is especially concerned with the consonantal text, particularly defective and plene spelling, and not with vowel and accent signs. It begins with a statement of general rules on the use of vowel letters in the Bible. It follows this with all the material from the Masorah

arranged by roots, giving under each root the words which can be written plene or defective, indicating how they are written. E.g. under the root אור

יְהִי אוֹר – אוֹר is always written plene with *waw* in the Torah.

מְאֹרֹת is twice written doubly defective--Gen 1:14, 16.

In Gen 1:15 וְהָיוּ לִמְאוֹרֹת is written plene, with the first *waw* but not the second (I.e. not לִמְאוֹרוֹת).

In Gen 1:16 אֶת הַמָּאוֹר is written plene, with *waw*, and מָאוֹר is always spelled this way in the Torah with one exception--the first case of שֶׁמֶן לַמָּאֹר in the *parashah* "*Terumah*" (Ex 25:6).

The end of the book contains collections of masoretic lists on the particles אֶת־, כָּל־, אֲשֶׁר, לֹא, etc., and notes on the correct way of writing the "songs" in the Torah, and lists of *petuḥot* and *setumot*. The sources from which the information was collected are not given, but they seem to have been Sefardic MSS and the masoretic notes in them.

Menaḥem ben Shelomo ha-Me'iri

161. Menaḥem ha-Me'iri (1249-1306) was author of the two-parts of the treatise *Qiryat Sefer*. The first of these parts contains the rules for writing Torah scrolls, including *qere/ketiv*, special forms of letters, dots, etc. The second part contains grammatical rules for the readers of the Bible on such features as *begad-kefat* letters following vowels, *shewa*, etc. After this various lists of words which are written plene or defective in the Torah are given: common nouns, personal or place names, (in alphabetical order), and other lists in the order of the Biblical text. An appendix lists the *petuḥot* and *setumot*, *taggim*, the number of *sedarim*, verses, words and letters.

Menaḥem ben Yehudah di Lonzano

162. Menaḥem di Lonzano (end of the sixteenth century) wrote the treatise *Or Torah*, which was first printed in his book *Shete Yadot* (Venice 1618), but was later printed alone. It contains notes on the Torah in the order of the Biblical text. In contrast to R. Me'ir ha-Levi Abulafia, and R. Menaḥem ha-Me'iri, this author concentrates on the vowel and

accent signs, and gives little information on the consonantal text. He corrects many of the printer's errors in V (and in other editions), which he treats in great detail. His work is based on both Ashkenazic and Sefardic MSS, and notes the opinions of R. Me'ir ha-Levi Abulafia, and R. Menaḥem ha-Me'iri, Eliahu ha-Levi, and others.

Yedidyah Shelomo Rafa'el ben Abraham (from) Norzi

163. Shelomo Yedidyah Norzi (first part of the seventeenth century), was author of *Minḥat Shay*, which remains the most important treatise in this area until the present day. It contains notes on the whole Bible, in the order of the Biblical text. The author concerns himself with the consonantal text (plene and defective spelling, *qere/ketiv*, and so on), and also with the vowel and accent signs. He also deals with the errors in the best editions of his day--particularly in V (relying heavily on Menaḥem di Lonzano's corrections to the Torah of that edition). He makes great use of the Masorah, relying on the works of scholars such as R. Me'ir ha-Levi Abulafia, and Lonzano, and also on Naqdanim and Grammarians such as R. David Qimḥi and Abraham ibn Ezra, and on commentaries such as that of Rashi. He makes use of the Aramaic Targums, the Talmud, and the Midrashim as sources of information, and also studied and made use of many Biblical manuscripts. The book has been printed as a commentary to the Bible below the text in the Mantua edition of 1742-4, or as an independent work (Vienna 1813-15). It also appears in various editions of the Bible, and in most "Rabbinic" Bibles, at the ends of the books, and is considered the final authority in matters of textual tradition. An introduction called *Miqdash Yah*, and an appendix on the *begad-kefat* letters following vowels, and on the rules for *qameṣ ḥaṭuf*, and the "*Ma'amar ha-Ma'arik*" (a treatise on the use of *gaᶜya*) is added to the book. The introduction was published in Jellinek, 1876.

Yaḥya Sāliḥ

164. Yaḥya Sāliḥ (Second half of the eighteenth century) wrote the treatise *Ḥeleq ha-Diqduq*, which contains notes on

selected passages from the whole Bible in the order of the text. It is concerned with the vowel and accent signs, *ga^c^ya*, the correct pronunciation of *shewa* and similar problems, not with the consonantal text. It is based on the Masorah, the Aramaic Targums, and the Arabic translation of R. Saadya Ga'on, and also on grammarians and masoretic scholars such as R. David Qimḥi, R. Abraham ibn Ezra, Lonzano, Eliahu ha-Levi, and others. It reveals its author's Yemenite origin in his reliance on the *Maḥberet ha-Tījān* (the "*Manuel du Lecteur*", #182), and on Yemenite MSS (referred to as *tījān*, sometimes qualified as "old" or "accurate" or "carefully corrected"). MSS are also mentioned under other names, such as "*Yerushalmiyim*".

Shelomo ben Yo'el (from) Dubno

165. Shelomo Dubno (1738-1813) was author of the treatise *Tiqqun Soferim* on Genesis, Exodus, and the Five Scrolls. His notes are given in complete or in abbreviated form in the various editions of the Bible with the "*Bi'ur*" commentary of Mendelssohn and his pupils. These notes deal with plene and defective spelling, and also with vowel and accent signs, in the manner of the *Minḥat Shay*, but whereas that work was based on manuscripts and on the earlier scholars, Shelomo Dubno based his work on printed editions and on more recent scholars.

Wolf Heidenheim

166. Wolf Heidenheim (1757-1832) was a most accurate *naqdan*, and wrote a book on the rules for the accents, *ga^c^ya* and *maqqef*. He published a number of editions of the Torah and other Biblical books. One of these includes the *^c^Eyn ha-Qore* of Yequti'el ha-Naqdan (#159) and the *^c^Eyn ha-Sofer* of Heidenheim himself, a collection of masoretic notes on plene and defective spellings, and on similar features. Another of his editions includes only the *^c^Eyn ha-Sofer* (Rödelheim 1818-21). Most of his other editions include some masoretic material.

Seeligmann Baer

167. Seeligmann Baer (1825-1897) was a most careful student of pointing. He published (with H.L. Strack) an edition of the *Diqduqe ha-Ṭeᶜamim* (#175). He also published (with F. Delitzsch) an edition of most of the Bible (see#3) on the basis of good MSS, with notes on various problems (mainly matters of vocalization and accentuation). This edition was based on the Masorah, on *Minḥat Shay*, and on many MSS. Selected masoretic notes on the variants between *Madinḥa'e* and *Maᶜarba'e*, bA and bN, *qere/ketiv*, etc., were also added. Baer also published *Tiqqun ha-Sofer weha-Qore* (Baer, 1866), containing a careful edition of the Torah and Esther without vowel and accent signs, but with notes on *qere/ketiv*, the dotted words, and the sacred names, for training in the copying and reading of Torah scrolls.

Many authors besides those just mentioned have collected and organized masoretic notes, or explained the masoretic abbreviations and terminology, such a Yoseph ha-Cohen in his *Minḥat Cohen*, David Viterbi in his *Em la-Masoret* (where the masoretic notes are arranged in a useful variety of categories), and Yoseph Qalman of Karlin, in his *Shaᶜar ha-Masorah* (on Genesis), and his *Mevo ha-Masoret*. Others could also be mentioned.

Midrash ha-Masorah

168. The Talmud already contains some midrashic interpretations based on *qere/ketiv*, plene and defective spelling, etc. Interpretations of this sort on *qere we-la ketiv* and *ketiv we-la qere* were published in the Baer-Strack edition of the *Diqduqe ha-Ṭeᶜamim*, #63-64, and an interpretation of the 15 dotted words in the Bible in #58 there. A small midrash, which appears in many forms under the name *Midrash Ḥaserot wi-Yeterot* presents midrashic interpretations based on many words written defective or plene, as רַגְלֵי חֲסִידָו (1S 2:9) "Written defective as if singular (not חֲסִידָיו) since the world is preserved for the sake of one righteous man". מַקְרִן מַפְרִיס (Ps 69:32) "מַקְרִן is written, (not מַקְרִין) since the bull which Adam offered had only one horn".

In later times the character of this midrash on the Masorah was changed, and the notes of the Masorah were themselves used as a subject for homiletic interpretations. The notes of the Masorah, usually that of V, were treated as a sacred text, as if there were some connection between the fragments of Biblical verses quoted in the Mp or Mm as references to the occurrence of particular forms. E.g. on בַּתֹּהוּ (Is 29:21 and Job 6:18)

(בֹּ דגשין וסימן) וַיַּטּוּ בַתֹּהוּ צַדִּיק, יַעֲלוּ בַתֹּהוּ וְיֹאבֵדוּ

"This means that whoever causes a righteous man to sin and err in nothingness and vanity (i.e. "turns aside the just with a thing of nought" Is 29:21) is unable to repent, but the two of them, beguiler and beguiled, "go up into nothingness and are destroyed (Job 6:18)". (Angel, 1622, No. 1114).

On וַיִּמְלְאוּ (Gen 25:24, 50:3).

(ב' באו' וסי') וַיִּמְלְאוּ לוֹ אַרְבָּעִים יוֹם, וַיִּמְלְאוּ יָמֶיהָ לָלֶדֶת

"The Masorah notes that "were fulfilled" occurs twice "And forty days were fulfilled for him", and "her days to give birth were fulfilled". This refers to the forty days required for the formation of an embryo".

On בְּמִרְמָה (Gen 27:35, 34:13)

(ב' באו' וסי') בָּא אָחִיךָ בְּמִרְמָה, וַיַּעֲנוּ בְנֵי יַעֲקֹב בְּמִרְמָה

"The Masorah notes that "with guile" occurs twice, "And thy brother (Jacob) came with guile" and "And the sons of Jacob answered with guile". This shows that because he acted towards his father with guile so his sons acted towards him with guile".

The best known work in this category is that of the Baᶜal ha-Ṭurim, from which the last two examples are taken. This work is generally printed in editions of the "Rabbinic Bible", and in popular editions of the Bible with commentaries. It has also appeared as a separate book *The Commentary of the Baᶜal ha-Ṭurim on the Torah* (R. Jacob ben R. Asher, 1971).

A few treatises have even derived mystic interpretations from the Masorah.

WORK ON THE MASORAH

(ii) The Study and Interpretation of Masoretic Materials

169. Subjects like the origin of the Masorah and the creators of it, the origin of various categories of notes (such

as the *qere/ketiv*), the explanation of the terminology, and of the various types of lists, have been studied by many scholars, Jewish and other, over the course of years. The following are the most important.

Eliahu Baḥur ben Asher ha-Levi Ashkenazi

Eliahu ha-Levi (also called Elias Levita, 1469-1549) wrote *Masoret ha-Masoret*, which has appeared in many editions, and has given him the position of the father of masoretic studies. In the introduction to this book, the author discusses various theories on the origin of the Masorah, vowel signs and accent signs, and establishes that they were not revealed at Sinai, but were developed by the Masoretes who lived after the period of the Talmud. In the first section "First Tablets", he deals with plene and defective spellings. In the second section "Second Tablets" he deals with a number of other features of the Masorah, categorizing the different types of *qere/ketiv* notes, explaining the most important technical terms, such as *dagesh* and *rafe* (לְאִישׁ is *rafe*, לָאִישׁ *dagesh*, מַחֲסֶה is *rafe*, מַחְסִי *dagesh*) *mille*ᶜ*el* and *millera*ᶜ (בַּדְּמָעוֹת is *mille*ᶜ*el*, בִּדְמָעוֹת is *millera*ᶜ, יִדְלֹף is *mille*ᶜ*el*, יִדָּלֵף is *millera*ᶜ, see #132 under רפ̇, מלע̇, דגש) and explaining the categories of masoretic lists סמיכין, דמיין, זוגין, שיטין, יחידאין and others. In the third section "The Broken Tablets" he explains the various abbreviations used, and lists a few names of Naqdanim and Masoretes. Eliahu ha-Levi also produced a concordance of the Bible called *Sefer ha-Zikronot* as an aid to the study of the Masorah. This is known in manuscript form, but only a small sample has ever been published (Goldberg, 1875).

Literature: Weil, 1963.

Johannis Buxtorf pater

170. The Elder Buxtorf (1564-1629) wrote *Tiberias*, a book on the Masorah based on the *Masoret ha-Masoret*. In this he outlines the history of the Masorah and the vowel and accent signs, and explains the masoretic terms in alphabetical order. As an example he gives the Mp and Mm to the first chapter of Genesis and explains them. At the end of the book he suggests

corrections to the Masorah on various passages.

Asher Anshil Worms

171. A.A. Worms, author of *Siyag la-Torah*, contests Eliahu ha-Levi's opinion on the date of the origin of the Masorah, vowel signs and accent signs from a traditional viewpoint, and gives explanations of masoretic terminology, abbreviations, etc. At the end he offers corrections to various masoretic notes.

Christian David Ginsburg

172. C.D. Ginsburg (1831-1914) collected in his *The Massorah Compiled from Manuscripts* an immense number of masoretic notes, lists and treatises (see #140). In his "*Introduction to the Massoretico-Critical Edition of the Hebrew Bible*", he discusses the basic subject matter and terminology of the Masorah, along with much material from different manuscripts, and he also describes a large number of Biblical MSS. He produced several editions of the Hebrew Bible. In the latest (Ginsburg, 1908, 1926), which is based on V, he lists variants from 75 manuscripts and 19 early editions including variants in vowel and accent signs, paying strict attention to various masoretic notes. He also published an edition and translation of the *Masoret ha-Masoret*, and of Jacob ben Ḥayyim's introduction to his edition of the Bible (V).

Paul Ernst Kahle

173. P.E. Kahle (1875-1965) advanced the study of the Masorah in two areas particularly: recognizing the nature and importance of the Babylonian and Palestinian traditions, and the importance of the manuscripts from the school of ben Asher. He was responsible for the fact that the text of L was used as the basis for the BHK edition (and so also the BHS edition).

Many other scholars besides those listed have worked on the Masorah, among them S.D. Luzatto, H. Graetz, L. Blau, and B.Z. Bacher.

THE MASORAH AND GRAMMAR

Grammatical matters in the Masorah

174. The function of the Masorah, which describes a text in order to preserve the tradition, is not that of grammar, which describes the language. Since both are descriptions of characteristic features of the Biblical text, however, much grammatical information is contained in the Masorah. The masoretic lists formed the basis for early grammatical descriptions in various ways. (1) Some of the terminology used in the Masorah was taken over by the grammarians. Terms such as masculine, feminine, singular, plural, the names of the letters, the vowel and accent signs, and other features of the pointing, the terms for accent position, *mille*ᶜ*el* and *millera*ᶜ, *dagesh*, *rafe*, *mappiq*, and also semantic terms such as תמיהה indicating a question, were all used by the Masoretes and taken over by the grammarians. (2) Since the Masoretes compared all the occurrences of particular words, their lists formed the basis for grammatical observations on changes in vowel patterns: either conditioned changes, such as changes in forms in contextual or pausal situations, changes in words with or without *maqqef*, with or without the definite article, or *waw* simple and *waw* consecutive, etc., or unconditioned variation in the vowelling of a word. In the same way the Masorah itself formulated rules on the vowelling of some words such as אֶת־/אֵת, כָּל־/כֹּל, and words of the form of לָמָּה, מַה, שֵׁם, בֵּן, etc. The Masorah also formulated rules on various features of the accentuation which were of use to later grammarians.

In some cases it is possible to trace the development of grammatical ideas in the Masorah. In some lists the Masorah does not distinguish words which have the same spelling but are grammatically different. Thus the verb form וְכָל (Is 40:12) can be included with forms of the particle כֹּל "all". In other lists, however, such grammatical differences are noted (see #132 under ליש 2 and 3, also מלע Jos 2:3). The development of terminology can also be traced, e.g. in *mille*ᶜ*el*/*millera*ᶜ and *dagesh*/*rafe* (see #132 for the different meanings of these terms) and also in the names of the vowel and accent signs.

Masoretico-Grammatical Treatises

175. At the end of the period of the Masoretes, treatises were produced which stood on the boundary between the areas of Masorah and of grammar.

Diqduqe ha-Ṭe^{c}*amim*. This work has been published in two editions, that of Baer-Strack (1879), and that of A. Dotan (1967). The Baer-Strack edition collects masoretic rules from various texts, most of them from the ends of Biblical MSS, without questioning whether they all formed a part of the same original treatise, or were the work of one author. In his edition, Dotan classifies the manuscripts, and establishes that the original *Diqduqe ha-Ṭe*^{c}*amim* contained 26 sections, which are reproduced in a fixed order in a few MSS which also give the name of the treatise and its author. The other sections in the Baer-Strack edition are not from the original treatise, but give various rules of unknown authorship which were added to the treatise in different MSS. Even the rules of the original *Diqduqe ha-Ṭe*^{c}*amim* are not all the work of Aharon ben Asher, but most of them were adapted by him from very early collections of masoretic lists called by Dotan קונטרסי המסורה "Masoretic Note-Books".

The original *Diqduqe ha-Ṭe*^{c}*amim* as edited by Dotan contains mostly rules on the accents and *ga*^{c}*ya*, with a few sections on subjects on the borderline between Masorah and grammar, such as the rules for pointing בֵּן, כֹּל, אֵת, לָמָּה, and forms from the roots חרב, הלך, גרש, and rules for the use of *dagesh* in certain forms such as תֹּאכַלְנָּה, תְּבִיאֶינָּה. The additional material in the Baer-Strack edition, includes material which is solely masoretic, such as *qere/ketiv*, *tiqqune soferim*, defective and plene spelling, and also material which is genuinely grammatical, such as the classification of the consonants according to their points of articulation, the pronunciation of *shewa*, the treatment of the *begad-kefat* letters after vowels, treatment of gutturals, vowel changes in inflected forms, "radical" and "servile" letters, distinction between construct and absolute forms, contextual and pausal forms, and information on the "tenses" of the verb and on other parts of speech.

Hidāyat al-qāri in its various forms, of which the most

important is the *Horayat ha-Qore*, is mainly concerned with grammatical matters, but it also includes lists of *qere we-la ketiv*, *ketiv we-la qere*, the list of the periods covered by the Biblical books, statements on the number of verses in the books, the poem on the letters ascribed to R. Saadya Ga'on (see #125), and *ḥillufim* between bA and bN on the Torah.

ᶜAdat Devorim by Joseph ha-Qosṭandini contains a grammatical section, and also the *Sefer ha-Ḥillufim* giving the variations between bA and bN for the whole Bible. It also contains many masoretic lists.

PART III

THE ACCENTS

INTRODUCTION

Literature

176. For a comprehensive survey, with bibliography, see Medan, 1968. For comparison with the Greek and Syriac accents, see Praetorius, 1901, and Segal, 1953. For a thorough study of the rules on the accents given in the *Diqduqe ha-Ṭe^{c}amim* (#175) see Dotan, 1967. For a study of the accents in A and related MSS, see Yeivin, 1968. For further literature, see #181-189 below.

The Function of the Accents

177. In addition to the vowel points, other signs are added to the letters of the Biblical text, which serve primarily to indicate the music of the Biblical chant. These signs are called "accents" (טעמים). They do not, like modern musical notation, indicate the pitch and duration of individual notes, but represent groups of notes (motifs, tropes) to which the words of the verse are chanted. The reader must, from his own knowledge, fit the musical motifs to the words marked, adapting them to the number of syllables, stress position, etc. Three additional signs, *paseq* (#283), *maqqef* (#290), and *ga^{c}ya* (#311) do not themselves indicate musical motifs (and so are not "accents") but give further indication how the music of the chant should be related to the words of the text.

In Tiberian texts, one system of accents is used in the 21 books--sometimes called the "Prose Books"--and in the prose sections at the beginning and end of the book of Job (Job 1:1-

3:2, 42:7-17). These are called the טעמי כ"א ספרים "Accents of the 21 Books". Another system is used in the three "Poetical" books, Psalms, Job, and Proverbs, called טעמי אמ"ת (אִיּוֹב, מִשְׁלֵי, תְּהִלִּים) or "Poetic accents". There are considerable differences between these two systems. In general the poetic accentuation is more intricate, and permits more variations than the prose. This book will concentrate on the prose accentuation, and will deal only briefly with the poetic system (#358).

Accents are also marked in texts with Palestinian and Babylonian pointing. Palestinian texts show different systems of accentuation in the prose and poetic books. In Babylonian texts the same system is used in all books.

178. Altogether the accents perform three functions. Their primary function, as already noted, is to represent the musical motifs to which the Biblical text was chanted in the public reading. This chant enhanced the beauty and solemnity of the reading, but because the purpose of the reading was to present the text clearly and intelligibly to the hearers, the chant is dependent on the text, and emphasizes the logical relationships of the words. Consequently the second function of the accents is to indicate the interrelationship of the words in the text. The accents are thus a good guide to the syntax of the text; but, since the reader was naturally presenting meaning, not structure, and accentuation marks semantic units, which are not always identical with syntactic units.

In the Tiberian system, the signs for most of the accents are marked above or below the letter representing the first consonant of the stress syllable. Thus the third function of the accents is to mark the position of the word stress. This is an important function, since stress is grammatically significant (phonemic). It may be the only feature distinguishing otherwise identical words, as שָׁבוּ֫ (root שבה) and שָׁ֫בוּ (root שוב).

In Babylonian texts, the accents were not originally marked on the stress syllable, and most scholars believe this of Palestinian texts also. Consequently the position of the word stress in these traditions is uncertain. In later Babylonian texts, especially those with "compound" pointing, the accent signs are marked on the stress syllable, as in Tiberian texts, under the influence of the Tiberian system.

Nowadays different communities (Ashkenazic, Sefardic, Babylonian, Yemenite, etc.) use different chants in their synagogue readings. In each community also, different forms of chant were used for the reading of the Torah, the *hafṭarah*, the book of Lamentations, and so on. There is no way of telling the extent to which these chants now in use reflect that used in Israel when the accent signs were fixed by the Tiberian Masoretes, although by study and comparison of the various traditions, musicologists are attempting to trace those features which have been preserved from early times.

179. This outline is mainly concerned with the form of the accent signs, the system of their use, their relationship to each other, and their value as syntactic markers. The music of the chant will only be mentioned if it is necessary for the understanding of the way in which the accents are used. It must be realized, however, that the sequence in which the accents are used is sometimes determined by musical considerations. Such considerations fix the maximum and minimum limits for the accents in a verse; they require that some accents must occur in certain positions, and that some accents cannot follow others. In some cases a particular accent cannot be used unless there is a certain number of words or syllables between it and the following accent, and so on. For this reason, different accentuation may be used on the same phrase in different passages, depending on its position in the verse, the length of the verse, and similar considerations. Such phenomena reflect the requirements of the musical basis of the accentuation, so, although the music does not directly concern us here, it must be remembered that it is the source of many of the rules governing the use of accents.

In this discussion of the accentuation, we will attempt to understand the accentuation of the Biblical texts, and to recognize the way in which the Masoretes expressed their understanding of the verse. We will deal with the forms of the accent signs, and the way they are marked in the MSS--particularly in the early MSS of the Tiberian tradition (those written before 1100--see #21). In general, the accentuation of these fully developed MSS differs from that of our printed editions only in minor details.

Scarcely any MSS early enough to reflect the stages by which the accentuation developed are preserved. Possibly the Geniza contains some fragments of this sort, but, if so, they have yet to be examined. For instance no Tiberian MS is known which marks an accent not in use today, or which fails to show one which is in use today. We find only a few Geniza fragments in which some verses are accentuated in a system wholly different from that of the fully developed texts. In the same way, a few Tiberian fragments are known in which the accent signs are not marked on the stress syllable.

Accents in Texts other than Biblical

180. The Targums, especially Targum Onqelos, are marked with accents corresponding to the accents of the Biblical text in some MSS and early printed editions.

Some verses of the Geniza fragments of the Book of Ben Sira are marked with "poetic" accentuation, and some later works, such as the "Scroll of Antiochus", and Saadya Ga'on's Hebrew introduction to his *Sefer ha-'Egron*, are marked with accents in imitation of the Biblical accentuation.

MSS of the Mishnah, and of other Rabbinic literature, with Tiberian, Palestinian, or Babylonian pointing, are sometimes provided with accents. The signs used are sometimes the same as those found in Biblical texts, but they do not follow the same rules of arrangement, and in fact the system of accentuation is quite different from the Biblical.

Accents are occasionally marked in texts of liturgical poetry (*piyyuṭ*). In both these last cases, accent signs are found only in MSS, and were not used in printed editions.

The Study of the Biblical Accentuation

181. The following treatises provide information on the accents:

Diqduqe ha-Ṭe^c*amim* (#175). This treatise, ascribed to Aharon ben Asher (#155) presents a list of the accents (of both prose and poetic systems). Some rules for the use of some accents are also given, but the accent system is not treated comprehensively; nor, in fact, is any individual accent. The rules given cover only "conjunctive" accents (#192), such as a single conjunctive used with *tevir* (#251), *merka* used on the same word as *tevir* (#253), the conjunctives used with *zarqa* (#259). Rules for the use of *paseq* (#283) and *gaᶜya* (#311) are also given.

182. *Hidāyat al-Qāri* (#175). This treatise was evidently written in Arabic in the tenth century. Parts are preserved in manuscript fragments, but only later treatises derived from it have been published. The most important for the accentuation is the *Sefer Ṭaᶜăme ha-Miqra* ascribed to Judah ben Balᶜam (Paris, 1565). This treatise gives a list of the disjunctive accents, states which of them can follow each other, and which conjunctives can be used with them. It also gives the disjunctives with which any conjunctive may be used, and describes the way the conjunctives are used with each disjunctive.

Another treatise based on the *Hidāyat al-Qāri*, generally known as the *Maḥberet ha-Tījān*, appears in a longer Hebrew form (published in Dérenbourg, 1870), and a shorter Arabic form (published in Neubauer, 1891). The information on the accents in these is much the same as in the *Hidāyat al-Qāri*.

A few chapters on the accents, wrongly ascribed to R. Yehudah Ḥayyuj, which add little to the material in the *Hidāyat al-Qāri*, were published in Nutt, 1870, in an addition (p. 120 ff of the Hebrew text. A translation of some parts, but not those dealing with accents, starts on p. 140 of the English.) Surveys of the accents are also given in *ᶜEṭ Sofer*, by R. David Qimḥi, (Lyck 1864), in *Arugat ha-Bosem* by Shemu'el Archevolti (Venice 1602-1606), and in *Miqneh Abram* by Abram di Balmes (Venice 1523).

183. Eliahu ha-Levi, in his book *Ṭuv Ṭaᶜam* (Venice, 1538) gives a description of the accents which is somewhat more complete and detailed than that in the *Hidāyat al-Qāri*. He notes that the disjunctive accents can be ranked according to their pausal value (see #196), but he does not deal with them under these rankings. He describes the forms of the accents, their names, the conjunctives used with them, and so on. He also describes the way the conjunctives are used with each

disjunctive, the combinations in which each conjunctive can be used, the accents which can follow each other, and so on.

184. R. Zalman Hanau in his *Sha*^{c}*are Zimra* (1718) added three features not found in earlier treatises: (1) a division of the disjunctives according to their rank in pausal value (#196, an innovation mainly favoured by Christian writers) (2) the recognition of a number of rules on substitution among the accents (3) a description of some features of the relation of accentuation to syntax. He was a sharpwitted scholar, but his work is marred by too much casuistry.

185. Y. L. Ben-Ze'ev in *Talmud Leshon* ^{c}*Ivri* gives a brief description of the disjunctives, the conjunctives used with them, and also a selection of rules for the relation of accentuation to syntax. This was the best organized and simplest manual from the "Haskala" period. Its importance lies in its popular approach and wide circulation.

186. The two most important treatises on the accents in Hebrew are, for the prose accents, W. Heidenheim's *Sefer Mishpeṭe ha-Ṭe*^{c}*amim* (Rödelheim, 1808). This is based on the *Sefer Ṭa*^{c}*ame ha-Miqra*, but adds many rules, masoretic notes on the accents, and material from the *Diqduqe ha-Ṭe*^{c}*amim*. It contains a complete description of the disjunctive and conjunctive accents, *maqqef*, and *ga*^{c}*ya*, but does not discuss the ways the different accents are combined. The most important treatise on the poetic accents is *Torat Emet* by S. Baer (Rödelheim, 1852). This gives a complete description of the disjunctive and conjunctive accents, with information on the possible combinations of accents.

From the later literature, M. Breuer, פיסוק טעמים שבמקרא (Jerusalem 1957) should be mentioned, and also J.L. Ne'eman צלילי המקרא (Tel Aviv, 1956), and M. Perlman, דפים ללימוד טעמי המקרא (Jerusalem, 1959-1972).

187. The most important books on this subject in English (and indeed very important generally), are those of W. Wickes (Wickes 1881, 1887, reprinted together, New York 1970, with a comprehensive introduction on the history of the study of the accents by A. Dotan). Wickes based his work on the study of

MSS and printed editions. He describes the forms of the accent signs, their names, and their use, with a detailed description of the conjunctives used with each disjunctive. The main part of each book describes the combinations in which the accents can occur. Instead of ranking the disjunctives by their pausal value, Wickes stresses the idea of "dichotomy" (#201) as the key to understanding them, and describes the way in which the dichotomy is related to the syntax. In an appendix in his second book, he describes the Babylonian accentuation of P (with "compound" pointing).

188. A. Spanier, in *Die massoretischen Akzente* (Berlin, 1927) discusses the accents mainly from the point of view of their relation to syntax. His book is important as it provides the first description of the accentuation of the early Babylonian Biblical MSS published from Geniza fragments by P. Kahle.

189. J.M. Japhet, in *Moreh ha-Qore* (*Die Accente der Heiligen Schrift*, Frankfurt, 1896) presents a detailed description of the accents in terms of the possible combinations, their relation to syntax, and also describes the disjunctives and their conjunctives individually in the traditional manner. This work is not based on the study of MSS, but does contain much valuable information collected from Grammarians and Biblical commentators.

The Date of the Development of the Accent System

190. The Talmud mentioned "*ṭe^{c}amim*" in connection with the reading of the Bible in several places. On Neh 8:8

וַיִּקְרְאוּ בַסֵּפֶר בְּתוֹרַת הָאֱלֹהִים מְפֹרָשׁ וְשׂוֹם שֶׂכֶל וַיָּבִינוּ בַּמִּקְרָא

TY *Megillah* 4:1 comments "וְשׂוֹם שֶׂכֶל refers to the טעמים", and in the corresponding passage (TB *Megillah* 3a) the Babylonian Talmud comments "וַיָּבִינוּ בַּמִּקְרָא refers to the פסקי טעמים". TB *^{c}Erubin* 21b remarks on the statement that Qohelet "taught knowledge to the people" (Qoh 12:9) that "he taught them the accent signs" (סימני טעמים). In TB *Nedarim* 37a it is noted that one can accept pay for teaching the פיסוק טעמים (though not for teaching the Torah). TB *Berakot* 62a mentions the use of the right hand to indicate the טעמי תורה, presumably referring to the practise known as "cheironomy", still in use in some Jewish communities, in which a leader uses his hands to indicate to the congregation the accentuation of the text being chanted. The other references to פיסוק טעמים, or even to "accent signs" also presumably refer to the Biblical chant, which acted as a sort of "oral punctuation" for the text, and is certainly very old. Written signs were not introduced in the Talmudic period.

It is not certain whether vowel signs or accent signs were first introduced into the text, but in any case the one was probably introduced soon after the other. The Talmud does not mention either accent signs or vowel signs by name. Even in the passage in *Bereshit Rabba* where *atnaḥta* is mentioned (36:8 in the MS Vatican 30, as noted by Y. Kutscher, referring to Neh 8:8) "שום שכל refers to the accents, ויבינו במקרא refers to the beginnings of verses. R. Ḥiyya ben R. Luliyany says that these are the הכרעות and the אתנחתא" the *atnaḥta* seems to refer to a pause or rest in the reading, not to a written sign. The names of vowel signs are used in a Geniza fragment containing a "Qaraite list of Terms" written, in the opinion of N. Allony, in the eighth century (Allony, 1964), but apart from this they are not mentioned until the mid ninth century. Mar Ṣemaḥ ben Ḥayyim Ga'on (883-896) mentioned ניקוד ומשרתות ופסקי טעמים "Vowel points and conjunctive and disjunctive accents", and the differences between the scholars of Babylon and Eretz Israel in the use of them.

The earliest Biblical MSS, such as C, already show a fully developed system of vowel and accent signs. This suggests that they must have been in use for at least 100 years. It would appear, then, that both vowel and accent signs must have been introduced sometime between the close of the Talmud (c. 600) and 750.

191. The accents in Greek and Syriac Biblical texts are the best known of the similar notation systems used by neighbouring peoples. Neither system shows any similarity to the Jewish systems either as regards the system as a whole, or in the way in which the signs are marked on individual words or phrases; although there is some similarity between the form of individual Syrian signs and some of those of the Palestinian

pointing, possibly due to Syrian influence. According to J.B. Segal, the development of the Syriac accent system began in the fifth century, and was completed in the seventh or eighth--more or less the period suggested for the development of the Jewish signs. The Greek system of "Ekphonetic neumes" appears, fully developed, in MSS from the ninth century on. Its origins must be earlier--according to some in the fourth century--but lack of evidence prevents any definite statement (see Segal, 1953, Höeg, 1935).

THE ACCENTS IN THE TWENTY-ONE BOOKS

Disjunctives and Conjunctives

192. The term טעמים is traditionally used for the accents in general, and also specifically for "disjunctive" accents in contrast to "conjunctive". Disjunctive accents are those marked on the last word of a clause or phrase, indicating a pause, or break in the sense. Conjunctive accents are marked on the words between the disjunctives, showing that they form part of a phrase ending at the next disjunctive. In the traditional terminology the conjunctives were spoken of as משרתים "servants" to the disjunctives, giving rise to the use of the latin term "servus" (plural servi) as a term for conjunctive accent--usually used of the conjunctives in relation to specific disjunctives. Where a word is closely joined to the following one, the two may form a single "accent unit". In this case the first word of the pair has *maqqef* (#290), showing that the two are to be treated as a single word, chanted to the motif indicated by the accent on the second word. Thus in the standard Tiberian text, every word has some form of accent sign.

In early Babylonian texts (and some Palestinian) only disjunctive accents are marked. In later Babylonian texts (those with "compound" vocalization) the Tiberian signs for conjunctive accents and *maqqef* are added to the Babylonian signs for disjunctives, producing a hybrid system. Later Palestinian texts often show signs for conjunctives, but these are not usually close to the Tiberian either in the form of the signs or in the way they are used.

193. Even the oldest Geniza fragments provide no evidence of a stage at which only disjunctives were marked in Tiberian texts, nor of a stage at which the accents were not marked on the stress syllable of the word. However many scholars believe that the Geniza fragments of Palestinian MSS show an early stage in which no conjunctives are used, and accent signs are not marked on the stress syllable, and a later stage in which conjunctives are used, and accent signs are marked on the stress syllable. Consequently it is argued that the Tiberian system did not develop from an earlier stage to a later one, but that it is a further development from the latest stage of the Palestinian accentuation.

(This statement represents the general opinion on the relationship of the Palestinian and Tiberian accentuation. The following facts should, however, be noted. (1) The MSS of "Group V" of Revell, 1977 use Tiberian vowel signs (but not those for *qameṣ*, *segol*, or *ḥaṭef shewa*) and sometimes also the Palestinian "o" sign, and use accent signs of which some are used in Palestinian and/or Tiberian MSS, while some are not. Conjunctive accents are usually not marked, but when they are, two different signs at most are used. (2) Some Palestinian MSS show signs for conjunctives which are quite close to the Tiberian in number and use (e.g. P206 of Revell, 1977), but in other texts the number of signs may be greater (P208) or smaller (P308), and their use is quite different. Furthermore texts which show a highly developed system of conjunctives do not necessarily mark the accent sign on the (Tiberian) stress syllable. P208 actually does this less frequently than most Palestinian MSS. Thus the Palestinian fragments do not fit a pattern of development from non-use of conjunctives + no marking of stress syllable to use of conjunctives + marking of stress syllable. Consequently the relationship of the Palestinian and Tiberian systems suggested above remains highly questionable. The situation was undoubtedly a good deal more complex than suggested there. For an alternative suggestion, see Revell, 1977, section 4.2-3. E.J.R.)

194. Some features of vocalization are determined by the distinction between conjunctives and disjunctives. The rule that a *begad-kefat* letter at the beginning of a word has *rafe*

if the preceding word ends in a vowel (#399) is valid only if the preceding word has a conjunctive accent or *maqqef*, not if it has a disjunctive. Similarly, the rules for the retraction of the accent (#307) and for *deḥiq* (#403) are also valid only when the first of the two words involved does not have a disjunctive.

Disjunctives are independent of conjunctives, and can appear without preceding conjunctives, but a conjunctive accent can only occur before a disjunctive, either alone, or as part of a chain of conjunctives dependent on that disjunctive. Some conjunctives are only used before one disjunctive, others may be used before several different disjunctives. All conjunctives have the same "joining" value, but the disjunctives have different grades of "pausal" value, some marking a major break; others a minor one (#196).

The following list gives the names and forms of the accents of the 21 books. Names inset denote a variant form of the preceding accent.

Disjunctives	
Silluq	דבֽר
Atnaḥ	דב֑ר
Segolta	דבר֒
Shalshelet	דב֓רי
Zaqef (qaṭan)	דב֔ר
Zaqef gadol	דב֕ר
Revia	דב֗ר
Ṭifḥa	דב֖ר
Zarqa	דבר֮
Pashṭa	דבר֙
Yetiv	מ֚לך
Tevir	דב֛ר
Geresh	דב֜ר
Gerhsayim	דב֞ר
Legarmeh	דב֣ר׀
Pazer (qaṭan)	דב֡ר
Pazer gadol	דב֟ר
Telisha (gedolah)	֠דבר

Conjunctives	
Munaḥ	דב֣ר
Mehuppak	דב֤ר
Merka	דב֥ר
Darga	דב֧ר
Azla	דב֨ר
Telisha qeṭannah	דבר֩
Galgal	דב֪ר
Merka kefulah	דב֦ר
Mayela	וֽיצא־נ֖ח

The Classification of Disjunctives

195. In early treatises on the accents (e.g. *Horayat ha-Qore* p. 75, Dérenbourg, 1870, p. 383) the accents are divided into three categories on a musical basis. The division is not identical in all sources; some accents are put in category 2 in some sources, in 3 in others. One example is

1. גֹּבַה (also ירים הקול ויעלהו)

   Pazer, telisha, geresh, shalshelet.

2. רוּם (also עלוי)

   Zarqa, revia, tevir, legarmeh.

3. שְׁחִיָּה (also נצב or העמדה)

   Pashṭa, zaqef, ṭifḥa, atnaḥ, silluq.

According to this division, the major pausal accents are in category 3, the names for which mean "low, standing, stopping", while the lesser pausal accents are in categories 1 "high, raising and exalting the voice" and 2 "high, raised". Thus the typical accent clause would seem to have followed a pattern like this  with a lesser pausal accent with a high tone at the high point of the arc, and a major pausal accent with a low tone at the end. As Eliahu ha-Levi says (*Ṭuv Ṭa^{c}am* chapter 4) "Certainly there is a difference between them as indicators of pause or a break between subjects...*shalshelet* and *telisha* which are 'great kings' (disjunctives chanted on a high note) do not mark a very great pause, like the 'lesser kings' (disjunctives chanted on a low note) mentioned. In the same way *qarne parah* (*pazer gadol*) has a sound like that of *pazer qaṭan*, and like two *telisha*s (i.e. it also is chanted on a high note). It scarcely marks a break between subjects at all. Thus where *zarqa* and *pazer* occur, the main pause generally occurs with the 'small' accents (accents chanted on low notes) which follow them. For example *zarqa* is always followed by *segolta*, and the main pause is at *segolta*, not at *zarqa*."

However this threefold classification is not based on the way the accents are combined, and further discussion of these musical phenomena would be beyond the scope of this study.

196. This classification based on music is the only one found in the Masorah or the early treatises. Christian scholars of the Renaissance classified the accents according to their pausal value into four grades, to which they gave

names such as "emperors, kings, dukes, counts". Some Jewish writers, such as Zalman Hanau and ben Ze'ev, also used this type of classification. Wickes opposes classification in this way (as did others before him), and indeed it does give a false impression of the accent system. One cannot argue that the pause after one accent must be longer than the pause after another. The value of the accents is relative. In one verse a disjunctive accent might be used for a particular reason on a word closely related to the following, while in another the two words might be joined by a conjunctive (cf. the accentuation of the lists of nations in Ex 3:17 and Ex 13:5).

197. The division of the accents into four grades can, however, provide a useful guide. The general tendency of the accentuation is to divide a larger unit into two smaller units, and as a rule a unit ending with a disjunctive of one grade is divided by one of the grade below. Thus a unit ending with a disjunctive of grade I is divided by one of grade II, not by one of grade III, and so on.

The four grades of pausal accents are:-

I. *Silluq, atnaḥ.*

II. *Segolta, shalshelet, zaqef, ṭifḥa.*

III. *Zarqa, pashṭa, tevir, revia.*

IV. *Pazer, telisha, geresh, legarmeh.*

The difference between the scheme proposed here and the earlier gradings into "emperors, kings, etc.", is that the pausal value of the grades in this scheme is relative, not absolute. I.e. disjunctives of grade II are not characterized by a longer pause than those of grade III, but by the fact that their clause is normally divided by a disjunctive of grade III. For this reason, in a short verse, the real disjunctive value (in terms of ordinary syntax) of a disjunctive of grade II might be less than that of a disjunctive of grade IV in a long verse or in different circumstances. Furthermore, because of the requirements of the music of the chant, some major disjunctives must be preceded by particular minor disjunctives. For this reason, minor disjunctives (e.g. grade III) may come to fill a position in which, from the point of view of syntax, a disjunctive of a superior grade (e.g. grade II) might be expected.

198.   If the same accent is used two or more times (without
an accent of a superior grade intervening), then the first
occurrence has greater pausal value than the next. E.g.

Ex 12:29   וַיהוָ֣ה הִכָּ֣ה כָל־בְּכוֹר֮ בְּאֶ֣רֶץ מִצְרַיִם֒

Gen 3:1   וַיֹּ֙אמֶר֙ אֶל־הָ֣אִשָּׁ֔ה אַ֚ף כִּֽי־אָמַ֣ר אֱלֹהִ֔ים לֹ֣א תֹֽאכְל֔וּ מִכֹּ֖ל עֵ֥ץ הַגָּֽן

Dt 6:10   אֲשֶׁ֨ר נִשְׁבַּ֧ע לַאֲבֹתֶ֛יךָ לְאַבְרָהָ֥ם לְיִצְחָ֖ק וּֽלְיַעֲקֹ֑ב

199.   One feature of the accentuation traditionally
connected with the pausal value of the accents is the pausal
vowelling. As a general rule, pausal forms appear with *atnaḥ*
and *silluq*, while contextual forms are used with the other
accents. However there are a number of cases in which a word
with *atnaḥ* or *silluq* appears in contextual form. The reason
for this is not clear. Such cases are listed in the Masorah
under the title פתח באתנח וסוף פסוק
"*pataḥ* with *atnaḥ* or *sof pasuq* (*silluq*)"
There are also many cases in which pausal vocalization occurs
with disjunctives of grade II (particularly *zaqef* and *segolta*).
E.g. Is 30:16   נִרְדָּ֔ף -- ב֞ זקף קמ֞ץ
"(One of) two cases where this word has *qameṣ* when marked with
zaqef". Occasionally pausal vocalization occurs with other
accents, as

Gen 15:14   אֲשֶׁ֥ר יַעֲבֹ֖דוּ

Lev 10:6   תִּפְרָ֔עוּ.. תִּפְרֹ֙מוּ֙

Gen 43:23   שָׁל֣וֹם לָכֶ֗ם אַל־תִּירָ֔אוּ

Ex 32:24   לְמִ֣י זָהָ֔ב הִתְפָּרָ֑קוּ

Hos 4:17   אֶפְרָ֑יִם

Mal 1:6   וְאִם־אָ֣ב אָ֔נִי... וְאִם־אֲדוֹנִ֣ים אָ֗נִי°

Mica 3:11   וְעַל־יְהוָה֙ יִשָּׁעֵ֔נוּ לֵאמֹ֔ר

    (It is probable that pausal forms in such positions
reflect an earlier stage of the reading tradition. For instance
items in lists are usually separated, by the accents, into
groups of two or three (see #205). Such groups may be treated
as separate verses, as Neh 12:1 ff. Where possible, the last
word in such a verse appears in pausal form, as Lev 14:54-56.

זֹ֣את הַתּוֹרָ֔ה לְכָל־נֶ֥גַע הַצָּרַ֖עַת וְלַנָּֽתֶק׃
וּלְצָרַ֥עַת הַבֶּ֖גֶד וְלַבָּֽיִת׃
וְלַשְׂאֵ֥ת וְלַסַּפַּ֖חַת וְלַבֶּהָֽרֶת׃

The list in Dt 5:14 is also marked by pausal forms in this way:-

לֹא־תַעֲשֶׂ֣ה כָל־מְלָאכָ֡ה אַתָּ֣ה וּבִנְךָֽ וּבִתֶּ֣ךָ

וְעַבְדּוֹ וַאֲמָתוֹ
וְשׁוֹרוֹ וַחֲמֹרוֹ וְכָל בְּהֶמְתּוֹ...

In this case however, the whole list is treated as part of a verse. Evidently when the vowel patterns were fixed the list here was read in short units, as was that of Lev 14:54-56, but later a different method (represented by the accents) became customary. Pausal forms with minor disjunctives seem to represent, then, a division of the text into syntactic and semantic units slightly different from that represented by the accents, but it is clear that the two systems of division were closely related (See Revell 1979). E.J.R.)

The Determination of the Accentuation of a Verse

200. The scholars who established the accentuation lived long ago, subject to different pressures from ours, and in a different thought-world. For this reason it is often difficult to understand the reason for some particular detail of the placing of the accent signs in a verse. Nevertheless one can obtain a general idea of the principles behind the placing of the accents. Two ways of explaining these principles are outlined below.

There is a comprehensive discussion of this subject in Hanau 1718, and a shorter discussion in Ben Ze'ev 1876. These scholars deal with problems such as the use of the disjunctives in lists, or in the similar case of words or phrases in parallel syntactic use, or where a statement introducing a subject is followed by a series of particularizing statements, and so on. In the view of these scholars, the verse is initially divided into two or three parts. If two, *atnaḥ*, is marked at the end of the first, and if three, then *segolta* is marked at the end of the first, and *atnaḥ* at the end of the second. After this, the relationship of each word is determined, to see whether it goes with the word which precedes or with the one which follows, and thus whether it should receive a disjunctive or a conjunctive accent. E.g. in הַמַּלְאָךְ | הַגֹּאֵל אֹתִי, the word הַגֹּאֵל is more closely connected to the word which follows it than to the one which precedes it, and so a mark indicating connection is placed after it, and a mark indicating separation is placed before it. After the relationship between all the words in one of the major divisions of the verse has been determined in this way, a disjunctive can be marked--according to the rules for their use, wherever separation has been marked, and a conjunctive--determined by the following disjunctive--wherever connection has been marked.

201. The second method of explaining the principles behind the placing of the accents in a verse is that of Wickes, based on the idea of dichotomy. This gives a more complete understanding, but there remain many places in the Bible where one must assume that an exception was made to the general rules, and anomalous accentuation was used for some specific purpose. According to Wickes' view, the verse is divided in two at the point of dichotomy; the two halves are themselves divided in two, and so the process of dichotomy continues until the whole verse is divided into single words, or groups of words joined by conjunctives. The particular disjunctive to be used at each point of dichotomy is determined by the rules for the use of the accents. Generally *atnaḥ* divides the verse, *zaqef* the verse halves, *pashṭa* or *revia* the unit ending with *zaqef*, and so on. In cases like this last, where one of two or more accents may be used to divide the unit, the choice of accent is usually determined by the number of words between the point of division and the end of the unit. The system can be shown thus:-

1st division			
2nd division		2nd division	
3rd division	3rd division	3rd division	3rd division

The process would be similar to the "immediate constituent" analysis sometimes used in modern descriptive linguistics.

Wickes explains the general principles by which the point of dichotomy is fixed in a unit in chapters III and IV of his book (Wickes 1887). However our intention is to understand the accentuation as it is, and not to speculate on the reasons for the use of the accents in individual verses, so this subject need not be pursued. Nevertheless a brief discussion is given below. This is followed by a discussion of the individual disjunctives. In the case of each disjunctive the subordinate disjunctive(s) used to divide its clause are indicated, and also the conjunctives used before it.

Some Principles Followed in Establishing the Point of Division of a Unit

202. i) The main division is generally placed about the middle of a verse, at a major syntactic division which is also a semantic division. Such a division can be between two clauses (as in Dt 32:9, Gen 2:2 below) or within a clause (Gen 2:4 below). The meaning of the second division can repeat that of the first:

Jer 4:24 רָאִיתִי הֶהָרִים וְהִנֵּה רֹעֲשִׁ֑ים וְכָל הַגְּבָעוֹת הִתְקַלְקָלוּ׃

Dt 32:9 כִּי חֵלֶק יְהוָה עַמּ֑וֹ יַעֲקֹב חֶבֶל נַחֲלָתוֹ׃

The meaning of the second division can extend a statement begun in the first:

Gen 2:2 וַיְכַל אֱלֹהִים בַּיּוֹם הַשְּׁבִיעִי מְלַאכְתּוֹ אֲשֶׁר עָשָׂ֑ה
וַיִּשְׁבֹּת בַּיּוֹם הַשְּׁבִיעִי מִכָּל מְלַאכְתּוֹ אֲשֶׁר עָשָׂה׃

Gen 1:8 וַיִּקְרָא אֱלֹהִים לָרָקִיעַ שָׁמָ֑יִם וַיְהִי עֶרֶב וַיְהִי בֹקֶר יוֹם שֵׁנִי׃

Gen 2:4 אֵלֶּה תוֹלְדוֹת הַשָּׁמַיִם וְהָאָרֶץ בְּהִבָּרְא֑ם בְּיוֹם עֲשׂוֹת יְהוָה אֱלֹהִים
אֶרֶץ וְשָׁמָיִם׃

Gen 2:12 וּזֲהַב הָאָרֶץ הַהִוא ט֑וֹב שָׁם הַבְּדֹלַח וְאֶבֶן הַשֹּׁהַם׃

The second division can add an explanation, etc., to the first:

Gen 2:17 וּמֵעֵץ הַדַּעַת טוֹב וָרָע לֹא תֹאכַל מִמֶּ֑נּוּ כִּי בְּיוֹם אֲכָלְךָ מִמֶּנּוּ
מוֹת תָּמוּת׃

There is a general tendency not to fix the main verse division after an introductory, unimportant part of the verse, such as an introduction to speech:

Gen 1:6 וַיֹּאמֶר אֱלֹהִים יְהִי רָקִיעַ בְּתוֹךְ הַמָּ֑יִם וִיהִי מַבְדִּיל בֵּין מַיִם לָמָיִם׃

Ex 12:43 וַיֹּאמֶר יְהוָה אֶל מֹשֶׁה וְאַהֲרֹן זֹאת חֻקַּת הַפָּ֑סַח כָּל בֶּן נֵכָר
לֹא יֹאכַל בּוֹ׃

(The main division does not come at אֱלֹהִים or אַהֲרֹן, after the introduction to speech, but within the speech itself.)

Similarly

Jer 4:9 וְהָיָה בַיּוֹם הַהוּא נְאֻם יְהוָה יֹאבַד לֵב הַמֶּלֶךְ וְלֵב הַשָּׂרִ֑ים
וְנָשַׁמּוּ הַכֹּהֲנִים וְהַנְּבִיאִים יִתְמָהוּ׃

Amos 4:2 נִשְׁבַּע אֲדֹנָי יְהוִה בְּקָדְשׁוֹ כִּי הִנֵּה יָמִים בָּאִים עֲלֵיכֶ֑ם
וְנִשָּׂא אֶתְכֶם בְּצִנּוֹת וְאַחֲרִיתְכֶן בְּסִירוֹת דּוּגָה׃

Here again the main division does not come after the introductory clause. There is also a tendency to mark the main division before some important feature of the verse, so as to emphasize it, as

Gen 22:10 וַיִּשְׁלַח אַבְרָהָם אֶת יָדוֹ וַיִּקַּח אֶת הַמַּאֲכֶ֑לֶת לִשְׁחֹט אֶת בְּנוֹ׃

Jer 24:3 וַיֹּאמֶר יְהוָה אֵלַי מָה אַתָּה רֹאֶה יִרְמְיָהוּ וָאֹמַר תְּאֵנִים
הַתְּאֵנִים הַטֹּבוֹת טֹבוֹת מְאֹד וְהָרָעוֹת רָעוֹת מְאֹד אֲשֶׁר לֹא תֵאָכַלְנָה מֵרֹעַ׃

203. ii) Two words which are subject and predicate, or have a similar grammatical relationship, are usually joined by a conjunctive, as

Gen 11:24 וַיְחִי נָחוֹר

Gen 24:1 וְאַבְרָהָם זָקֵן

But if a further word is involved, such as a modifier, the first word has a disjunctive accent, as

Gen 21:1 וַיהוָה פָּקַד אֶת־שָׂרָה

Gen 18:33 וְאַבְרָהָם שָׁב לִמְקֹמוֹ

204. iii) A word in construct to a following word is generally joined to it by a conjunctive, as

Gen 20:18 אֵשֶׁת אַבְרָהָם

Neh 2:20 אֱלֹהֵי הַשָּׁמַיִם

If a phrase contains two or more words in construct, the last of these will have the conjunctive, but the preceding construct forms are likely to have disjunctives, the strongest at the beginning of the phrase, as

Nu 2:3 דֶּגֶל מַחֲנֵה יְהוּדָה

Ex 23:19 רֵאשִׁית בִּכּוּרֵי אַדְמָתְךָ

Dt 3:10 עָרֵי מַמְלֶכֶת עוֹג

Nu 3:32 פְּקֻדַּת שֹׁמְרֵי מִשְׁמֶרֶת הַקֹּדֶשׁ

Nu 3:25 וּמָסַךְ פֶּתַח אֹהֶל מוֹעֵד

However if, in similar cases, only the first two words are closely joined, the disjunctive will come on the second, as

2S 17:14 אֶת־עֲצַת אֲחִיתֹפֶל הַטּוֹבָה

Note the difference in the accentuation of

Dt 28:61 בְּסֵפֶר הַתּוֹרָה הַזֹּאת (where זאת goes with תוֹרָה)

and Dt 29:20 בְּסֵפֶר הַתּוֹרָה הַזֶּה (where זֶה goes with סֵפֶר)

(See #286).

205. iv) In lists, and similar cases of words in parallel syntactic usage, two words (or phrases) are joined by a conjunctive accent, as

Lev 25:44 עֶבֶד וְאָמָה

If the list is composed of three words, the first usually has a conjunctive, the second a disjunctive, as

Ex 25:3 זָהָב וָכֶסֶף וּנְחֹשֶׁת
1C 1:1 אָדָם שֵׁת אֱנוֹשׁ
Jer 25:27 שְׁתוּ וְשִׁכְרוּ וּקְיוּ
Jer 13:14 לֹא־אֶחְמוֹל וְלֹא־אָחוּס וְלֹא אֲרַחֵם
Nu 31:9 וְאֵת כָּל־בְּהֶמְתָּם וְאֶת־כָּל־מִקְנֵהֶם וְאֶת־כָּל־חֵילָם

A list of four words is generally divided into two pairs, as

Ex 1:4 דָּן וְנַפְתָּלִי גָּד וְאָשֵׁר
Is 19:15 רֹאשׁ וְזָנָב כִּפָּה וְאַגְמוֹן
Ex 20:17 וְעַבְדּוֹ וַאֲמָתוֹ וְשׁוֹרוֹ וַחֲמֹרוֹ

206. v) There is a certain tendency to mark small words, like הוּא, אַתָּה, אָנֹכִי, אֲנִי, לְמַעַן, אַחֲרֵי, עוֹד, אֵת, אֲשֶׁר, גַּם, כִּי, etc., with a disjunctive accent. Hanau and Ben Ze'ev state as a general rule that if the following word has a disjunctive, one of these small words will have a conjunctive, but if the following word has a conjunctive, the small word will have a disjunctive, as

1K 2:2 אָנֹכִי הֹלֵךְ
Is 45:12 אָנֹכִי עָשִׂיתִי אֶרֶץ

In fact, however these small words very commonly have *maqqef*, so that the rule should be formulated as follows: If the following word has a disjunctive, the small word has a conjunctive or *maqqef*, as

Gen 3:19 עַד שׁוּבְךָ
Gen 13:15 עַד־עוֹלָם

but if the following word has a conjunctive, the small word has a disjunctive or *maqqef*, as

2K 17:41 עַד הַיּוֹם הַזֶּה
Gen 15:18 עַד־הַנָּהָר הַגָּדֹל

The use of *maqqef* is governed by many rules (#290), but they cannot be discussed here. It must simply be noted that in the case of prepositions, conjunctions, and similar small words, which commonly have no accent of their own, and are joined to the following word by *maqqef*, the opposite tendency may also appear, so that they, and not the following longer word, are marked with a disjunctive accent.

This selection of the principles by which the point of division in a unit is fixed can only give a preliminary guide to the division of simple phrases and short verses. The longer the verse and the more complex the phrase, the more difficult it is to analyze this feature.

THE DISJUNCTIVE ACCENTS: THE COMBINATIONS POSSIBLE AND THEIR SERVI

207. The description of the accents, the form of the signs and their use, given below, covers both what is found in modern printed editions and what is found in ancient MSS. As regards the form of the accent signs, those composed of lines show, as a rule, straight lines in MSS (and in BHK and BHS) and curved lines in modern editions. As shown in the list (#194) the majority of accent signs are "impositive"--placed above or below the first consonant of the stress syllable. If there is a vowel sign below the same letter, the accent sign is generally placed to the left of the vowel sign. A few accents are "prepositive"--placed on the first letter of the word, or "postpositive"--placed on the last letter.

In the description of the conjunctives used with each disjunctive, the position "first", "second", etc., is counted back from the disjunctive, so that the "first" conjunctive is always the one immediately before the disjunctive.

'Silluq' סילוק

208. *Silluq* is also called סוֹף פָּסוּק. This is the accent on the last word in the verse, marked by a stroke under the stress syllable (סִילֽוּק). In printed editions the stroke is vertical. In MSS it is often slanted to the left (סִילֽוּק), either a little (as in A, L, B) or a lot (as in C, S, S^1)--in fact up to 45 degrees from the vertical in S.

At the end of the verse, after the word bearing *silluq* two dots are usually marked. In MSS, these are usually small, and marked in the upper half of the line, as אַבְרָהָם׃. In some early MSS--mostly Geniza fragments with Babylonian pointing, a small circle is used instead of two dots, and in some MSS a single dot is marked at the end of the verse.

In most MSS, such as L, C, S, these two dots are marked at the end of every verse, but this is not always the case. In A, for instance, the two dots are only marked at the end of one half or one third of the verses in the 21 books, and in the three poetical books, only at the end of about one tenth. B and S^1 show a similar inconsistency in the use of these dots, and in L[20] they are not used at all.

In most MSS *silluq* is marked on all words, but in a few MSS in which every verse in the three poetic books ends at the end of a line and is followed by the two dots, *silluq* is only marked if the word has penultimate stress. This may occur even in early MSS, such as L[13]. V seems to show traces of this convention, even though the verses do not end only at the end of a line.

209. *Silluq* can only be preceded by one conjunctive, and this is *merka* מֵרְכָ֖א, as בֵּ֥ית אָבִֽיו (Gen 34:19). This accent, also called מַאֲרִיךְ or מְאַרְכָא, is the most common conjunctive, and occurs before several accents. In the MSS it is marked by a straight line below the stress syllable, usually pointing somewhat to the left (מֵרְכָ֖א), but sometimes vertical (often identical to *silluq*) or even slanted to the right (like *tifḥa*). In printed editions it is pointed to the left, and is curved (מֵרְכָ֥א).

210. In five places, the word bearing *silluq* has, in addition, a secondary accent like *tifḥa* in form. This is marked in an open syllable suitable for *ga*[c]*ya* (#326). The cases are:-

Lev 21:4	לְהֵ֖חַלּֽוֹ
Nu 15:21	לְדֹרֹ֖תֵיכֶֽם
Is 8:17	וְקִוֵּ֖יתִי־לֽוֹ
Hos 11:6	מִמֹּעֲ֖צוֹתֵיהֶֽם
1C 2:53	וְהָאֶֽשְׁתָּ֖אֻלִֽי

In these cases *silluq* has neither *tifḥa* nor a conjunctive before it, so that it seems as if *tifḥa* and *silluq* are appearing on the same word. It also seems likely that this sign represented a musical motif similar to that of *tifḥa*. Nevertheless the Masorah treats this as a conjunctive, with the name *mayela* (מָאיְלָא, also called נְטוּיָה or דְּחוּיָה). It may be called specifically *mayela* with *silluq*, as the same sign occurs under similar conditions with *atnaḥ* (#216). In some MSS *ga*[c]*ya* may be marked in an open syllable between *mayela* and *silluq*, as וְהָאֶֽשְׁתָּ֖אֻלִֽי (A, L, 1C 2:53).

211. The accent which most commonly marks the main

division in the unit ending with *silluq*--the verse--is *atnaḥ*. *Atnaḥ* is always used in longer verses, and in any case where the point of division is distant from *silluq*. In short verses *atnaḥ* may not be used, in which case the main division is marked by *zaqef* or *ṭifḥa*, depending on the distance of the point of division from *silluq*, or on the syntactical importance of the division. Thus the division is marked by *ṭifḥa* in

Gen 46:23 וּבְנֵי־דָן חֻשִׁים׃ (The shortest verse in the Bible, with only two accents)

Gen 1:13 וַיְהִי־עֶרֶב וַיְהִי־בֹקֶר יוֹם שְׁלִישִׁי׃

Ex 15:18 יְהוָה יִמְלֹךְ לְעֹלָם וָעֶד׃

Lam 3:6 בְּמַחֲשַׁכִּים הוֹשִׁיבַנִי כְּמֵתֵי עוֹלָם׃

The division is marked by *zaqef* in

Gen 23:12 וַיִּשְׁתַּחוּ אַבְרָהָם לִפְנֵי עַם הָאָרֶץ׃

Qoh 4:5 הַכְּסִיל חֹבֵק אֶת־יָדָיו וְאֹכֵל אֶת־בְּשָׂרוֹ

Lam 5:19 אַתָּה יְהוָה לְעוֹלָם תֵּשֵׁב כִּסְאֲךָ לְדֹר וָדוֹר׃

Lam 5:21 הֲשִׁיבֵנוּ יְהוָה אֵלֶיךָ וְנָשׁוּבָה חַדֵּשׁ יָמֵינוּ כְּקֶדֶם

Dt 18:13 תָּמִים תִּהְיֶה עִם יְהוָה אֱלֹהֶיךָ׃

However *atnaḥ* may also be used to divide relatively short verses as 2S 22:27 עִם־נָבָר תִּתָּבָר וְעִם־עִקֵּשׁ תִּתַּפָּל׃

1S 2:6 יְהוָה מֵמִית וּמְחַיֶּה מוֹרִיד שְׁאוֹל וַיָּעַל׃

212. The disjunctive *ṭifḥa* regularly appears before *silluq*, even where the word bearing *silluq* is closely connected with the preceding, as

Gen 1:16 ...לְמֶמְשֶׁלֶת הַלַּיְלָה וְאֵת הַכּוֹכָבִים

Lev 2:6 -- מִנְחָה הִוא

Dt 10:13 -- לְטוֹב לָךְ׃

Ṭifḥa fails to appear only in those cases where no accent at all intervenes between *atnaḥ* and *silluq*, as

Gen 1:3 וַיֹּאמֶר אֱלֹהִים יְהִי אוֹר וַיְהִי־אוֹר׃

Gen 1:11 ...עַל־הָאָרֶץ וַיְהִי־כֵן

Gen 41:21 וּמַרְאֵיהֶן רַע כַּאֲשֶׁר בַּתְּחִלָּה וָאִיקָץ

There is, in some MSS, one exceptional case in which *merka* is the only accent between *atnaḥ* and *silluq*:

Mic 6:3 in A, L, C, S^1 וּמָה הֶלְאֵתִיךָ עֲנֵה בִי

'Atnaḥ' - אתנח, אתנחה, אתנחתא

213. The first vowel of the name may be "e" (*segol*) or "a" (*pataḥ*). This accent is marked by an inverted "v" shape under

the stress syllable, formed with straight lines in the MSS (אַתְנָ֑ח), but with curved in most printed texts (אַתְנָ֑ח). It occurs in most verses, marking the main verse division, and can only appear once in any verse.

Atnah̩ generally has only one servus, and this is *munah̩* (marked by a backwards "L" shape under the stress syllable, מוּנַ֣ח). This name is short for "*shofar munah̩*", as this accent belongs to the *shofar* category. In the three books, there is a conjunctive called *shofar* *ᶜilluy* (#363), marked by the *munah̩* sign placed above the stress syllable. Some early treatises use this name and *shofar mekarbel*, along with *shofar munah̩*, to describe conjunctives used with particular accents, or combinations of accents, in the 21 books (see #220), but in standard Tiberian texts the *munah̩* sign is used in all the positions named. *Mehuppak*, the conjunctive used before *pasht̩a* (#240) also belongs to the *shofar*-class, as its alternative name, שׁוֹפָר הָפוּךְ, shows.

214. In about 30 cases *atnah̩* has two servi, both *munah̩*s. This form of accentuation generally occurs when the word immediately before *atnah̩* is a monosyllable, and the word before that is כִּי, as

Gen 40:16 כִּ֣י ט֣וֹב פָּתָ֑ר

1K 2:37, 42 כִּ֣י מ֣וֹת תָּמ֑וּת

It is, however, occasionally used in other situations, as

Lam 1:18 כִּ֣י פִ֣יהוּ מָרִ֑יתִי

Amos 3:8 מִ֣י לֹ֣א יִירָ֑א

Ez 8:6 מֵהֶ֣ם (מָ֣ה הֵ֣ם ק) עֹשִׂ֑ים

1C 4:12 אֲבִ֣י עִ֣יר נָחָ֑שׁ

215. In two cases *munah̩* is used as a secondary accent in the same word as *atnah̩*, marked on an open syllable suitable for *gaᶜya* (#326). The cases are

2S 12:25 יְדִֽידְיָ֑הּ

1C 5:20 שֶׁ֣עִמָּהֶ֑ם

(This last case shows a secondary accent on the prefixed particle, -שֶׁ֣, a fairly common occurrence (#233, 241).

216. In ten or eleven cases in the Bible, a sign of the same form as *t̩ifh̩a* appears as a secondary accent on the same

word as *atnaḥ*. This sign, which is also generally marked on an open syllable suitable for *gaᶜya*, is called *mayela*, or specifically *mayela* with *atnaḥ*, to differentiate it from the same sign used with *silluq* (#210). *Ṭifḥa* does not occur before *mayela*, but in three cases a conjunctive is used before it:

merka in Jer 2:31 אִם אֶרֶץ מַאְפֵּלְיָה

azla in Dan 4:9, 18 וּמָזוֹן לְכֹלָּא־בֵהּ

Merka is the regular servus of *ṭifḥa* (which *mayela* resembles in form), but *azla* before *ṭifḥa* would be an anomaly. In the other cases of *mayela* before *atnaḥ*, no conjunctive precedes *mayela*.

Gen 8:18 וַיֵּצֵא־נֹחַ

Nu 28:26 בְּשָׁבֻעֹתֵיכֶם

2K 9:2 וּבָאתָ־שָּׁמָּה

Ez 7:25 קְפָדָה־בָא

Ez 10:13 לָאוֹפַנִּים (but *mayela* is not used here in some early MSS)

Ez 11:18 וּבָאוּ־שָׁמָּה

Rut 1:10 וַתֹּאמַרְנָה־לָּהּ

2C 20:8 וַיֵּשְׁבוּ־בָהּ (note that *mayela* occurs here on the syllable immediately before *atnaḥ*).

In a number of MSS, *gaᶜya* may be marked on the syllable between *mayela* and *atnaḥ*, if it is open, as in L[18]

Ez 11:18 וּבָאוּ־שָׁמָּה

217. As with *silluq*, *ṭifḥa* regularly appears before *atnaḥ*, even if *atnaḥ* is only preceded by one word which is closely connected to it, as

Lev 19:11 לֹא תִּגְנֹבוּ

Is 10:8 כִּי יֹאמַר

Jer 10:15 מַעֲשֵׂה תַּעְתֻּעִים

Ṭifḥa fails to appear only where *atnaḥ* is the first accent in the verse, as

Gen 35:5 וַיִּסָּעוּ

Dt 11:27 אֶת־הַבְּרָכָה

Ez 34:19 וְצֹאנִי

218. The use of disjunctives to mark the divisions in the two halves into which the verse is divided is much the same in both halves. As a general rule, if the main division comes on the word immediately before *atnaḥ* or *silluq*, it is marked by *ṭifḥa*, as

Gen 3:9 וַיֹּאמֶר לוֹ אַיֶּכָּה

Gen 26:33 וַיִּקְרָא אֹתָהּ שִׁבְעָה

If the main division comes on the second word before *silluq* or *atnaḥ*, it may be marked either by *ṭifḥa* or by *zaqef*. Thus with *ṭifḥa*, Gen 2:16 מִכֹּל עֵץ־הַגָּן אָכֹל תֹּאכֵל

Gen 21:1 וַיהוָה פָּקַד אֶת־שָׂרָה כַּאֲשֶׁר אָמָר

With *zaqef*, Lev 10:20 וַיִּשְׁמַע מֹשֶׁה וַיִּיטַב בְּעֵינָיו

Gen 1:15 וְהָיוּ לִמְאוֹרֹת בִּרְקִיעַ הַשָּׁמַיִם לְהָאִיר עַל־הָאָרֶץ

As these examples show, where the main division is marked by *zaqef*, *ṭifḥa* is always used between this *zaqef* and the *atnaḥ* or *silluq*, according to the rules of the accent system.

If the main division in the verse half occurs on the third word or further before *atnaḥ* or *silluq*, it is marked by *zaqef*. If there are two or more major divisions in the verse-half, *zaqef* is repeated at each of them. Where a series of *zaqef*s is used in this way, the one closest to *silluq* or *atnaḥ* has, as a general rule, the least pausal value, and the one farthest from *silluq* or *atnaḥ* the greatest, as

1C 22:7 בְּנוֹ (בני ק) אֲנִי הָיָה עִם־לְבָבִי לִבְנוֹת בַּיִת לְשֵׁם יְהוָה אֱלֹהָי

Gen 12:7 וַיֵּרָא יְהוָה אֶל־אַבְרָם וַיֹּאמֶר לְזַרְעֲךָ אֶתֵּן אֶת־הָאָרֶץ הַזֹּאת

There is one difference in the accentuation of the two halves of the verse. In the first half (the unit ending with *atnaḥ*), if the main division is distant from *atnaḥ*, it may be marked with *segolta* in place of *zaqef*. *Segolta* can only mark the first major division in the *atnaḥ* clause, and cannot be preceded by *zaqef*, as

Gen 44:1 וַיְצַו אֶת־אֲשֶׁר עַל־בֵּיתוֹ לֵאמֹר מַלֵּא אֶת־אַמְתְּחֹת הָאֲנָשִׁים אֹכֶל
כַּאֲשֶׁר יוּכְלוּן שְׂאֵת

'Zaqef' - זקף, זקפא

219. This accent is marked by two dots in vertical line above the stress syllable (זָקֵף). It is sometimes called *zaqef qaṭan* to distinguish it from its variant form, *zaqef gadol*, which is marked by the same two dots with a vertical stroke to the left of them (זָקֵף). The two signs have the same pausal value, as noted in the *Horayat ha-Qore* p. 96 (Dérenbourg, 1870, p. 404) "We have already mentioned that *zaqef* has two forms. It is sometimes called *zaqef qaṭan*, and sometimes *zaqef gadol*, according to the musical motif". A further variation on the *zaqef* melody is marked by a diagonal stroke leaning towards the

left (like *azla* or *pashṭa*) in the same word as *zaqef*. This form is known as *methiga-zaqef* (the diagonal stroke is also given various other names in the masoretic literature, as חוטֵר, מַקֵּל, דַּרְבָּן). In many cases also *munaḥ* is marked as a secondary accent on the same word as *zaqef* and this combination is considered as a fourth variant of the *zaqef* melody. These variants all have the same pausal value as *zaqef qaṭan*, but differ in melody.

Zaqef is the most common disjunctive accent. It appears in most verses of the Bible, and may be used one or more times in both halves of the verse.

220. *Zaqef* usually has one or two servi. Both are *munaḥs*. Two are used only where *zaqef* is preceded by *pashṭa*, as

Ex 12:13 הַבָּתִּים֒ אֲשֶׁ֣ר אַתֶּ֣ם שָׁ֔ם

There is one exception to this rule (Breuer):

Ez 16:23 --^-- א֣וֹי א֣וֹי לָ֔ךְ

The standard Tiberian system uses the ordinary *munaḥ* sign in all cases before *zaqef*, but some treatises mention different forms of conjunctive. E.g. *Sefer Ṭa**ame ha-Miqra* fol. Eii: "*Zaqef qaṭan* never has more than two servi:*shofar mekarbel* and *shofar* *ᶜilluy*. The rules on this are as follows:

If *zaqef* has one servus, and it is marked on the first letter of the word (representing the first consonant of the stress syllable), then the servus is *shofar mekarbel*, as in

Dt 4:8 גּ֣וֹי גָּד֔וֹל

Jer 18:7 רֶ֣גַע אֲדַבֵּ֔ר

Jer 44:10 לֹ֣א דֻכְּא֔וּ

If the accent is not marked on the first letter of the word, the servus is *shofar ᶜilluy*, as

Jer 36:24 וְלֹ֣א פָחֲד֔וּ

Jer 18:9 וְרֶ֣גַע אֲדַבֵּ֔ר

If *zaqef* has two servi, the first of these (i.e. the second before *zaqef*) is always *shofar mekarbel*, whether it is on the first letter of the word or no, and the one immediately before *zaqef* is *shofar ᶜilluy*, as

Ex 29:33 אֲשֶׁ֣ר כֻּפַּ֣ר בָּהֶ֔ם

Gen 15:4 אֲשֶׁ֣ר יֵצֵ֣א מִמֵּעֶ֔יךָ etc."

Shofar ᶜilluy and *shofar mekarbel* are distinguished from *shofar munaḥ* in some MSS pointed in the Expanded Tiberian

system, as Vatican MS Urbinati 2 (but it is inconsistent). A single servus marked on the first letter (*shofar mekarbel*) is distinguished as in Ez 7:13 (2nd) לֹא יָשׁוּב. If the servus is not on the first letter, (*shofar* ^{c}*illuy*) it is marked as in
Ez 7:12 הִגִּיעַ הַיּוֹם.
Two servi (*mekarbel* and ^{c}*illuy*) are marked as in
Ez 4:4 אֲשֶׁר תִּשְׁכַּב עָלָיו.

The "*mekarbel*" sign, composed of *munaḥ* and two *merkas* is found occasionally even in V, and is remarked on by Menaḥem di Lonzano in his '*Or Torah*', e.g. on Dt 1:17 "אֲשֶׁר should be without the two strokes", Dt 1:23 "שְׁנַיִם should be without the two strokes" (Breuer). This sign is also mentioned in the MS of *Token Ezra* "וַיְדַבֵּר *shofar mekurbal* and two *merkas*". In the Codex Reuchlinianus (R), which also has expanded Tiberian pointing, *mekarbel* is marked by a sign similar to *mehuppak*, but ^{c}*illuy* is not distinguished from *shofar munaḥ*. Thus עֹשֶׂה כֹּל (Is 44:24) has *mekarbel*, but in דְּבַר עַבְדּוֹ (Is 44:26), the ordinary *munaḥ* sign is used where the treatises require *shofar* ^{c}*illuy*. (See Kahle, 1930, p. 59*).

Some Palestinian MSS also use three different signs where the standard Tiberian text has *munaḥ* (e.g. P208 of Revell 1977), but the rules for their use seem to differ from those given in the treatises.

The Variants of 'Zaqef'

221. *Zaqef qaṭan* is always used where *zaqef* is preceded by *munaḥ*. Where *zaqef* is not preceded by *munaḥ*, however, other variants of *zaqef* may occur.

i) *Munah-zaqef*. This combination is used when the *zaqef* word includes an open syllable suitable for *ga*^{c}*ya* (#326) which is not the first syllable, as

Gen 4:1 וְהָאָדָם (at the beginning of the verse)
Ex 18:19 בְּקֹלִי אִיעָצְךָ

If the syllable suitable for *ga*^{c}*ya* is the first in the word, then *ga*^{c}*ya* is marked, and not *munaḥ*, as

Dt 28:37 הָעַמִּים

There are four exceptions to this

1K 17:23, 2K 2:11 אֵלִיָּהוּ
Hos 5:4 מַעַלְלֵיהֶם
Qoh 2:18 שֶׁאַנִּיחֶנּוּ

If the word also contains a closed syllable suitable for *ga*ga^{c}ya*, and its structure is "fully regular" (#319), the *ga^{c}ya* is marked, and not the *munaḥ*, as

Dt 34:9 וַֽיַּעֲשׂ֔וּ (not וַיַּעֲשׂ֔וּ)

Rut 4:14 אֶל־נָֽעֳמִ֔י (not אֶל־נָעֳמִ֔י)

But Neh 9:24 הַֽכְּנַעֲנִ֔ים forms an exception.

If the structure of the word is "not fully regular" (#322), the *munaḥ* is marked, and not the *ga^{c}ya*, as

1K 22:31, 2C 18:30 הִלָּחֲמ֔וּ (not הִלָּֽחֲמ֔וּ)

But Jer 28:16 מְשַׁלֵּֽחֲךָ֔ forms an exception.

In a few further cases *ga^{c}ya-shewa* is marked rather than a possible *munaḥ*, as

Zech 1:16 בְּֽרַחֲמִ֔ים (not בְּרַחֲמִ֔ים)

In a few cases also *ga^{c}ya* on an open syllable with a full vowel at the beginning of a word is marked rather than *munaḥ*, as 2S 2:23 מֵֽאַחֲרָ֔יו (not מֵאַחֲרָ֔יו)

Occasionally *ga^{c}ya* occurs in place of *munaḥ* when the open syllable is not the first in the word,as

Ex 38:23 וּבָֽאַרְגָּמָ֔ן

Jud 16:26, 1K 7:21, cf. 1C 18:8 אֶת־הָֽעַמֻּדִ֔ים

Is 8:9, Joel 1:2 וְהַֽאֲזִ֔ינוּ

These variations on *zaqef* may appear both where *pashṭa* precedes the *zaqef* and where it does not. The other variations, however, appear only where *pashṭa* does not precede the *zaqef*.

222. *(ii)* *Zaqef gadol*. If *pashṭa* does not precede the *zaqef*, and if the word bearing *zaqef* is not suitable for *munaḥ-zaqef* (nor for *methiga-zaqef* either, see #223), then *zaqef gadol* is used, as Ex 35:28 לַמָּא֕וֹר

Jer 31:3 מֵֽרָח֕וֹק

Zaqef gadol appears exceptionally after *pashṭa* in

2C 17:11 לו׳ צֹ֕אן

Zaqef gadol may be repeated, as in

Ex 16:6 עֶ֕רֶב וִֽידַעְתֶּ֕ם

If the word is of "regular" structure suitable for *ga^{c}ya* on a closed syllable (#319), this *ga^{c}ya* is marked and *zaqef qaṭan* is used, not *zaqef gadol*, as

Jer 20:1, 26:7 אֶֽת־יִרְמְיָ֔הוּ

There are seven exceptions in which *zaqef gadol* is used, as

Jud 9:35, 1K 8:55 וַֽיַּעֲמֹ֔ד (not וַיַּֽעֲמֹ֔ד)
In a few cases *ga^cya* with *zaqef qaṭan* is used rather than *zaqef gadol* where the structure is not regular (#324), as
Jud 18:22 נִֽזְעֲק֔וּ
In some cases *ga^cya* with *shewa* (#333) with *zaqef qaṭan* is used rather than *zaqef gadol*, as
1K 8:18 הֱֽטִיבֹ֔תָ
Haggai 1:14 וְֽאֶת־ר֔וּחַ
Zaqef gadol may not be used even where the *ga^cya* stands on an open syllable (#326), as
1S 13:12 וָֽאֶתְאַפַּ֔ק
1S 9:15 and elsewhere וַֽיהוָ֔ה
Despite the cases in which these exceptions occur, however, *zaqef gadol* is a very common accent occurring on hundreds of words in the Bible.

223. *iii) <u>Methigah-zaqef</u>.* If the *zaqef* is not preceded by *pashṭa*, and if the word bearing *zaqef* contains a closed syllable which is separated from the stress syllable by a full vowel--or at least by a vocal *shewa*, and if this closed syllable is not the first in the word, the *methigah-zaqef* is used, as
Ex 35:9 וְאַ֨בְנֵי־שֹׁ֔הַם (compare Ex 25:7 אַבְנֵי־שֹׁ֔הַם where the closed syllable is the first in the word).
Est 9:10 וּבַ֨בִּזָּ֔ה
Lev 13:54 וְכִ֨בְּס֔וּ
In general, where the word is of regular structure suitable for *ga^cya* on a closed syllable (#319), this *ga^cya* is marked with *zaqef qaṭan* rather than the *methigah-zaqef*, but there are exceptions, as
Dt 28:52 בְּכָ֨ל־אַרְצְךָ֔
Lev 25:7 וְלִ֨בְהֶמְתְּךָ֔
In a few exceptional cases, *methigah* occurs on the first syllable of a word, as
1K 1:37 מִ֨כִּסֵּ֔א
Jer 22:28 אִ֨ם־כְּלִ֔י

224. A phenomenon called נסיגת המתיגה "the retraction of *methigah*" also occurs, as in Jer 29:4 לְכָ֨ל־הַגּוֹלָ֔ה--where the *methigah* would be expected on the -הַ, but is retracted to the preceding syllable. As the result of such retraction, *methigah*

may occur on the first syllable of a word, even though this is
abnormal for it, as

1S 27:11   כָּל־הַיָּמִים (not כָּל־הֲיָמִים)

The retraction of *methigah* is differently marked in different
MSS, evidently following different rules.

The marking of *methigah* itself also differs in different
MSS. It is marked consistently in A and B. It is not marked
at all in S, where all words where *methigah* is expected have
zaqef qaṭan alone. In other MSS, such as L and S[1], *methigah*
is generally, but not always, marked where expected.

Methigah-zaqef is not repeated on successive words.

The above definition states that *methigah-zaqef* does not
occur after *pashṭa*, but in some MSS, such as C and L[15],
methigah-zaqef occurs consistently after *pashṭa*, and in other
MSS this occurs sporadically.

225.   As a general rule, *methigah* and *ga^{c}ya* are not used on
the same word. Similarly, in some MSS, *ga^{c}ya* is not used on the
same word as *zaqef gadol*--notably in A, and also in C, S, L[11].
In some other early MSS, *ga^{c}ya* is used with *zaqef gadol*, as

B, L, Ex 28:21   תְּהְיֶ֫יןָ

L, Dt 4:22   וִירִשְׁתֶּ֫ם

Disjunctives used to Divide the 'Zaqef' Clause

226.   If the *zaqef* clause consists of two words, *pashṭa* is
used on the first, if the word bearing *zaqef* is long, as

Gen 21:24   וַיֹּ֨אמֶר֙ אַבְרָהָ֔ם

Nu 16:28   בְּזֹאת֙ תֵּֽדְעוּ֔ן

If the word bearing *zaqef* is short, the preceding word has
munaḥ, as

Gen 15:3   וַיֹּ֣אמֶר אַבְרָ֔ם

Ex 7:17   בְּזֹ֣את תֵּדַ֔ע

This is the general rule, but there are many exceptions to it.

If the *zaqef* clause contains three or more words, where
the main division comes on the first word before *zaqef* it is
marked by *pashṭa*, as

Gen 4:9   וַיֹּ֤אמֶר יְהוָה֙ אֶל־קַ֔יִן

If the main division occurs on the second word before *zaqef*,
pashṭa may still be used, as

Gen 1:31   וַיַּ֤רְא אֱלֹהִים֙ אֶת־כָּל־אֲשֶׁ֣ר עָשָׂ֔ה

Gen 2:10 וְנָהָר יֹצֵא מֵעֵדֶן

The main division may also be marked by *revia*, in which case *pashṭa* is used on the word between *revia* and *zaqef*, as

Gen 22:3 וַיַּשְׁכֵּם אַבְרָהָם בַּבֹּקֶר וַיַּחֲבֹשׁ אֶת־חֲמֹרוֹ

If the main division is on the third word before *zaqef*, it is still, in a few cases, marked with *pashṭa*, as

Gen 3:12 הָאִשָּׁה אֲשֶׁר נָתַתָּה עִמָּדִי

However *revia* is usually used, with *pashṭa* between it and *zaqef*, as

Gen 1:2 וְהָאָרֶץ הָיְתָה תֹהוּ וָבֹהוּ

If the main division is on the fourth word or further before *zaqef*, it is marked by *revia*, with *pashṭa* between it and *zaqef*, as Gen 1:9

וַיֹּאמֶר אֱלֹהִים יִקָּווּ הַמַּיִם מִתַּחַת הַשָּׁמַיִם אֶל־מָקוֹם אֶחָד

If needed, *revia* can be repeated to mark a further division, but still the disjunctive immediately before *zaqef* is *pashṭa*, as

Jud 2:20 וַיֹּאמֶר יַעַן אֲשֶׁר עָבְרוּ הַגּוֹי הַזֶּה אֶת־בְּרִיתִי
אֲשֶׁר צִוִּיתִי אֶת־אֲבוֹתָם

However one *revia* can follow another only if there are at least three words between them. If this is not the case, then *pashṭa* is used in place of the *revia* closer to *zaqef*, with a second *pashṭa* between this "transformed *revia*" and the *zaqef*, as

Gen 7:11 בַּיּוֹם הַזֶּה נִבְקְעוּ כָּל־מַעְיְנוֹת תְּהוֹם רַבָּה

If three divisions are required, they may be marked by two *revia*s followed by *pashṭa* (with a second *pashṭa* before the *zaqef*) as

Jud 16:5 וַיַּעֲלוּ אֵלֶיהָ סַרְנֵי פְלִשְׁתִּים וַיֹּאמְרוּ לָהּ פַּתִּי אוֹתוֹ
וּרְאִי בַּמֶּה כֹּחוֹ גָדוֹל

More commonly *revia-pashṭa-revia* is used--again with a second *pashṭa* immediately before the *zaqef*, as

Mic 6:5 עַמִּי זְכָר־נָא מַה־יָּעַץ בָּלָק מֶלֶךְ מוֹאָב

Gen 27:37

וַיַּעַן יִצְחָק וַיֹּאמֶר לְעֵשָׂו הֵן גְּבִיר שַׂמְתִּיו לָךְ וְאֶת־כָּל־אֶחָיו
נָתַתִּי לוֹ לַעֲבָדִים

Pashṭa is not repeated under other conditions (i.e. where it is not preceded by *revia*) save in one exceptional case

1S 2:16 וְאָמַר לוֹ (לא ק) כִּי עַתָּה תִתֵּן

(where the second *pashṭa* occurs in the variant form *yetiv*). Similarly three *pashṭa*s occur together only in one exceptional case,

Ezra 7:25

וְאַנְתְּ עֶזְרָא כְּחָכְמַת אֱלָהָךְ דִּי־בִידָךְ מַנִּי שָׁפְטִין וְדַיָּנִין
דִּי־לֶהֱוֺן דָּאנִין (דאינין ק) לְכָל־עַמָּה דִּי בַּעֲבַר נַהֲרָה

'Segolta' and 'Shalshelet' - שלשלת -- סגול, סגלתא

227. *Segolta*, or *segol*, is not usually mentioned by name in the Masorah, but it is called, with reference to *zarqa* which always precedes it, "follower of *zarqa*" - הָרוֹדֵף לְזַרְקָא or עוֹקֵב הַזַּרְקָא. Occasionally also the name קָבְלָה is used, as in the Mp of L (and BHK, but not BHS,) at

Jud 9:36

עָם -- יז קמצ וכל אתנ וקבל וסופ פסוק דכות ב מ ב

"The word is pointed with *qameṣ* is all but two cases where the accent is *atnaḥ*, *segolta*, or *sof pasuq*, and in 17 other cases".

The sign for this accent in standard Tiberian MSS is the *segol* sign, upside down and postpositive (סְגֹלְתָּא֒). In MSS with expanded Tiberian pointing, (and occasionally in some others) the sign is repeated on the stress syllable of words with penultimate stress (הַמֶּ֒לֶךְ֒). The three dots usually form a triangle pointing upwards, but other orientations occur, as סְגֹלְתָּא in S^1, L^1, L^8, or סְגֹלְתָּא in C.

228. *Segolta* regularly marks the first major division in the first half of the verse (before *atnaḥ*). In one case alone *atnaḥ* is not used, and *segolta* marks the main verse division:

Ezra 7:13

מִנִּי שִׂים טְעֵם דִּי כָל־מִתְנַדַּב בְּמַלְכוּתִי מִן־עַמָּה יִשְׂרָאֵל
וְכָהֲנוֹהִי וְלֵוָיֵא לִמְהָךְ לִירוּשְׁלֶם עִמָּךְ יְהָךְ׃

Zaqef cannot precede *segolta*, but usually follows it, marking divisions between it and *atnaḥ*.

Segolta may be preceded by one or two servi, both *munaḥ*, as

Nu 30:13 בְּיוֹם שָׁמְעוֹ

Is 8:23 לַאֲשֶׁר מוּצָק לָהּ

229. *Segolta* is always preceded by *zarqa* (#230). Where *segolta* would stand on the first word in the verse (which occurs in seven cases), the accent *shalshelet* (also called מַרְעִים in the Masorah) is used instead of *segolta*. *Shalshelet* is marked by a zigzag line above the stress syllable, and a vertical line

(*paseq*) after the word (שַׁלְשֶׁ֓לֶת׀). In the accentuation of the three books, the zigzag line is used to mark a conjunctive *shalshelet*, and also a disjunctive one, which is distinguished from the conjunctive by the following *paseq*. It seems that in the accentuation of the 21 books, where no distinction of the sort is needed, the *paseq* was used in imitation of the poetic accentuation. The seven cases where *shalshelet* occurs are:-

Gen 19:16	וַיִּתְמַהְמָ֓הּ׀	Gen 24:12, Amos 1:2	וַיֹּאמַ֓ר׀
Gen 39:8	וַיְמָאֵ֓ן׀	Lev 8:23	וַיִּשְׁחָ֓ט׀
Is 13:8	וְנִבְהָ֓לוּ׀	Ezra 5:15	וַאֲמַר־לֵ֓הּ׀

Disjunctives used to Divide the 'Segolta' Clause

230. The rules for the division of the *segolta* clause are similar to those for the *zaqef* clause.

If *segolta* is preceded by one word, it is marked with *zarqa*, as *segolta* never occurs without *zarqa* before it, as

Gen 2:23 וַיֹּאמֶר֮ הָֽאָדָם֒

If *segolta* is preceded by two or more words, and the main division occurs on the first word before *segolta*, it is marked by *zarqa*, as

Gen 1:7 וַיַּ֣עַשׂ אֱלֹהִים֮ אֶת־הָֽרָקִיעַ֒

If the main division is on the second word before *segolta*, it is still usually marked with *zarqa*, as

Gen 6:4 הַנְּפִלִ֞ים הָי֣וּ בָאָ֘רֶץ֮ בַּיָּמִ֣ים הָהֵם֒

The division may be marked with *revia*, in which case *zarqa* is used between the *revia* and *segolta*, as

Dt 1:41 וַתַּעֲנ֣וּ׀ וַתֹּאמְר֣וּ אֵלַ֗י חָטָ֘אנוּ֮ לַֽיהוָה֒

If the main division is on the third word or further before *segolta*, it is marked by *revia*, with *zarqa* used between the *revia* and *segolta*, as

Is 53:12 לָכֵ֞ן אֲחַלֶּק־ל֣וֹ בָרַבִּ֗ים וְאֶת־עֲצוּמִים֮ יְחַלֵּ֣ק שָׁלָל֒

If necessary, *revia* can be repeated to mark further divisions, with *zarqa* still used between the *revia*s and *segolta*, as

2C 7:22 וְאָמְר֗וּ עַל֩ אֲשֶׁ֨ר עָזְב֜וּ אֶת־יְהוָ֣ה׀ אֱלֹהֵ֣י אֲבֹתֵיהֶ֗ם
אֲשֶׁ֣ר הוֹצִיאָם֮ מֵאֶ֣רֶץ מִצְרַיִם֒

However one *revia* can follow another only if they are separated by three or more words. Where this is not the case, the first *revia* before *segolta* is replaced by *pashṭa*, with *zarqa* between it and *segolta*, as

Dt 12:18 כִּ֣י אִם־לִפְנֵי֩ יְהוָ֨ה אֱלֹהֶ֜יךָ תֹּאכְלֶ֗נּוּ בַּמָּקוֹם֙ אֲשֶׁ֨ר יִבְחַ֜ר

יְהוָה אֱלֹהֶיךָ בּוֹ

Even this transformation can occur only where the *pashṭa* is separated from the following *zarqa* by two or more words. Where this is not the case, the first *revia* before *segolta* is replaced by *zarqa* (instead of by *pashṭa*), so that, in this situation, which is quite common, *segolta* is preceded by two *zarqa*s, as

Ex 12:29 וַיְהִי בַּחֲצִי הַלַּיְלָה וַיהוָה הִכָּה כָל־בְּכוֹר בְּאֶרֶץ מִצְרַיִם

In one case alone the application of these rules produces three consecutive *zarqa*s. This is

2K 1:16 כֹּה־אָמַר יְהוָה יַעַן אֲשֶׁר־שָׁלַחְתָּ מַלְאָכִים לִדְרֹשׁ בְּבַעַל זְבוּב
אֱלֹהֵי עֶקְרוֹן

Elsewhere no more than two *zarqa*s occur together, and two consecutive *zarqa*s occur only after *revia*, except in two cases:

1S 2:15 גַּם בְּטֶרֶם יַקְטִרוּן אֶת־הַחֵלֶב

and also Is 45:1 (quoted in #258).

'Ṭifḥa' - טפחא

231. Also called טַרְחָא. The sign for this accent is a diagonal stroke below the stress syllable, sloping to the right (טִפְחָא). In most printed editions the stroke is curved (טִפְחָא).

Ṭifḥa is very common, occurring twice in most verses of the Bible, once before *atnaḥ* and once before *silluq*. In the Tiberian accentuation no distinction is made between these two positions, but in the Babylonian accentuation different signs are used: -ˇ- before *atnaḥ* and -ב- before *silluq*.

Ṭifḥa frequently appears with no servus, and rarely has more than one. The single servus is *merka*.

232. In fourteen cases two servi are used before *ṭifḥa*: *darga* and *merka kefulah* . *Darga* (also called שִׁישְׁלָא) is marked in most MSS by a zigzag stroke (דַּרְגָּא or even דַּרְגָּא) below the stress syllable. In some MSS and most printed editions, the stroke is curved (דַּרְגָּא). *Darga* is also used before other disjunctives. *Merka kefulah* (double *merka*, also called תְּרֵין חוּטְרִין) is used only before *ṭifḥa* (although the same sign is common in the accentuation of Rabbinic literature). *Darga* is used before *merka kefulah* in this combination. Since *darga* is most commonly used before *tevir*, it is assumed that *merka kefulah* is a variant of *tevir*, used as a conjunctive. In most

of the cases in which these two servi are used before *ṭifḥa*, they appear on successive syllables (as shown in the left hand column below). They are separated by one or more syllables only in the few cases shown in the right hand column.

Lev 10:1	אֲשֶׁר לֹא צִוָּה	Gen 27:25	וַיָּבֵא לוֹ יַיִן
Nu 14:3	הֲלוֹא טוֹב לָנוּ	Ex 5:15	לָמָּה תַעֲשֶׂה כֹה
Nu 32:42	וַיִּקְרָא לָה נֹבַח	Ez 14:4	נַעֲנֵיתִי לוֹ בָהּ (בא ק)
1K 10:3, 2C 9:2	אֲשֶׁר לֹא הִגִּיד	2C 20:30	וַיָּנַח לוֹ אֱלֹהָיו
1K 20:29	וַיַּחֲנוּ אֵלֶּה נֹכַח־אֵלֶּה		
Hab 1:3	וַיְהִי רִיב וּמָדוֹן		
Zech 3:2	הֲלוֹא זֶה אוּד		
Ezra 7:25	וְדִי לָא יָדַע		
Neh 3:38	וַיְהִי לֵב לָעָם		

233. In 8 cases *merka* occurs as a secondary accent on the same word as *ṭifḥa*, generally on an open syllable suitable for *ga*ᶜ*ya*. These cases are:

Lev 23:21	בְּכָל־מוֹשְׁבֹתֵיכֶם	2K 15:16	כָּל־הֶהָרוֹתֶיהָ
Jer 8:18	מַבְלִיגִיתִי	Ez 36:25	וּמִכָּל־גִּלּוּלֵיכֶם
Ez 44:6	מִכָּל־תּוֹעֲבוֹתֵיכֶם	1C 15:13	לְמַבָּרִאשׁוֹנָה
Dan 5:17	וּנְבִזְבְּיָתָךְ	Song 6:5	שֶׁהֵם

This last case shows a secondary accent on the prefixed particle -שֶׁ, a fairly common occurrence (#215, 241).

Disjunctives used to Divide the 'Ṭifḥa' Clause

234. The rules for the division of *ṭifḥa* clauses are similar to those for clauses ending with *zaqef* and *segolta*. If the main division in the *ṭifḥa* unit is on the word preceding *ṭifḥa*, it is marked by *tevir*, as

Gen 1:4 וַיַּרְא אֱלֹהִים אֶת־הָאוֹר

If the division is on the second word before *ṭifḥa*, it is also generally marked by *tevir*, as

Gen 3:10 וָאִירָא כִּי־עֵירֹם אָנֹכִי

Gen 22:12 וְלֹא חָשַׂכְתָּ אֶת־בִּנְךָ אֶת־יְחִידְךָ

But *revia* is sometimes used, particularly if one of the two words is long. In this case *tevir* is used on the word before *ṭifḥa*, as

Jos 9:17 וַיִּסְעוּ בְנֵי־יִשְׂרָאֵל וַיָּבֹאוּ אֶל־עָרֵיהֶם

If the main division is on the third word or further before *ṭifḥa*, it is always marked by *revia*, with *tevir* between it and the *ṭifḥa*, as

Gen 32:1 וַיַּשְׁכֵּם לָבָן בַּבֹּקֶר וַיְנַשֵּׁק לְבָנָיו וְלִבְנוֹתָיו

If necessary, *revia* may be repeated to mark further divisions before *ṭifḥa*, with *tevir* between the last *revia* and the *ṭifḥa*, as Jer 29:14 וְשַׁבְתִּי אֶת־שְׁבִיתְכֶם (שבותכם ק)

וְקִבַּצְתִּי אֶתְכֶם מִכָּל־הַגּוֹיִם וּמִכָּל־הַמְּקוֹמוֹת אֲשֶׁר הִדַּחְתִּי אֶתְכֶם שָׁם

However one *revia* can follow another only if three or more words occur between them. Where this is not the case, *pashṭa* is used instead of the first *revia* before the *ṭifḥa*, with *tevir* between it and the *ṭifḥa*, as

Dt 20:20 וּבָנִיתָ מָצוֹר עַל־הָעִיר אֲשֶׁר־הִוא עֹשָׂה עִמְּךָ מִלְחָמָה

This use of *pashṭa* is only possible, however, if it is separated from the *tevir* by two or more words. If this is not the case, *tevir* and not *pashṭa* is used instead of the first *revia* before *ṭifḥa*, so that in this situation, which is quite common, *ṭifḥa* is preceded by two *tevirs*, as

Is 37:24 וַתֹּאמֶר בְּרֹב רִכְבִּי אֲנִי עָלִיתִי מְרוֹם הָרִים

Two *tevirs* in succession appear only after *revia* , with three exceptions:

Qoh 4:8 --- גַּם־זֶה הֶבֶל וְעִנְיַן רָע

Qoh 6:2 --- זֶה הֶבֶל וָחֳלִי רָע

Jos 20:4 --- וְדִבֶּר בְּאָזְנֵי זִקְנֵי־הָעִיר הַהִיא

'Revia' - רביע

235. *Revia* is marked by a dot above the stress syllable (רְבִיעַ). In printed editions this dot is distinguished from the vowel points by its heavy square form, but this is not the case in most MSS.

Revia may have up to three servi. The first servus before *revia* is *munaḥ*, as

Gen 19:30 וַיֵּשֶׁב בָּהָר

The second servus before *revia* is *darga*, as

Gen 24:15 וְהִנֵּה רִבְקָה יֹצֵאת

In one exceptional verse most versions (A, L, S^1, etc.) show the servi of *revia* as two *munaḥs* (Is 45:1 quoted in #258). A third servus--also *munaḥ*--occurs only in the following cases:

Nu 4:14 אֲשֶׁר יְשָׁרְתוּ עָלָיו בָּהֶם

2S 21:2 לֹא מִבְּנֵי יִשְׂרָאֵל הֵמָּה

1K 19:21 וַיִּקַּח אֶת־צֶמֶד הַבָּקָר וַיִּזְבָּחֵהוּ

2K 20:3, Is 38:3 אֵת אֲשֶׁר הִתְהַלַּכְתִּי לְפָנֶיךָ

Is 5:25 וַיֵּט יָדוֹ עָלָיו וַיַּכֵּהוּ
Qoh 4:8 גַּם בֵּן וָאָח אֵין־לוֹ
Ezra 6:12 דִּי שַׁכִּן שְׁמֵהּ תַּמָּה

236. In five cases *munah* appears as a secondary accent in the same word as *revia*. In some cases (but not in all) it is marked on an open syllable suitable for *ga^{c}ya* (#326).
The cases are:

Gen 45:5	אַל־תֵּעָצְבוּ	Ex 32:31	אָנָּא
Zech 7:14	וְאֵסָעֲרֵם	Qoh 4:10	וְאִילוֹ
Dan 1:7	בֵּלְטְשַׁאצַּר		

Disjunctives used to Divide the 'Revia' Clause

237. The division of the textual unit ending with *revia* is marked by *legarmeh*, *geresh*, *telisha*, and *pazer*. The last three are also used to divide clauses ending with *pashta*, *tevir*, and *zarqa*, but *legarmeh* occurs (with rare exceptions) only before *revia*. *Legarmeh* is generally marked on the second word before *revia*, with the servus *munah* on the intervening word, as

Dt 14:28 מִקְצֵה ׀ שָׁלֹשׁ שָׁנִים

However *legarmeh* may stand immediately before *revia*, as

Gen 3:15 וְאֵיבָה ׀ אָשִׁית

Legarmeh is often the only disjunctive used in the *revia* clause but, if another division occurs, it is marked by *geresh*, as

Gen 27:1 וַיִּקְרָא אֶת־עֵשָׂו ׀ בְּנוֹ הַגָּדֹל

Occasionally two successive *legarmeh*s are used, preceded by *geresh*, as

Gen 19:14 וַיֵּצֵא לוֹט וַיְדַבֵּר ׀ אֶל־חֲתָנָיו ׀ לֹקְחֵי בְנֹתָיו

As a general rule, where several divisions are marked in the *revia* clause, and one is marked by *legarmeh*, it is preceded by *geresh*.

Disjunctives subordinate to *revia* (other than *legarmeh*) generally occur in the order *pazer*, *telisha*, *geresh*, with greater pausal value the farther they stand from *revia*. They occur in various combinations:

Geresh alone, as Ex 36:11 וַיַּעַשׂ לֻלְאֹת תְּכֵלֶת

As a general rule, *geresh* is used immediately before *revia* only where *revia* is preceded by two words, with the division immediately before the *revia*, as Gen 1:28 וַיֹּאמֶר לָהֶם אֱלֹהִים.

If there is only one word before *revia*, *geresh* is rarely used, unless the word marked by *revia* is very long, as

Lev 26:30 וְהִשְׁמַדְתִּ֞י אֶת־בָּמֹתֵיכֶ֗ם

2C 4:20 וְאֶת־הַמְּנֹר֞וֹת וְנֵרֹתֵיהֶ֗ם

Telisha and *geresh* before *revia*:

Is 7:4 וְאָמַרְתָּ֣ אֵלָ֠יו הִשָּׁמֵ֨ר וְהַשְׁקֵ֜ט אַל־תִּירָ֗א

Pazer and *geresh* before *revia*:

2S 11:1 וַיִּשְׁלַ֣ח דָּוִ֡ד אֶת־יוֹאָב֩ וְאֶת־עֲבָדָ֨יו עִמּ֜וֹ וְאֶת־כָּל־יִשְׂרָאֵ֗ל

Pazer, telisha and *geresh*:

2K 3:25

וְהֶעָרִ֣ים יַהֲרֹ֡סוּ וְכָל־חֶלְקָ֣ה טוֹבָ֠ה יַשְׁלִ֨יכוּ אִישׁ־אַבְנ֜וֹ וּמִלְא֗וּהָ

Pazer, telisha, geresh, and *legarmeh*:

Dt 13:7

כִּ֣י יְסִֽיתְךָ֡ אָחִ֣יךָ בֶן־אִמֶּ֠ךָ אוֹ־בִנְךָ֨ אוֹ־בִתְּךָ֜ א֣וֹ ׀ אֵ֣שֶׁת חֵיקֶ֗ךָ

There are a few cases in which different arrangements of these disjunctives subordinate to *revia* occur. If further divisions need to be marked, *pazer* is repeated.

'Pashṭa' and 'Yetiv' - יתיב, פשטא

238. These names usually designate different signs representing variant forms of the same accent, but the names יְתִיב, פַּשְׁטָא, and יְתִיב־פַּשְׁטָא may be applied to either form. The sign for *pashṭa* is postpositive--a diagonal stroke at the left side of the last letter of the word, above it, and pointing to the left. The stroke is straight in most MSS (פַּשְׁטָא֙), curved in most printed editions (פַּשְׁטָא֙). If the word has penultimate stress, the sign is repeated on the stress syllable (הַמֶּ֙לֶךְ֙). *Pashṭa* is nearly always subordinate to *zaqef*.

The Repetition of the 'Pashṭa' Sign

239. *Pashṭa* is the only accent sign in standard Tiberian MSS which is regularly repeated on a penultimate stress syllable. In standard printed editions, the *pashṭa* sign is repeated on every word in which the stressed vowel is not the last (i.e. every word with penultimate stress, including words with *pataḥ* "furtive"). Most early MSS - for instance L and C - follow the same system, but some MSS show a different convention.

In A, S, and some other MSS, the sign is only repeated where at least one letter stands between the two letters to be marked with the signs, as הַשְׁמִ֨יעַ֙ (Is 62:11), לְפָנֶ֨יךָ֙ (Is 58:8). Where this is not the case, the pashṭa sign is not repeated, as מִזְבֵּחַ֙ (Is 19:19), הֱטִיבֹתָ֙ (2K 10:30), יְרוּשָׁלַ֙ם (Is 52:1) וְשַׂמְתִּ֙הָ (Hos 2:5). This system of marking pashṭa is mentioned in some treatises, such as Qimḥi's ᶜEṭ Sofer, p. 31b. "When the two letters (on which the pashṭa signs would be marked) are separated only by one vowel, with no vowel letter, there is a difference of opinion. Some read two pashṭas, others only one, as in הָרִ֫ימִי בַכֹּ֙חַ (Is 40:9)".

In B and S^1, and some other MSS, pashṭa is not repeated not only where the two letters on which it would be marked are not separated by a third, but also in other situations as well, as לַחֹ֙דֶשׁ (B, Ex 12:18), מִשְׁפַּחַת֙ (B, Nu 3:33). This usage is not consistent, however, as pashṭa sometimes is repeated on such words.

In L^2 pashṭa is never repeated. Thus תָּבוֹאתָה֙ (Dt 33:16) זְבָחֵימוֹ֙ (Dt 32:38).

In some cases, where the position of the word stress might be in doubt, the pashṭa sign is repeated on a stressed final syllable, as שׁוּבָ֨לִ֙ (C, S^1, Jer 31:19), שָׁבֽ֨וּ֙ (S^1, 2C 25:12), וְכוֹבַ֨ע֙ (S^1, Ez 27:10).

In many MSS pointed in the expanded Tiberian system, pashṭa is repeated on every word in which the last letter does not represent the first consonant of the stress syllable, as בָּרְבִ֨יעִ֙י (Ez 1:1), כְּכַ֨ף֙ (Ez 1:7), גָּד֨וֹל֙ (Ez 1:4).

The Servi of 'Pashṭa'

240. *Pashṭa* may have up to six servi. The first servus before *pashṭa* is usually *mehuppak*. This is one of the *shofars* (#213), also called מַהְפָּךְ, שׁוֹפָר הָפוּךְ, or שׁוֹפָר מְהוּפָּךְ, and its sign seems to be in origin the sign for *shofar munaḥ* (-ֻ--) turned round (מְהוּפָּךְ). In most MSS and printed editions the sign has developed to a "v" shape on its side (מְהוּפָּךְ), but some MSS show a rounded form מְהוּפָּךְ, as noted by Eliahu ha-Levi in his book *Ṭuv Ṭaᶜam*, chapter 5: "The form of *mehuppak* is a *kaf* reversed, ⊂ . This is the form used in Ashkenazi texts, but in Sefardi texts the form is like *nun* reversed, ⌊ . For this reason it is called *shofar hafuk*."

Mehuppak appears as servus to *pashṭa* only where the two stressed syllables are separated by some sort of a vowel--at least a vocal *shewa*, as

Gen 1:7 בֵּ֤ין הַמַּ֙יִם֙

Gen 18:6 שְׁלֹ֤שׁ סְאִים֙

If the two stress syllables are not separated, the servus is *merka*, as

Gen 1:2 הָֽיְתָ֥ה תֹ֙הוּ֙

Lev 25:10 יוֹבֵ֥ל הִוא֙

This is still true even if the two words are separated by *paseq*, as

Jer 12:5 רַגְלִ֥ים ׀ רַ֙צְתָּה֙

241. In five cases *mehuppak* appears as a secondary accent on the same word as *pashṭa*. It is marked on an open syllable suitable for *ga*^{c}*ya*, which happens to be formed, in all cases, by the prefixed particle -שֶׁ (cf. #215, 233).

Song 1:7 שֶֽׁאָהֲבָה֙ Song 1:12 עַד־שֶׁ֤הַמֶּ֙לֶךְ֙
Song 3:4 שֶׁ֤הֲבֵיאתִיו֙ Qoh 1:7 שֶׁ֤הַנְּחָלִים֙
Qoh 7:10 שֶׁ֤הַיָּמִים֙

242. Where *pashṭa* has two servi, the first before *pashṭa* is *mehuppak* or *merka* (according to the rule given above). Where the second servus is marked on the first letter of its word, *munaḥ* is used, as

Gen 13:14 שָׂ֣א נָ֤א עֵינֶ֙יךָ֙

Ex 12:42 לֵ֣יל שִׁמֻּרִ֥ים הוּא֙

Where the second servus is not marked on the first letter of its word, *azla* (also called קַדְמָא) is used. The sign for this accent is a diagonal line pointing to the left. It is marked above the letter representing the first consonant of the stress syllable, and this is usually enough to distinguish it from *pashṭa* (which is marked by a similar stroke). Where both would be marked on the same letter, they are distinguished by the fact that *azla* is marked over the middle of the letter, *pashṭa* at the left of it. Thus

אֲשֶׁ֨ר (Dt 29:14) shows *azla* אֲשֶׁר֙ (Dt 29:11) shows *pashṭa*
וֶֽהֱשִׁיבְךָ֨ (Dt 28:68) shows *azla* לְבָבְךָ֙ (Dt 28:67) shows *pashṭa*

Azla appears as second servus before *pashṭa* in

Is 30:10 אֲשֶׁ֨ר אָמְר֤וּ לָרֹאִים֙

Gen 8:1 וַיַּעֲבֵר אֱלֹהִים רוּחַ

There is one exception to this general rule, in which the second servus before *pashṭa* is not marked on the first letter, but nevertheless *munaḥ* is used:

Est 9:15 °--- בְּיוֹם אַרְבָּעָה עָשָׂר

243. Where *pashṭa* has two servi, it may sometimes appear that the second before *pashṭa* has a certain pausal value, but not the first, as

Gen 7:13 בְּעֶצֶם הַיּוֹם הַזֶּה

2K 9:5 וְהִנֵּה שָׂרֵי הַחַיִל

Usually, however, the first servus before *pashṭa* appears to have the greater pausal value, as

Gen 12:10 וַיֵּרֶד אַבְרָם מִצְרַיְמָה

Gen 22:9 וַיִּבֶן שָׁם אַבְרָהָם

Rut 1:22 וְרוּת הַמּוֹאֲבִיָּה כַלָּתָהּ

In such cases it is suggested that the first servus, *mehuppak*, has been transformed from *geresh*. That is, the accentuation should be וירד אברם מצרימה, ויבן שם אברהם, ורות המואביה כלתה, but the *geresh* before *pashṭa* is replaced by *mehuppak*, since *geresh* is not used immediately before *pashṭa* unless the word bearing *pashṭa* is very long, as

Lev 9:7 וַעֲשֵׂה אֶת־חַטָּאתְךָ

Ex 9:14 אֲנִי שֹׁלֵחַ אֶת־כָּל־מַגֵּפֹתַי

Is 25:6 יְהוָה צְבָאוֹת לְכָל־הָעַמִּים

and some half dozen other cases in the whole Bible. This transformation would explain why the second servus and further before *pashṭa* are the same accents which function as the servi of *geresh*.

244. In eight places the two servi of *pashṭa* are marked on the same word, the second of them marked as a secondary accent generally on an open syllable suitable for *ga^cya* (#326). These cases are:

Lev 25:46	וּבְאַחֵיכֶם בְּנֵי־יִשְׂרָאֵל	Nu 20:1	כָּל־הָעֵדָה מִדְבַּר־צִן
Dt 8:16	הַמַּאֲכִלְךָ מָן	Lam 4:9	שֶׁהֵם יָזוּבוּ
Ez 43:11	וְכָל־צוּרֹתָו וְכָל־תּוֹרֹתָו	Dan 3:2	גְדָבְרַיָּא דְתָבְרַיָּא
Ezra 7:24	זַמָּרַיָּא תָרָעַיָּא	2C 35:25	בְּקִינוֹתֵיהֶם עַל־יֹאשִׁיָּהוּ

245. In one case, the two servi of *pashṭa*, *azla* and

mehuppak are marked on the same letter.

Ez 20:31 אַתֶּם נִטְמְאִים לְכָל־גִּלּוּלֵיכֶם

246. The servus in the third place before *pashṭa* is *telisha qeṭannah*. The sign for this accent is postpositive. In MSS it is marked by a small circle above the line תְּלִישָׁא. In printed texts the circle is joined to the letter by a small stroke (תְּלִישָׁא). The same sign, differentiated by its prepositive position, is used to mark the disjunctive *telisha gedolah* (#270). The two accents are sometimes distinguished as *telisha śemol* (*telisha* left, conjunctive) and *telisha yamin* (*telisha* right, disjunctive).

In standard Tiberian texts, *telisha qeṭannah* is not usually repeated on the stress syllable of words with penultimate stress, although this does occur occasionally--probably to point out the stress position where it might easily be mistaken, as וַיֹּאמְרוּ לוֹ (A, L, C, S^1, Jud 18:19), מֵתָה (L, S^1, Gen 48:7), שָׁבוּ (L, S^1, Jer 11:10). In a very few cases the sign is marked twice on the last syllable of the word to point out that the stress is final, as לָמָּה (N, Jer 44:7). In some printed editions, however, the sign is repeated on the stress syllable where this is penultimate, and this is regularly done in MSS with expanded Tiberian pointing.

Telisha qeṭannah is always followed by *azla*. Consequently where *pashṭa* has three servi, the second is always *azla*, whether it is marked on the first letter or no, as

Nu 18:19 בְּרִית מֶלַח עוֹלָם הוּא

Zech 14:4 וְנִבְקַע הַר הַזֵּיתִים מֵחֶצְיוֹ

247. The fourth, fifth and sixth servi before *pashṭa* are *munaḥ*s, as

Dt 28:49 יִשָּׂא יְהוָה עָלֶיךָ גּוֹי מֵרָחוֹק

2K 18:14

וַיִּשְׁלַח חִזְקִיָּה מֶלֶךְ־יְהוּדָה אֶל־מֶלֶךְ־אַשּׁוּר לָכִישָׁה לֵאמֹר חָטָאתִי

'Yetiv'

248. *Yetiv* has the same pausal value as *pashṭa*, but indicates a musical variant. It is used where the accent sign is to be placed on the first letter of the word on which *pashṭa* is expected, and no servi precede it. Thus:- Where the accent

stands on the first letter, *yetiv* is used, as

Nu 7:88 זֹ֚את חֲנֻכַּ֣ת הַמִּזְבֵּ֔חַ

Otherwise *pashṭa* is used, as

Nu 16:28 בְּזֹאת֙ תֵּֽדְע֔וּן

With no servus, *yetiv* is used, as

Gen 4:10 ק֚וֹל דְּמֵ֣י אָחִ֔יךָ

With a servus, *pashṭa* is used, as

Ex 32:18 אֵ֤ין קוֹל֙

The *yetiv* sign has the same form as that for *mehuppak*, and is also marked under the stress syllable, but is usually placed a little before the letter. It is characteristically differentiated from *mehuppak*, which is marked to the left of the vowel sign, by the fact that it is placed to the right. Thus in Dt 20:19 כִּ֚י מִמֶּ֣נּוּ תֹאכֵ֔ל shows *yetiv*, but כִּ֤י הָֽאָדָם֙ shows *mehuppak*. If there is no vowel sign under the letter, *mehuppak* is written under the middle of the letter, *yetiv* to its right. Thus in Lev 5:23 א֤וֹ אֶת־הָעֹ֙שֶׁק֙ אֲשֶׁ֣ר עָשָׁ֔ק א֚וֹ אֶת־הַפִּקָּד֔וֹן the first of the signs is *mehuppak*, the second *yetiv*.

249. *Mehuppak* and *yetiv* are also distinguished by the accents which follow them. *Mehuppak* is always followed by *pashṭa*. *Yetiv* is generally followed by *zaqef*. Since one *pashṭa* can follow another (where one is a transformation of *revia*, see #226), *yetiv* can follow *pashṭa*, as

Dt 11:30 אַחֲרֵי֙ דֶּ֚רֶךְ מְב֣וֹא הַשֶּׁ֔מֶשׁ

In the same way, *pashṭa* can follow *yetiv*, but even in this case *yetiv* is clearly distinguished if the *pashṭa* is preceded by *mehuppak*, as in Gen 22:16 יַ֚עַן אֲשֶׁ֤ר עָשִׂ֙יתָ֙ where the first sign is *yetiv*, the second *mehuppak*. When *yetiv* comes immediately before *pashṭa*, however, it can easily be taken for *mehuppak*. For this reason the Masorah lists the eleven cases where this occurs. They are

Lev 5:2	א֚וֹ בְנִבְלַ֙ת֙	Jer 14:14	שֶׁ֚קֶר הַנְּבִאִים֙
Dt 1:4	אֵ֚ת סִיחֹן֙	Dan 2:10	דִּ֚י כָּל־מֶ֙לֶךְ֙
Is 5:24	אֵ֚ת תּוֹרַת֙	Dan 7:27	דִּ֚י מַלְכְוָת֙
Is 30:32	כֹּ֚ל מַעֲבַר֙	Ezra 6:8	דִּ֚י מִדַּת֙
Jer 16:12	אִ֚ישׁ אַחֲרֵי֙	Ezra 9:4	כֹּ֚ל חָרֵד֙
Jer 22:30	אִ֚ישׁ יֹשֵׁב֙		

There is no case in the Bible where two *yetiv*s occur in succession.

Disjunctives used to Divide the 'Pashṭa' Clause

250. The same disjunctives are used to divide the textual unit ending in *pashṭa* as are used in that ending in *revia* (#237), but there are two differences in their use:

1) *Legarmeh* is not generally used before *pashṭa*, though it is common before *revia*.

2) *Geresh* may come immediately before *revia*, but, as noted above (#243), it rarely occurs immediately before *pashṭa*, and only where the word bearing *pashṭa* is long. Elsewhere *geresh* is transformed into the servus of *pashṭa*. Thus in Gen 43:3 the accentuation is הָעֵ֣ד הֵעִ֩ד בָּ֜נוּ הָאִ֤ישׁ לֵאמֹ֙ר

although הע֣ד הע֩ד ב֜נו הא֨יש לאמר֙

would be expected.

The disjunctives subordinate to *pashṭa* are *pazer*, *telisha*, and *geresh*, usually used in that order. They are used in various combinations:

1) *Geresh* alone

Lev 23:10 דַּבֵּ֞ר אֶל־בְּנֵ֤י יִשְׂרָאֵל֙

But in this situation, as already noted, *geresh* is usually transformed into the servus of *pashṭa*, as

Dt 9:21 וָאֶכֹּ֨ת אֹת֤וֹ טָח֙וֹן

2) *Telisha* and *geresh*

Gen 14:7 וַיָּשֻׁ֩בוּ וַיָּבֹ֜אוּ אֶל־עֵ֤ין מִשְׁפָּט֙

Or, with *geresh* transformed into the servus of *pashṭa*,

Is 43:10 לְמַ֣עַן תֵּ֠דְעוּ וְתַאֲמִ֨ינוּ לִ֤י וְתָבִ֙ינוּ֙

3) *Pazer* and *geresh*

Qoh 5:18 גַּ֣ם כָּל־הָאָדָ֡ם אֲשֶׁ֣ר נָתַן־ל֣וֹ הָאֱלֹהִ֩ים עֹ֨שֶׁר וּנְכָסִ֜ים
וְהִשְׁלִיטוֹ֙ לֶאֱכֹ֤ל מִמֶּ֙נּוּ֙

Or, with *geresh* transformed into the servus of *pashṭa*.

Jer 30:10 וְאַתָּ֡ה אַל־תִּירָ֩א עַבְדִּ֨י יַעֲקֹ֤ב נְאֻם־יְהוָה֙

4) *Pazer*, *telisha* and *geresh*

Ez 14:21 אַ֣ף כִּי־אַרְבַּ֣עַת שְׁפָטַ֣י ׀ הָרָעִ֡ים חֶ֠רֶב וְרָעָ֞ב וְחַיָּ֤ה רָעָה֙

Or, with *geresh* transformed into the servus of *pashṭa*,

Gen 22:2 וַיֹּ֡אמֶר קַח־נָ֠א אֶת־בִּנְךָ֨ אֶת־יְחִידְךָ֤ אֲשֶׁר־אָהַ֙בְתָּ֙

'Tevir' - תביר

251. *Tevir*, also called תְּבִירָא, is marked by a stroke (like *merka*) under the stress syllable, with a dot to the left of its centre: תְּבִ֛יר in MSS, תְּבִ֛יר in most printed editions. It is generally subordinate to *ṭifḥa*.

Tevir may be preceded by up to four servi. The first servus before *tevir* is generally *darga*, but *darga* is only used where the two stress syllables are separated by more than a single syllable - that is by at least one full vowel and one vocal *shewa*, otherwise *merka* is used. Thus in Gen 19:5 אַיֵּה הָאֲנָשִׁים two vowels and *shewa* occur between the two stress syllables, so *darga* is used, but in Dt 31:22 וַיִּכְתֹּב מֹשֶׁה only one vowel separates the two stress syllables, so the servus is *merka*.

In most situations a *shewa* plus a full vowel create enough separation between the two stress syllables for *darga* to be used. This occurs where the *shewa* is

1) at the beginning of a word Lev 19:9 לֹא תְכַלֶּה
Gen 19:24 הִמְטִיר עַל־סְדֹם

2) under a letter with *dagesh* "forte"
Dt 1:30 עָשָׂה אִתְּכֶם

3) the second of two *shewa*s within a word
Est 2:7 לְקָחָהּ מָרְדֳּכַי
Lev 19:5 וְכִי תִזְבְּחֻהוּ

4) a *ḥaṭef shewa* Gen 27:22 וַיִּגַּשׁ יַעֲקֹב
Nu 16:30 כִּי נִאֲצוּ

However a *shewa* following a "long" vowel within a word does not form a sufficient separation, so that *merka* is used, as

1K 15:7 הַמִּלְחָמָה הָיְתָה 2S 24:17 נָא יָדְךָ
2S 17:17 לֹא יוּכְלוּ Jer 42:6 שֹׁלְחִים אֹתְךָ

(Note that from the point of view of the early treatises, *shewa* in this situation is silent, see #379).

If *paseq* occurs between the servus and *tevir*, the servus is always *darga*, no matter how close the two stressed syllables are, as

Gen 42:13 אַחִים׀ אֲנַחְנוּ
2C 20:8 לְךָ׀ בָּהּ

252. There are about 15 exceptions to the above rule, in which *darga* is used, even though it is separated from *tevir* by only one syllable. In general in these cases the syllable which separates the two accents is suitable for *ga*[c]*ya*, and this may be the reason for the exception. In these cases, the accents are separated by:

1) A long vowel followed by *shewa*

Qoh 9:10 תִּמְצָ֤א יָדְךָ֖

2C 30:3 לֹ֤א יָכְל֖וּ

2C 18:33 (ידך ק) הֲפֹ֤ךְ יָדְיךָ֖ (but the parallel הֲפֹ֥ךְ יָדְךָ֖ in 1K 22:34 shows *merka*).

2) A vowel plus a *ḥaṭef-shewa* under a non-guttural

Ez 28:16 מָלֽ֤וּ תוֹכְךָ֖

Is 19:25 אֲשֶׁ֤ר בֵּֽרֲכ֖וֹ

3) The first syllable of an imperfect *qal* form of היה (which is suitable for *ga*

suitable for *ga*^{c}*ya*, see #355)

Gen 18:18 הָי֤וֹ יִֽהְיֶ֖ה

Lev 7:33 ל֤וֹ תִֽהְיֶ֛ה

But there are three other cases of the same situation in the Bible in which the servus is *merka*:

Is 24:13 כֹּ֥ה יִֽהְיֶ֖ה

Is 39:8 כִּ֥י יִֽהְיֶ֛ה

Ex 23:26 לֹ֥א תִֽהְיֶ֖ה

4) A syllable containing a "long" vowel joined by *maqqef* to the following word, which is stressed on the first syllable (a situation suitable for *ga*^{c}*ya*, see #337)

Jos 8:9, 12 בֵּ֤ין בֵּֽית־אֵ֖ל

2K 7:10, A וְהִנֵּ֤ה אֵֽין־שָׁ֛ם (L, וְהִנֵּ֥ה)

1S 30:17 מֵא֤וֹת אִֽישׁ־נַ֖עַר

Ex 21:35 יִגֹּ֤ף שֽׁוֹר־אִ֛ישׁ

Dt 14:10 אֲשֶׁ֤ר אֵֽין־ל֛וֹ

In the three other examples of this situation in the Bible, the servus is *merka*:

Amos 2:11 הַאַ֥ף אֵֽין־זֹ֖את

Lev 11:12 אֲשֶׁ֥ר אֵֽין־ל֛וֹ

Nu 25:15 אֻמּ֥וֹת בֵּֽית־אָ֛ב

5) A syllable marked with *ga*^{c}*ya*, either "phonetic" (#350)

2S 20:6 יֵֽרַ֤ע לָ֛נוּ

or "musical" (#324)

Hos 10:14 כְּשֹׁ֤ד שַֽׁלְמַ֛ן

Most of these exceptions are listed in the *Diqduqe ha-Ṭe*^{c}*amim* (Dotan, 1967, section 3), and often elsewhere in masoretic literature. There is one further exception to the general rule, in which the two accents are separated by a full vowel and a *ḥaṭef shewa*, but the servus is nevertheless *merka*:

Ezra 9:15 אֵ֥ין לַעֲמ֖וֹד

'Merka-tevir' and the Servi of 'Tevir'

253. In some hundred cases *merka* is marked as a secondary accent on the same word as *tevir*. (Of the secondary accents, the use of *munaḥ-zaqef*, #221, is more frequent). Unlike *munaḥ* with *zaqef*, *merka* can be used in this way even on the first letter of the word, but only in cases where the servus is marked on a long vowel, and is separated from the *tevir* by a vocal *shewa* alone. Examples of *merka-tevir* are:

Jud 9:44 פָּשְׁטוּ
Dt 13:16 אֶת־יֹשְׁבֵי
2S 4:7 וַיֵּלְכוּ

Merka may still occur if the two accents are separated by a *ḥaṭef shewa* under a non-guttural, as Ez 33:28, A וְשָׁמֲמוּ (L, S[1] וְשָׁמְמוּ) but not where they are separated by a *ḥaṭef shewa* under a guttural, by a full vowel, or more, as

Gen 30:25 כַּאֲשֶׁר
Gen 36:18 אָהֳלִיבָמָה
Jer 25:31 הָרְשָׁעִים

There are, however, three exceptions where *merka* is used before a *ḥaṭef shewa* under a guttural:

Ez 36:3 וַתַּעֲלוּ
2C 13:12 אַל־תִּלָּחֲמוּ
2C 31:9 עַל־הַכֹּהֲנִים

If another conjunctive is used before *tevir*, *merka* is not used in the same word as *tevir* (as Ex 12:22 לֹא תֵצְאוּ) except in three cases in which *darga* is used on the preceding word:

Song 2:7, 3:5 אִם־תָּעִירוּ וְאִם־תְּעוֹרְרוּ

and the similar passage in Song 8:4.

254. The rules for the use of *merka* and *tevir* on the same word are outlined in the *Diqduqe ha-Ṭeᶜamim* (Dotan, 1967, section 4), and often elsewhere in masoretic literature, but because of the similarity of the signs for *merka* and *gaᶜya*, the two became confused, and the usage was forgotten. Already in L *gaᶜya* occurs in most of the cases where *merka* is expected. The rules are generally followed faithfully in MSS written before 1000, but after that they were abandoned little by little, and are not followed in printed editions at all.

255. The rules for the second, third, and fourth servi before *tevir* are the same as for those before *pashṭa*. The second servus is *azla* or *munaḥ*, as

Dt 26:2 אֲשֶׁ֥ר תָּבִ֛יא מֵאַרְצְךָ֖

Nu 13:3 וַיִּשְׁלַ֨ח אֹתָ֥ם מֹשֶׁ֛ה

Gen 36:21 אֵ֣לֶּה אַלּוּפֵ֥י הַחֹרִ֛י

Is 1:5 עַ֣ל מֶ֥ה תֻכּ֛וּ

As with *pashṭa*, it may sometimes appear that the second of two servi before *tevir* has a certain pausal value which the other does not, as

Ex 15:25 שָׁ֣ם שָׂ֥ם ל֛וֹ

Generally, however, it is the first servus before *tevir* which seems to have the pausal value, as

Gen 12:17 וַיְנַגַּ֨ע יְהוָ֧ה ׀ אֶת־פַּרְעֹ֛ה

As with *pashṭa*, it is suggested that in these cases the word with the first servus before *tevir* should have had *geresh*, but that this *geresh* was transformed into a servus for musical reasons, since *geresh* is not used immediately before *tevir* unless the word bearing *tevir* is very long. This occurs in a few cases, as

Ez 43:11 וְיִשְׁמְר֞וּ אֶת־כָּל־צוּרָת֛וֹ

Nu 33:2 וַיִּכְתֹּ֣ב מֹשֶׁ֗ה אֶת־מוֹצָאֵיהֶ֛ם

Jos 3:17 הָאָר֜וֹן בְּרִית־יְהוָ֗ה בֶּחָרָבָ֛ה

256. In eight cases the two servi of *tevir* are marked on the same word, with the *azla* on an open syllable suitable for *ga*^{c}*ya*:

Is 30:16 וַתֹּ֨אמְר֥וּ לֹא־כִ֛י

Is 32:15 עַד־יֵ֨עָרֶ֥ה עָלֵ֛ינוּ

Job 1:15, 16, 17, 19 וָאִמָּ֨לְטָ֥ה רַק־אֲנִ֛י

Neh 11:7 בֶּן־קוֹלָיָ֥ה בֶן־מַעֲשֵׂיָ֖ה

2C 17:8 וַאֲדֹנִיָּ֣הוּ וְטוֹבִיָּ֣הוּ

257. The third servus before *tevir* is *telisha qeṭannah*, as

Dt 34:8 וַיִּבְכּ֨וּ בְנֵ֧י יִשְׂרָאֵ֛ל אֶת־מֹשֶׁ֖ה

The fourth is *munaḥ*, as

Amos 9:7 הֲל֣וֹא כִבְנֵי֩ כֻשִׁיִּ֨ים אַתֶּ֥ם לִ֛י

The rules for the disjunctives marking the divisions in the textual unit ending with *tevir* are the same as those given above (#250) for *pashṭa*.

'Zarqa' - זרקא

258. *Zarqa* is also known as צִינּוֹר or צִינּוֹרִי. The sign, זַרְקָא֮ in MSS, זַרְקָא֮ in printed editions, is postpositive, marked above the top left corner of the last letter of the word--possibly to distinguish it from *ṣinnorit* (a secondary accent in the poetic accentuation, see #372). In standard Tiberian MSS *zarqa* is normally not repeated on the stress syllable of words with penultimate accent, although this does occasionally occur, as אָנֹ֮כִי֮ (L and C, 2S 3:8), חֲנָ֮נִי֮ (L, 2C 19:2).

Zarqa is a disjunctive subordinate to *segolta*. *Segolta* regularly follows *zarqa* (or a pair of *zarqas*, as the accent can be repeated). There is only one exception to this:
Is 45:1 כֹּה־אָמַ֣ר יְהוָה֮ לִמְשִׁיחוֹ֮ לְכ֣וֹרֶשׁ אֲשֶׁר־הֶחֱזַ֣קְתִּי בִֽימִינוֹ֒ (so A, L, S[1], etc., C לְכ֣וֹרֶשׁ).
It is suggested that for exegetic reasons the *segolta* expected on לְכוֹרֶשׁ (which appears in R) was replaced by *munaḥ*. Early MSS read לְכוֹרֶשׁ here with *munaḥ*, and not *legarmeh*, and this is the only place in the Bible where two *munaḥs* are used before *revia*. See Rashi's remarks on this verse (#286).

259. *Zarqa* may have up to four servi. A single servus is usually *munaḥ*, as

Gen 1:28 וַיְבָ֣רֶךְ אֹתָם֮

There are, however, ten exceptions, in which *merka* is used:

Ex 6:6	אֱמֹ֥ר לִבְנֵֽי־יִשְׂרָאֵל֮	1C 5:18	וַחֲצִ֥י שֵֽׁבֶט־מְנַשֶּׁה֮
Ex 30:12	אֶת־רֹ֥אשׁ בְּנֵֽי־יִשְׂרָאֵל֮	1C 14:11	וַיַּעֲל֥וּ בְּבַֽעַל־פְּרָצִים֮
2S 7:7, 1C 17:6			בְּכֹ֥ל אֲשֶׁר־הִתְהַלַּכְתִּי֮
1K 1:19, 25	שׁ֥וֹר וּמְרִיא־וְצֹאן֮	1C 21:12	נִסְפֶּ֥ה מִפְּנֵֽי־צָרֶיךָ֮
Rut 4:4	נֶ֥גֶד הַיֹּשְׁבִים֮		

In these cases the word bearing *zarqa* is generally long and has *ga*[c]*ya*, but there are similar cases where *munaḥ*, and not *merka* occurs, as

Nu 26:20 וַיִּהְי֣וּ בְנֵֽי־יְהוּדָה֮

260. The second servus before *zarqa* is marked according to the rules for that before *pashṭa* or *tevir* (#242). If it is on the first letter of the word it is *munaḥ*, otherwise *azla*. Thus

Nu 6:21 זֹ֣את תּוֹרַ֣ת הַנָּזִיר֮ shows *munaḥ*

Gen 16:5 וַתֹּ֨אמֶר שָׂרַ֣י אֶל־אַבְרָם֮ shows *azla*

261. In two cases, however, the second servus before *zarqa* is marked on the first letter of the word, but is *merka*, not *munaḥ*. These cases are:

2C 6:32 לֹ֣א מֵעַמְּךָ֣ יִשְׂרָאֵל֮

2K 8:5 ה֣וּא מְסַפֵּ֣ר לַמֶּלֶךְ֮

If *zarqa* is repeated, and the second *zarqa* has two servi, the second servus before this *zarqa* is always *munaḥ*, even if it does not come on the first letter, as

Jos 22:5 ---֮ אֲשֶׁ֣ר צִוָּ֣ה אֶתְכֶם֮

Is 20:2 ---֮ בְּיַ֣ד יְשַׁעְיָ֣הוּ בֶן־אָמוֹץ֮

but this only occurs in five cases in the Bible.

262. Where *zarqa* has two servi, the first before *zarqa* is usually *munaḥ*, as

Ex 8:5, A וַיֹּ֤אמֶר מֹשֶׁ֣ה לְפַרְעֹה֮ (L ו֣יאמר)

However if the first servus before *zarqa* is followed by *paseq* (#283), that servus is *merka*, as

Ex 34:6 וַיַּעֲבֹ֨ר יְהוָ֥ה׀ עַל־פָּנָיו֮

There are two exceptions to this rule, in which the first of two servi before *zarqa* is *munaḥ*, even though it is followed by *paseq*:

Gen 37:22 וַיֹּ֨אמֶר אֲלֵהֶ֥ם ׀ רְאוּבֵן֮ 2K 4:13 ---֮ הִנֵּ֣ה חָרַ֣דְתְּ׀ אֵלֵינוּ֮

In the same way, if there is a *ga*ᶜ*ya* in the word bearing *zarqa*, the first of two servi before the *zarqa* is *merka*. Thus, with *ga*ᶜ*ya* on a closed syllable in a word of regular structure (#319)

Jer 18:18 לְכ֞וּ וְנַחְשְׁבָ֤ה עַל־יִרְמְיָהוּ֮

Ex 36:6 וַיַּעֲבִ֨ירוּ ק֤וֹל בַּֽמַּחֲנֶה֮

So also where the structure is not regular (#324)

Jos 11:8 וַיִּתְּנֵ֨ם יְהוָ֤ה בְּיַד־יִשְׂרָאֵל֮

Nu 10:10 וּבְי֨וֹם שִׂמְחַתְכֶ֤ם וּֽבְמוֹעֲדֵיכֶם֮

Also with *ga*ᶜ*ya* on a closed syllable with a long vowel (#337)

Jud 3:10 וַתְּהִ֨י עָלָ֤יו רֽוּחַ־יְהוָה֮

1C 5:1 וּבְנֵ֨י רְאוּבֵ֤ן בְּֽכוֹר־יִשְׂרָאֵל֮

Where *ga*ᶜ*ya* is used in an open syllable, the situation is less clear, since this category of *ga*ᶜ*ya* is not marked consistently in the early MSS. If all the words in which *ga*ᶜ*ya* could occur on an open syllable are considered, the servus before them is usually *merka*, as

Jos 23:16 אֶת־בְּרִ֨ית יְהוָ֤ה אֱלֹהֵיכֶם֮

Neh 8:15 וְיַעֲבִירוּ קוֹל בְּכָל־עָרֵיהֶם

There are four exceptions to this rule, in which the servus is *munaḥ*, even though the word bearing *zarqa* could have *ga*^{c}*ya* on an open syllable:

1S 23:25 וַיֵּלֶךְ שָׁאוּל וַאֲנָשָׁיו

2K 4:29 וְקַח מִשְׁעַנְתִּי בְיָדְךָ

Ez 10:9 וְהִנֵּה אַרְבָּעָה אוֹפַנִּים

Ex 10:3 וַיָּבֹא מֹשֶׁה וְאַהֲרֹן

However if the second servus before *zarqa* is *munaḥ*, then the first is also *munaḥ* in this situation even if there is *ga*^{c}*ya* on the word accented with *zarqa*, as

Nu 15:24 אִם מֵעֵינֵי הָעֵדָה

Lev 17:5 --- אֲשֶׁר הֵם זֹבְחִים

There are also eight exceptions to the general rule, in which the first of two servi before *zarqa* is *merka*, and not *munaḥ* as expected, even though *ga*^{c}*ya* does not occur on the word bearing *zarqa*:

Jos 18:14 אֲשֶׁר עַל־פְּנֵי בֵית־חֹרוֹן

2S 5:11, 1C 14:1 חִירָם מֶלֶךְ־צֹר מַלְאָכִים

2S 4:8 אֶת־רֹאשׁ אִישׁ־בֹּשֶׁת אֶל־דָּוִד

2S 3:8 הֲרֹאשׁ כֶּלֶב אָנֹכִי (L אנכי to show the penultimate stress)

Dan 6:13 קְרִבוּ וְאָמְרִין קֳדָם־מַלְכָּא

Nu 30:15 יַחֲרִישׁ לָהּ אִישָׁהּ

Dt 19:5 יָבֹא אֶת־רֵעֵהוּ בַיַּעַר

There are also two further exceptions in which the two servi, *azla* and *merka*, are marked on the same word:

Jud 21:21 אִם־יֵצְאוּ בְנוֹת־שִׁילוֹ

Neh 12:44 לָאוֹצָרוֹת לַתְּרוּמוֹת

There is one further example in which the two servi are marked on the same word, but here they are followed by *paseq*, so that it is not properly included among the exceptions to the rule.

Lev 10:12 וְאֶל־אִיתָמָר בָּנָיו

263. These rules for the servi of *zarqa* and a list of exceptions to them, occur in the *Diqduqe ha-Ṭe*^{c}*amim* (Dotan, 1967, section 9) and often elsewhere in the masoretic literature. However neither the rules nor the exceptions are given completely.

The MSS show different systems of marking the two servi before *zarqa*. In some MSS (e.g. C) the first of two servi before *zarqa* is always *munaḥ*. In some (e.g. S) the second of two servi is always *munaḥ*. The *Sefer ha-Ḥillufim* lists many variations between bA and bN in the servi of *zarqa*, and the printed editions show many variants when compared to the MSS.

264. The rules for the third and fourth servi before *zarqa* are the same as for those before *pashṭa* and *tevir* (#246), that is, the third is *telisha qeṭannah*, as

1C 21:15 וַיִּשְׁלַח הָאֱלֹהִים מַלְאָךְ לִירוּשָׁלִַם

and the fourth is *munaḥ*, as

Ex 17:6 הִנְנִי עֹמֵד לְפָנֶיךָ שָּׁם עַל־הַצּוּר

Similarly the rules for the disjunctives used to divide the *zarqa* clause are the same as those used to divide clauses ending in *pashṭa* or *tevir* (#250).

'Geresh' and 'Gershayim' - גרש, גרשים

265. *Geresh*, also called טֶרֶס, is one of the disjunctives subordinate to *revia*, *pashṭa*, *tevir*, and *zarqa*. It appears in two forms, both marked above the stress syllable: a single diagonal stroke, pointing right (גֶּרֶשׁ in MSS, גֶּרֶשׁ in printed texts), or a double stroke, *gershayim* or double *geresh* (דָּבָר in MSS, דָּבָר in printed texts). These two forms represent variations in the musical motif of the accent, and have the same pausal value. In some MSS--mostly those with expanded Tiberian vocalization--the single *geresh* sign is used in all cases, and *gershayim* is not distinguished.

Geresh is marked on a word when it has penultimate stress, or when it is preceded by *azla*. *Gershayim* is used when the word has final stress, and is preceded either by no servus at all, or by *munaḥ*. Thus *geresh* occurs

1) On a word with penultimate stress
   - with no servus Gen 14:7 וַיָּבֹאוּ
   - with *munaḥ* Dt 5:24 (21) הֵן הֶרְאָנוּ
2) With preceding *azla*, on a word where the stress is
   - penultimate Gen 11:31 וַיִּקַּח תֶּרַח
   - or final Gen 22:6 וַיִּקַּח אַבְרָהָם

Gershayim occurs on words with final stress

1) with no servus Ex 12:17 וּשְׁמַרְתֶּם
2) with preceding *munaḥ* Dt 26:12 כִּי תְכַלֶּה
   Ex 3:16 לֵךְ וְאָסַפְתָּ

266. The rules for the servi of *geresh* are the same as those for the second servus before *pashṭa*, *tevir*, or *zarqa*: If the servus is marked on the first letter of the word it is *munaḥ*, otherwise it is *azla*. However if the servus is preceded by *telisha qeṭannah*, it is *azla* in all cases, since *telisha qeṭannah* is always followed by *azla* (#246), as

Nu 25:14 וְשֵׁם אִישׁ יִשְׂרָאֵל

Jud 3:16 וַיַּעַשׂ לוֹ אֵהוּד

267. The second servus before *geresh* is *telisha qeṭannah*. Any servus before that is *munaḥ*, as

Dt 1:19 אֵת כָּל־הַמִּדְבָּר הַגָּדוֹל וְהַנּוֹרָא הַהוּא

Jer 8:1

וְיֹצִיאוּ (יוציאו ק) אֶת־עַצְמוֹת מַלְכֵי־יְהוּדָה וְאֶת־עַצְמוֹת־שָׂרָיו
וְאֶת־עַצְמוֹת הַכֹּהֲנִים

'Azla-geresh' on One Word

268. *Azla* is often marked as a secondary accent on the word bearing *geresh*. This occurs under conditions similar to those governing the marking of *munaḥ* on the word bearing *zaqef*, or *merka* on the word bearing *tevir* (#221, 253).

If there is no servus before the word bearing *geresh*, and if this word contains an open syllable suitable for *ga*^{c}*ya*, (#326), and this syllable is not the first syllable, then *azla* is likely to be marked on that word, and not *ga*^{c}*ya*. The combination *azla-geresh* generally occurs where the *geresh* is subordinate to *pashṭa*, *tevir*, or *zarqa*, but not where it is subordinate to *revia*. Compare, for instance, the use of *azla-geresh*

in Jer 25:9 וַהֲבִאֹתִים עַל־הָאָרֶץ הַזֹּאת

Ex 16:15 וַיֹּאמְרוּ אִישׁ אֶל־אָחִיו

to the use of *ga*^{c}*ya* and *gershayim* in

Is 56:7 וַהֲבִיאוֹתִים אֶל־הַר קָדְשִׁי

Gen 11:2 וַיֹּאמְרוּ אִישׁ אֶל־רֵעֵהוּ

There are, however, a few cases in which *azla-geresh* is subordinate to *revia*, generally when the word on which the combination is used is long, and is preceded by *telisha qeṭannah*, as

1K 12:24 לֹא־תַעֲלוּ וְלֹא־תִלָּחֲמוּן עִם־אֲחֵיכֶם בְּנֵי־יִשְׂרָאֵל

also the similar case in

2C 11:4 לֹא־תַעֲלוּ וְלֹא־תִלָּחֲמוּ עִם־אֲחֵיכֶם

or where it is preceded by *telisha gedolah*, as

Ez 31:12 אֶל־הֶהָרִים וּבְכָל־גֵּאָיוֹת נָפְלוּ דָלִיּוֹתָיו

But the combination does occasionally occur where no *telisha* precedes, as

Dt 34:11 לְכָל־הָאֹתֹת וְהַמּוֹפְתִים

Dt 8:15 הַמּוֹלִיכְךָ בַּמִּדְבָּר הַגָּדֹל וְהַנּוֹרָא

269. There are also some exceptions to the general rule where the word bearing *geresh* is subordinate to *pashṭa*, *tevir*, or *zarqa*. In such cases *azla-geresh* is expected, but is sometimes not marked. Thus where the word bearing *geresh* is of fully regular structure, suitable for *ga*ᶜ*ya* on a closed syllable (#319) this *ga*ᶜ*ya* is preferred to *azla*, as

2C 24:13 וַיַּעֲמִידוּ אֶת־בֵּית הָאֱלֹהִים

However if the structure is not fully regular (#322), *azla* is preferred to *ga*ᶜ*ya*, as

Ez 31:16 וַיִּנָּחֲמוּ בְּאֶרֶץ תַּחְתִּית

Sometimes *ga*ᶜ*ya* is preferred to *azla* on a closed syllable where the structure is non-regular (#324), as

1S 17:26 אֶל־הָאֲנָשִׁים הָעֹמְדִים עִמּוֹ

Sometimes *shewa-ga*ᶜ*ya* is preferred to *azla*, as

Jer 38:10 וְהַעֲלִיתָ אֶת־יִרְמְיָהוּ הַנָּבִיא

Jos 10:24 כְּהוֹצִיאָם אֶת־הַמְּלָכִים הָאֵלֶּה

In some cases *ga*ᶜ*ya* and *azla* are both marked on the word bearing *geresh* (a phenomenon which does not occur with *munaḥ-zaqef*), as

Nu 27:11 וְהָיְתָה לִבְנֵי יִשְׂרָאֵל

1S 8:16 וְאֶת־שִׁפְחוֹתֵיכֶם וְאֶת־בַּחוּרֵיכֶם הַטּוֹבִים

Sometimes *ga*ᶜ*ya* on a more distant syllable (#328) is preferred to *azla* on a syllable closer to *geresh*, as

Neh 4:7 וָאַעֲמִיד מִתַּחְתִּיּוֹת לַמָּקוֹם (instead of וָאַעֲמִיד)

There are also a few other cases of exception, as

Ez 16:3 וְאָמַרְתָּ כֹּה־אָמַר אֲדֹנָי יְהוִה

Jer 5:19 וַתַּעַבְדוּ אֱלֹהֵי נֵכָר

'Telisha (gedolah)' - תלישא גדולה

270. *Telisha* is one of the accents subordinate to *revia*, *pashṭa*, *tevir*, or *zarqa*. It is prepositive, apparently to distinguish it from *telisha qeṭannah*, which is postpositive

(#246). The sign (like that of *telisha qeṭannah*) is a small circle תְּ֠לִישָׁא to which a stroke is added in printed texts תְּ֠לִישָׁא. If this accent is marked on a group of words joined by *maqqef* to form a single accent unit, it is marked on the last of them, as Nu 18:9 כָּל־קָרְבָּנָם

In MSS with standard Tiberian pointing the *telisha* sign is generally not repeated on the stress syllable, although there are exceptions, such as הוֹצִיאִי (L, Jos 2:3, S^1 has הוֹצִיאִי) וּמָאַסְתִּי (S^1, 2K 23:27), וּמִכּוּתָה (S^1, 2K 17:24). In standard printed editions the sign is never repeated, but there are editions in which every accent sign which is not marked on the stress syllable is repeated, and in these the *telisha* sign is repeated wherever the first letter of the word does not represent the first consonant of the stress syllable - and so even where the first vowel is *shewa* and the second vowel is stressed, as כְּכֹל (Nu 8:20). *Telisha* is also repeated in most MSS with expanded Tiberian pointing.

271. *Telisha gedolah* and *telisha qeṭannah* have similar musical motifs, and for this reason there are many variants in the marking of them in the MSS and printed editions. Probably for the same reason, *telisha gedolah* and *telisha qeṭannah* are always separated by at least one other accent, with one exception only:

2S 14:32 בֹּא הֵנָּה וְאֶשְׁלְחָה אֹתְךָ אֶל־הַמֶּלֶךְ

Neither *telisha gedolah* nor *telisha qeṭannah* is repeated on successive words.

272. In five cases in the Bible, *telisha gedolah* and *geresh* are marked on the same word. In printed editions, the *telisha* sign is marked at the beginning of the word, and the *geresh* sign on the stress syllable, even though the reader is warned to read the *geresh* before the *telisha*. In MSS the accent signs are marked in the order in which they are to be read, with the *geresh* before the *telisha*. Thus in MSS

Ez 48:10 וּלְאֵלֶּה

Zeph 2:15 זֹאת

Lev 10:4 קִרְבוּ

Gen 5:29 זֶה

2K 17:13 שֻׁבוּ

but in printed editions ז֜֠את, ה֠לְאֵלֶּה etc.
This order of these two accents is surprising, since where they are subordinate to *pashṭa*, *tevir*, or *zarqa*, *telisha* usually precedes *geresh* (#237).

273. *Telisha* may have up to five servi, all *munaḥ*s, as

Gen 17:8	וְנָתַתִּ֣י ֠לְךָ
Ex 18:21	וְאַתָּ֣ה תֶחֱזֶ֣ה מִכָּל־֠הָעָם
Ez 47:12	וְעַל־הַנַּ֣חַל יַעֲלֶ֣ה עַל־שְׂפָת֣וֹ מִזֶּ֣ה׀ וּמִזֶּ֣ה׀ כָּל־עֵֽץ־֠מַאֲכָל

'Pazer' - פזר

274. There are two forms of *pazer*, *pazer gadol* (also called, in late texts, קַרְנֵי פָרָה or עֶגְלָה) which is marked in MSS by a "v" shaped sign above the stress syllable, (פָּזֵ֟ר), and in printed editions by the same, with circles added (פָּזֵ֟ר), and *pazer qaṭan*, or simply *pazer*, marked in MSS by a "T" shape on its side (פָּזֵ֡ר), and in printed texts by an inverted "h" shape (פָּזֵ֡ר). In masoretic treatises, *pazer gadol* is described as being "like *ṭet*" in form (ט = ˅) and *pazer qaṭan* as "like *ṣade*" (ץ = ץ, a form found in many MSS). The signs for both forms of *pazer* are marked above the stress syllable.

Pazer is used as a disjunctive subordinate to *revia*, *pashṭa*, *tevir*, or *zarqa*.

Pazer gadol occurs only sixteen times in the Bible. It never has fewer than two servi, and is usually preceded by a long string of them. The first servus before *pazer gadol* is *galgal* (גַּלְגַּל, also called יֶרַח בֶּן יוֹמוֹ or אוֹפַן in late treatises). This is marked by a sign below the stress syllable - a semicircle open at the top in MSS, (גַּלְגַּ֪ל), a "v" shape in printed texts (גַּלְגַּ֪ל). All other servi of *pazer gadol* are *munaḥ*s.

275. *Pazer gadol* occurs in the Bible as follows:

with two servi

1. Nu 35:5 אֶת־פְּאַת־קֵ֣דְמָה אַלְפַּ֪יִם בָּאַמָּ֟ה
2. 2C 24:5 צְא֣וּ לְעָרֵ֪י יְהוּדָ֟ה
3. Neh 13:5 וְשָׁ֣ם הָ֪יוּ לְפָנִ֟ים
4. Neh 5:13 כָּ֣כָה יְנַ֪עֵר הָאֱלֹהִ֟ים

with three servi

5. 2K 10:5 וַיִּשְׁלַ֣ח אֲשֶׁר־עַל־הַבַּ֣יִת וַאֲשֶׁ֪ר עַל־הָעִ֟יר

6. Jer 38:25 וּבָאוּ אֵלֶיךָ וְאָמְרוּ אֵלֶיךָ
7. 2C 35:7 וַיָּרֶם יֹאשִׁיָּהוּ לִבְנֵי הָעָם
8. Est 7:9 גַּם הִנֵּה־הָעֵץ אֲשֶׁר עָשָׂה הָמָן
9. Neh 13:15 וּמְבִיאִים הָעֲרֵמוֹת וְעֹמְסִים עַל־הַחֲמֹרִים
with four servi
10. Neh 1:6 תְּהִי נָא אָזְנְךָ־קַשֶּׁבֶת וְעֵינֶיךָ פְתוּחוֹת
11. Jer 13:13 הִנְנִי מְמַלֵּא אֶת־כָּל־יֹשְׁבֵי הָאָרֶץ הַזֹּאת
12. 2S 4:2 וּשְׁנֵי אֲנָשִׁים שָׂרֵי־גְדוּדִים הָיוּ בֶן־שָׁאוּל
with five servi
13. Jos 19:51 אֲשֶׁר נִחֲלוּ אֶלְעָזָר הַכֹּהֵן וִיהוֹשֻׁעַ בִּן־נוּן
14. 1C 28:1 שָׂרֵי הַשְּׁבָטִים וְשָׂרֵי הַמַּחְלְקוֹת הַמְשָׁרְתִים אֶת־הַמֶּלֶךְ
with six servi
15. Ez 48:21 וְהַנּוֹתָר לַנָּשִׂיא מִזֶּה וּמִזֶּה לִתְרוּמַת־הַקֹּדֶשׁ וְלַאֲחֻזַּת הָעִיר
16. Ezra 6:9 וּבְנֵי תוֹרִין וְדִכְרִין וְאִמְּרִין לַעֲלָוָן לֶאֱלָהּ שְׁמַיָּא

The reason for the use of *pazer gadol* in these verses is described in the *Horayat ha-Qore* p.91 (Dérenbourg, 1870, p.400) "They say that *pazer gadol* is marked in these cases because (the words on which it is marked in) these verses require special emphasis so the voice was raised more than usual, making (ordinary *pazer* into) *pazer gadol*.

276. *Pazer* (*qaṭan*) is a common accent. It may have up to six servi, all *munaḥ*s, as Ex 28:27 וְנָתַתָּה אֹתָם
Dt 22:6 כִּי יִקָּרֵא קַן־צִפּוֹר לְפָנֶיךָ
Est 2:15 וּבְהַגִּיעַ תֹּר־אֶסְתֵּר בַּת־אֲבִיחַיִל דֹּד מָרְדֳּכַי

In one case, אָנָּא (Gen 50:17) the servus *munaḥ* is marked as a secondary accent on the word bearing *pazer*.

Pazer is frequently repeated, especially in lists of personal names, as
Neh 12:36 וְאֶחָיו שְׁמַעְיָה וַעֲזַרְאֵל מִלְלַי גִּלְלַי מָעַי נְתַנְאֵל וִיהוּדָה
1C 15:18 זְכַרְיָהוּ בֵּן וְיַעֲזִיאֵל וּשְׁמִירָמוֹת וִיחִיאֵל וְעֻנִּי אֱלִיאָב וּבְנָיָהוּ
וּמַעֲשֵׂיָהוּ וּמַתִּתְיָהוּ וֶאֱלִיפְלֵהוּ וּמִקְנֵיָהוּ וְעֹבֵד אֱדֹם

'*Legarmeh*' - לגרמיה

277. The full name of this accent is "*munaḥ legarmeh*", that is "(The motif of) *munaḥ* (used) by itself (as a disjunctive)". It is marked by the *munaḥ* sign under the stress syllable, with *paseq* following the word. The corresponding accent in the Babylonian system, *nigda*, is marked by its own sign, נִיגְדָא, and similarly in Palestinian texts the sign for the

corresponding accent is distinct from that for any of the conjunctives. The Tiberian poetic accentuation shows three similar signs, formed from the sign for a conjunctive followed by *paseq*: these are *mehuppak legarmeh* and *azla legarmeh* (#370), and *shalshelet gedolah* (also used as a disjunctive in the 21 books, see #229) which contrasts in the poetic accentuation with the conjunctive *shalshelet qeṭannah* (#371).

Paseq is marked by a vertical stroke. In MSS it is usually shorter than an average letter, and is marked in the upper half of the line, although it may be marked in the middle of the line or lower down: פָּסֶק׀, פָּסֶק׀. In printed texts it occupies the whole height of the letter.

278. *Legarmeh* is usually used as a minor disjunctive subordinate to *revia*. In this situation the conjunctive *munaḥ* generally occurs between *legarmeh* and *revia*, as

Gen 41:5 וְהִנֵּ֣ה ׀ שֶׁ֣בַע שִׁבֳּלִ֗ים

Gen 7:2 מִכֹּ֣ל ׀ הַבְּהֵמָ֣ה הַטְּהוֹרָ֗ה

Sometimes two conjunctives stand between *legarmeh* and *revia*, as

Gen 31:29 אֶ֣מֶשׁ ׀ אָמַ֧ר אֵלַ֣י לֵאמֹ֗ר

and sometimes *legarmeh* stands immediately before *revia*, as

Ex 30:13 זֶ֣ה ׀ יִתְּנ֗וּ

Lev 13:3 הָפַ֣ךְ ׀ לָבָ֗ן

Where *paseq* is expected immediately before *revia*, it is converted into *legarmeh*, as

Jos 5:14 וַיֹּ֣אמֶר ׀ ל֗א

2K 2:12 אָבִ֣י ׀ אָבִ֗י

The Masorah notes only one case in which *paseq* is used immediately before *revia*:

Is 42:5 הָאֵ֣ל ׀ יְהוָ֗ה

Legarmeh can be repeated, as

Gen 7:23 וַיִּ֜מַח אֶֽת־כָּל־הַיְק֣וּם ׀ אֲשֶׁ֣ר ׀ עַל־פְּנֵ֣י הָאֲדָמָ֗ה

279. *Legarmeh* precedes *revia* in the vast majority of cases, but in the following cases, this accent is subordinate to other disjunctives:

1) *Geresh* - 11 cases

Gen 28:9 אֶֽת־מָחֲלַ֣ת ׀ בַּת־יִשְׁמָעֵ֜אל בֶּן־אַבְרָהָ֝ם

1S 14:3 אִֽי־כָב֣וֹד ׀ בֶּן־פִּֽינְחָ֜ס בֶּן־עֵלִ֝י

1S 14:47 בְּמוֹאָ֣ב ׀ וּבִבְנֵֽי־עַמּ֜וֹן וּבֶאֱד֝וֹם

2S 13:32 יוֹנָדָב בֶּן־שִׁמְעָה אֲחִי־דָוִד

2K 18:17 אֶת־תַּרְתָּן וְאֶת־רַב־סָרִיס וְאֶת־רַבְשָׁקֵה מִן־לָכִישׁ

(A reads אֶת־תַּרְתָּן)

Jer 4:19 מֵעַי מֵעַי אחולה (אוחילה ק)

(The first accent is *legarmeh*, the second *azla-paseq*)

Jer 38:11 וַיִּקַּח עֶבֶד־מֶלֶךְ אֶת־הָאֲנָשִׁים

Jer 40:11 אֲשֶׁר־בְּמוֹאָב וּבִבְנֵי־עַמּוֹן וּבֶאֱדוֹם

Ez 9:2 בָּאִים מִדֶּרֶךְ־שַׁעַר הָעֶלְיוֹן

Haggai 2:12 הֵן יִשָּׂא־אִישׁ בְּשַׂר־קֹדֶשׁ

2C 26:15 וַיַּעַשׂ בִּירוּשָׁלַםִ חִשְּׁבֹנוֹת

2) *Pashta* - 3 cases

Lev 10:6 רָאשֵׁיכֶם אַל־תִּפְרָעוּ וּבִגְדֵיכֶם לֹא־תִפְרֹמוּ

Lev 21:10 אֲשֶׁר־יוּצַק עַל־רֹאשׁוֹ שֶׁמֶן הַמִּשְׁחָה

Rut 1:2 וְשֵׁם שְׁנֵי־בָנָיו מַחְלוֹן וְכִלְיוֹן

3) *Tevir* - 1 case

Is 36:2 וַיִּשְׁלַח מֶלֶךְ־אַשּׁוּר אֶת־רַבְשָׁקֵה מִלָּכִישׁ יְרוּשָׁלַ͏ְמָה

4) *Pazer* - 2 cases

Dan 3:2 לְמִכְנַשׁ לַאֲחַשְׁדַּרְפְּנַיָּא

Neh 8:7 וְשֵׁרֵבְיָה יָמִין

280. Apart from these cases, *legarmeh* comes only before *revia*. Thus every case of *munah* followed by the *paseq* stroke occurring before *revia* is *legarmeh*, except for that at Is 42:5 (as noted in #278). Where the vertical stroke is used after any other conjunctive, and also after *munah* before any other disjunctive (save for the cases listed in #279) it represents *paseq* following a conjunctive. The Masorah lists all cases of *paseq* in the Bible (see the accurate list in Wickes, 1887, p. 127-129). Some MSS - particularly those with expanded Tiberian pointing - mark every case of the vertical stroke as *paseq* (פ̇ ,פס̇) or *legarmeh* (לג̇ ,לגר̇). In some MSS in which this is not done systematically, the stroke is identified in cases where confusion is likely, as in the Mp of L, where the note לגר̇ is given against the two cases where this accent precedes *pazer* (#279.4), and the note פסק̇ is given at Is 42:5.

281. A single servus before *legarmeh* is *merka*, as

2K 1:13 וַיִּכְרַע עַל־בִּרְכָּיו

Ex 14:10 וְהִנֵּה מִצְרַיִם

282. *Legarmeh* has two servi in only five cases. The first is *merka*, and the second - where it comes on the first letter - is *munaḥ*, as

1S 27:1 כִּ֣י הִמָּלֵ֥ט אִמָּלֵ֣ט ׀

Where the second servus comes on the second letter, and the first vowel is *shewa*, the second servus is *merka*, as

Ez 8:6 אֲשֶׁ֥ר בֵּ֥ית יִשְׂרָאֵ֣ל ׀

In other cases where the second servus does not come on the first letter, *azla* is used:

1K 14:21, 2C 12:13 וּשְׁבַ֨ע עֶשְׂרֵ֥ה שָׁנָ֣ה ׀

Qoh 6:2 וְֽאֵינֶ֨נּוּ חָסֵ֥ר לְנַפְשׁ֣וֹ ׀

However there is much variation in MSS and printed texts in the marking of either one or two servi before *legarmeh*.

'Paseq' - פסק

283. As already noted (#277), *paseq* (or פְּסִיק) is marked by a vertical stroke between one word and the next. It is marked after a word with a conjunctive accent, and shows that a slight pause should be made in the reading, but not pause enough to require a disjunctive accent. It seems probable that *paseq* was established after the system of conjunctives and disjunctives, as it completes it. If so, the lateness of its introduction would explain the lack of system in its use.

Paseq is one of the מבטלים--phenomena which nullify the normal rules for the use of *rafe* in *begad-kefat* letters at the beginning of a word (#400). Thus in אֹת֣וֹ ׀ בָּאֵ֗שׁ (Dt 9:21) *bet* has *dagesh*, even though it follows a word which ends in a vowel and has a conjunctive accent, because the words are separated by *paseq*. *Paseq* may also affect the choice of a conjunctive, as with *tevir* (#251) and *zarqa* (#262). Its effect here can be described in general terms as causing the choice of the conjunctive used where many syllables separate conjunctive and disjunctive, rather than that used where a few separate them. The rules for *paseq* are comprehensively outlined in the *Diqduqe ha-Ṭeᶜamim* (Dotan, 1967, section 16).

284. Wickes recognizes two classes of *paseq* (Wickes, 1887, p. 122); ordinary and extraordinary.

1) Ordinary *paseq* may occur after any conjunctive. It is used to separate two words for a variety of reasons.

(i) Where one word ends, and the next begins, with the same consonant, *paseq* is used to avoid running the words together, as

1C 22:3 וּבַרְזֶ֣ל ׀ לָרֹ֗ב

Neh 2:12 וַאֲנָשִׁ֣ים ׀ מְעַט֮

So also where the sounds are similar but not identical, as

Nu 21:1 וַיִּ֥שְׁבְּ ׀ מִמֶּ֖נּוּ

(ii) *Paseq* separates similar or identical words, as

Ex 16:5 י֥וֹם ׀ י֖וֹם

Gen 22:11 אַבְרָהָ֣ם ׀ אַבְרָהָ֑ם

Is 21:2 הַבּוֹגֵ֤ד ׀ בּוֹגֵד֙ וְהַשּׁוֹדֵ֣ד ׀ שׁוֹדֵ֔ד

Dt 7:26 שַׁקֵּ֧ץ ׀ תְּשַׁקְּצֶ֛נּוּ וְתַעֵ֥ב ׀ תְּתַֽעֲבֶ֖נּוּ

Ez 3:27 הַשֹּׁמֵ֤עַ ׀ יִשְׁמָע֙ וְהֶחָדֵ֣ל ׀ יֶחְדָּ֔ל

(iii) *Paseq* is used where the context might suggest that words should go together, but the correct sense requires that they be separated, as

Gen 18:15 וַיֹּ֥אמֶר ׀ לֹ֖א (not וַיֹּאמֶר לוֹ)

Gen 18:21 עָשׂ֣וּ ׀ כָּלָ֑ה (כָּלָה is not the object of עָשׂוּ)

(iv) *Paseq* is used to avoid irreverent use of the divine name, as

Is 37:24 חֵרַ֣פְתָּ ׀ אֲדֹנָ֗י

(v) *Paseq* is used to mark separation for emphasis, as

Ex 15:18 יְהוָ֥ה ׀ יִמְלֹ֖ךְ

Dt 6:4 יְהוָ֥ה ׀ אֶחָֽד

285. 2) Extraordinary *paseq* (Wickes, 1887, p. 124) is used to mark a slight pause in a series of conjunctives which could not otherwise be marked. Thus, before *pashṭa*, *tevir*, and *zarqa*:

Gen 1:5 וַיִּקְרָ֨א אֱלֹהִ֤ים ׀ לָאוֹר֙

Is 10:14 וַתִּמְצָ֨א כַקֵּ֤ן ׀ יָדִי֙

Est 10:1 וַיָּשֶׂם֩ הַמֶּ֨לֶךְ אֲחַשְׁרֹ֧שׁ ׀ (אחשורוש ק) מַ֛ס

Gen 3:14 וַיֹּאמֶר֩ יְהוָ֨ה אֱלֹהִ֥ים ׀ אֶֽל־הַנָּחָשׁ֮

This is especially common before *geresh*, *pazer*, and *telisha*, as

Est 9:27 קִיְּמ֣וּ וְקִבְּל֣ (וקבלו ק) הַיְּהוּדִים֩ ׀ עֲלֵיהֶ֨ם ׀ וְעַל־זַרְעָ֜ם

Lev 5:12 וְקָמַ֣ץ הַכֹּהֵ֣ן ׀ מִ֠מֶּנָּה

Nu 11:26 וַיִּשָּׁאֲר֣וּ שְׁנֵֽי־אֲנָשִׁ֣ים ׀ בַּֽמַּחֲנֶ֡ה שֵׁ֣ם הָאֶחָ֣ד ׀ אֶלְדָּ֡ד

In some cases a *paseq* would fit both ordinary and extraordinary classes, as

Lam 2:8 חָשַׁ֨ב יְהוָ֤ה ׀ לְהַשְׁחִית֙

Dt 4:32 אֲשֶׁר֩ בָּרָ֨א אֱלֹהִ֤ים ׀ אָדָם֙

Paseq is not marked consistently in any one of these categories. Sometimes it is used, and sometimes it is not, and the cases where it might be expected but does not occur are far more numerous than those where it does occur.

ACCENTUATION AND INTERPRETATION

The Commentators and the accents

286. Commentators--and also the versions--generally understand the text in a way consistent with the accents. Commentators sometimes refer to the accentuation of a verse, and only rarely do they explain the text in a way which conflicts with the accentuation. For information on this subject, see Breuer, 1957, p. 135-158, Melammed, 1970, p. 195-199, Yalon, 1971, p. 331. In his *Sefer Moznayim* Ibn Ezra says "You should not listen to, or agree with, any interpretation which is not consistent with the accentuation ".

Rashi sometimes cites the accents as support for his interpretation of a verse. For example on עָשׂ֥וּ ׀ כָּלָ֑ה (Gen 18:21) "For this reason *paseq* is used between עָשׂוּ and כָּלָה to separate the two words". Rashbam says "There is a *paseq* between the two words to show that they are not closely connected and the meaning is 'If they have acted thus, I will make an end of them'".

The following examples give further illustrations of reference to the accentuation by Rashi (and other where noted)".

Ex 15:17 מִקְּדָּ֕שׁ אֲדֹנָ֖י כּוֹנְנ֥וּ יָדֶֽיךָ

"The accent on מִקְּדָּשׁ is *zaqef gadol*, to separate this word from the divine name, indicating "The sanctuary which thy hands have established, O God."

Ex 24:5 וַיִּשְׁלַ֗ח אֶת־נַעֲרֵי֙ בְּנֵ֣י יִשְׂרָאֵ֔ל וַיַּעֲל֖וּ עֹלֹ֑ת וַיִּזְבְּח֞וּ זְבָחִ֧ים שְׁלָמִ֛ים לַיהוָ֖ה פָּרִֽים

TB *Ḥagiga* 6b. "Rav Ḥisda asked 'How is this verse to be understood? They offered burnt offerings (namely lambs), and sacrificed peace-offerings of oxen? Or were both offerings of oxen? What difference does it make? Mar Zuṭra said 'In regard to the פיסוק טעמים'. R. Aḥa son of Rabba said 'If one says I vow to offer a burnt offering like the burnt offering that Israel offered in the desert - should he offer oxen or lambs?'. It remains in doubt". Rashi's comment on the words פיסוק טעמים

is "It refers to the accentuation. If two types of offering are involved (lambs and oxen), a disjunctive must be marked on וַיַּעֲלוּ עוֹלוֹת: *atnaḥ*, as in our text, or *zaqef qaṭan*, or any other accent which marks the end of a unit of text. If only one type of offering is mentioned (oxen), one of the other accents which have less pausal force, such as *pashṭa* or *revia* should be used".

Dt 11:30 אַחֲרֵי דֶּרֶךְ מְבוֹא הַשֶּׁמֶשׁ

"Further on from the Jordan on the West side. The accentuation shows that the first two words are separate. אַחֲרֵי has *pashṭa* and דֶּרֶךְ has *mushpal* (= *yetiv*), and there is *dagesh* in the *dalet*, whereas if אַחֲרֵי דֶרֶךְ formed a single phrase, אַחֲרֵי would have *shofar hafuk*, a conjunctive, דֶּרֶךְ would have *pashṭa*, and the *dalet* would be *rafe*".

Rashbam: "אַחֲרֵי דֶּרֶךְ has the equivalent of two *pashṭas*. However because the accent sign is marked on the first letter of דֶּרֶךְ the actual sign is (the same as) *shofar mehuppak*."

Dt 29:20 בְּסֵפֶר הַתּוֹרָה הַזֶּה

"Above (Dt 28:61) it says בְּסֵפֶר הַתּוֹרָה הַזֹּאת. זֹאת is feminine, modifying תּוֹרָה, while זֶה is masculine, modifying סֵפֶר. The phrases are divided into two parts by the accents. In Dt 28:61 *tifḥa* is used under סֵפֶר, and הַתּוֹרָה is joined by a conjunctive to הַזֹּאת, which it modifies, but here (Dt 29:20) *tifḥa* is used under הַתּוֹרָה, so that the words סֵפֶר הַתּוֹרָה are closely joined, and the masculine הַזֶּה is separated, as it refers to סֵפֶר."

Jos 7:15 וְהָיָה הַנִּלְכָּד בַּחֵרֶם יִשָּׂרֵף בָּאֵשׁ אֹתוֹ וְאֶת־כָּל־אֲשֶׁר־לוֹ

"His tent and goods 'will be burned with fire', while 'he and all he owns' - referring to cattle - will be stoned, as made clear below. The *zaqef* on בָּאֵשׁ shows that this word is separated from אֹתוֹ, for we find elsewhere that this accent is used at the end of a unit of text."

2S 3:8 (In the best MSS) הֲרֹאשׁ כֶּלֶב אָנֹכִי

"However according to the pointing there is an accent under הֲרֹאשׁ, (and the words כֶּלֶב אָנֹכִי are joined by *maqqef*). This represents the interpretation--הֲרֹאשׁ 'even if I wanted to be a chief in your house' כֶּלֶב אָנֹכִי 'it would be better for me to be a dog--an insignificant private person--in David's household'. This is also the interpretation of Targum Jonathan". (Rashi's text showed different accentuation, with *merka* or *munaḥ* on the first word, see #262, and <u>cf</u>. V הראש כלב־אנכי).

1K 10:28 מִמִּצְרָיִם וּמִקְוֵה סֹחֲרֵי הַמֶּלֶךְ יִקְחוּ מִקְוֵה בִּמְחִיר
"The accent *zaqef gadol* is used on וּמִקְוֵה to show that the word stands by itself, and is not joined to what follows."
Is 45:1 כֹּה־אָמַר יְהוָה לִמְשִׁיחוֹ לְכוֹרֶשׁ אֲשֶׁר־הֶחֱזַקְתִּי בִימִינוֹ
TB *Megilla* 12a: "R. Naḥman bar R. Ḥisda interpreted 'What does the passage quoted mean? Was Cyrus Messiah? The text means God said to the Messiah, I have a complaint on your behalf against Cyrus'".
Rashi: "Two words written as if joined to each other (i.e. as if "Cyrus" was in apposition to "Messiah"), but the accentuation reflects the interpretation given, for *zarqa* is always followed by *segolta*, but here we have לִמְשִׁיחוֹ with *zarqa* and לְכוֹרֶשׁ with *ma'arik* to set it apart and separate it from לִמְשִׁיחוֹ (see #258).
Jer 3:8 וָאֵרֶא כִּי עַל־כָּל־אוֹדוֹת אֲשֶׁר נִאֲפָה מְשׁוּבָה יִשְׂרָאֵל
שִׁלַּחְתִּיהָ וָאֶתֵּן אֶת־סֵפֶר כְּרִיתֻתֶיהָ אֵלֶיהָ
"The accentuation shows the correct interpretation". יִשְׂרָאֵל has *zaqef*, and so is separated from שִׁלַּחְתִּיהָ. שִׁלַּחְתִּיהָ has *zaqef gadol* and stands by itself. It should be interpreted thus: 'I watched her to punish her'. Why? 'because for the very reason that backsliding Israel had committed adultery'. What was my vengeance? 'I sent her away from me'".
Ez 1:11 וּפְנֵיהֶם וְכַנְפֵיהֶם פְּרֻדוֹת מִלְמָעְלָה
"If I did not see *zaqef gadol* on וּפְנֵיהֶם I would not be able to explain this passage, but the accentuation shows where the divisions should be made. Thus וּפְנֵיהֶם is separated from what follows, and the interpretation is 'These were their faces, and their wings were spread out above their faces, covering them...' This chapter provides another example (Ez 1:18 וְגַבֵּיהֶן וְגֹבַהּ לָהֶם וְיִרְאָה לָהֶם where the word וְגַבֵּיהֶן is set apart by the accentuation)."
Redaq: "The word וּפְנֵיהֶם is separated by the accent, showing that it is not joined to what follows. The text means 'Their faces were as described, and their wings grew from the body, and were spread out above to fly'."
Song 8:6 --רְשָׁפֶיהָ רִשְׁפֵּי אֵשׁ שַׁלְהֶבֶתְיָה
"'Coals of fierce fire coming from the power if the flames of Gehenna'. The *zaqef gadol* on רִשְׁפֵּי shows that אֵשׁ should be joined (not to it but) to שַׁלְהֶבֶתְיָה, indicating fire of

supernatural flame."

Hos 12:12 אִם־גִּלְעָד אָוֶן אַךְ־שָׁוְא הָיוּ בַּגִּלְגָּל שְׁוָרִים זִבֵּחוּ

Redaq: "...otherwise the accent on הָיוּ would join it to בַּגִּלְגָּל. But even though *zaqef* is used on this word, the sense of the interpretation suggested is not always consistent with the accentuation."

Examples from the Three Books:

Ps 73:24 בַּעֲצָתְךָ תַנְחֵנִי וְאַחַר כָּבוֹד תִּקָּחֵנִי

Rashi: "If there were a disjunctive accent on כָּבוֹד, the interpretation would be 'After you have dealt with Sennacherib, you would take back all the glory you allotted to him. You have made wonderful miracles for Israel, and destroyed Sennacherib'. However since the disjunctive is on וְאַחַר, the interpretation is as follows 'After this you will take me for honour--draw me to yourself for honour and glory'."

Job 36:33 יַגִּיד עָלָיו רֵעוֹ מִקְנֶה אַף עַל־עוֹלֶה

Rashi: "However the fact that מִקְנֶה is pointed with *segol* shows that it is not in construct to אַף, for if it were it would have *ṣere*, and would not have a disjunctive accent as it does in our text, where it has *revia* (*mugrash*)".

Literature: Ackermann, 1893, Shereshevsky, 1972.

Accentuation and Syntax

287. The following passages used to illustrate points of syntax and interpretation raised by the accentuation are collected mainly from Wickes, 1887 (Appendix I, p. 130 ff., and elsewhere) and Breuer, 1957 (p. 135 ff.).

The use of the accents is affected not only by the syntax and meaning of the text, but also by certain rules of accentuation (see #179). One of these requires that if a phrase is composed of two words, they are joined by a conjunctive, as

Gen 35:2 (אֶת) אֱלֹהֵי הַנֵּכָר

If a third word is added at the end of the phrase the second word may be considered as more closely connected with it than with the first, so that the two words of the original phrase seem to be put in a different relationship, as in Dt 31:16 אֱלֹהֵי נֵכַר־הָאָרֶץ where נֵכַר is joined more closely to הָאָרֶץ (by *maqqef*) than to אֱלֹהֵי, to which it is more closely joined in meaning. Further examples in which the two words of a phrase appear to be dislocated in this way are:-

Ezra 10:14 חֲרוֹן אַף־אֱלֹהֵינוּ with the phrase חֲרוֹן אַף
Dt 31:25 אֲרוֹן בְּרִית־יְהוָה " " " אֲרוֹן בְּרִית
2C 13:20 וְלֹא־עָצַר כֹּחַ־יָרָבְעָם " " " עָצַר כֹּחַ
Nu 9:3 בְּאַרְבָּעָה עָשָׂר־יוֹם " " " אַרְבָּעָה עָשָׂר
Gen 19:2 הִנֶּה נָּא־אֲדֹנַי " " " הִנֵּה נָא
Dt 4:28 מַעֲשֵׂה יְדֵי אָדָם " " " מַעֲשֵׂה יְדֵי
Is 7:3 וּשְׁאָר יָשׁוּב בְּנֶךָ " " " שְׁאָר יָשׁוּב
Ez 8:5 סֵמֶל הַקִּנְאָה הַזֶּה " " " סֵמֶל הַקִּנְאָה

288. When a third word is added at the beginning of a phrase, the opposite tendency is shown. The additional word (especially if *maqqef* is commonly used with it) is joined to the first word of the original phrase, so again the two words of the original phrase seem to be dislocated, as in

Nu 33:7 עַל־פִּי הַחִירֹת with the phrase פִּי הַחִירֹת
Hos 1:8 אֶת־לֹא רֻחָמָה " " " לֹא רֻחָמָה
Dt 8:8 אֶרֶץ־זֵית שֶׁמֶן " " " זֵית שֶׁמֶן

This phenomenon does not show that the Masoretes took a different view of the syntax from ours, but stems from the conventions of accentuation.

The Accentuation of Selected Verses

289.

Gen 1:11 עֵץ פְּרִי עֹשֶׂה פְּרִי לְמִינוֹ

עֵץ פְּרִי has *geresh* subordinate to *pashta*. Therefore "Fruit-bearing trees of various types" are indicated, and not "fruit trees bearing fruit according to the type of tree" (as the Rabbis explained).

Gen 6:9 נֹחַ אִישׁ צַדִּיק תָּמִים הָיָה בְּדֹרֹתָיו

צַדִּיק has *tevir*, and so is separated from תָּמִים, which is joined to הָיָה--and so also

Lev 23:15 שֶׁבַע שַׁבָּתוֹת תְּמִימֹת תִּהְיֶינָה

and Nu 29:13 כְּבָשִׂים בְּנֵי־שָׁנָה אַרְבָּעָה עָשָׂר תְּמִימִם יִהְיוּ

Gen 19:1 וַיִּשְׁתַּחוּ אַפַּיִם אָרְצָה

אַפַּיִם is joined to וַיִּשְׁתַּחוּ, and separated from אָרְצָה (as is usual with this idiom).

Cf. 1K 1:31 וַתִּקֹּד בַּת־שֶׁבַע אַפַּיִם אֶרֶץ

and Is 49:23 אַפַּיִם אֶרֶץ יִשְׁתַּחֲווּ לָךְ

Gen 20:13 וַיְהִי כַּאֲשֶׁר הִתְעוּ אֹתִי אֱלֹהִים מִבֵּית אָבִי

The word אֱלֹהִים has *zarqa*, but is preceded by *revia*, and so is more closely joined to what follows than to what precedes. This is presumably to avoid the suggestion that God "misled" Abraham. (Cf. *Bereshit Rabba* 52:11)

Gen 24:60 וַיֹּ֣אמְרוּ לָ֔הּ אֲחֹתֵ֕נוּ אַ֥תְּ הֲיִ֖י לְאַלְפֵ֣י רְבָבָ֑ה

Zaqef gadol separates אֲחֹתֵ֕נוּ from what follows, showing that it is a "vocative", and not part of a clause "You are our sister".

Gen 39:17 בָּֽא־אֵלַ֞י הָעֶ֧בֶד הָֽעִבְרִ֛י אֲשֶׁר־הֵבֵ֥אתָ לָּ֖נוּ לְצַ֥חֶק בִּֽי

The disjunctive *ṭifḥa* is used on לָּ֖נוּ, so לְצַ֥חֶק בִּֽי modifies בָּא not הֵבֵ֥אתָ.

Ex 33:19 וְקָרָ֧אתִֽי בְשֵׁ֛ם יְהוָ֖ה

Ex 34:5 וַיִּקְרָ֥א בְשֵׁ֖ם יְהוָֽה

In both passages, בְּשֵׁם is separated from יְהוָה by a disjunctive. The meaning is "He called God by name". The meaning "He called on the name of God" is distinguished by the use of a conjunctive on בְּשֵׁם, as in

Gen 12:8 וַיִּקְרָ֖א בְּשֵׁ֥ם יְהוָֽה

Lev 13:38

וְאִישׁ֙ אֽוֹ־אִשָּׁ֔ה כִּֽי־יִהְיֶ֥ה בְעוֹר־בְּשָׂרָ֖ם בֶּהָרֹ֑ת בֶּהָרֹ֖ת לְבָנֹֽת

The main verse division is at the first בֶּהָרֹת.

Lev 14:23 וְהֵבִ֨יא אֹתָ֜ם בַּיּ֧וֹם הַשְּׁמִינִ֛י לְטָהֳרָת֖וֹ אֶל־הַכֹּהֵ֑ן

The word הַשְּׁמִינִ֛י is joined to what precedes, and is separated from what follows by the disjunctive *tevir*, meaning "He will bring it on the eighth day for the purpose of purification".

Lev 16:30

כִּֽי־בַיּ֥וֹם הַזֶּ֛ה יְכַפֵּ֥ר עֲלֵיכֶ֖ם לְטַהֵ֣ר אֶתְכֶ֑ם מִכֹּל֙ חַטֹּ֣אתֵיכֶ֔ם
לִפְנֵ֥י יְהוָ֖ה תִּטְהָֽרוּ

The main division is at אֶתְכֶ֑ם, and מִכֹּל֙ חַטֹּאתֵיכֶ֔ם has the disjunctive *zaqef*, meaning "You will be cleansed before God from all your sins". The Rabbis did not make a division here, interpreting "You will be cleansed from all your sins before God"--i.e. those between man and God only (Mishnah *Yoma* 8:9)

Dt. 11:13

לְאַהֲבָ֞ה אֶת־יְהוָ֤ה אֱלֹהֵיכֶם֙ וּלְעָבְד֔וֹ בְּכָל־לְבַבְכֶ֖ם וּבְכָל־נַפְשְׁכֶֽם

The disjunctive *zaqef* is used on וּלְעָבְד֔וֹ, indicating that God must be both loved and served with one's whole heart and soul.

Dt 26:5 אֲרַמִּי֙ אֹבֵ֣ד אָבִ֔י

The accentuation corresponds with the Rabbinic interpretation "An Aramaean (Laban) was seeking to destroy my father" (so

Onqelos, Rashi), not to "My father was an Aramaean about to perish".

Dt 32:5 שִׁחֵת לוֹ לֹא בָּנָיו מוּמָם

The *ṭifḥa* on לֹא marks the main division of this unit, as Onqelos and Rashi take it. However Ibn Ezra and others take לֹא בָּנָיו together, against the accentuation.

Dt 33:17 בָּהֶם עַמִּים יְנַגַּח יַחְדָּו אַפְסֵי־אָרֶץ

יַחְדָּו has the disjunctive *ṭifḥa*, indicating "With them he shall push the peoples together--even the ends of the earth."

Jos 2:5 וַיְהִי הַשַּׁעַר לִסְגּוֹר בַּחֹשֶׁךְ וְהָאֲנָשִׁים יָצָאוּ

לִסְגּוֹר has the disjunctive *revia*, showing that בַּחֹשֶׁךְ goes with what follows: "The men went out in the dark".

Jud 5:18 זְבֻלוּן עַם חֵרֵף נַפְשׁוֹ לָמוּת וְנַפְתָּלִי עַל מְרוֹמֵי שָׂדֶה

The main verse division is at וְנַפְתָּלִי. Rashi remarks "So also Naphtali, עַל מְרוֹמֵי שָׂדֶה means 'At Mt. Tabor'", but Redaq says "Naphtali in the same way will fight strongly on the high places of the land", ignoring the accentuation.

Jud 6:24 וַיִּבֶן שָׁם גִּדְעוֹן מִזְבֵּחַ לַיהוָה וַיִּקְרָא־לוֹ יְהוָה שָׁלוֹם

The accents show יְהוָה as the subject of וַיִּקְרָא, in contrast to all the commentators, who make יְהוָה שָׁלוֹם the name of the altar.

1S 3:3

וְנֵר אֱלֹהִים טֶרֶם יִכְבֶּה וּשְׁמוּאֵל שֹׁכֵב בְּהֵיכַל יְהוָה
אֲשֶׁר־שָׁם אֲרוֹן אֱלֹהִים

The main verse division is at שֹׁכֵב, so that בְּהֵיכַל יְהוָה... modifies וְנֵר אֱלֹהִים טֶרֶם יִכְבֶּה. However Targum Jonathan translates "Samuel was lying in the Temple court of God", and so Rashi. (Cf. LXX, Jerome).

1K 16:24

וַיִּקְרָא אֶת־שֵׁם הָעִיר אֲשֶׁר בָּנָה עַל שֶׁם־שֶׁמֶר אֲדֹנֵי הָהָר שֹׁמְרוֹן

The meaning is not "He called the city 'Shomron' after the name of Shemer, ruler of the mountain" but "He called the name of the city after the name of Shemer, ruler of the mountain called Shomron".

2K 10:15

וַיֹּאמֶר אֵלָיו הֲיֵשׁ אֶת־לְבָבְךָ יָשָׁר כַּאֲשֶׁר לְבָבִי עִם־לְבָבֶךָ
וַיֹּאמֶר יְהוֹנָדָב יֵשׁ וָיֵשׁ תְּנָה אֶת־יָדֶךָ

The disjunctive *tevir* separates יֵשׁ from וָיֵשׁ, although the commentators join them (as Redaq, who comments "Repetition for emphasis").

2K 19:13 (Is 37:13)

אַיּ֤וֹ מֶֽלֶךְ־חֲמָת֙ וּמֶ֣לֶךְ אַרְפָּ֔ד וּמֶ֖לֶךְ לָעִ֣יר סְפַרְוָ֑יִם
הֵנַ֖ע וְעִוָּֽה

The main verse division is at סְפַרְוָ֑יִם because הֵנַ֖ע וְעִוָּֽה are taken as verbs, as in Targum Jonathan. If they were taken as names, (as in the RV) the division would be elsewhere.

2K 24:15 הוֹלִ֛יךְ גּוֹלָ֖ה מִירוּשָׁלִַ֖ם בָּבֶֽלָה

The disjunctive *tevir* separates הוֹלִ֛יךְ from גּוֹלָ֖ה indicating "He carried away to Babylon as spoil from Jerusalem".

Is 1:5 עַ֣ל מֶ֥ה תֻכּ֖וּ ע֣וֹד תּוֹסִ֣יפוּ סָרָ֑ה

The main division of this unit is marked by the disjunctive *tifḥa* at ע֣וֹד, which must therefore be taken with תֻכּ֖וּ, not תּוֹסִ֣יפוּ.

Is 1:9 לוּלֵי֙ יְהוָ֣ה צְבָא֔וֹת הוֹתִ֥יר לָ֛נוּ שָׂרִ֖יד כִּמְעָ֑ט
כִּסְדֹ֣ם הָיִ֔ינוּ לַעֲמֹרָ֖ה דָּמִֽינוּ

The main verse division is at כִּמְעָ֑ט, which therefore goes with שָׂרִ֖יד "A small remnant", and not with כִּסְדֹ֣ם "We had been almost like Sodom"--as some take it.

Is 1:13 לֹ֣א תוֹסִ֗יפוּ הָבִיא֙ מִנְחַת־שָׁ֔וְא קְטֹ֥רֶת תּוֹעֵבָ֛ה הִ֖יא לִ֑י

The accentuation joins קְטֹ֥רֶת and תּוֹעֵבָ֛ה, indicating "Bring no more vain oblation. It is 'abominable incense' to me" not "Incense is an abomination to me" (as the RV).

Is 6:2 שְׂרָפִ֨ים עֹמְדִ֤ים מִמַּ֙עַל֙ ל֔וֹ

Pashṭa rather than a conjunctive is used on מִמַּ֙עַל֙, to create a division and thus avoid anthropomorphism.

Is 9:5 וַיִּקְרָ֨א שְׁמ֜וֹ פֶּ֠לֶא יוֹעֵץ֙ אֵ֣ל גִּבּ֔וֹר

פֶּ֠לֶא has *telisha* immediately after *geresh* before *pashṭa*, a most surprising combination, intended, for whatever reason, to separate פֶּלֶא from יוֹעֵץ.

Is 25:1 יְהוָ֤ה אֱלֹהַי֙ אַ֔תָּה

The accents indicate "You are the Lord my God" not "O Lord, you are my God".

Is 25:9 הִנֵּ֨ה אֱלֹהֵ֤ינוּ זֶ֛ה קִוִּ֥ינוּ ל֖וֹ וְיוֹשִׁיעֵ֑נוּ

זֶ֛ה is separated from what follows by the disjunctive *tevir*, indicating "This is our God; we have waited for him" (as RV).

Is 28:6

וּלְר֖וּחַ מִשְׁפָּ֑ט לַיּוֹשֵׁב֙ עַל־הַמִּשְׁפָּ֔ט וְלִ֨גְבוּרָ֔ה מְשִׁיבֵ֥י מִלְחָמָ֖ה שָֽׁעְרָה

The main verse division is at מִשְׁפָּ֑ט, and not at עַל־הַמִּשְׁפָּ֔ט as would be expected from the parallelism.

Is 29:16 הַפְכְּכֶם אִם־כְּחֹמֶר הַיֹּצֵר יֵחָשֵׁב

The accentuation joins כְּחֹמֶר הַיּוֹצֵר, indicating "Your inversions will be considered as potter's clay" and not "Will the potter be considered as clay" (as RV).

Is 38:13 שִׁוִּיתִי עַד־בֹּקֶר כָּאֲרִי כֵּן יְשַׁבֵּר כָּל־עַצְמוֹתָי

The main division of the unit is marked by *zaqef* at כָּאֲרִי, thus the interpretation is not "He breaks all my bones like a lion" (as RV), but as Rashi "I have gained strength like a lion to bear chastisement all night, but the illness breaks all my bones",

Is 40:3 קוֹל קוֹרֵא בַּמִּדְבָּר פַּנּוּ דֶּרֶךְ יְהוָה

Where the same disjunctive appears twice, the first generally has the greater pausal value (#198). Thus the main division is at קוֹרֵא, indicating "The voice of one that crieth 'Prepare ye in the wilderness...'" (as RV). (Matthew 3:3 "The voice of one crying in the wilderness" shows that a different interpretation was current in the first century, but the Qumran "Manual of Discipline", 1QS 8:13-14, shows that the interpretation indicated by the accents was also current at that time).

Is 40:13 מִי־תִכֵּן אֶת־רוּחַ יְהוָה

The word רוּחַ has the disjunctive *ṭifḥa*, thus "The Lord" must be taken as the answer to the question "Who has measured the wind?" (as Targum Jonathan, Rashi, and others, against RV). Possibly accentuation to avoid anthropomorphism.

Is 43:17

הַמּוֹצִיא רֶכֶב־וָסוּס חַיִל וְעִזּוּז יַחְדָּו יִשְׁכְּבוּ בַּל־יָקוּמוּ דָּעֲכוּ כַּפִּשְׁתָּה כָבוּ

The main verse division is at וְעִזּוּז, so that יַחְדָּו goes with what follows "They will lie down together and not rise" (as RV).

Is 45:16

בּוֹשׁוּ וְגַם־נִכְלְמוּ כֻּלָּם יַחְדָּו הָלְכוּ בַכְּלִמָּה חָרָשֵׁי צִירִים

The main verse division is at כֻּלָּם, so that יַחְדָּו goes with what follows: "They shall go together..." (as RV).

Is 53:2

וַיַּעַל כַּיּוֹנֵק לְפָנָיו וְכַשֹּׁרֶשׁ מֵאֶרֶץ צִיָּה לֹא־תֹאַר לוֹ וְלֹא הָדָר
וְנִרְאֵהוּ וְלֹא־מַרְאֶה וְנֶחְמְדֵהוּ

The main verse division is at הָדָר, so that Rashi comments "When we saw him from the beginning without form, how could we desire him?"

Is 56:9 כֹּל חַיְתוֹ שָׂדָי אֵתָיוּ לֶאֱכֹל כָּל־חַיְתוֹ בַּיָּעַר

The accentuation requires the interpretation "All you beasts of the field (vocative), come and eat all the beasts of the forest" (So Targum Jonathan and Rashi--also RV footnotes--but not Redaq and others--and RV text).

Is 60:19 לֹא־יִהְיֶה־לָּךְ עוֹד הַשֶּׁמֶשׁ לְאוֹר יוֹמָם וּלְנֹגַהּ הַיָּרֵחַ לֹא־יָאִיר לָךְ

The disjunctive *zaqef gadol* separates וּלְנֹגַהּ from הַיָּרֵחַ "For brightness the moon will not give you light" (as RV).

Jer 4:1 אִם־תָּשׁוּב יִשְׂרָאֵל נְאֻם־יְהוָה אֵלַי תָּשׁוּב

The disjunctive on אלי indicates "The Lord said to me 'You will return'", not "unto me shalt thou return" (as RV).

Jer 10:3 כִּי־עֵץ מִיַּעַר כְּרָתוֹ

There is a disjunctive on עֵץ, indicating "A tree which he cut out of the forest", not "He cut a tree from the forest" (as RV).

Jer 15:18 לָמָּה הָיָה כְאֵבִי נֶצַח וּמַכָּתִי אֲנוּשָׁה
מֵאֲנָה הֵרָפֵא הָיוֹ תִהְיֶה לִי כְּמוֹ אַכְזָב מַיִם לֹא נֶאֱמָנוּ

The main verse division comes at אֲנוּשָׁה. Nevertheless all commentators apply "refusing to be healed" to מַכָּתִי.

Jer 46:17 קָרְאוּ שָׁם פַּרְעֹה מֶלֶךְ־מִצְרַיִם שָׁאוֹן הֶעֱבִיר הַמּוֹעֵד

The accentuation marks פַּרְעֹה מֶלֶךְ־מִצְרַיִם שָׁאוֹן as a unit, showing that the construct מֶלֶךְ has two nouns dependent on it. He is מֶלֶךְ מִצְרַיִם and מֶלֶךְ שָׁאוֹן "Pharaoh King of Egypt who was King of a great multitude" (Redaq).

Ez 15:2 מַה־יִּהְיֶה עֵץ־הַגֶּפֶן מִכָּל־עֵץ הַזְּמוֹרָה אֲשֶׁר הָיָה בַּעֲצֵי הַיָּעַר

The main verse division is at מִכָּל־עֵץ so that עֵץ הַזְּמוֹרָה should not be joined. As Rashi says "I am not speaking about the cultivated vine, but the wild vine of the forests"

Ez 44:22 וְהָאַלְמָנָה אֲשֶׁר תִּהְיֶה אַלְמָנָה מִכֹּהֵן יִקָּחוּ

The disjunctive *zaqef* is used on אַלְמָנָה, so that אַלְמָנָה מִכֹּהֵן should not be joined. Thus מִכֹּהֵן "some of the priests"--but not the high priest--may marry a widow.

Amos 6:6 הַשֹּׁתִים בְּמִזְרְקֵי יַיִן

The disjunctive *pashta*, rather than a conjunctive, is used on מִזְרְקֵי, indicating "Who drink wine from bowls" (although מִזְרְקֵי is construct where absolute would be expected) and not "Who drink from bowls of wine". Possibly "Who drink wine from bowls of (gold and silver)" was intended.

Zech 4:7 וְהוֹצִיא אֶת־הָאֶבֶן הָרֹאשָׁה תְּשֻׁאוֹת חֵן חֵן לָהּ

According to the accentuation, the meaning is not "Shoutings of 'Grace, grace...'" (as RV), but "He will bring out...with shouting. Grace be to it" (against Rashi).

1C 3:17 וּבְנֵי֙ יְכָנְיָ֣ה אַסִּ֔ר

The accentuation is more fitting to the interpretation "The sons of Jeconiah the prisoner" (as RV), than to the accepted interpretation which takes אַסִּר as the name of a son of Jeconiah.

1C 7:3

וּבְנֵ֥י עֻזִּ֖י יִֽזְרַחְיָ֑ה וּבְנֵ֣י יִֽזְרַחְיָ֗ה מִ֣יכָאֵ֜ל וְעֹבַדְיָ֧ה וְיוֹאֵ֛ל יִשִּׁיָּ֥ה חֲמִשָּׁ֖ה רָאשִׁ֥ים כֻּלָּֽם

The word חֲמִשָּׁ֖ה has the disjunctive *ṭifḥa*, indicating "There are five, and they are all chiefs".

2C 24:14 וַיַּעֲשֵׂ֨הוּ כֵלִ֤ים לְבֵית־יְהוָה֙ כְּלֵ֣י שָׁרֵ֔ת וְהַעֲל֕וֹת וְכַפּ֖וֹת וּכְלֵ֣י זָהָ֣ב וָכָ֑סֶף

The accentuation appears to take הַעֲלוֹת as the name of some implement (cf. Redaq in his *Sefer ha-Shorashim*) or activity "raising candles and hands" (cf. Ibn Janāḥ in his *Sefer ha-Shorashim*).

Literature. Freedman and Cohen, 1974.

'MAQQEF'

290. Where two words are read together with a single accent, as if they were a single word, *maqqef* is marked between them to indicate this. *Maqqef* therefore shows that two words are closely connected, but it has no musical motif of its own, and is therefore not considered an "accent", either conjunctive or disjunctive. The number of words joined in this way is most commonly two, as אֶת־הָעָ֔ם (Ex 13:17), but may be three, as אֶת־לֶב־פַּרְעֹה֙ (Ex 14:4), or, rarely, four, as עַֽל־כָּל־דְּבַר־פֶּ֡שַׁע (Ex 22:8).

This joining marked by *maqqef* affects not only the musical accent, but also the vowel pattern. Since a word followed by *maqqef* is part of the same stress unit as the following word, all its syllables are likely to be distant from the main stress syllable, so that vowel change frequently occurs. The most common changes are *segol* replacing *ṣere*, as שֵׁם/שֶׁם־, יְקַטֵּל/יְקַטֶּל־, אֵת/אֶת־ and *qameṣ ḥaṭuf* replacing *ḥolem*, as כֹּל/כָּל־, יִקְטֹל/יִקְטָל־, רֹב/רָב־, עֹז/עָז־, חֹק/חָק־, קְטֹל/קְטָל־.

291. In the early MSS, the *maqqef* sign is thinner and shorter than it is in the printed editions. If the word bearing *maqqef* was followed by an unusually large space (as was

often left between words which otherwise would not fill out the line) the *maqqef* was not lengthened or repeated, as it is in printed editions, but was written as usual, leaving a space between it and the following word, as אֶת־ הָאוֹר. Occasionally no space was left between words, and this was considered sufficient to show that they were joined by *maqqef*, as אֶתעָנְיִי. (A, Ps 31:8).

292. As this shows, *maqqef* could be considered a superfluous sign, since it indicates the absence of any (other) accent sign. In the best MSS, however, *maqqef* is consistently marked after every word which does not have its own accent, and is only very rarely omitted. In A, for instance, *maqqef* is lacking in only about fifty of the many thousands of cases where it is required. The omission of *maqqef* is also very rare in L, and does not seem to occur in C and S at all. In B and S^1, its omission is somewhat more common than in A. In inferior MSS, and also in some of those with expanded Tiberian pointing, the omission of *maqqef* is much more frequent.

293. In a number of MSS, *maqqef* is occasionally marked after a word with a conjunctive accent. This is most common where the word has penultimate stress, as שֹׂנְאֵי־בָצַע (L^3, Ex 18:21), וַתֹּאמֶר־אֶסְתֵּר (L Est 7:6). This is possibly intended to show that the last syllable of the word has no accent.

The MS L^2 omits *maqqef* quite commonly after a short word, as כָּל קְדֹשָׁיו (Dt 33:3), and also marks *maqqef* after words with conjunctive accents, as וְעֵזֶר־מִצָּרָיו (Dt 33:7), showing, in this respect, a tradition somewhat different from the standard.

Literature on 'Maqqef'

294. Masoretic literature includes a few rules involving *maqqef*. The *Diqduqe ha-Ṭeᶜamim* lists vowel changes in a few words: אֵת, כֹּל, בֵּן, when followed by *maqqef*, and other masoretic treatises do the same for additional words, such as שֵׁם, חֵן and others.

The early grammarians wrote much on vowel change in words followed by *maqqef*, but they did not draw up general rules on the use of the sign. Yequti'el ha-Naqdan seems to have done this in a small treatise which was never printed, but is known in manuscript, and was evidently used by later scholars, particularly Heidenheim. Eliahu ha-Levi devoted chapter eight of his *Ṭuv Ṭaᶜam* to *maqqef*, and similar chapters are found in the *Miqneh Abram* of Abram di Balmes (at the end of his book based, according to Heidenheim, on Yequti'el ha-Naqdan), the *Arugat ha-Bosem* of Shemu'el Archevolti (chapter 11). The most complete statement is found in W. Heidenheim's *Mishpeṭe ha-Ṭeᶜamim* (Rödelheim, 1808, section 3, chapter 3).

There is a useful short section on *maqqef* in Bergsträsser 1918 (Vol. 1, #11); a comprehensive treatment, with new rules, in Praetorius, 1897, p. 9-21, and a few interesting paragraphs in Spanier, 1927, p. 130-142.

The Principles of the Use of 'Maqqef'

295. *Maqqef*, which occurs more than 50,000 times in the Bible (making it one of the most common signs) appears for three main reasons: to avoid the occurrence of two main stress syllables one after the other, to avoid giving a short word its own accent, and to avoid the use of an additional accent.

i) Avoiding two main stress syllables one after the other. The occurrence of two main stress syllables one after the other was evidently disliked. Where two words are closely connected in meaning this does sometimes occur, as

Is 52:7 מְבַשֵּׂר טוֹב
Is 1:23 אֹהֵב שֹׁחַד
Is 5:8 מַגִּיעֵי בַיִת

There is, however, a tendency to avoid it. Two methods are used. One is the retraction of the stress on the first word (#307), as

Gen 21:6 עָשָׂה לִי
Hos 14:10 וְיָבֵן אֵלֶּה, יֵלְכוּ בָם, יִכָּשְׁלוּ בָם

However this retraction can occur only under specific conditions (#308). The second method of preventing the occurrence of two successive stress syllables is to read the two words with a single accent, as

Gen 20:13 אִמְרִי־לִי instead of אִמְרִי לִי. So also
Jer 41:8 נִמְצְאוּ־בָם
Jer 36:2 מְגִלַּת־סֵפֶר
Is 48:9 אֶחֱטָם־לָךְ
Is 8:9 מֶרְחַקֵּי־אָרֶץ

296. ii) <u>Small words</u>. There is a tendency to treat short words as enclitic--that is, as part of the same stress unit as the following word. Thus they often have *maqqef*. Short words show this tendency in different degrees. This does not seem to depend on meaning or syntax, but on word structure. The particles אַף and אֵי are treated in the same way as the construct nouns יַד and מֵי respectively. Three groups can be recognized.

297. 1) Words made up of a closed syllable with a short vowel show a strong tendency to take *maqqef*. In a two-word phrase, they generally are marked with it, as אֶל־אַבְרָהָם (Gen 20:10). There are, however, differences among them. Some, like אֶל, אַל, בַּל, בֶּן, בַּת, מַה, פֶּן, almost always have *maqqef*. Others, like אֶת, כָּל, עַל, אִם, עִם, אַף, גַּם, עַד, אַךְ, רַק, and אֲשֶׁר, the nouns גַּו, דַּם, הַר, יַד, etc., and דְּבַר, נְהַר, שְׂפַת, חֹק, רֹב, הֵן, יֵשׁ, שֵׁם, have it somewhat less commonly. (Note that vocal *shewa* does not form a syllable, see #376.)

298. 2) Words consisting of a single open syllable, like כִּי, לֹא, לוֹ, אוֹ, מָה, מִי, פֹּה, אִי, חֵי, מֵי, יְדֵי, בְּנֵי, יְמֵי, פִּי, הֲלֹא, זֶה, הִנֵּה, הוּא, הִיא, show a lesser tendency to take *maqqef* than those of the preceding group, and in a two-word phrase they generally do not have it, as כִּי נִמְצָאוּ (1S 9:20). They do have *maqqef*, however, where two stress syllables would otherwise come together, as כִּי־טוֹב (Gen 1:4).

299. 3) Words consisting of a single closed syllable with a long vowel, as אֵין, בֵּין, בֵּית, אִישׁ, קְצִיר, שְׂעִיר, תּוֹךְ, יוֹם, קוֹל, אוֹי, show the least tendency to take *maqqef*. In two word phrases they do not have *maqqef* whether two stress syllables come together (as אֵין כֹּל Nu 11:6) or no (as אֵין אֹתוֹ Gen 40:8).

If the short word has a prefixed particle (as מִכֹּל, וְאֵת, מִפְּנֵי, כַּאֲשֶׁר), the tendency to take *maqqef* is reduced in all groups.

300. iii) <u>Economy of Accents</u>. Sometimes words which are closely connected, but which do not come under the above two categories, are joined with *maqqef*. The purpose of this appears to be to avoid the use of an additional accent. Thus in Jer 40:4 עָלַיִךְ וְאִם־רַע בְּעֵינַיִךְ לָבוֹא־אִתִּי בָבֶל חֲדָל

If לָבוֹא did not have *maqqef*, a completely different accentuation would be required, as *ṭifḥa* only takes one servus. This would inevitably increase the pausal value of the accents on אִתִּי and בְּעֵינֶיךָ, thus: עָלֶיךָ ואם־רַע בעינֶיךָ לָבוֹא אִתִּי בֹּבָל חֲדָל.
Similarly in Dt 32:44

וַיָּבֹא מֹשֶׁה וַיְדַבֵּר אֶת־כָּל־דִּבְרֵי הַשִּׁירָה־הַזֹּאת בְּאָזְנֵי הָעָם

If הַשִּׁירָה did not have *maqqef*, the accentuation would have to be

ויבֹא משה וידבֵּר את־כל־דברֵי השירָה הזֹאת באזנֵי העָם.

The use of *maqqef* for "economy" is frequent before *geresh*, *pazer*, and *telisha*, to avoid long strings of conjunctives, as
Jer 11:4 בְּיוֹם הוֹצִיאִי־אוֹתָם מֵאֶרֶץ־מִצְרַיִם מִכּוּר הַבַּרְזֶל
2C 13:11

עֹלוֹת בַּבֹּקֶר־בַּבֹּקֶר וּבָעֶרֶב־בָּעֶרֶב וּקְטֹרֶת־סַמִּים וּמַעֲרֶכֶת לֶחֶם

Group (iii) shows that the use of *maqqef* is not dependent only on morphology and syntax, but also on the requirements of the accentuation. This cannot be discussed further here, but unfortunately no complete study is available.

301. The MSS show more variants in the use of *maqqef* than in the use of the accents, but in the early MSS with standard Tiberian pointing, such variations are not too common. Notes on variations in the use of *maqqef* occasionally appear in the margins of MSS. About eighty of the variations between bA and bN (or cases where they agree, but differ from other scholars) involve *maqqef*, as

Gen 26:22 bA	כִּי־עַתָּה	bN	כִּי
Gen 39:6 bA	יְפֵה־תֹאַר	bN	יְפֵה
Is 45:3 bA	כִּי־אֲנִי יְהוָה	bN	כִּי
Is 34:11 bA	קַו תֹהוּ	bN	קַו־תֹהוּ (also A, L, S^1 I)

302. From the point of view of the accentuation, words joined by *maqqef* are considered as a single unit, and are treated so in the marking of conjunctives, secondary accents, and *ga*^{c}*ya*. For instance in אֶל־הָאִשָּׁה, the combination *munaḥ-zaqef* can be used, because אֶל is joined by *maqqef* to the following word, and so -הָ is not the first syllable (#221). In כְּתֹנֶת־בַּד קֹדֶשׁ, the servus is *azla*, not *munaḥ*, since the word in question is not stressed on its first syllable, due to the use of *maqqef*(#265). *Ga*^{c}*ya* is marked in similar combinations, as Dt 17:2 אוֹ־אִשָּׁה (*ga*^{c}*ya* in an open syllable, two places before

the stress, #326), or 1S 9:20 אֶת־לִבְּךָ֑ (*ga*^{c}*ya* on a closed syllable in a word of fully regular structure, #319).

303. When *ga*^{c}*ya* is used on a word with *maqqef* (as טֽוֹבַת־שֶׂ֫כֶל, 1S 25:3), it represents neither an accent nor an accent retracted. The marking of *ga*^{c}*ya* on a combination of words joined by *maqqef* is governed by the same rules as govern the marking of *ga*^{c}*ya* on a single word. Nevertheless, from the point of view of the accent system, the accent is never retracted where *ga*^{c}*ya* cannot be used, as

Jos 10:27 נֶחְבְּאוּ־שָׁ֑ם
Gen 3:16 יִמְשָׁל־בָּֽךְ׃
Gen 40:8 סַפְּרוּ־נָ֖א

'Maqqef' as Determined by Linguistic or Musical Phenomena

304. *Maqqef* is used for two basic reasons: i) Linguistic. *Maqqef* follows words which are short, and which in normal speech would tend to be enclitic--included with the following word in a single stress unit. Even many words given a conjunctive accent in the Bible would be joined with the following word in a single stress unit in everyday speech. ii) Musical. *Maqqef* may be used for reasons connected with the accent system (#300). In most cases it can be assumed that *maqqef* is used both for linguistic and for musical reasons, as

1S 7:11 מִן־הַמִּצְפָּ֔ה
Dt 33:20 אַף־קָדְקֹֽד
Gen 41:12 וַנְּסַפֶּר־ל֔וֹ וַיִּפְתָּר־לָ֖נוּ

In some words the use of *maqqef* involves a change in the vowel pattern (#290). Thus in

Lev 25:5

אֵ֣ת סְפִ֤יחַ קְצִֽירְךָ֙ לֹ֣א תִקְצ֔וֹר וְאֶת־עִנְּבֵ֥י נְזִירֶ֖ךָ לֹ֣א תִבְצֹ֑ר

את occurs in two parallel phrase, once with *ṣere* and no *maqqef*, and once with *segol* and *maqqef*. Clearly this is not determined by linguistic phenomena. Grammatically, either vocalization is acceptable. Here, then, the use of *maqqef* must be determined by the musical requirements of the accentuation, and the linguistic phenomenon--the use of two different vowel patterns --is consistent with the musical.

305. In some cases, however, the linguistic and musical

phenomena do not correspond; that is, the vowel pattern is not that expected with the accentuation. *Ḥolem* is usually replaced by *qameṣ* before *maqqef*, as in Ex 21:11 וְאִם־שְׁלָשׁ־אֵלֶּה (where two stress syllables would come together but for the *maqqef*). In Jos 21:33 שְׁלֹשׁ־עֶשְׂרֵה עִיר (where two stress syllables would not come together) *ḥolem* is retained, despite the use of *maqqef*. Here it can be said that *maqqef* is used for musical reasons, but the linguistic situation does not require it.

Further examples can be found with רֹב. Before a word stressed on the first syllable, רָב־ has *maqqef* and *qameṣ*, as רָב־כָּעַס Qoh 1:18. Here the musical and linguistic situations correspond. Where the following word is not stressed on the first syllable, the word may have an accent and *ḥolem*, as Lev 25:16 רֹב הַשָּׁנִים. Again the musical and linguistic situations correspond. However the word may also have *maqqef* and *ḥolem* under these conditions, as Is 1:11 לָמָּה־לִּי רֹב־זִבְחֵיכֶם Lam 1:5 עַל רֹב־פְּשָׁעֶיהָ. Here the musical situation requires *maqqef*, but the linguistic situation does not.

In some cases a short vowel replaces a long one even where two stress syllables do not come together. Thus in Lev 6:11 חָק־עוֹלָם the musical and linguistic situations correspond, and the same is true in Ez 45:14 וְחֹק הַשֶּׁמֶן. However in Job 26:10 חֹק־חָג the *maqqef* has a musical, but not a linguistic source, and *ḥolem* is used with *maqqef*, even though two stress syllables come together.

Further examples can be found in infinitive construct forms. For instance the musical and linguistic situations correspond in

Is 54:9 וּמִגְּעָר־בָּךְ

where *maqqef* and *qameṣ* are used, and in

Nu 34:18 לִנְחֹל אֶת־הָאָרֶץ

where an accent and *ḥolem* occur. However in

Jos 19:49 וַיְכַלּוּ לִנְחֹל־אֶת־הָאָרֶץ

where *maqqef* and *ḥolem* are used, the source of *maqqef* is musical, and the linguistic situation is not consistent with it.

The same phenomenon occurs where the independent form has *ṣere* in the final syllable. Thus יֵשׁ normally shows *segol* with *maqqef*, as Gen 44:20 יֶשׁ־לָנוּ, and *ṣere* with an accent, as

Gen 28:16 יֵשׁ יְהוָה

but in

Qoh 6:11 יֵשׁ־דְּבָרִ֥ים הַרְבֵּ֖ה

where *ṣere* and *maqqef* occur, the source of *maqqef* is musical, and the linguistic situation is not consistent with it.

Again in Gen 25:19 בֶּן־אַבְרָהָ֑ם (־בֶּן has *segol* and *maqqef*) and in Gen 30:17 בֵּ֥ן חֲמִישִֽׁי (בֵּן has *ṣere* and an accent) the musical and linguistic situations correspond. However in the *Diqduqe ha-Ṭeᶜamim* (Dotan, 1967, section 6), four cases are listed where ־בֵּן has *ṣere* and *maqqef*, showing that the source of *maqqef* is musical, but the linguistic situation does not correspond. These are

Gen 30:19 וַתֵּ֥לֶד בֵּן־שִׁשִּֽׁי

1S 22:20 וַיִּמָּלֵ֣ט בֵּן־אֶחָ֗ד

2S 9:12 וְלִמְפִיבֹ֥שֶׁת בֵּן־קָטָ֑ן

Ez 18:10 וְהוֹלִ֥יד בֵּן־פָּרִ֖יץ

The same section lists seven cases where בֶּן has *segol* and an accent, showing that the source of *maqqef* is linguistic, but the musical phenomena do not correspond. These are:-

Lev 24:10 בֶּ֚ן הַיִּשְׂרְאֵלִ֔ית (with the disjunctive *yetiv*!)

Lev 1:5 אֶת־בֶּ֣ן הַבָּקָ֑ר

Neh 6:18 בֶּ֣ן בֶּרֶכְיָ֑ה

Is 8:2 בֶּ֥ן יְבֶרֶכְיָֽהוּ

1C 9:21 בֶּ֣ן מְשֶׁלֶמְיָ֔ה

Est 2:5 בֶּ֥ן יָאִ֛יר בֶּן־שִׁמְעִ֥י

Gen 17:17 הַלְּבֶ֤ן מֵאָה־שָׁנָה֙

Further examples where the source of *maqqef* is musical, and the linguistic situation does not correspond, are Job 7:12 הֲיָם־אָ֭נִי, Ez 14:4 דַּבֵּר־אוֹתָם and where the source of *maqqef* is linguistic, but the musical situation does not correspond. With כל (see Dotan 1967, section 8):-

Ps 35:10 כָּ֥ל עַצְמוֹתַ֨י Prov 19:7 כָּ֥ל אֲחֵי־רָ֨שׁ

with an imperative form:

Jud 19:5 סְעָ֥ד לִבְּךָ֛

The use of 'Maqqef' with Short Words

306. There is a tendency to use *maqqef* with short words. It was noted above (#206) that under certain circumstances, short words are not marked with a conjunctive accent, but a disjunctive of greater pausal value than the accent on the following word. When not marked with a disjunctive, short

words tend to loose any musical accent of their own, and are joined to the following word, and so marked with *maqqef*. This can be seen in

Gen 23:19 אֶת־שָׂרָה אִשְׁתּוֹ and Gen 20:14 אֵת שָׂרָה אִשְׁתּוֹ

שָׂרָה has a conjunctive in both cases. In Gen 23:19 אֶת־ is marked with *maqqef* (of lesser pausal value than the conjunctive), but in Gen 20:14, אֵת has the disjunctive *ṭifḥa* (of greater pausal value). This is a general tendency in the Biblical accentuation.

RETRACTION OF THE ACCENT - נסיגה, נסוג אחור

307. Retraction of the accent is one of the ways of avoiding the occurrence of accents on two successive syllables (#295). Where two words are closely connected, and the accent of the first is marked on its final syllable, and that of the second on its first syllable, the accent of the first word may be retracted to the penultimate syllable to avoid the occurrence of accents on two successive syllables. Retraction only occurs where the first word of the pair has a conjunctive accent. There is one exception:

Nu 23:23 מַה־פָּעַל אֵל (bN reads פָּעַל). Two further considerations affect this retraction: i) the structure of the first word of the pair ii) the meaning of the pair of words.

308. i) Word structure and Retraction of the Accent.

1) The accent is not likely to be retracted from a closed syllable pointed with a long vowel, as

Ex 15:27 עֵינֹת מַיִם Prov 9:4, 16 יָסֻר הֵנָּה

1K 14:13 דָּבָר טוֹב

As a general rule, a vowel of this sort cannot be shortened enough to permit the retraction. Where *ṣere* is involved, however, this rule does not apply. Words with *ṣere* in a final closed syllable are treated in three different ways: (a) The accent is not retracted, and the *ṣere* remains, as

Is 1:23 אֹהֵב שֹׁחַד

Prov 13:3 נֹצֵר פִּיו

Is 5:2 חָצֵב בּוֹ

Jer 46:14 וְהָכֵן לָךְ

Is 51:8 יֹאכְלֵם עָשׁ

Dan 8:19 לְמוֹעֵד קֵץ

(b) The accent is retracted, and the *sere* is replaced by *segol*, as Is 41:7 אֶת־הוֹלֶם פָּעַם (The only example with a participle)

Song 4:6 אֵלֶךְ לִי

Zech 13:8 יִוָּתֶר בָּהּ

Gen 39:14 לְצַחֶק בָּנוּ

Dt 21:17 לָתֶת לוֹ

Job 41:10 תָּהֶל אוֹר

Hos 9:2 יְכַחֶשׁ בָּהּ

(c) The accent is retracted; the *ṣere* remains, and is marked with *ga*^{c}*ya* (see #338), as

Prov 12:1 אֹהֵב דָּעַת

Is 49:7 לִמְתָעֵב גּוֹי

Jud 8:10 שֹׁלֵף חָרֶב

Ez 26:15 בֵּהָרֵג הֶרֶג

Jer 23:29 יְפֹצֵץ סָלַע

This occurs occasionally even where the *ṣere* is followed by *pataḥ* "furtive", as

Is 63:12 בּוֹקֵעַ מַיִם

Prov 11:26 מֹנֵעַ בָּר

2) The accent can only be retracted to an open syllable, as

Ps 65:10 מָלֵא מָיִם 1S 25:3 וִיפַת תֹּאַר

If the stress syllable is preceded by *shewa*, the accent may even be retracted to a preceding open syllable with a long vowel, as 2S 5:13 וַיִּוָּלְדוּ עוֹד, or where the *shewa* is a *ḥaṭef*.

Mic 6:8 וְאַהֲבַת חֶסֶד Nu 2:31 לְמַחֲנֵה דָן

Gen 45:15 וְאַחֲרֵי כֵן Is 47:2 וְטַחֲנִי קָמַח

If the penultimate syllable is closed, the accent is not retracted, save in a few exceptional cases:

(a) וַיִּהְיוּ שָׁם (Jos 4:9 and elsewhere)

(b) אַלְלַי לִי (Mic 7:1, but אַלְלַי לִי Job 10:15)

(c) Perfect verb forms with *waw* "consecutive", as

Dt 16:2 וְזָבַחְתָּ פֶּסַח Ex 25:12 וְיָצַקְתָּ לּוֹ

3) The accent is retracted to the antipenultimate syllable in a few words which have a closed penultimate syllable, but an open syllable before that, as

Ex 15:8 נֶעֶרְמוּ מַיִם Dt 33:28 יַעַרְפוּ טָל

Is 50:8 נַעַמְדָה יָּחַד

also Gen 49:20 מַעֲדַנֵּי מֶלֶךְ (but מַעֲדַנֵּי has *maqqef* in most MSS).

4) The accent on the first word may be retracted even where the

accented vowel of the second word is preceded by *shewa*, although this is rare. Examples are:

Gen 1:11 עֹ֣שֶׂה פְּרִי֙ Gen 15:7 לָ֥תֶת לְךָ֛
1C 28:10 בָּ֥חַר בְּךָ֛ Hab 3:11 עָ֣מַד זְבֻ֑לָה

5) There are a few categories of word in which the accent is only very rarely retracted:-

(a) Words with "heavy" suffixes or verbal endings such as --ֶן, --ֶכֶן, --ֶם, --כֶם etc., as

Lev 20:11 דְּמֵיהֶ֥ם בָּֽם Gen 41:21 וּמַרְאֵיהֶ֣ן רַ֔ע
Jud 14:15 קְרָאתֶ֥ם לָ֖נוּ Jos 2:16 וְנַחְבֵּתֶ֨ם שָׁ֜מָּה

Retraction in this group occurs mostly in qal verb forms from ל"ה or ל"א roots, but it is rare. Examples are:-

Dt 4:25 וַעֲשִׂ֤יתֶם פֶּ֙סֶל֙ Jer 11:4 וִהְיִ֤יתֶם לִי֙
Ez 36:22 אֲשֶׁר־בָּ֥אתֶם שָֽׁם

(b) Retraction does not occur on words ending with a doubly closed syllable (marked by two *shewa*s), as

Gen 16:11 וְיֹלַ֣דְתְּ בֵּ֔ן Jud 4:20 וְאָמַ֖רְתְּ אָֽיִן

(c) Retraction does not occur where the final syllable of the word is --ַי, as

Gen 48:9 בָּנַ֣י הֵ֔ם Is 20:4 וַחֲשׂוּפַ֥י שֵׁ֖ת
Ps 69:5 אֹיְבַ֣י שֶׁ֑קֶר

(d) Retraction does not occur on words ending with the suffix --ךָ, as

Ps 5:5 יְגֻרְךָ֥ רָֽע 1S 26:19 הֱסִיתְךָ֣ בִי֙
Gen 46:3 אֲשִֽׂימְךָ֥ שָֽׁם

(e) Retraction is rare where the two words are accented with *azla* and *geresh*, as

Gen 19:14 וַיֵּצֵ֨א ל֜וֹט, compare Gen 4:16 וַיֵּ֥צֵא קַ֖יִן

309. ii) <u>Meaning and the Retraction of the Accent</u>: (1) Two-word units.

Retraction of the accent is more likely to occur where two words form a semantic unit, more closely related to each other than to the words before and after them. The most common categories are:-

(a) The second word has prefixed *lamed* or *bet*, and modifies the first. The structure may be verbal, as

Ps 44:11 שָׁ֣סוּ לָֽמוֹ Job 3:3 אִוָּ֣לֶד בּ֑וֹ

or nominal, as Ps 119:99 שִׂ֣יחָה לִֽי

Prov 17:21 לְת֣וּגָה ל֑וֹ Prov 15:16 וּמְה֥וּמָה בֽוֹ

There are a few exceptions, as Is 5:29   שָׁאַג֮ לוֹ֒

(b) The two words are a verb and its subject or object, as

Gen 3:19   תֹּ֥אכַל לֶ֖חֶם   Song 2:13   נָתְנ֥וּ רֵ֖יחַ

Ps 10:11   שָׁ֥כַח אֵ֖ל   Mal 1:9   הָיְתָ֣ה זֹּ֔את

(c) The two words form a construct phrase, as

Joel 1:20   אֲפִ֖יקֵי מָֽיִם   Gen 46:32   רֹ֥עֵי צֹ֖אן

Retraction occurs rarely in other situations:-

Where the two words are noun and adjective, as

Ps 68:12   צְבָ֥א רָֽב

Subject and verb, as 2S 13:30   וְהַשְּׁמֻעָ֣ה בָ֔אָה

Predicate and pronominal subject of a nominal clause, as

Lev 14:44   טָמֵ֥א הֽוּא   Jud 12:5   הַֽאֶפְרָתִ֣י אַ֔תָּה

Number and noun numbered, as

1S 17:17   וַעֲשָׂרָ֥ה לֶ֖חֶם   Gen 22:23   שְׁמֹנָ֥ה אֵ֖לֶּה

However the number 100 forms an exception, as retraction is
usual with מֵאָה, as

2K 4:43   מֵ֥אָה אִֽישׁ   2C 5:21   מֵ֥אָה אָֽלֶף

310.   (2) <u>Larger Units</u>. In three-word units, where the
pair in which retraction might occur is closely connected with
the word preceding or following it, retraction is much less
common.

a) Where the pair is connected to the following word, as

Gen 1:2   הָיְתָ֥ה תֹ֨הוּ֙ וָבֹ֔הוּ

Here the accent on the first word is not retracted, as the
second word is more closely connneted to the third word than to
the first. Again in Lev 22:10, לֹֽא־יֹ֥אכַל קֹ֑דֶשׁ is (in the accent
system) a two-word unit, so retraction occurs on יֹאכַל, but in
Lev 22:14   כִּֽי־יֹאכַ֥ל קֹ֖דֶשׁ בִּשְׁגָגָ֑ה retraction does not occur, because
a third word is involved. In Ps 53:6 לֹֽא־הָ֥יָה פָ֑חַד shows
retraction in a two word unit, but 1K 17:7, Jer 14:4
לֹֽא־הָיָ֥ה גֶ֨שֶׁם בָּאָ֑רֶץ shows no retraction as a third word is involved.
So also

Dt 29:17   פֹּרֶ֥ה רֹ֖אשׁ וְלַעֲנָֽה

Ez 34:27   וְנָתַ֤ן עֵ֣ץ הַשָּׂדֶ֗ה

Gen 2:20   לֹֽא־מָצָ֥א עֵ֖זֶר כְּנֶגְדּֽוֹ

Hab 2:12   בֹּ֥נֶה עִ֖יר בְּדָמִ֑ים

But note Gen 4:17   וַֽיְהִי֙ בֹּ֣נֶה עִ֔יר

b) Where the pair is connected to the preceding word, as

Prov 24:27   וְעִתְּדָ֥הּ בַּשָּׂדֶ֖ה לָ֑ךְ

Here the accent on בַּשָּׂדֶ֔ה is not retracted as this word is more closely connected to the word before it than to the one after it. So also in

Ps 31:4 כִּֽי־סַלְעִ֣י וּמְצוּדָתִ֣י אָ֑תָּה

In four word units which can be conveniently split into two pairs, the tendency to retraction reappears, as

Rut 4:15 ט֣וֹבָה לָּ֔הּ מִשִּׁבְעָ֖ה בָּנִֽים

Ez 42:20 ח֣וֹמָה ל֗וֹ סָבִ֣יב ׀ סָבִ֔יב

and compare Gen 6:8 מָ֥צָא חֵ֖ן בְּעֵינֵ֥י יְהוָֽה

(a four word unit in which retraction occurs), with

Jer 31:1 מָ֥צָא חֵן֙ בַּמִּדְבָּ֔ר where retraction does not occur. So also

Job 31:40 תַּ֤חַת חִטָּ֨ה ׀ יֵ֣צֵא ח֗וֹחַ with retraction and

Hab 3:5 וְיֵצֵ֥א רֶ֖שֶׁף לְרַגְלָֽיו with no retraction. Also

Ps 35:13 וַאֲנִ֤י ׀ בַּחֲלוֹתָ֗ם לְב֫וּשִׁ֥י שָׂ֗ק with retraction and

Ps 69:12 וָאֶתְּנָ֣ה לְבוּשִׁ֣י שָׂ֑ק with no retraction.

These are the basic principles governing the retraction of the accent, but there are many exceptions to them. Some of these occur where retraction is dependent on the structure of the word, but most occur where the relation of the two words to each other and to the surrounding context determines whether or no the accent should be retracted.

Literature. Wijnkoop, 1881, Praetorius, 1897.

'*GA^{c}YA*'

Literature.

311. Some information on *ga^{c}ya* is included in the rules on the accents given in the *Diqduqe ha-Ṭe^{c}amim* (Dotan, 1967, sections 14, 15, 20, and elsewhere). The statements on *ga^{c}ya* in the masoretic literature and the works of the early grammarians are few and unsystematic. The most detailed treatment of the rules for *ga^{c}ya* is that given by Yequti'el ha-Naqdan (published in Gumpertz, 1958). It was Yequti'el who set up different categories of the use of *ga^{c}ya*, introduced the terms "light *ga^{c}ya*" (*ga^{c}ya* in an open syllable) and "heavy *ga^{c}ya*" (*ga^{c}ya* in a closed syllable).

The survey of the rules for *ga^{c}ya* in the *Miqneh Abram* of Abram di Balmes, and in Heidenheim's *Sefer Mishpeṭe ha-Ṭe^{c}amim* (45a - 60b) was based on those of Yequti'el ha-Naqdan. Eliahu ha-Levi also gives detailed rules on the use of *ga^{c}ya*--though less systematic than those of Yequti'el ha-Naqdan, in *Ṭuv Ṭa^{c}am* chapter 7. The same is true of Shelomo Yedidyah Norzi's *Ma'amar ha-Ma'arik*.

The most comprehensive survey of the rules for *ga^{c}ya* is that in Baer 1869. These rules were derived from the study of *ga^{c}ya* in late MSS, and in some cases Baer imposes a system where none is evident in his sources. Nevertheless, Baer's rules were adopted in scholarly grammars, such as Bergsträsser 1918 (vol. 1, #11).

A few surveys of the system of marking *ga^{c}ya* in early MSS have been published. The system used in C is briefly described in Harṭom, 1952. The use of *ga^{c}ya* in several MSS is briefly described in Greenspan, 1961. A detailed description of the marking of *ga^{c}ya* in A is given in Yeivin, 1968, p. 89-194 (on the 21 books), and p. 241-277 (on the three books).

The Name 'Ga^{c}ya'

312. *Ga^{c}ya* (גִּיעְיָה, גַּעְיָה) is the older name for this sign (a short vertical stroke under the word), and is used in the masoretic literature. The absence of *ga^{c}ya* is called *ḥaṭef*, as in the Mm of A at

Prov 4:16 איוב לא יִשְׁנוּ חטף משלי לא יִֽשְׁנוּ געי

"יִשְׁנוּ (לא) in Job 29:22 has no *ga^{c}ya*, but in Proverbs it has *ga^{c}ya*." (Note that the word has a different meaning in the two cases.) *Metheg* (מֶתֶג), the later name for the sign, and that common today, is first known from the work of Yequti'el ha-Naqdan (first half of the thirteenth century). Eliahu ha-Levi (beginning of the sixteenth century) already suggests that *metheg* is the correct term, and that *ga^{c}ya* was only a name for one of the classes of *metheg* (that with *shewa*).

The 'Ga^{c}ya' Sign

313. *Ga^{c}ya* is marked by a short vertical stroke under the word (generally on a syllable before the main stress syllable, on which an accent sign is marked). In printed texts the stroke is really vertical, and this is also the case in most MSS, but in some MSS it is slanted a little to the right (to distinguish it from *merka*, which is slanted to the left). In the *Horayat ha-Qore* it is said that bA and bN use this form of the sign, but it is characteristic of only a few early MSS.

Ga^{c}ya forms part of the accent system, and is generally marked only in MSS in which the accent signs are marked, but not in those which show only vowel signs. *Ga^{c}ya* is not easily confused with the accent signs, as it is generally marked before the stress syllable, while most accent signs are marked on the stress syllable.

314. *Ga^{c}ya* is generally written to the left of a vowel sign marked under the same letter. In some MSS, such as A and L, this convention is carefully maintained, with very few exceptions--and those usually due to correction, or to lack of space in the regular position. In other MSS, such as C, S, S^{1}, *ga^{c}ya* is often written to the right of the vowel sign, without any particular reason. With *shewa* also, *ga^{c}ya* is generally written to the left of the *shewa* sign, but there are MSS in which it is often written to the right. The same is generally true of *ḥaṭef shewa* signs, but in some MSS, such as L and S^{1}, the *ga^{c}ya* sign may be written between the two parts of the *ḥaṭef* sign; -ֲ-. This does not occur in A and C.

The Function of 'Ga^{c}ya'

315. *Ga^{c}ya* has no musical motif of its own, but indicates that the reading of the syllable on which it is marked is to be slowed down, and not slurred over, as noted in *Horayat ha-Qore* p. 77 (Dérenbourg, 1870, p. 385) "But *ga^{c}ya*, which has the form of a stroke inclined backwards, and is found under some words, is neither a disjunctive nor a conjunctive accent, but indicates that the syllable must be lengthened a bit". It is probable that this slowing down of the reading of the syllable is the main function of *ga^{c}ya*, not the raising or trilling of the tone. It is possible, however, that, as time went on, *ga^{c}ya* came to be viewed as a secondary accent, and the rules for its use were changed, so that it came to be read with a raising of the pitch, and a short motif of its own.

The Categories of 'Ga^{c}ya'

316. The use of *ga^{c}ya* can be divided into two groups of categories:

i) Musical: categories determined by the needs of the Biblical chant. The marking of *ga^{c}ya* in these categories is dependent

on the syllabic structure of the word, and on the accent on that word or the one preceding or following. Most examples of $ga^{c}ya$ belong in these categories.
ii) Phonetic: Categories dependent on the consonants and vowels of the word, or of the preceding or following words. Few examples of $ga^{c}ya$ belong in these categories.

It is not always possible to determine the reason for which $ga^{c}ya$ is marked. In some cases it could be either musical or phonetic, but this is of no importance. Whatever the reason for marking $ga^{c}ya$, its function is always the same: to slow the reading of the syllable, whether this is required for musical reasons at the beginning of a particular motif, or for phonetic reasons, to ensure the clear pronunciation of all the sounds of a word.

317. The use of $ga^{c}ya$ in different sources differs greatly. In general, most categories of $ga^{c}ya$ are not marked consistently in MSS, while in printed texts a number of categories are marked systematically. For the study of the early MSS it is most important to note the categories of $ga^{c}ya$ which are mentioned in masoretic treatises, and those mentioned in the *Sefer ha-Ḥillufim*, since the use of $ga^{c}ya$ is the area in which bA and bN differ most frequently. The categories of $ga^{c}ya$ are as follows:-

i) Musical.
(a) $Ga^{c}ya$ on a closed syllable ("small" or "heavy" $ga^{c}ya$) in a word the structure of which can be "regular" or "not regular".
(b) $Ga^{c}ya$ on an open syllable ("great" or "light" $ga^{c}ya$)
(c) *Shewa* $ga^{c}ya$
(d) $Ga^{c}ya$ on a closed syllable with a "long" vowel.

ii) Phonetic.
(a) $Ga^{c}ya$ used to render a following *shewa* vocal.
(b) $Ga^{c}ya$ used on account of a guttural.
(c) $Ga^{c}ya$ used in the roots היה and חיה.

MUSICAL '$GA^{C}YA$'

318. The names "heavy" and "light" $ga^{c}ya$ (געיה כבדה, געיה קלה) for the two basic categories of musical $ga^{c}ya$ were introduced by Yequti'el ha-Naqdan, and were, as Dotan has remarked, an unfortunate innovation. Dotan, in his

edition of the *Diqduqe ha-Ṭeᶜamim* uses the terms "small" and "great" *gaᶜya* (געיה קטנה, געיה גדולה), terms which are used in the Masorah. These terms are not appropriate either, for although in the Masorah the term "small *gaᶜya*" is used for *gaᶜya* in a closed syllable, it may also include *gaᶜya* in an open syllable, and it seems quite likely that the term "great *gaᶜya*" in the Masorah refers to an accent. For this reason the descriptive names "*gaᶜya* on a closed syllable" and "*gaᶜya* on an open syllable" are used here.

'Gaᶜya' on a Closed Syllable

319. Regular Structure. A word of the same structure as מִתְקַטְּלִים, which has a closed syllable, separated from the stress syllable by another (the "buffer" syllable) followed by vocal *shewa* (simple or *ḥaṭef*) is said to have "regular" structure. In words of such structure, the initial closed syllable has *gaᶜya* if the word has a disjunctive accent, as נִתְחַכְּמָה. In the pattern מִתְקַטְּלִים, the vocal *shewa* stands under a letter with *dagesh* "forte" (follows a doubled consonant). It may also be the second of two *shewas*, in a form of pattern מִתְפַּלְפְּלִים, as הַכַּרְמְלִי (1S 30:5), or a *ḥaṭef shewa* in a form of pattern מִתְפַּעֲלִים, as מִשְׁתַּחֲוִים (Gen 37:9). Further examples are:-

מִתְקַטְּלִים Dt 31:22 וַיְלַמְּדָהּ
Ez 4:8 מִצִּדְּךָ
Jud 20:32 וַנְתַקְּנֻהוּ

and made up of two words joined by *maqqef*:-

1S 9:20 אֶת־לִבְּךָ

מִתְפַּלְפְּלִים Gen 49:23 וַיִּשְׂטְמֻהוּ
Gen 49:14 הַמִּשְׁפְּתָיִם
2S 23:20 מִקַּבְצְאֵל

and made up of words joined by *maqqef*:-

1C 28:13 וּלְכָל־מְלֶאכֶת
1C 5:10 עַל־כָּל־פְּנֵי
Lev 18:17 אֶת־בַּת־בְּנָהּ
Ez 10:15 בִּנְהַר־כְּבָר

מִתְפַּעֲלִים Jer 23:17 לִמְנַאֲצַי
Gen 41:3 וַתַּעֲמֹדְנָה
Jud 5:22 מִדַּהֲרוֹת
Is 57:8 וַתַּעֲלִי

and made up of words joined by *maqqef* :-

2K 11:10 אֶת־הַחֲנִית

This category of *ga*^{c}*ya* is mentioned in the *Diqduqe ha-Ṭe*^{c}*amim* (Dotan, 1967, section 15). An expanded statement is given in the *Qunṭrese ha-Masorah*, as indicated in the notes there, and in Yeivin, 1968, p. 96.

"Fully Regular" Structure

320. Words of the patterns described in #319 are said to have "fully regular" structure. If a word of this structure has a disjunctive accent, *ga*^{c}*ya* is generally marked, but if the accent is conjunctive, *ga*^{c}*ya* is generally not marked. This general rule holds good in about 90% of the cases, but there are exceptions. In a few dozen cases the accent is disjunctive, but *ga*^{c}*ya* is not marked, as

Jud 16:3	וַיֶּאֱחֹז	Lev 11:7, Dt 14:8	וְאֶת־הַחֲזִיר
Neh 1:3	מִן־הַשֶּׁבִי	Gen 34:3	וַיֶּאֱהַב
Ex 28:5	וְאֶת־הַתְּכֵלֶת		

There are about 200 cases in which the accent is conjunctive, but *ga*^{c}*ya* is nevertheless marked, as

Ez 37:23	יִטַּמְּאוּ	Gen 11:2	וַיִּמְצְאוּ
2C 30:24	וַיִּתְקַדְּשׁוּ	--and in words joined by *maqqef*	
Is 14:29	אַל־תִּשְׂמְחִי	Jud 3:28	אֶת־מַעְבְּרוֹת
Nu 11:22	אֶת־כָּל־דְּגֵי	Jos 22:20	וְעַל־כָּל־עֲדַת

321. These exceptions are one of the major subjects of variation between ben Asher and ben Naftali;and indeed of marginal notes on variants in general. For example:-

(i) Words with disjunctive accents

Ex 7:13, 9:35	וַיֶּחֱזַק	bN has *ga*^{c}*ya*
Lev 13:56	מִן־הַשְּׁתִי	bN has *ga*^{c}*ya*
Gen 13:12	וַיֶּאֱהַל	bA and bN agree on lack of *ga*^{c}*ya*
1K 7:4, 5	אֶל־מֶחֱזָה	bA and bN agree on lack of *ga*^{c}*ya*

(ii) Words with conjunctive accents

2C 20:17	הִתְיַצְּבוּ	bN has *ga*^{c}*ya*
Jer 27:15	הַנִּבְּאִים	bN has no *ga*^{c}*ya*
1K 20:29	וַיַּחֲנוּ	bA and bN agree on presence of *ga*^{c}*ya*
2K 25:5	וַיִּרְדְּפוּ	bA and bN agree on lack of *ga*^{c}*ya*

"Not Fully Regular" Structure

322. Words with patterns similar to those described in #319, but showing slight differences in structure, are said to be of "not fully regular" structure. Words in this category show slightly less tendency to the use of *gaᶜya* than words with fully regular structure. The following patterns are included in this category:-

1) Where the closed syllable is followed by vocal *shewa*, i.e. the "buffer" syllable begins with a vocal *shewa*, as

1C 2:3	הַֽכְּנַעֲנִ֑ית	Ex 16:23	אֲשֶׁר־תְּֽבַשֵּׁ֗לוּ

2) Where the "buffer" syllable has a long vowel, such as *qameṣ*, followed by a *ḥaṭef shewa*, as

Jos 10:36	וַיִּֽלָּחֲמוּ	2K 14:10	וּֽנְשָׂאֲךָ֖
2S 22:8	וַיִּֽתְגָּעֲשׁוּ	1S 17:36	אֶת־הָֽאֲרִי֙

or, with *ṣere*, Gen 32:27 אֲשַׁלֵּֽחֲךָ

or, with *ḥolem*, 1K 8:42 וּֽזְרֹעֲךָ֖

Rut 2:20	מִגֹּֽאֲלֵ֖נוּ	Lev 23:44	אֶת־מֹֽעֲדֵ֖י

Words with patterns like הַפּֽוֹעֲלִים (as הַשֹּׁעֲרִים, הַכֹּהֲנִים, etc.) usually do not have *gaᶜya*, and in general the number of exceptions to the rule in this category is much greater than among words with fully regular structure.

3) Where the "buffer" syllable has a long vowel followed by simple *shewa* (as in מִתְבָּרְכִים) *gaᶜya* is generally not marked. There are, however, a few exceptions, as

Dt 30:14 (and elsewhere) בִּֽלְבָבְךָ

Lev 19:5 (and elsewhere) לִֽרְצֹנְכֶ֖ם

2S 5:1 וּֽבְשָׂרְךָ֖

4) Where the stress syllable is preceded by a *ḥaṭef*--or even a simple *shewa*--which separates two identical consonants (or a *ḥaṭef* under some other non-guttural letter). If this *ḥaṭef* is preceded by a short vowel, *gaᶜya* is marked as in words with fully regular structure, as

Jud 16:24	וַֽיְהַלְל֗וּ	1K 8:30	יִֽתְפַּלְל֖וּ

If the vowel preceding the *ḥaṭef* is long, the marking of *gaᶜya* follows the rule given in (2) above, as

Zeph 2:1	הִֽתְקוֹשְׁשׁוּ	Jos 22:6	וַֽיְבָרְכֵ֖ם
Dt 32:6	וַֽיְכֹנְנֶֽךָ		

323. *Gaᶜya* is sometimes marked on a closed syllable in words of similar structure, but where the stress syllable is

not preceded by *shewa* or *ḥaṭef*, but the buffer syllable has, or could have, *ga*ᶜ*ya*.

1) Words composed of a closed syllable followed by some form from the root היה or חיה which could have *ga*ᶜ*ya* on the first syllable (see #355), as Is 10:22 אִם־יִהְיֶה--bN has אִֽם־.

2) Words in which the buffer syllable is marked with *ga*ᶜ*ya* before a guttural with *shewa* (#354), as 1C 5:32 וְזַרְחְיָה (the first *ga*ᶜ*ya* is musical, the second phonetic). Also

1C 27:19 יִשְׁמַעְיָהוּ 1S 26:19 יִשְׁמַע־נָא

Jer 5:7 אֶסְלֽוֹח־לָךְ (אסלח ק)

It would be possible to include words of pattern מִתְבָּרְכִים (class 3 in #322) in this group, since the buffer syllable could have *ga*ᶜ*ya* (on an open syllable) in those too.

*Ga*ᶜ*ya* in words of regular structure is the most common use of *ga*ᶜ*ya* on a closed syllable.

Non-regular structure

324. Words with structure which is not "regular"--that is not patterned like מִתְקַטְּלִים or its variants described above)--rarely show *ga*ᶜ*ya* on a closed syllable, and the use of *ga*ᶜ*ya* on such words has no fixed rules.

1) In some 15 cases *ga*ᶜ*ya* is marked on the fourth syllable before the accent, as Dt 12:2 אֶֽת־כָּל־הַמְּקֹמוֹת

2) In some 200 cases *ga*ᶜ*ya* is marked on the third syllable before the accent. This occurs mainly when the accent is one of the "high" trilled disjunctives (#195). Thus with

geresh Jos 13:3 מִֽן־הַשִּׁיחוֹר

pazer Jud 18:2 מִֽמִּשְׁפַּחְתָּם

telisha Lev 11:4, Dt 14:7 אֶֽת־הַגָּמָל

zarqa Gen 17:20 וּֽלְיִשְׁמָעֵאל

However it may occur with other disjunctives, as

1S 1:4 וּֽלְכָל־בָּנֶיהָ Ex 15:20 כָֽל־הַנָּשִׁים

And even with conjunctives, as

Dt 5:22 (19) אֶֽת־הַדְּבָרִים Gen 9:10 וּֽבְכָל־חַיַּת

3) In some 30 cases *ga*ᶜ*ya* is marked on the second syllable before the accent--most commonly on a word with penultimate stress marked with *pashṭa*, as

Jer 11:9 נִמְצָֽא־קֶשֶׁר

Lev 23:21 and elsewhere מִקְרָֽא־קֹדֶשׁ

2S 23:16, 1C 11:18 וַיִּשְׁאֲבוּ־מַיִם

However it also occurs with other accents, as

Ex 17:6 עַל־הַצּוּר Jos 11:4, 1S 13:5 עַל־שְׂפַת־הַיָּם

Dt 9:2 עַם־גָּדוֹל

This category contains a number of words in which the *ga^{c}ya* could be classified as phonetic (#350).

4) In some 60 cases *ga^{c}ya* is marked on the syllable immediately before the accent. In this position *ga^{c}ya* is rarely marked for musical reasons. Examples are:-

Ez 42:1 וַאֲשֶׁר־נֶגֶד Jud 18:22 נִזְעֲקוּ

2C 30:11 נִכְנְעוּ 1S 30:28 בְּשִׂפְמוֹת

Hos 10:14 שַׁלְמַן Gen 1:11 תַּדְשֵׁא

2S 22:17 יַמְשֵׁנִי

Ga^{c}ya in this position is usually marked for phonetic reasons (#350) and this may be the case even in some of the examples given above.

'Ga^{c}ya' before 'paseq'

325. This is most commonly found in cases like 1K 2:30 וַיֹּאמֶר׀ לֹא, where it is evidently used to mark a separation between the two words greater than that indicated by the *paseq*. *Ga^{c}ya* is only marked in this position in early MSS, and is rare even there.

'Ga^{c}ya' on an Open Syllable, or a syllable with a Long Vowel before 'Shewa'

326. *Ga^{c}ya* may be marked on an open syllable with either a long or a short vowel, and also on a syllable marked with a long vowel before *shewa*. This is the *ga^{c}ya* called "light" by Yequti'el ha-Naqdan, and "great" by Dotan. The Masoretes regarded *shewa* after a long vowel within a word as silent (לא יצא בפה see #386) so that in a word like קָטְלוּ the syllable marked by *ga^{c}ya* is, in their view, closed, not open. However because the rules for *ga^{c}ya* in this situation are similar to those for its use on an open syllable, the two situations are described together. Note, however, that two different types of syllable are involved.

This section, then, describes the use of *ga^{c}ya* (i) on an open syllable before a full vowel, as אָנֹכִי (ii) on an open syllable before a *ḥaṭef shewa*, as שָׁאֲלָה, יַעֲמֹד (iii) on a syllable with a long vowel before a *shewa* as קָטְלוּ. The use of *ga*^{c}*ya* in these cases is not affected by the accent on the word. It occurs both with disjunctive and with conjunctive accents. Thus, situation (i)

Gen 22:14	יֵֽאָמֵר		

and in words joined by *maqqef*

Gen 22:17	כִּֽי־בָרֵךְ	Gen 22:9	אָֽמַר־לוֹ
Gen 24:43	הַשְׁקִֽינִי־נָא		

Situation (ii)

Gen 21:30	בַּֽעֲבוּר		

and in words joined by *maqqef*

Ez 37:14	כִּֽי־אֲנִי		

Situation (iii)

Gen 22:12	יָֽדְךָ	Gen 22:5	נֵֽלְכָה
Gen 47:4	וַיֹּֽאמְרוּ		

and in words joined by *maqqef*

Gen 22:12	כִּֽי־יְרֵא		

327. If the second syllable before the stress syllable is closed, and therefore not suitable for this *ga*^{c}*ya*, but some preceding syllable is open, or has a long vowel followed by *shewa*, then *ga*^{c}*ya* is used on that syllable, as

Ex 27:10, 11	הָֽעַמּוּדִים	1S 26:19	מֵֽהִסְתַּפֵּחַ
Ez 42:5	מֵֽהַתַּחְתֹּנוֹת	Gen 23:18	שַֽׁעַר־עִירוֹ
Gen 9:2	הָֽאֲדָמָה	Gen 23:19	וְאַֽחֲרֵי־כֵן
Gen 23:11	לֹֽא־אֲדֹנִי	Est 8:10	הָֽאֲחַשְׁתְּרָנִים
Gen 18:21	אֵֽרְדָה־נָּא	Gen 21:3	אֲשֶֽׁר־יָֽלְדָה־לּוֹ

If *ga*^{c}*ya* is marked on some syllable of a word, and before that syllable is another on which *ga*^{c}*ya* could be marked (as before an accent) according to the rules given above, then the second *ga*^{c}*ya* may be marked, as

Gen 49:18	לִֽישׁוּעָֽתְךָ	Nu 8:2	בְּֽהַֽעֲלֹתְךָ
Ez 6:9	תּֽוֹעֲבֹֽתֵיהֶם	Nu 26:31	הָֽאַשְׂרְאֵלִי
Gen 31:33	בְּאֹֽהֶל־יַֽעֲקֹב		

Two *ga*^{c}*ya*s are often marked on the same word in printed texts, but this is rare in MSS.

328. If a word contains two syllables which are open, or contain a long vowel followed by *shewa*, and so are suitable for *ga*^{c}*ya*, and these come one after the other, then *ga*^{c}*ya* is usually marked on the one close to the accent in preference to

the other, as

1S 19:1 וִיהוֹנָתָן 2S 2:22 , מֵאַחֲרָי

1S 30:15 וְאוֹרִדְךָ

and in words joined by *maqqef*, Jos 10:20 גְּדוֹלָה־מְאֹד

This is the system used in printed texts, and in some MSS, such as A. In some other MSS, however, the *gaᶜya* farther from the accent is given preference, either consistently or sporadically, as

2C 20:2, L לִיהוֹשָׁפָט, A לִיהוֹשָׁפָט

Amos 4:1 C הָרֹצְצוֹת, הָאֹמְרֹת

Lev 13:7 B הֵרָאֹתוֹ

However if the *gaᶜya* farther from the accent is on a word joined with *maqqef*, and so preserves something of the original main stress of that word, then this further *gaᶜya* is given preference over the nearer one in the MSS, as

Gen 47:20 כִּי־מָכְרוּ Gen 31:52 לֹא־תַעֲבֹר

Gen 35:22 בְּנֵי־יַעֲקֹב Is 60:5 כִּי־יֵהָפֵךְ

Dt 9:3 הוּא־הָעֹבֵר

There are a few exceptions to this rule in the MSS, but not many. However printed texts still give preference to the *gaᶜya* nearer the accent, as כִּי־מָכְרוּ, etc.

329. As a general rule, *gaᶜya* is only marked on an open syllable if there is some sort of "buffer" (a vowel or a *ḥaṭef*) between the open syllable and the stress syllable, but occasionally in the MSS *gaᶜya* is marked even where there is no such buffer, as

Gen 42:35, B וַיִּירָאוּ

1S 26:20, L דָּמִי

This occurs most commonly in cases where two words are joined by *maqqef*, as

Jer 17:4, A, L כִּי־אֵשׁ Is 10:12, A עַל־פְּרִי־גֹדֶל

Nah 2:4, A אַנְשֵׁי־חַיִל Gen 45:12, B כִּי־פִי

Ex 4:6, B הָבֵא־נָא

L[20] and some other MSS use *gaᶜya* in this position quite frequently in the same word as the accent, especially if the accent is *pashṭa*, as

Jer 15:2 לַחֶרֶב Jer 26:2 הַבָּאִים

Some MSS with expanded Tiberian pointing also use *gaᶜya* in these positions quite frequently, as Vatican MS Urbino 2, in

Ez 1:1 בִּשְׁלֹשִׁים Ez 1:3 הָיֹה הָיָה

Ga^{c}*ya* is not used in these situations in printed texts.

330. The use of *ga*^{c}*ya* in an open syllable is not described in the masoretic literature or in other early sources, and there are only scattered references to this *ga*^{c}*ya*. In the *Diqduqe ha-Ṭe*^{c}*amim* (Baer-Strack 1879, #32) it is said

י(י)ראו meaning fear has *ga*^{c}*ya*, as Gen 20:8 וַיִּירְאוּ

יראו meaning see has no *ga*^{c}*ya*, as Nu 17:24 וַיִּרְאוּ

In the *Horayat ha-Qore* p. 90 (Dérenbourg, 1870, p. 398) it is said that "*ga*^{c}*ya* sometimes distinguishes meaning, as in the rule 'forms from ירא have *ga*^{c}*ya*, forms from ראה do not' and as in תִּשְׁנוּ (Neh 13:21) which means 'do again' (שנה), and יִשְׁנוּ (Prov 4:16) which means 'sleep' (ישן)". Yequti'el ha-Naqdan was the first to draw up rules for the use of this *ga*^{c}*ya*, and he has been followed by later scholars.

331. *Ga*^{c}*ya* on an open syllable, or after a long vowel followed by *shewa* is the most common category of *ga*^{c}*ya* in the Bible, and occurs in thousands of words. In the early MSS, this *ga*^{c}*ya* is not marked on all the words where it could be, but only on some of them, and in some MSS it is marked more commonly than in others. It seems probable that it was not considered important to mark it--possibly because it made less difference to the pronunciation of the word than did *ga*^{c}*ya* on a closed syllable.

In A, this *ga*^{c}*ya* is most commonly marked on words with *pashṭa* or *zaqef*, less commonly on those with other disjunctives, and only rarely on words with conjunctives. It is marked in about 30% of the possible cases.

In L and S it is marked in about 40% of the possible cases. In B and S^{1} it is marked in about 20% of the possible cases. In C this *ga*^{c}*ya* is marked much more commonly--in about 75% of the possible cases.

The other early MSS mark this *ga*^{c}*ya* in varying proportions of the possible cases. It is not always true that earlier MSS mark it less, as is shown by B and C, which are roughly contemporary. It is, however, generally true that later MSS mark this *ga*^{c}*ya* more commonly, and the printed texts mark *ga*^{c}*ya* on an open syllable regularly on every syllable suitable for it.

'Ga^c^ya on an Open Syllable after the Accent

332. A special case of *ga^c^ya* on an open syllable is *ga^c^ya* marked after the accent. If a word with the accent on the penultimate syllable ends in an open syllable, and stands before a word with the accent on the first syllable, *ga^c^ya* may be marked on the open syllable after the accent at the end of the first word, as

2K 1:13	עֲבָדֶ֫יךָ אֵ֫לֶּה	1S 15:6	עָשִׂ֫יתָה חֶ֫סֶד
Jer 9:20	עָלָ֫ה מָ֫וֶת	Is 52:11	ס֫וּרוּ ס֫וּרוּ
Ez 21:16	הוּחַ֫דָּה חֶ֫רֶב	1C 12:26	גִּבּ֫וֹרֵי חַ֫יִל
Is 14:31	הֵילִ֫ילִי שַׁ֫עַר		

This *ga^c^ya* is only rarely marked. It is most common in early MSS, but occurs only in scattered places in them.

This *ga^c^ya* occurs more often where the vowel of the stress syllable of the second word is preceded by *shewa*, as

Gen 28:2 and elsewhere	פַּדֶּ֫נָה אֲרָ֫ם	Dt 32:13	וַיֵּנִקֵ֫הוּ דְבַ֫שׁ
Ez 41:7	לְמַ֫עְלָה לְמַ֫עְלָה	Jer 9:18	בֹּ֫שְׁנוּ מְאֹ֫ד

This *ga^c^ya* also is marked most in early MSS, and is not marked in printed texts.

'Ga^c^ya' with 'Shewa'

333. *Ga^c^ya* marked with *shewa* (or a *ḥaṭef*) at the beginning of a word indicates (as elsewhere) that that syllable must be slowed or lengthened. Consequently that *shewa* becomes a vowel--probably equivalent to an ordinary short vowel. This *ga^c^ya* is rare in the twenty one books (only some 200 cases occur) but is common in the three books. This is a musical *ga^c^ya*, but it is often used with *shewa* before a guttural, which suggests that there may be phonetic reasons for its use. The system of marking it is similar to that for *ga^c^ya* in a closed syllable, but there are no firm rules for its use.

This *ga^c^ya* is marked on the second, third, or fourth syllable before the accent. It is usually used with "high" accents (#195), and so with *geresh*.

2K 24:14	וְֽאֵת־כָּל־הַשָּׂרִ֜ים	Gen 10:14, 1C 1:12	וְֽאֶת־פַּתְרֻסִ֜ים
Jos 10:24	כְּֽהוֹצִיאָ֜ם		
with *pazer* Ez 43:11	וְֽכָל־צוּרֹתָ֡יו	1C 12:41	וּֽבַבָּקָ֡ר
with *telisha* Jer 42:5	כְּֽכָל־הַדָּבָר		

with *zarqa* Gen 24:30 וְאֶת־הַצְּמִדִים Ez 35:12 וְיָדַעְתָּ

It also occasionally occurs with other accents, as

Ez 41:9 אֲשֶׁר־לַצֵּלָע Jud 4:9 בְּיַד־אִשָּׁה

1K 6:22 אֲשֶׁר־לַדְּבִיר (where *ga*[c]*ya* with *shewa* is given preference over *ga*[c]*ya* in a closed syllable in a word with "regular" structure).

Ga[c]*ya* is also used on *shewa* before the vowel of the syllable immediately before the stress syllable. This occurs mostly on words marked with *zaqef*, as

Song 1:5 וְנָאוָה Jer 51:61 וְרָאִיתָ וְקָרָאתָ

Is 13:2 שְׂאוּ־נֵס

This does occasionally occur with other accents, as

Song 1:8 צְאִי־לָךְ Jer 34:3 וְעֵינֶיהָ

334. A special category of words which take *ga*[c]*ya* with *shewa* is formed by words of structure similar to the "regular" structure of words suitable for *ga*[c]*ya* in a closed syllable but which have a consonant with *shewa* in place of the initial closed syllable, as מְקַטְּלִים, מְפַלְפְּלִים (like מִתְקַטְּלִים, מִתְפַּלְפְּלִים see #319). Examples are:-

2S 5:24, 1C 14:15 כְּשָׁמְעֲךָ Jer 34:14 תְּשַׁלְּחוּ

also מְפַעֲלִים (like מִתְפַּעֲלִים)

1K 8:1 and elsewhere לְהַעֲלוֹת Zech 8:23 וְהֶחֱזִיקוּ

2C 32:33 בְּמַעֲלֵה Hos 8:2 יְדַעֲנוּךָ

Dt 7:26 תְּתַעֲבֶנּוּ also Ez 48:1 לְבוֹא־חֲמָת

This *ga*[c]*ya* may also occur in forms like מְבָרְכִים (like מִתְבָּרְכִים which has "regular" structure, but not "fully regular", see #322) as Is 28:4 and elsewhere וְהָיְתָה

Joel 2:17 וְיֹאמְרוּ

Zech 8:21 וְהָלְכוּ Ez 41:7 וְנָסְבָה

335. The above describes *ga*[c]*ya* with *shewa* in words with disjunctive accents. This *ga*[c]*ya* also occurs occasionally in words with conjunctives, especially unusual combinations of conjunctives, as

Ez 34:10 -´-- -ֽ-- וְדָרַשְׁתִּי -´-- -`-- where *darga* follows *geresh*, and is the second servus before *revia*, or

2K 25:19 -ֽ-- אֲשֶׁר־הוּא -ֽ-- on a word (which is long and begins with *shewa*) which has *merka* as a servus to *legarmeh*.

Occasionally *ga*[c]*ya* with *shewa* is used in words with other

conjunctives, as with
mehuppak Ex 14:11 הֲמִבְּלִי and elsewhere
azla Ex 29:23 וְחַלַּת and elsewhere.

In the three poetical books there are a few cases of *ga^{c}ya* with *shewa* within a word, as

Ps 1:1	אַשְׁרֵי	Ps 89:25	וֶאֱמוּנָתִי
Ps 64:7	יַחְפְּשׂוּ		

336. *Ga^{c}ya* with *shewa* is regularly marked in early MSS, but the rules for it are not described in early sources, nor even by Yequti'el ha-Naqdan. Heidenheim and Baer were the first to establish these rules. The pronunciation of *shewa* with *ga^{c}ya* is described in the masoretic literature (as in the *Diqduqe ha-Ṭe^{c}amim* , Baer-Strack 1879, #11--see also Morag, 1963, p. 160 ff.). They state that *shewa* at the beginning of a word was generally pronounced as a small *pataḥ*, (פתחה קטנה) but that when it was marked with *ga^{c}ya* it was pronounced like a full *pataḥ* (בפתחה גדולה תצא). Before gutturals, the *shewa* was pronounced as a short vowel of the same quality as the vowel following the guttural, but when it was marked with *ga^{c}ya* it had the sound of a full vowel of that quality (thus בְּהֹנוֹת Jud 1:7 would be pronounced with three *ḥolems*). *Shewa* at the beginning of a word before *yod* was pronounced like a short *ḥireq*, but when marked with *ga^{c}ya*, it was pronounced like a full *ḥireq*.

'Ga^{c}ya' in a Closed Syllable with a Long Vowel

337. *Ga^{c}ya* may be marked in a closed syllable with a long vowel. In Hebrew such syllables usually have the accent, and when they do not have the accent they usually have *maqqef*. In this last situation, *ga^{c}ya* may be marked before either a disjunctive or a conjunctive accent.

This *ga^{c}ya* is marked regularly in most printed texts, but in MSS it is usually marked only if the closed syllable with the long vowel stands immediately before the stress syllable, as

Hos 8:7	אֵין־לוֹ	Jud 17:7	גָּר־שָׁם
Jos 12:16	בֵּית־אֵל	2K 4:26	רוּץ־נָא

If the closed syllable in question is the second before the accent, *ga^{c}ya* is usually not marked, as

Gen 41:45	שֵׁם־יוֹסֵף	Jos 23:6	סוּר־מִמֶּנּוּ

Jos 15:41 בֵּית־דָּגוֹן Jos 3:3 בְּרִית־יְהוָה

If the syllable in question is the third before the accent, *ga^{c}ya* is more likely to be marked, as

Jos 9:7 אִישׁ־יִשְׂרָאֵל Rut 2:23 קְצִיר־הַשְּׂעֹרִים

Jud 2:5 and elsewhere שֵׁם־הַמָּקוֹם

In general the marking of this *ga^{c}ya* in the early MSS is more regular than the marking of *ga^{c}ya* on an open syllable, but less regular than the marking of *ga^{c}ya* on a closed syllable of the "regular" type. However the regularity varies from MS to MS.

'Ga^{c}ya' on a closed syllable with 'Ṣere' after the Accent

338. Where a word ending in a closed syllable pointed with *ṣere* has its accent retracted, and the *ṣere* remains, it is marked by *ga^{c}ya* (see #308, 1c), as

Nu 17:23 וַיָּצֵץ צִיץ Is 66:3 עֹרֵף כֶּלֶב, מְבָרֵךְ אָוֶן

Is 40:7, cf. 8 נָבֵל צִיץ

This *ga^{c}ya* is marked both in MSS and in printed texts.

The System of Preference for Musical 'Ga^{c}ya'

339. In early MSS, such as A, L, C, two *ga^{c}ya*s are only rarely marked on the same word (or on a group of words joined by *maqqef*). Where a word or word group could have more than one *ga^{c}ya*, only one of them is generally marked, as

Ezra 9:12 בְּנוֹתֵיכֶם Jer 31:20 אֲרַחֲמֶנּוּ

where *ga^{c}ya* is marked under the initial *shewa* but not in the following open syllable, or Ex 15:26 כָּל־הַמַּחֲלָה, where *ga^{c}ya* in the initial closed syllable (a "non-regular" type) is marked, while that of the regular type, under the *he*, is not. Contrariwise, in A in 2K 23:12 וְאֶת־הַמִּזְבְּחוֹת, *ga^{c}ya* in a closed syllable of the regular type is marked, while that of the non-regular type, under the *alef*, and *ga^{c}ya* with the initial *shewa*, are not. (The *ga^{c}ya* with *shewa* was marked by bN).

340. The choice of which of two or more *ga^{c}ya*s should be marked under a word is determined by certain general principles, although these are affected by many detailed considerations which cannot be described here. The basic principle is that *ga^{c}ya* on a closed syllable is given preference over *ga^{c}ya* on an open syllable, or *ga^{c}ya* after a long vowel followed by *shewa*.

Examples are:-

Jud 18:12 וַֽיַּעֲלוּ Jud 19:29 הַֽמַּֽאֲכֶלֶת

Here *ga^cya* on the initial closed syllable (of the regular type) is marked, but that on the following open syllable (before the *ḥaṭef*) is not. So also

Dt 31:20 אֶֽל־הָֽאֲדָמָה Nu 17:21 כָּֽל־נְשִׂיאֵיהֶם

Here *ga^cya* is marked on the initial closed syllable of non-regular type, but not on the following open syllable. This general principle is common to all the early MSS.

On the problem of preference in words which could have more than one *ga^cya* on an open syllable (or on a syllable with a long vowel followed by *shewa*) see #328.

341. In the case of words which could have *ga^cya* on an open syllable and on a closed syllable with a long vowel (#337), the general rule is that if the closed syllable comes immediately before the stress syllable, *ga^cya* is marked on it, as Rut 1:11 הַֽעוֹד־לִי Job 2:11 לָֽנוּד־לוֹ

However if this is not the case, the *ga^cya* on the open syllable is preferred, as

Is 8:11 and elsewhere הָֽעָם־הַזֶּה Jos 11:12 הַֽמְּלָכִים־הָאֵלֶּה

Dt 7:1 גּֽוֹיִם־רַבִּים

The Marking of 'Ga^cya' in Manuscripts and Printed Texts

342. In early MSS, *ga^cya* on a closed syllable of regular or non-regular type, and *ga^cya* with *shewa*, are usually carefully and accurately marked. In some MSS this is also the case with *ga^cya* on a closed syllable with a long vowel. MSS following this system show the following characteristics:

1) The system of marking these *ga^cya*s is generally consistent throughout the MS.

2) The system of marking these *ga^cya*s is similar in different MSS. That is, *ga^cya* is generally marked in the same position on the same word in all early MSS.

3) Variations involving *ga^cya* noted in lists of *ḥillufim* or in marginal notes in the MSS are almost solely concerned with *ga^cya* in these categories.

These characteristics show the importance to the Masoretes of *ga^cya* in these categories, as opposed to *ga^cya* in an open syllable (or after a long vowel followed by *shewa*).

The lesser importance of *ga*^{c}*ya* in these latter categories is also shown by the fact that

1) The system of marking *ga*^{c}*ya* in an open syllable (or after a long vowel followed by *shewa*) is not consistent in any single MS.

2) The early MSS do not share the same system for marking *ga*^{c}*ya* in these categories, and they show no uniformity in the words on which *ga*^{c}*ya* in these categories is marked.

3) Lists of *ḥillufim* are almost bare of examples of variants involving *ga*^{c}*ya* in these categories.

343. In later MSS and in printed texts, a different system of marking *ga*^{c}*ya* is used. In printed texts, *ga*^{c}*ya* on an open syllable (or after a long vowel followed by *shewa*) is generally consistently and systematically marked, but *ga*^{c}*ya* on a closed syllable is marked only sporadically, or not at all.

344. This difference is reflected in the system of preference for marking *ga*^{c}*ya*. If a word could have *ga*^{c}*ya* both on a closed syllable and on an open syllable, that on the open syllable is marked in printed text, as Ex 14:19 וַיַּעֲמֹד whereas that on the closed syllable would be marked in early MSS (וַיַּעֲמֹד).

In a number of scholarly editions, such as those of Baer, Heidenheim, Qoren, and others, *ga*^{c}*ya* is marked as completely as possible, so that both *ga*^{c}*ya*s are marked in a word like וַיַּעֲמֹד. Similar usage is found in a number of MSS, as noted by Eliahu ha-Levi in his *Ṭuv Ṭa*^{c}*am* chapter 7. "When there is *dagesh* in the second letter of a word, and this letter is followed by א, ה, ח, or ע pointed with *ḥaṭef pataḥ*, then that word has two *methegs*: one on the first letter -- the principal *metheg*, one on the letter before the guttural--but only if the word has a disjunctive accent, as וַיַּעֲמֹד, וַיַּעֲבֹר."

PHONETIC 'GA^{C}*YA'*

345. Some *ga*^{c}*ya*s are not affected by the syllabic structure of the word, or by its accent. They have a phonetic, not a musical function. They have several purposes, among them *ga*^{c}*ya* with a short vowel (or even a long vowel) to show that a following *shewa* is vocal, and *ga*^{c}*ya* before a guttural to

slow down the reading of the vowel so that the guttural may be pronounced properly. It is not always clear what particular fault in pronunciation phonetic *ga^{c}ya* was intended to remedy. However the effect of phonetic *ga^{c}ya* is the same as that of musical *ga^{c}ya*: the slowing down of the reading.

'Ga^{c}ya' marking a following 'Shewa' as vocal

346. This *ga^{c}ya* is marked in various situations: before a consonant which has lost its historical doubling, before a sibilant consonant, before a group of similar consonants, etc. In some cases not only is the vowel before such a consonant marked with *ga^{c}ya*, but a *ḥaṭef* is marked after it as well (#391), but this is not done consistently either with words of the same structure, or with the same words in different MSS. Some MSS mark the *ḥaṭef* frequently (and this is one of the unique characteristics of A). Others mark it rarely. The quality of this *ḥaṭef* is determined by the Tiberian rules for the pronunciation of vocal *shewa* (#336, 387). Before a non-guttural other than *yod*, or a guttural pointed with *pataḥ*, *ḥaṭef pataḥ* is used. Before a guttural pointed with *qameṣ*, *ḥaṭef qameṣ* is used. Such a *ḥaṭef* is unlikely to occur before a guttural pointed with other vowels, or before *yod*.

'Ga^{c}ya' on a Short Vowel

347. (i) <u>On initial ה with 'pataḥ' before מ</u>. *Ga^{c}ya* is often marked before *mem* under word initial *he* with *pataḥ* representing either the definite article or *he* "interrogative". *Ga^{c}ya* is generally not marked if the *he* begins the syllable immediately before the stress syllable, as הַמְעַ֫ט (Is 7:13), and similarly it is not marked if the *he* begins the <u>third</u> syllable before the stress syllable, as הַמְקֻשָּׁרוֹת (Gen 30:41). However if the syllable in question is the <u>second</u> before the stress syllable, *ga^{c}ya* generally is marked, as

2S 10:3	הַֽמְכַבֵּד	Is 40:20	הַֽמְסֻכָּן
1C 27:21	הַֽמְנַשֶּׁה	Job 3:21	הַֽמְחַכִּים
Nu 20:19	בַּֽמְסִלָּה		

In all cases but the last (which is not preserved) A has *ḥaṭef pataḥ* under the *mem*.

In some cases, where simple *shewa* is used under the *mem*, where the word in question fits the description of regular structure, suitable for *gaᶜya* on an initial closed syllable, as Ez 46:24, A הַֽמְבַשְּׁלִים 2C 32:31, L (A מֲ) הַֽמְשַׁלְּחִים It is uncertain whether the *gaᶜya* is phonetic *gaᶜya*, in which case the following *shewa* is vocal, or musical *gaᶜya*, in which case the following *shewa* is silent. However where *ḥaṭef pataḥ* is used under the *mem*, as in A in 2C 32:31, it is certain that the *gaᶜya* is phonetic.

There are a number of exceptions to this rule, in which *gaᶜya* is not marked before *mem*, as לַֽמְנַצֵּחַ (Hab 3:19, and so always). In some other words *gaᶜya* is not marked and the *mem* has *dagesh* (and so the *shewa* is vocal), as Jos 19:13, הַמְּתֹאָר Qoh 11:5 הַֽמְּלֵאָה.

348. *Gaᶜya* is occasionally marked under initial *he* with *pataḥ* before other consonants as well, as (after *he* interrogative)

1S 18:23	הֲֽנְקַלָּה	Gen 27:38	הַֽבְרָכָה

Or after the definite article

Ez 40:43	וְהַֽשְׁפַתַּיִם	Ps 104:18	לַֽשְׁפַנִּים
2K 2:1, 11	בַּֽסְעָרָה	Jer 33:10	הַֽנְשַׁמּוֹת
Ex 7:29 and elsewhere	הַֽצְפַרְדְּעִים	2K 17:31	וְהַֽסְפַרְוִים

A shows *ḥaṭef pataḥ* in the cases in 1S, Ezekiel, Psalms, as does B in the case in Exodus.

349. (ii) <u>'*Gaᶜya*' on conjunctive '*waw*' pointed as '*shureq*'.</u> *Gaᶜya* in this situation is especially common before sibilants, but also appears before other consonants. Thus, in the syllable immediately before the stress,

Before שׁ	Jud 5:12	וּֽשֲׁבֵה	2K 19:16 and elsewhere	וּֽשְׁמָע
	Qoh 9:7	וּֽשֲׁתֵה		
Before שׂ	Lev 25:34	וּֽשֲׂדֵה		
Before ס	Is 26:20	וּֽסֲגֹר	1K 13:7	וּֽסְעָדָה
Before ז	Gen 2:12	וּֽזֲהַב	Jer 48:20 (וזעקו ק)	וּֽזְעָקִי
Before צ	Jer 22:20	וּֽצְעָקִי		
Before ק	Is 34:16	וּֽקְרָאוּ	(A וּֽקֲרָאוּ)	

In the second syllable before the stress syllable:

Before ס	Is 45:14	וּֽסְחַר־כּוּשׁ	(A וּֽסֲחַר)
	2K 7:18	וּֽסְאָה־סֹלֶת	(S[1] וּֽסֳאָה־)
Before ת	Ez 26:21		וּֽתְבֻקְשִׁי (A וּֽתֲבֻקְשִׁי)
	Jer 3:25		וּֽתְכַסֵּנוּ (A וּֽתֲכַסֵּנוּ)

Before ל Gen 1:18, Lev 10:10 וּֽלֲהַבְדִּ֫יל

350. (iii) <u>'Ga^{c}ya' on Other Short Vowels</u>. 1) Before a consonant which has lost its historical doubling:

Jos 11:2 כִּֽנְר֑וֹת (A כִּֽנֲר֑וֹת)
Ps 17:14 מִֽמְתִ֡ים
Nu 1:18 וַיִּֽתְיַלְד֥וּ
Jud 16:16 וַתְּֽאַלְצֵ֑הוּ (A וַתְּֽאַֽלֲצֵ֑הוּ)
Gen 1:24 וְחַֽיְתוֹ־אֶ֖רֶץ
Gen 2:23 לֻֽקֳחָה־זֹּֽאת
Ez 7:24 מְקַֽדְּשֵׁיהֶֽם and others.

2) Before a syllable beginning with a guttural.

1S 5:12 שַֽׁוְעַ֥ת
2S 22:2 סַֽלְעִ֥י
Is 65:8 הַֽשְׁחִ֥ית
Job 1:3 שִֽׁבְעַ֣ת
Gen 21:6 יִֽצְחַק־לִֽי (some have יִֽצֲחַק־)
1K 17:11 לִֽקְחִי־נָ֥א

3) Before a syllable beginning with a *begad-kefat* letter which is *rafe*:

Jer 12:16 דַּֽרְכֵ֗י
Jer 20:9 כַּֽלְכֵ֥ל
Is 54:12 כַּֽדְכֹּ֗ד
Lev 13:48 בְּֽשְׁתִ֗י
Is 20:1 סַֽרְג֗וֹן
Job 33:25 רֻֽטְפַ֣שׁ (A, L רֻֽטֲפַ֣שׁ)
Gen 30:38 בְּֽשִׁקֲת֣וֹת

4) Other situations:

Dan 9:19 הַֽקְשִׁ֥יבָה (L הַֽקֲשִׁ֥יבָה)
2S 22:12 חַֽשְׁרַת־מַ֗יִם (A חַֽשֲׁרַת־)

'Ga^{c}ya' before the First of a Pair of Identical Consonants

351. *Ga^{c}ya* is usually marked in this situation whether the first of the pair of consonants was historically doubled (and has lost this doubling) or not. Thus, historically doubled

Is 62:9 וְהִֽלְל֗וּ Is 64:10 הִֽלְל֫וּךָ
Jud 5:11 מְֽחַצְצִ֗ים 2S 16:7 בְּֽקַלְל֑וֹ
1S 2:25 יְֽפַלְל֣וֹ Ez 31:6 קִֽנְנ֗וּ

With no historical doubling

Ez 4:12 בְּֽגֶלְלֵ֗י Jer 51:49 חַֽלְלֵ֥י, חַֽלֲלֵ֑י

2C 20:2 בְּחַצְצוֹן Jud 9:57 קִלְלַת
Mic 6:7 בְּרִבְבוֹת Zech 11:3 יִלְלַת

In most such cases A marks a *ḥaṭef shewa* under the first of the two consonants.

In a few cases of this phenomenon *ga*^{c}*ya* is not marked, as הִנְנִי (always), and Job 10:15 אַלְלַי, and in some similar cases, the first of the two consonants has *dagesh*, and no *ga*^{c}*ya* is marked, as 1K 1:40 מְחַלְּלִים

Is 34:15 קִנְּנָה Ps 95:1 נְרַנְּנָה

'Ga^{c}*ya' on a Long Vowel*

352. A syllable containing a long vowel followed by *shewa* generally has musical *ga*^{c}*ya* (#326). However in some MSS *ḥaṭef shewa* is used in a number of such cases, so that it can be assumed that in a number of cases *ga*^{c}*ya* under a long vowel followed by *shewa* is phonetic *ga*^{c}*ya*. Examples are:

Before ר Job 31:37 אֲקָרְבֶנּוּ
Nu 16:32 כָּל־הָרְכוּשׁ (B, L, הָרֲכוּשׁ, S הָרְכוּשׁ)

and so often in forms from the roots ברך, גרש, ירד (#379).

Before other consonants:

Jer 22:28 הוּטְלוּ (A הוּטֲלוּ)
Ez 9:8 וְנֵאשְׁאַר Est 1:6 רִצְפַּת (many MSS רִצֲפַּת)

and so also in certain circumstances in forms from the roots אכל, הלך , and others, (see #380).

353. Even where a long vowel is followed by two identical consonants the first of which is pointed with *shewa*, the long vowel is often marked with *ga*^{c}*ya*, and the *shewa* is a *ḥaṭef*, as

Ez 26:12, 39:10 וּבָזְזוּ (A וּבָזֲזוּ)
Is 58:9 מְתּוֹכְכָה (A מְתּוֹכֲכָה)
Jer 6:6 סֹלְלָה (A סֹלֲלָה)

This usage is not consistent, however. Sometimes both *ga*^{c}*ya* and *ḥaṭef* appear. Sometimes *ga*^{c}*ya* is not marked, and the *shewa* is simple. Sometimes there is no *ga*^{c}*ya*, but a *ḥaṭef shewa* is used, and sometimes *ga*^{c}*ya* is used, but the *shewa* is simple. Different methods are used in different MSS, and there is no agreement between them. It appears that the general rule was that *shewa* after a long vowel was silent, but that if this *shewa* stood under the first of two identical consonants it was always vocal. This latter fact could be marked either by a *ḥaṭef shewa* or by *ga^{c}ya*, so either one may be used alone, but sometimes both are used, and sometimes no indication is given. (See #385).

'Ga^{c}ya' on a Short Vowel before a Guttural

354. (i) 'Ga^{c}ya' before a Guttural which closes a Syllable. *Ga^{c}ya* is sometimes marked before a guttural pointed with *shewa* either within a word or at the end of a word joined to a second by *maqqef*--especially if the second word begins with *lamed* or *nun*. Thus, within a word

1C 5:4	שְׁמַֽעְיָה	Is 1:1	יְשַֽׁעְיָהוּ
Neh 11:24	וּפְתַֽחְיָה		

Before *maqqef*

1K 1:51	יִשָּֽׁבַע־לִי	Jud 14:3	קַֽח־לִי
1S 28:22	שְׁמַֽע־נָא		

Ga^{c}ya is similarly sometimes used on the last syllable of a word with penultimate stress if it ends with a guttural and the following word begins with *lamed* or *nun*, as

Rut 1:21	הֵרַֽע לִי	1K 2:8	וָאֶשָּֽׁבַע לוֹ
Ez 1:4, 27	וְנֹגַֽהּ לוֹ		

Ga^{c}ya may even be marked in a similar situation after *pataḥ* "furtive", as

Jud 19:25	לִשְׁמֹעַֽ לוֹ	Dt 29:19	סְלֹחַֽ לוֹ

This *ga^{c}ya* is consistently used with the numbers אַרְבַּֽע־עֶשְׂרֵה, שְׁבַֽע־עֶשְׂרֵה, תְּשַֽׁע־עֶשְׂרֵה.

355. (ii) 'Ga^{c}ya' in Forms of היה and חיה. *Ga^{c}ya* is used in many forms from these roots to prevent the slurring over of the *he* or *ḥet*. It occurs in two classes of forms:

1) Before *he* or *ḥet* with *shewa*, as יִֽהְיוּ, יִֽהְיֶה, תִּֽהְיֶה, תִּֽהְיֶינָה, תִּֽהְיוּ, לִֽהְיוֹת, בִּֽהְיוֹתוֹ, מִֽהְיוֹתָהּ, וִֽהְיוּ, וֶֽהְיֵה, נִֽהְיְתָה and so on (and in the corresponding forms from חיה).

2) Before the *yod* of the pronominal prefix where it has *shewa*, as in וַֽיְהִי, וַֽיְחִי.

This *ga^{c}ya* is most commonly used where the word has a disjunctive accent, but may also occur with conjunctives. The tendency to mark it differs in different forms, and it is not consistent in individual MSS, nor is its use uniform in any group of MSS, and it does not appear in the lists of *ḥillufim*. This *ga^{c}ya* is, however, as a rule marked consistently when the word in question is joined by *maqqef* to a word stressed on the first syllable, as

Ez 45:8 יִֽהְיֶה־לּוֹ Jer 7:23 תִּֽהְיוּ־לִי
Gen 1:5 וַֽיְהִי־עֶרֶב וַֽיְהִי־בֹקֶר

The System of Preference for Phonetic 'Ga^{c}ya'

356. It was noted above (#339) that only one musical *ga^{c}ya* was normally marked on a word, even where more than one could appear. This is not, however, the case where a phonetic *ga^{c}ya* is involved. In this case two *ga^{c}yas* are marked on the same word even in MSS like A and L, where this is otherwise very rare. Examples of different combinations of *ga^{c}yas* are given below:

1) Musical *ga^{c}ya* on a closed syllable with regular structure (#324) and phonetic *ga^{c}ya* before a pair of identical consonants.

Job 42:10 בְּהִֽתְפַּֽלְלוֹ 2C 7:14 וְיִֽתְפַּֽלְלוּ

2) Musical *ga^{c}ya* on an open syllable, and phonetic *ga^{c}ya* on forms from היה and חיה.

Ez 13:9 לֹֽא־יִֽהְיוּ Ez 36:3, A לִֽהְיֽוֹתְכֶם

3) Phonetic *ga^{c}ya* before *mem* following *he* with *pataḥ*, and phonetic *ga^{c}ya* before a pair of identical consonants

Jud 7:7, A הַֽמְֽלַקְקִים

4) Musical *ga^{c}ya* on an open syllable (#326) and phonetic *ga^{c}ya* before a guttural with *shewa*

Lam 5:5 הֽוּנַֽח־לָֽנוּ

5) Musical *ga^{c}ya* on a closed syllable (#323) and phonetic *ga^{y}ya* before a guttural with *shewa*

1C 7:3 יִֽזְרַֽחְיָה Is 38:4 אֶֽל־יְשַֽׁעְיָהוּ
Jer 44:17 וַֽנִּֽשְׂבַּֽע־לֶחֶם Hos 4:17 הַֽנַּֽח־לוֹ
1C 2:19, 2C 11:18 וַֽיִּֽקַּֽח־לוֹ 2C 2:7 וּֽשְׁלַֽח־לִי

6) Musical *ga^{c}ya* with *shewa* (#333) and phonetic *ga^{c}ya* before a guttural with *shewa*

Neh 6:10, L שְֽׁמַֽעְיָה 1S 22:12, Jer 37:20 שְֽׁמַֽע־נָא
2C 2:6 שְֽׁלַֽח־לִי

This system of marking the two *ga^{c}yas* on one word is not common to all the early MSS. In some only one *ga^{c}ya* is marked, either the musical or the phonetic.

'Maqqef' after 'Ga^{c}ya'

357. In some MSS *maqqef* is marked--sometimes consistently,

sometimes sporadically--after a word marked with *ga*^{c}*ya* after the accent. This occurs in words where *ga*^{c}*ya* is marked on a final open syllable (#332), as בּוֹשָׁה־חֲמָת (Jer 49:23 in C), where *ga*^{c}*ya* is marked on a final closed syllable with a long vowel, (#338), as לְבָעֵר־קָיִן (Nu 24:22 in S) and where phonetic *ga*^{c}*ya* is marked before a guttural with *shewa* after the accent (#354), as וַתּוֹשַׁע־לוֹ (Is 59:16 in A, C) לִשְׂבֹּעַ־לָחֶם (Lam 5:6 in L[13]).

The purpose of this *maqqef* is to indicate that, even though *ga*^{c}*ya* is marked after the accent, so that the reading of that syllable must be slowed down, the word must be joined to the following word, and no break should be made between them. That is, *ga*^{c}*ya* sometimes indicates a pause of some sort. The *maqqef* is used to show that no pause should be made in these cases. As is said in Nutt, 1870, text p. 129 (ascribed to Ḥayyuj) "*Ga*^{c}*ya* is the opposite of *maqqef*, because *maqqef* joins words while *ga*^{c}*ya* separates them."

THE ACCENTS OF THE THREE BOOKS

358. Some of the accent signs used in the Twenty-One Books are also used in the Three Books, and some are only found in the Three Books. The signs used in the Three Books are:-

Disjunctives		Conjunctives	
Silluq	דבֽר	*Munaḥ*	דבֽ֣ר
^{c}*Oleh we-yored*	ד֫ב֥ר	*Merka*	דב֥ר
Atnaḥ	דב֑ר	^{c}*Illuy*	דב֬ר
Revia	דב֗ר	*Ṭarḥa*	דב֖ר
Revia mugrash	ד֝ב֗ר	*Galgal*	דב֪ר
Shalshelet gedolah	דב֓ר׀	*Mehuppak*	דב֤ר
Ṣinnor	דבר֘	*Azla*	דב֨ר
Deḥi	֭דבר	*Shalshelet qeṭannah*	דב֓ר
Pazer	דב֡ר	*Ṣinnorit*	֘דבר
Mehuppak legarmeh	דב֤ר׀		
Azla legarmeh	דב֨ר׀		

The following paragraphs describe these accents, and the basic rules for their use. It is not the intention to give a complete description of this accentuation, however, so details such as the reasons for the use of different conjunctives, or rare combinations of accents, are not included.

Literature: Wickes, 1881; Dotan 1967, particularly sections 10, 11, 12, 13; Baer, 1852; Yeivin 1968, p. 281-356.

'Silluq' - סילוק

359. *Silluq* is used at the end of every verse, as in the twenty-one books. In the three books, it may have up to four servi. A single servus is usually *munaḥ*, as

Ps 1:1 לֹ֣א יָשָֽׁב

or *merka*, as

Ps 1:2 יוֹמָ֥ם וָלָֽיְלָה

Two servi are usually *ṭarḥa* (טַרְחָא, marked with the sign used in the twenty-one books for *ṭifḥa*, but nevertheless a conjunctive) and *munaḥ*, as

Ps 1:6 וְדֶ֖רֶךְ רְשָׁעִ֣ים תֹּאבֵֽד

Various accents appear as the third and fourth servi before *silluq*, and their use is governed by intricate rules. Examples are: with three servi

Ps 9:11 כִּ֤י לֹא־עָזַ֖בְתָּ דֹרְשֶׁ֣יךָ יְהוָֽה

Ps 89:49 יְמַלֵּ֣ט נַפְשׁ֖וֹ מִיַּד־שְׁא֣וֹל סֶֽלָה

with four servi

Ps 42:2 כֵּ֤ן נַפְשִׁ֨י תַעֲרֹ֖ג אֵלֶ֣יךָ אֱלֹהִֽים

Other combinations of servi are also used.

If the verse is long, and the main division is distant from *silluq*, it is marked by *ᶜoleh we-yored*, as

Ps 46:10 מַשְׁבִּ֣ית מִלְחָמוֹת֮ עַד־קְצֵ֪ה הָ֫אָ֥רֶץ
קֶ֣שֶׁת יְ֭שַׁבֵּר וְקִצֵּ֣ץ חֲנִ֑ית עֲ֝גָל֗וֹת יִשְׂרֹ֥ף בָּאֵֽשׁ

If the verse is short, and the main division is relatively close to *silluq*, it is marked by *atnaḥ*, as

Ps 46:2 אֱלֹהִ֣ים לָ֭נוּ מַחֲסֶ֣ה וָעֹ֑ז עֶזְרָ֥ה בְ֝צָר֗וֹת נִמְצָ֥א מְאֹֽד

'ᶜOleh we-yored' - עולה ויורד

360. This accent, used to mark the main verse division, is indicated by a sign composed of two elements: a sign like *merka* is used below the stress syllable (*yored*), and a sign like *mehuppak* is used above the preceding syllable (*ᶜoleh*), as לְנַ֫פְשִׁ֥י (Ps 3:3). Where this accent is marked on two words which should be joined by *maqqef*, and the second of the two is stressed on the first syllable, the two signs are divided between the end of the first word and the beginning of the second, as לֹ֫א לָ֥נוּ (Ps 115:1) (*maqqef* is not usually marked). This is true even where a conjunctive occurs, if the preceding word has penultimate stress, as in סְפַ֫רְתָּ֥ה אָ֥תָּה (Ps 56:9), in which case the conjunctive is marked on the stress syllable.

If the preceding word has a disjunctive (*revia*), the first component of the ^{c}*oleh we-yored* sign is not marked, as in קֶדֶם סֶלָה (Ps 55:20). This is also the case where the final word of the verse half is stressed on its first syllable, and the preceding word is stressed on its last syllable, as לְאֵל חָי (Ps 42:3) וְאֵשֵׁב רֹאשׁ (Job 29:25). This is the convention in MSS. In printed texts, however, the upper sign may be marked on the same letter as the lower as in וְאֵשֵׁב רֹאשׁ, or between the two words, as וְאֵשֵׁב רֹאשׁ.

Words with ^{c}*oleh we-yored* regularly appear in pausal form, as Ps 30:10 אֶל שָׁחַת, Ps 137:7 יְרוּשָׁלָ͏ִם.

361. ^{c}*Oleh we-yored* has only one servus. In the MSS, this characteristic servus is marked by a "v" shaped sign marked under the stress syllable. In later MSS this is confused with *galgal*, the servus of *pazer*, so that the servus of ^{c}*oleh we-yored* has the same semi-circular form as the servus of *pazer*. The extent to which the angular form of the servus of ^{c}*oleh we-yored* is distinguished from the semi-circular form of the servus of *pazer* serves as an indicator of the accuracy and purity of the tradition of the accentuation in a manuscript.

If the word bearing the servus is stressed on its first syllable, the servus is *mehuppak* in the MSS, although the *galgal* sign is usually used here in printed texts also. Occasionally the servus is *merka*.

As a rule, where ^{c}*oleh we-yored* has no servus, it is preceded by the disjunctive *revia*, as

Ps 3:6 אֲנִי שָׁכַבְתִּי וָאִישָׁנָה

If ^{c}*oleh we-yored* has a servus, it is preceded by the disjunctive *ṣinnor*, as Ps 48:3 יְפֵה נוֹף מְשׂוֹשׂ כָּל־הָאָרֶץ. Either *revia* or *ṣinnor* is always used before ^{c}*oleh we-yored*, for which reason it is called עוקב הרביע "Follower of *revia*" or עוקב הזרקא "Follower of *zarqa*" (*zarqa* is another name for *ṣinnor*) in the masoretic literature.

The main divider of the unit ending with ^{c}*oleh we-yored*, which is used before *revia* or *ṣinnor*, is *revia gadol*, as

Ps 1:3 וְהָיָה כְּעֵץ שָׁתוּל עַל־פַּלְגֵי מָיִם

'Atnaḥ' - אתנח

362. *Atnaḥ* in the Three Books has the same form as in the

twenty-one books, and a similar use, but its pausal value is less than that of ^{c}*oleh we-yored* and similar to that of *zaqef* in the Twenty-One Books. It has up to five servi.

If *atnaḥ* is preceded by the disjunctive *deḥi*, a single servus is *munaḥ*, as

Ps 2:1 לָמָּה רָגְשׁוּ גוֹיִם

If it is not preceded by *deḥi*, a single servus is *merka*, as

Ps 6:3 -- רְפָאֵנִי יְהוָה

Two servi before *atnaḥ* are both *munaḥ*s, as

Ps 2:4 יוֹשֵׁב בַּשָּׁמַיִם יִשְׂחָק

However if *paseq* is used before the *atnaḥ*, the servi are *ṭarḥa* (see #359) and *merka*, as

Ps 57:10 אוֹדְךָ בָעַמִּים׀ אֲדֹנָי

As with *silluq*, various conjunctives are used as the third and further servi before *atnaḥ*. Examples are:-

With three servi, Ps 2:5 אָז יְדַבֵּר אֵלֵימוֹ בְאַפּוֹ

With four servi, Ps 96:4 כִּי גָדוֹל יְהוָה וּמְהֻלָּל מְאֹד

Five servi before *atnaḥ* occur only in Prov 3:12.

The main division in the unit ending with *atnaḥ* is usually marked by *deḥi* if it is close to the *atnaḥ*, and by *revia* (*gadol*) if it is distant from the *atnaḥ*.

'Revia gadol' - רביע גדול

363. *Revia gadol* is used subordinate to ^{c}*oleh we-yored* and to *atnaḥ*.

Three types of *revia* are distinguished in the three books. *Revia mugrash*, which is used in the second half of the verse, before *silluq*, is usually distinguished by the addition of a *geresh*-like stroke (#366). *Revia gadol* and *revia qaṭan* are marked by the same sign, a dot above the stress syllable (as the *revia* of the Twenty-One Books) but differ in their use. *Revia qaṭan* is used immediately before ^{c}*oleh we-yored*. *Revia gadol* is used as the main divider in the unit ending with *atnaḥ* or ^{c}*oleh we-yored*. *Revia* also appears as the main verse divider where *atnaḥ* is not used, as

Ps 58:1 לַמְנַצֵּחַ אַל־תַּשְׁחֵת לְדָוִד מִכְתָּם

This is *revia mugrash* without the "*geresh*" (#367).

If two *revia*s are used in such a verse, as

Ps 57:9 עוּרָה כְבוֹדִי עוּרָה הַנֵּבֶל וְכִנּוֹר אָעִירָה שָּׁחַר

the first of the two is *revia gadol*, and the second *revia mugrash* without the "*geresh*".

Revia gadol rarely has more than one servus, but several conjunctives may occur in this position, depending on the circumstances.

The servus may be *merka*, as

Ps 18:16 אֲפִ֥יקֵי מַ֗יִם

It may be *mehuppak*, as Ps 54:5 קָ֤מוּ עָ֗לַי

Mehuppak meṣunnar--i.e. *mehuppak* with *ṣinnorit* (#372) used as a "helping tune" on the open syllable before the stress--is also used, as Ps 40:10 בְּקָ֘הָ֤ל רָ֗ב

ᶜIlluy (One of the shofar accents (#213), marked by the *munaḥ* sign above the stress syllable) may also act as servus to *revia* as Ps 5:9 נְחֵ֬נִי בְצִדְקָתֶ֗ךָ

Revia gadol has two servi only in Ps 27:6, 55:24.

In the unit ending with *revia gadol*, a division which is near the *revia*, or of little significance, is marked by *legarmeh* (#370), as

Ps 37:28 כִּ֤י יְהוָ֨ה ׀ אֹ֘הֵ֤ב מִשְׁפָּ֗ט

A division more distant from the *revia*, or more significant, is marked by *pazer* (#369), as

Ps 11:2 כִּ֤י הִנֵּ֪ה הָרְשָׁ֡עִים יִדְרְכ֬וּן קֶ֗שֶׁת

Both accents may occur, as

Ps 2:12 נַשְּׁקוּ־בַ֡ר פֶּן־יֶאֱנַ֤ף ׀ וְתֹ֬אבְדוּ דֶ֗רֶךְ

'*Deḥi*' - דחי

364. *Deḥi* is used subordinate to *atnaḥ*. It is marked by a stroke under the word, slanting to the right, like *ṭifḥa* in the Twenty-One Books, or the conjunctive *ṭarḥa* in the Three Books. It is distinguished from *ṭarḥa* by its prepositive position, as תַּ֭סְתִּירֵנִי (Ps 64:3). If two words are joined by *maqqef*, the *deḥi* is marked on the second, as נְֽסָה־עָ֭לֵינוּ (Ps 4:7). In some MSS, the stress syllable of a word marked by *deḥi* is indicated (where confusion might occur) by a stroke below the stress syllable, slanted to the left (like *merka*), as ע֭וּרָ֥ה (Ps 57:9, 108:3), אָ֭נָ֥ה (Ps 139:7), אָ֭נֹכִ֥י (Prov 24:32, Job 29:16).

In MSS with expanded Tiberian pointing, the *tevir* sign is used, below the stress syllable, to mark *deḥi*, and indeed *deḥi* and *tevir* do have similar pausal value.

Deḥi may have up to three servi.

One servus is *munaḥ*, as Ps 5:8 בְּרֹ֣ב חַ֭סְדְּךָ

If the word bearing *deḥi* contains an open syllable with a long vowel followed by *shewa*, suitable for *ga^cya*, if this is not the first syllable, and if no servus precedes, then *munaḥ* is marked on the open syllable in the same word as *deḥi*, as

Ps 106:28 וַיִּצָּמְדוּ

Various conjunctives appear as the second servus before *deḥi*, for example *mehuppak*, as Ps 28:2 שְׁמַע קוֹל תַּחֲנוּנַי

A third servus before *deḥi* is found only in Ps 56:10, Job 34:37.

Divisions in the unit ending with *deḥi* are marked by *legarmeh*, as Ps 12:5 אֲשֶׁר אָמְרוּ לִלְשֹׁנֵנוּ נַגְבִּיר

or by *pazer*, as Ps 28:5 כִּי לֹא יָבִינוּ אֶל־פְּעֻלֹּת יְהוָה

or by both together, as

Ps 45:8 עַל־כֵּן מְשָׁחֲךָ אֱלֹהִים אֱלֹהֶיךָ

'Ṣinnor' - צינור

365. *Ṣinnor* is used subordinate to *^coleh we-yored*. This accent is marked by the sign used for *zarqa* in the Twenty-One Books (which here, as there, is above the word and postpositive) and the accent is called *zarqa* in the masoretic literature. The MSS show a few cases where the sign is repeated to indicate the stress syllable, as שְׁאוֹל (Ps 49:15).

Ṣinnor may have one or two servi. A single servus is either *merka*, as מִי זֶה (Ps 24:8) or *munaḥ*, as אָשִׁיר עֻזֶּךָ (Ps 59:17). Two servi are usually *merka* and *munaḥ*, as

Ps 14:7, 53:7 מִי יִתֵּן מִצִּיּוֹן

However sometimes *mehuppak* and *munaḥ* are used, as

Ps 24:10 מִי הוּא זֶה

The two servi are occasionally marked on the same word, as

Ps 37:14 פָּתְחוּ רְשָׁעִים Ps 79:11 תָּבוֹא לְפָנֶיךָ

Divisions subordinate to *ṣinnor* are marked by *legarmeh*, as

Ps 18:7 בַּצַּר־לִי אֶקְרָא יְהוָה

or by *pazer*, as Ps 31:11 כִּי כָלוּ בְיָגוֹן חַיַּי

or by both together as

Ps 32:6 עַל־זֹאת יִתְפַּלֵּל כָּל־חָסִיד אֵלֶיךָ

'Revia mugrash' - רביע מוגרש

366. *Revia mugrash* occurs only in the second half of the verse, after *atnaḥ*, as the last disjunctive before *silluq*. In the masoretic literature it is called *ṭifḥa*, and it has, in fact, a function similar to that of *ṭifḥa* in the Twenty-One

Books (#231). It is marked by the *revia* dot over the stress syllable, with a *geresh*-like stroke (after which it is named) marked above the beginning of the word (prepositive), as וְחַטָּאִים (Ps 1:5). If two words are joined by *maqqef*, the stroke is marked on the second, as עַל־צִיּוֹן (Ps 2:6). If the word is stressed on the first syllable, the dot and the stroke are usually marked above the same letter, as תַּמּוּ (Ps 73:19), although in some MSS, such as A, only the stroke is used in this situation.

367. Where *atnaḥ* is not used in a verse, the word which should have *revia mugrash* is marked with the *revia* dot alone, as "*revia mugrash* without *geresh*". This accent usually acts, like *atnaḥ*, as the mark of the main verse division, and, for this reason, its servi differ a little from those usual with *revia mugrash*. In some MSS, the full *revia mugrash* sign, with the stroke, is used even in verses which have no *atnaḥ*.

Revia mugrash may have one or two servi, but *revia mugrash* without *geresh* may have up to four. A single servus is *merka*,
as Ps 7:13 קַשְׁתּוֹ דָרַךְ
This is occasionally marked on the same word as *revia mugrash*,
as Ps 119:61 תּוֹרָתְךָ
Two servi of *revia mugrash* are both *merkas*, as
Ps 52:11 וַאֲקַוֶּה שִׁמְךָ כִי־טוֹב
But two servi of *revia mugrash* without *geresh* are *ṭarḥa* and *merka*, as Ps 119:140 צְרוּפָה אִמְרָתְךָ מְאֹד
However the MSS vary on this point.
Revia mugrash without *geresh* rarely has three servi. One example is Ps 129:7 שֶׁלֹּא מִלֵּא כַפּוֹ קוֹצֵר
Four servi occur only in Ps 68:36.

'Revia qaṭan' - רביע קטן

368. *Revia qaṭan* occurs only as a subordinate disjunctive immediately before *ᶜoleh we-yored*. It may have up to three servi. One servus is *merka*, as
Ps 3:6 אֲנִי שָׁכַבְתִּי
Two servi are *mehuppak* and *merka*, as
Ps 139:14 עַל כִּי נוֹרָאוֹת
The two servi are sometimes marked on one word, as
Ps 13:6 יָגֵל לִבִּי

And sometimes two *merka*s are marked on one word as servi to *revia qaṭan*, as Ps 67:5 יִשְׂמְחוּ וִירַנְּנוּ
Three servi occur only in Ps 1:2.

The only disjunctive used subordinate to *revia qaṭan* is *legarmeh*, as in Ps 63:2 אֱלֹהִים׀ אֵלִי אַתָּה

'Pazer' - פזר

369. *Pazer* in the Three Books is usually marked by the same sign as *pazer* (*qaṭan*) in the Twenty-One Books, -֡- (the "*ṣade*" form). In some MSS, however, this form is used only where the accent has no servi, and the "*ṭet*" form (-֟- the *pazer gadol* sign of the Twenty-One Books, #274) is used where the accent has servi. The presence or absence of this distinction is a useful characteristic by which MSS can be classified.

Pazer may have up to three servi. A single servus is only rarely used. It is usually *merka*, as
Ps 4:3 בְּנֵי אִישׁ
Different MSS show different systems of marking two servi of *pazer*, and these reflect differences between the Masoretes, such as bA and bN. The system used in A and L is as follows:- The servus immediately before *pazer* is *galgal* (as before *pazer gadol* in the Twenty-One Books). The second servus is *mehuppak* where the word is stressed on its first syllable, as
Ps 126:2 אָז יִמָּלֵא שְׂחוֹק
Where this is not the case, it is *azla*, as
Ps 5:12 וְיִשְׂמְחוּ כָל־חוֹסֵי בָךְ
Various conjunctives act as the third servus before *pazer*, for example *mehuppak* in
Ps 22:25 כִּי לֹא־בָזָה וְלֹא שִׁקַּץ
The only disjunctive used subordinate to *pazer* is *legarmeh*, as
Ps 104:35 יִתַּמּוּ חַטָּאִים׀ מִן־הָאָרֶץ

'Legarmeh' - לגרמיה

370. *Legarmeh*, in the Three Books as in the Twenty-One (#277), is marked by the sign for a conjunctive accent followed by *paseq*. Two conjunctives are used in the three books, *azla* and *mehuppak*. The resulting signs are distinguished as *azla legarmeh* and *mehuppak legarmeh*, but these represent variant forms of the same accent.

If the accent has a servus, *azla legarmeh* is used. If it has no servus, and the word is short, *mehuppak legarmeh* is used, as Ps 4:2 עֲנֵנִי׀
If the word is long, *azla legarmeh* is used even with no servus, as Ps 60:2 בְּהַצּוֹתוֹ׀
However if the accent is the first disjunctive before *silluq*, *mehuppak legarmeh* is used in all cases, even if the word is long, as
Job 37:14 וְהִתְבּוֹנֵן׀ נִפְלְאוֹת אֵל

Legarmeh may have one or two servi. Various conjunctives are used to mark a single servus, but the most common is *mehuppak*, as
Ps 1:3 אֲשֶׁר פִּרְיוֹ׀
However the servus may be *ᶜilluy*, as
Ps 23:5 תַּעֲרֹךְ לְפָנַי׀
and it may be *merka*, as
Ps 35:10 כָּל עַצְמוֹתַי׀
Each of these may be marked in the same word as *legarmeh*. Thus *mehuppak*,
Ps 18:16 וַיֵּרָאוּ׀
ᶜilluy, Ps 42:6, 12, 43:5 מַה־תִּשְׁתּוֹחֲחִי׀
merka, Ps 2:2 יִתְיַצְּבוּ׀
Two servi occur before *legarmeh* in three places only, for example Ps 117:2 כִּי גָבַר עָלֵינוּ׀

'Shalshelet' - שלשלת

371. *Shalshelet* is marked by a zigzag stroke above the stress syllable. In the three books, this accent is used both as a disjunctive, *shalshelet gedolah*, distinguished by the *paseq* stroke after the word (as in the Twenty-One Books, #229), and as conjunctive, *shalshelet qeṭannah*.

Shalshelet gedolah is used in the second half of the verse, and is followed by the two servi of *silluq*, as
Ps 7:6 וּכְבוֹדִי׀ לֶעָפָר יַשְׁכֵּן סֶלָה
As a general rule, *shalshelet gedolah* has no servi, but in Ps 89:2 it has one servus, and in two places it has two servi, for example Job 32:6 עַל־כֵּן זָחַלְתִּי וָאִירָא׀ מֵחַוֹּת דֵּעִי אֶתְכֶם

Shalshelet qeṭannah (conjunctive *shalshelet*) is distinguished by the fact that *paseq* does not occur after the word. It occurs in only eight cases as one of a chain of

conjunctives before *silluq*, *atnaḥ*, or *revia mugrash* without *geresh*, as Ps 65:2 לְךָ דֻמִיָּה תְהִלָּה אֱלֹהִים בְּצִיּוֹן
Ps 68:15 בְּפָרֵשׂ שַׁדַּי מְלָכִים בָּהּ

'Ṣinnorit' - צינורית

372. *Ṣinnorit* serves as a secondary accent in words with conjunctive accents. It is marked by a sign like that of *ṣinnor*, but slanted to the right. As a rule it is marked on an open syllable immediately before the stress syllable. The vowel of the open syllable may be long, as יָשׁוּבוּ (Ps 56:10), or short, as וְנִעֵר (Ps 136:15). *Ṣinnorit* is not used before a *shewa* or a *ḥaṭef shewa*.

In standard Tiberian texts *ṣinnorit* is generally used with *mehuppak*, and occurs rarely also with *merka*, in various combinations of servi, for example
Ps 118:25 הוֹשִׁיעָה נָּא
In MSS with the expanded Tiberian pointing, *ṣinnorit* is regularly used with *merka*, and with *munaḥ* as well, and it is also used on an open syllable before a *shewa* or a *ḥaṭef shewa*, as in Vatican MS Urbino 2 in Ps 1:5 בַּעֲדַת

'Methigah' - מתיגה

373. This accent is marked by the same sign as the *methigah* used before *zaqef* in the Twenty-One Books (#223). It also is used as a secondary accent on words with conjunctive accents. It occurs only with *merka* acting as a servus before *revia mugrash* or *silluq*. It is found in some Genizah fragments and in some standard Tiberian texts, but not, for instance, in A, L, or S[1]. Most texts with expanded Tiberian pointing do not use it either.

Methigah is marked on the syllable (open or closed) immediately before the stress syllable, as
Ps 18:15 וּבְרָקִים רָב Ps 51:8 חָכְמָה תוֹדִיעֵנִי

Other Features of the Accentuation of the Three Books

374. A few other phenomena reflect the special form of chant used in the three books.
1) The large number of words on which two accents are marked--even in rare combinations. The secondary accent is sometimes marked on an open syllable suitable for *ga*^{c}*ya*, as הָאַלְמָנָה

(Ps 31:19, *revia qaṭan*), וֶאֱמוּנָתוֹ (Ps 98:3), and sometimes on a closed syllable which is generally not suitable for *gaʿya*, as בַּמַּכְתֵּשׁ (Prov 27:22), בַּמִּדְבָּר (Job 24:5, *revia gadol*), בֵּרַכְנוּכֶם (Ps 118:26).

2) The retraction of the accent to the beginning of the word, a phenomenon which appears to have a musical origin, and results in the marking of the accent on an unexpected syllable, as

Ps 66:15 אֶעֱשֶׂה בָקָר עִם־עַתּוּדִים סֶלָה

Ps 1:1 אַשְׁרֵי הָאִישׁ

Ps 141:5 יֶהֶלְמֵנִי צַדִּיק

Prov 29:13 מֵאִיר עֵינֵי שְׁנֵיהֶם יְהוָה

Ps 98:9 לִפְנֵי יְהוָה

This phenomenon is admittedly rare, but in the Twenty-One Books it does not occur at all.

APPENDIX

NOTES ON *SHEWA* AND ON *DAGESH* AND *RAFE*

INTRODUCTION

375. Masoretic treatises, such as the *Kitāb al-Khilaf* (*Sefer ha-Ḥillufim*), the *Diqduqe ha-Ṭe^c amim*, the "Treatise on the *Shewa*", and the *Horayat ha-Qore*, naturally deal with matters of vocalization. These are outside the scope of this book, but two phenomena, *dagesh* and *shewa*, form such an important part of the subject matter of such treatises that it seems advisable to include a discussion of them in an appendix. It must be noted, however, that they are discussed here from the point of view of the masoretic treatises, which is different from that of modern grammarians, so that statements made here may conflict with those of modern grammars (and particularly introductory grammars), which are based on historical considerations.

SHEWA - שבא, שוא

376. The distinction of silent from vocal *shewa* was a great concern for the Masoretes for two reasons: (1) This was necessary for correct pronunciation, since vocal *shewa* was realized as an ultra-short vowel, but silent *shewa* as no vowel (2) *Shewa* acted as a guide to the syllable structure of the word. It was not considered as forming a syllable, but as

dependent on one of the "full vowels"; silent *shewa* on the preceding vowel, and vocal *shewa* on the following vowel. Thus in וַיִּשְׁכְּנוּ (Gen 25:18) the silent *shewa* under the *shin* shows that it goes with what precedes, and the vocal *shewa* under the *kaf* shows that it goes with what follows, so that the word is divided וַיִּשְׁ-כְּנוּ. So with a word like וְהָאֲחַשְׁדַּרְפְּנִים (Est 9:3), the *shewa*s show that the syllabic structure is וְהָ-אֲחַשְׁ-דַּרְ-פְּנִים. Phonetic *ga^{c}ya* (#346) could change silent *shewa* to vocal, and so change the syllabic structure of a word. The word וּזְהַב without *ga^{c}ya* is divided וּזְ-הַב, but with *ga^{c}ya* (Gen 2:12) it becomes וּ-זֲהַב. In the same way at the end of a word, silent *shewa* (whether marked or only potential) marks the division. In בְּרֵאשִׁית בָּרָא (Gen 1:1), if the *shewa* were vocal the division would be בְּרֵא-שִׁי-תְבָ-רָא.

The Recognition of Vocal 'Shewa' (i) The General Rule

377. At the beginning of a word, *shewa* is vocal. The only exception to this is found in the forms of שְׁתַּיִם. Here the initial *shewa* is considered silent, a pronunciation made possible among the Tiberians (according to some sources, e.g. Levi, 1936, p. ט, translation p. 8*) by the use of a helping vowel, as אֶשְׁתַּיִם. This helping vowel was evidently the source of the disagreement over the accentuation of the word when it has *pashṭa* with no preceding conjunctive (Lev 23:17, Ez 1:11, 41:24, 24). Those who pronounced this initial helping vowel as a full vowel considered that the word was not stressed on its first syllable, so that the *pashṭa* sign was required, as שְׁתַּ֙יִם֙. Those who did not pronounce the helping vowel as a full vowel considered the word as stressed on its first syllable, and so marked it with *yetiv* (see #248). Even in this there was disagreement, however, as bA put the accent sign before the *shewa*, as שְׁ֚תַּיִם (so A, L), while bN put it after, as שְׁתַּ֚יִם.

378. At the end of a word, *shewa* is silent. Most sources also say that when two *shewa*s come together at the end of a word, as וַיֵּבְךְּ עֲלֵיהֶם (Gen 45:15), both are silent. However some sources state that the first is silent and the second vocal, unless the word occurs at a major pause, as וַיֵּבְךְּ (Gen 29:11), in which case all agree that both are silent.

379. Within a word, where *shewa* is marked on two successive letters, the first is silent and the second vocal. *Shewa* under a letter marked with *dagesh* is vocal. Apart from these two clear cases, *shewa* within a word is considered silent, with the exception of several special categories of *shewa* which are noted in various masoretic sources.

Shewa below *resh*. The Masorah gives rules on the subject of *shewa* under *resh*, but these are not the same in different sources. It is said that, in nouns, if *resh* is the second letter, and has *qameṣ* or *ṣere* before it, then *shewa* under the *resh* is vocal, as

Ex 8:11 הָרְוָחָה Ex 19:2 מֵרְפִידִים

If it has *ḥireq* or *ḥolem* before it, however, *shewa* under the *resh* is silent, as

Jud 19:17 בִּרְחֹב Jud 9:37 יוֹרְדִים

Rules on *shewa* under *resh* in verb forms are given for particular roots:

גרשׁ -- If there is *segol* under the *shin*, then *shewa* under the *resh* is vocal, as Ex 23:30 אֲגָרְשֶׁנּוּ. Otherwise the *shewa* is silent, as Jud 11:2 וַיְגָרְשׁוּ, with the exception of Ps 34:1 וַיְגָרְשֵׁהוּ, where the *shin* has *ṣere*, but the *shewa* under the *resh* is vocal in the opinion of bA (although bN considers it silent).

ברך -- If the accent sign is on the *bet*, *shewa* under the *resh* is silent, as 1C 29:20 בָּרְכוּ נָא. If the accent is on the *kaf*, *shewa* under the *resh* is vocal, as Gen 27:34 בָּרְכֵנִי, with the exception of Dan 4:31 בָּרְכֵת, where the *shewa* is considered silent, even though the accent sign is on the *kaf* (*Diqduqe ha-Ṭe*ᶜ*amim*, Dotan 1967, section 21).

Shewa under *resh* is considered vocal also in Gen 18:21 אֵרְדָה־נָּא (*Diqduqe ha-Ṭe*ᶜ*amim*), Ps 83:13 נִירְשָׁה לָּנוּ (given as a case of agreement between bA and bN), and, according to bA, Job 31:37 אֲקָרְבֶנּוּ (Where A and L have *ḥaṭef pataḥ*. However bN considers the *shewa* silent in this case).

380. Shewa under other Letters. The Masorah gives rules for the pronunciation of *shewa* in some other verb forms:

אכל -- If the *lamed* has *segol*, then *shewa* under the *kaf* is vocal, as Dt 12:24 תֹּאכְלֶנּוּ. Otherwise the *shewa* is silent as Nu 11:19 תֹּאכְלוּן, with the exception of Qoh 5:10 אֹכְלֶיהָ where the *shewa* is considered silent even though the *lamed* has *segol*.

This is stated in *Diqduqe ha-Ṭe*^{c}*amim* (Dotan 1967, section 22), and is also given in the *Sefer ha-Ḥillufim* as the opinion of bA However bN regards the *shewa* under the *kaf* as silent in all cases.

הלך -- *Shewa* under the *lamed* is silent except in the long form of the imperfect where the accent is retracted to the first syllable, and the following word has conjunctive *dagesh* (#405), as Ex 4:18 אֵלְכָה נָּא (*Diqduqe ha-Ṭe*^{c}*amim*, Dotan 1967, section 25. L has *ḥaṭef pataḥ*).

The Recognition of Vocal 'Shewa' (ii) Special Cases

381. *Shewa* following Phonetic *Ga*^{c}*ya* . *Shewa* following a short vowel is usually silent, even where this vowel has musical *ga*^{c}*ya* (#319). However if the short vowel has phonetic *ga*^{c}*ya* intended to show that the following *shewa* is vocal, it is, of course, vocal. The situation in which phonetic *ga*^{c}*ya* is used are described above (#345). The Masorah gives rules covering some of these situations.

382. *Shewa* under *Mem* following *He* with *Pataḥ* at the Beginning of a Word. (cf. #347)

These rules apply not only to *he*, but also to *kaf*, *lamed*, or *bet* representing a preposition with the vowel of the definite article.

Where the *he* has *ga*^{c}*ya*, if it is musical *ga*^{c}*ya*, the following *shewa* is silent, but if it is phonetic *ga*^{c}*ya*, the following *shewa* is vocal. The *Diqduqe ha-Ṭe*^{c}*amim* (Dotan, 1967, section 14) states that, as a rule, *ga*^{c}*ya* in this situation is phonetic, so the *shewa* is vocal. Various examples are given, mainly in two categories.

1) Words on which musical *ga*^{c}*ya* would not be used for reasons of structure, as Amos 6:3 הַֽמְנַדִּים.

2) Words which could take musical *ga*^{c}*ya* on a closed syllable of regular type, but which have a conjunctive accent, so that such a *ga*^{c}*ya* would not normally be marked (see #319-320), as 2C 32:31 הַֽמְשַׁלְּחִים.

In words in these two categories, then, the *ga*^{c}*ya* is phonetic and the *shewa* vocal. This is followed by a list of words in which the *shewa* is silent. Most of these are words which could take musical *ga*^{c}*ya* in a closed syllable of the regular type, and which have a disjunctive accent, as

1S 18:7 הַֽמְשַׂחֲקוֹת Nu 5:19, 24, 24 הַֽמְאָרְרִים

Some, however, have a conjunctive accent, as

2K 23:5 הַֽמְקַטְּרִים

and in some the structure is not regular, as

Is 23:12 הַֽמְעֻשָּׁקָה

In these cases the *ga*^c^*ya* is musical, and the *shewa* is silent.

Some sources give rules for determining whether *shewa* is vocal or silent in such cases by the number of letters in the word. If it has five letters, as הַֽמְסֻכָּן (Is 40:20) then the *shewa* is vocal. If it has six or more letters, and the accent sign is on the fifth or sixth, as הַֽמְצַפְצְפִים (Is 8:19), then the *shewa* is silent, but if the accent sign is on the fourth letter, as הַֽמְחַכִּים (Job 3:21), then the *shewa* is vocal. Some exceptions to these rules are also listed.

The rule given in the *Diqduqe ha-Ṭe*^c^*amim* covers most of the cases, but not all. The other rules, however, cover an even smaller proportion. In some MSS, notably in A, the *mem* in this situation is pointed with *ḥaṭef pataḥ* when the *shewa* is vocal, which gives a clear indication of the pronunciation.

383. Shewa after Phonetic Ga^c^ya in Other Situations.

Shewa under other letters is vocal when it follows phonetic *ga*^c^*ya*. Examples are:-

1) On *he* with *pataḥ* (or *kaf*, *lamed*, or *bet* with the vowel of the definite article) at the beginning of a word (#348) as

1S 18:23 הַֽנִקְלָה 2K 2:1, 11 בַּֽסְעָרָה

Jud 16:21 בַּֽנְחֻשְׁתַּיִם

2) On conjunctive *waw* pointed as *shureq* (#349), as

2K 9:17 וּֽשְׁלַח Job 17:9 וּֽטְהָר־יָדַיִם

3) After other short vowels (#350), as

Jer 22:15 הֲֽתִמְלֹךְ Ps 80:11 אַֽרְזֵי־אֵל

(In the latter case bA and bN agree that the *shewa* is vocal).

384. Shewa Standing Between Merka used as a Secondary Accent and the Main Accent or Ga^c^ya .

This situation occurs in the three books, mainly among the servi of *revia gadol* (#363), *revia qaṭan* (#368), *ṣinnor* (#365), and *legarmeh* (#370). According to the *Diqduqe ha-Ṭe*^c^*amim* (Dotan, 1967, section 13), the *shewa* is vocal. Examples are:-

Prov 28:22	נִבְהָל לַהוֹן	Ps 73:28	קִרְבַת אֱלֹהִים
Ps 65:5	תִּבְחַר וּתְקָרֵב		
Ps 39:13	שִׁמְעָה תְפִלָּתִי		
Ps 31:12	וְלִשְׁכֵנַי		

There are four exceptions in which *shewa* in this situation is silent:-

Ps 69:21	שִׁבְרָה לִבִּי	Ps 86:2	שָׁמְרָה נַפְשִׁי
Ps 140:6	טָמְנוּ־גֵאִים	Prov 8:13	יִרְאַת יְהוָה

385. <u>*Shewa* under the First of a Pair of Identical Letters</u>. In the *Diqduqe ha-Ṭeᶜamim* (Dotan, 1967, section 5), and in other masoretic treatises, the rule is given that if *gaᶜya* is used before the first of a pair of identical letters, *shewa* under that letter is vocal, as

Zech 11:3	יִלְלַת	1K 21:19	לָקְקוּ

If there is no *gaᶜya*, then the *shewa* is silent, as in הִנְנִי, הִנְנוּ, חִקְקֵי־אָוֶן (Is 10:1).

There are six exceptions to this rule, in which the pair of identical letters comes after the vowel of the stress syllable, as יְשַׁחֲרֻנְנִי Prov 1:28. This rule makes no distinction between *gaᶜya* after a short vowel, which is certainly phonetic, and *gaᶜya* after a long vowel, as צָלְלוּ Ex 15:10, which could be musical.

This rule is not reflected in the MSS,--even those in which *ḥaṭef shewa* is frequently used under non-guttural letters. Some words are marked according to the rule, as (in A)

Is 62:9	וְהִלְלוּ	Is 58:9	מִתּוֹכְכָה
Dt 33:2	מֵרִבְבֹת	Jer 51:48	הַשּׁוֹדְדִים

Here a *ḥaṭef shewa* is used where *gaᶜya* is marked, but not where *gaᶜya* is not marked. However other words show vocalization which is not consistent with the rule, as

Jer 25:12	לְשִׁמְמוֹת	(L20 לְשִׁמֲמוֹת)	
Is 59:10	נְגַשֲׁשָׁה	Jer 51:53	שֹׁדְדִים

The study of the pointing of A in this situation, and comparison of it with other early MSS, reveals a somewhat different rule. If there is a short vowel before the first of a pair of identical letters, the *shewa* is silent unless it follows *gaᶜya* or is marked as a *ḥaṭef* (whether *gaᶜya* is marked or not). If the preceding vowel is long, the *shewa* is always vocal, whether *gaᶜya* is marked or not (for a long vowel before *shewa* may always take *ga^{c}ya*, #326).

386. In addition to these rules, a number of cases of *ḥillufim* also concern the pronunciation of *shewa* within the word. Examples are:-

Ez 16:18 וְקִטַּרְתְּ bN and "Tiberias" וְקִטַּרְתְּ
Ez 21:28 פְּקִסָּם־שָׁוְא bN קְסָם־ R. Pinḥas קְסָם־

The MSS also show some other words, not mentioned in the rules given above, in which a *ḥaṭef shewa* is used where a simple *shewa* is expected. Examples are:-

Under *resh*
S[1] in Ez 28:13 וּבָרֲקַת S[1] in Ps 22:27 דֹּרְשָׁיו
After *ga^{c}ya* or an accent sign on a long vowel
A in Joel 3:3 וְתִימְרֲוֹת A and S[1] in Dt 32:36 אָזֲלַת
S[1] in Dan 4:33 הוּסֲפַת לִי
After a short vowel with no phonetic *ga^{c}ya*
A in 1S 28:8 קָסֳומִי־נָא (L, C, S[1], קָסֳומִי)
A in Ps 74:5 בִּסֲבָךְ־עֵץ (L־בִּסֲבָךְ)

It seems probable that, although the rules given above cover most of the cases in which *shewa* within a word was considered vocal, they do not cover them all. Apart from those cases mentioned in the rules, however, and the few exceptional cases, *shewa* within a word was considered silent, whether it followed a short vowel, as וַיִּשְׁלַח (Gen 8:9), or a long vowel, (even if it had musical *ga^{c}ya*), as שָׁמְעוּ (Gen 43:25).

The Pronunciation of 'Shewa'

387. From the point of view of quantity, *shewa* represented an ultra-short vowel--even shorter than a short vowel. From the point of view of quality, *shewa* usually had the same sound as *pataḥ*. If it was followed by a guttural, however, the *shewa* had the same quality as the vowel following the guttural; Thus in בְּאֵר the *shewa* was pronounced as a very short *ṣere*, in מְאֹד as a very short *ḥolem*, and in לְקָחָה־זֹּאת as a very short *qameṣ*. (For the Tiberians, the sign ָ always represented the same vowel quality, "ɔ", so *ḥaṭef qameṣ* and *qameṣ ḥaṭuf* differed from *qameṣ gadol* only in quantity.). If the *shewa* was itself under a guttural, however, it was pronounced with the quality of *pataḥ* even where it was followed by a guttural, as
Job 9:13 שָׁחֲחוּ Ps 98:8 יִמְחֲאוּ־

Nu 13:22 אֲחִימַן

Before a consonantal *yod*, vocal *shewa* was pronounced as a very short *ḥireq*, as in בְּיוֹם, לְיָקִים (1C 24:12). However if *shewa* before *yod* stood under a guttural, it was not pronounced as *ḥireq*, but as *ḥaṭef pataḥ* or some other *ḥaṭef*, as

Ez 16:6 חֲיִי Jud 18:19 הֱיוֹתְךָ

Ps 88:5 אֱיָל

The pronunciation of *shewa* with *gaᶜya* is described in #336.

'Ḥaṭef Shewa' under a Non-Guttural Letter

388. The Tiberian pointing regularly distinguishes vocal *shewa* from silent only under gutturals. In many cases, however, *shewa* under other consonants is represented by a *ḥaṭef* to indicate that it is vocal, in some--sometimes in most--of the MSS and printed texts. This may occur either for morphological or for phonetic reasons.

(i) <u>*Ḥaṭef Shewa* Used for Morphological Reasons</u>. This occurs most commonly where the *shewa* derives from a "u" or "o" vowel, in which case the sign used is *ḥaṭef qameṣ*. This is especially common under *qof*, *gimel*, the other *begad kefat* letters, *ṭet*, and the sibilants *ṣade* and *shin*. Presumably the tendency to preserve the original "o/u" sound was greater with them than with other consonants. Examples are:-

At the beginning of a word:

הֳמִי, צֳרִי, קֳבֵל, קֳדָם, אֶל־הַקֳּבָּה (Nu 25:8), וְאֶת־קֳדָשָׁיו (2K 12:19).

Sometimes a full vowel sign, not a *ḥaṭef*, is used in this position:

קָדָשִׁים, קָדְמוֹנִי, קָטָנִּי (1K 12:10), קָבְלוֹ (Ez 26:9), קָבָל־עָם (2K 15:10), שָׁרָשָׁיו, סָובָאִים (Ez 23:42). (See Dotan, 1972, p. 241-247). Within a word--under a letter with *dagesh* אֶצֳּרֶנָּה (Is 27:3), תִּקֳּבֶנּוּ (Nu 23:25), כֻּתֳּנֹת (Ex 28:40), הַגֳּרָנוֹת (Joel 2:24), שִׁבֳּלִים, but שִׁבֲּלֵי (Zech 4:12), צִפֳּרִים, but Aramaic צִפֲּרַיָּא (Dan 4:9), סֻבֳּלוֹ (Is 9:3). Under the second of a pair of letters with *shewa* יֶהְדֳּפֶנּוּ (Nu 35:20), וָאֶשְׁקֳלָה (Ezra 8:25), but וָאֶשְׁקְלָה (Ezra 8:26), קָדְקֳדוֹ, הַבַּרְקֳנִים (Jud 8:7), מָרְדֳּכַי.

389. In some cases (as noted above) *ḥaṭef pataḥ* occurs where this "morphological" *ḥaṭef qameṣ* is expected. Presumably this indicates that the original "o/u" colouring of the vowel was no longer audible, so it was treated as a *ḥaṭef pataḥ* (i.e.

the normal sound of vocal *shewa*). Examples are:-
At the beginning of a word קֳשִׁי (L[1] Dt 9:27)
Under a letter with *dagesh* מִסֻּבֳּכוֹ (Jer 4:7)
Under the second of a pair of letters with *shewa* יִרְדֳּפֶךָ (Ez 35:6, 6), אֶשְׁפֳּטֶךָ (Ez 35:11), אֶכְתֳּבֶנָּה (L, Jer 31:33).

The "morphological" use of *ḥaṭef segol* is rare in Hebrew--one example is וּבְצֶלְצֱלִים (A, C, 2S 6:5) but it is more common in Aramaic words, as בֱּנַיְתַהּ (Dan 4:27), קֱרִי (Ezra 4:18), גֱּלִי (Dan 2:30), but גֱּלִי (Dan 2:19), וּמַדֱּקָה (Dan 7:7), מְמַלֱּלָה (Dan 7:11).

390. (ii) Ḥaṭef Shewa Used for Phonetic Reasons. *Ḥaṭef qameṣ* is the most common in this category also. It occurs most commonly before a guttural with *qameṣ*. However *ḥaṭef qameṣ* in these cases replaces a simple *shewa* which is vocal according to the standard rules, so that error in pronunciation would not be likely. Presumably the *ḥaṭef* sign was intended to prevent incorrect pronunciation resulting from lack of attention. Examples are:-
At the beginning of a word קֳהָת, וְכָל־קֳהָלָהּ (Ez 32:22)
Under a consonant with *dagesh* הַקֳּהָתִי, הַקְּעָרֹת (Nu 4:6), שִׂמֳּחָהוּ (L, Jer 20:15), פִּתֳּחָה (C, Is 48:8), בְּסַאסְּאָה (Is 27:8)
Under the second of a pair of letters with *shewa* לְיָקְמֳעָם (1K 4:12), הִתְמַהְמֳהָם (Jud 3:26), וְנִשְׁקֳעָה (Amos 8:8)
Ḥaṭef pataḥ is used similarly for phonetic reasons in וַתְּצַדֲּקִי (Ez 16:51), מִגְרֲשֵׁי (1C 5:16), אַשְׁכֲּנַז (L, Gen 10:3)

391. In some MSS, such as A, *ḥaṭef shewa* is commonly used under non-guttural letters in all the categories described. In others, like S, this is rare. Clearly the Masoretes considered the use of a *ḥaṭef shewa* sign to mark vocal *shewa* under a guttural as necessary, but under other letters as optional. Thus, for instance, the *Diqduqe ha-Ṭeᶜamim* (Dotan, 1967, section 19) says "Some scribes, following a valid tradition, read *ḥaṭef qameṣ* in many places...while others, also following a valid tradition, do not, but there is no (authoritative) source but the preference of the scribes." Similarly it is said in the *Horayat ha-Qore* p. 64 (Dérenbourg, 1870, p. 372) "If one argues that the *dalet* of 'Mordecai' (and other letters in other words) has *ḥaṭef qameṣ*, tell him, 'but this sign is only

a device used by some scribes to warn that the consonants should be pronounced fully, and not slurred over'. *Ḥaṭef qameṣ* is written in some texts. It is not used in others, but the reader nevertheless pronounces the word in the same way when he comes to read it."

Prefixes with 'Shewa' before 'Yod' with 'Ḥireq'

392. According to the rules given above, initial *shewa* before *yod* followed by *ḥireq* should sound like a very short *ḥireq*, as *lĭyiśrɔ'el* for לְיִשְׂרָאֵל. However the combination of two "i" vowels separated by *yod* is likely to develop into a long "i" vowel, *līśrɔ'el*, and this gave rise to a systematic variation between ben Asher and ben Naftali. Ben Asher admits the long "i" in only three words: וִֽילְלַ֫ת (Jer 25:36), לִֽיקְּהַת־אֵ֫ם (Prov 30:17), and כִּֽיתְר֫וֹן (S[1], Qoh 2:13). In these cases the *shewa* following the *yod* is vocal, so that the *ḥireq* occurs in an open syllable. Elsewhere, bA marks the two vowels (*shewa* and *ḥireq*) separately, but bN requires the long "i" vowel where the word begins with the preposition ב, כ, or ל before the words יִרְאַת, יִרְאָה, יִזְרְעֶאל, יִשְׂרָאֵל, and with some other individual words, as וִיטַ֫ב (Jud 19:6), לִירְאָתֶֽךָ (Ps 119:38), וִיחֵ֫לּוּ (Job 29:21). In words which are not included in this list, or which have prefixes other than ב, כ, or ל, as וְיִשְׂרָאֵל, or which have two prefixes, as וּבְיִשְׂרָאֵל, bN does not require the long "i", and so agrees with bA.

393. Most of the early MSS point these words as bA, but C, and, in the main, S, use the bN system.

There are a few words in the Bible pointed with *shewa* followed by *yod* and *ḥireq* where long "i" would be expected, as וַיְיִף (Ez 31:7), לְיִסּ֫וֹד (2C 31:7). This is possibly the result of hyper-correction--the long "i" was avoided even where it should have been used.

The system of puncutation used in these situations in the MSS with expanded Tiberian pointing is related to the system of bN, but in these MSS long "i" is marked when any prefix is followed by *yod* with *ḥireq*. Thus, in R, וִיתֵּן (1S 2:10), וִירַשׁ (Is 57:13). This contrasts with the real ben Naftali system.

'Dagesh' (and 'Rafe') Indicating that a Letter Represents a Consonant (or a Vowel).

394. *Dagesh* and *rafe* may be used to show whether the letters ו, ה, א, represent consonants or vowels. (i) *He*

Consonantal *he* at the end of a word is marked by a dot (identical in form to *dagesh*) called *mappiq*. Non-consonantal final *he* is generally (but not always) marked with *rafe*. In some MSS consonantal *he* may be marked with *mappiq* even within a word, especially where it is pointed with *shewa*, as

Lev 26:43, L and S בָּהְשַׁמָּה Nu 34:28, S פְּדַהְאֵל

Ez 16:53, L[10] בְּתוֹכָהְנָה

395. (ii) *Alef* is marked with *dagesh* in four words in the Bible. Three derive from the root בוא: Lev 23:17 תָּבִיאּוּ לֶחֶם

Gen 43:26 וַיָּבִיאּוּ לוֹ Ezra 8:18 וַיָּבִיאּוּ לָנוּ

These represent most of the cases in which these words are followed by a word beginning with *lamed* and stressed on the first syllable. Possibly there was a tendency to slur over the *alef* in this situation (Cf. the similar tendency with gutturals before *shewa*, #354). The fourth case of *alef* with *dagesh* is רֻאּוּ (Job 33:21). Possibly the *dagesh* here is intended to emphasize the need to use the glottal stop rather than a "w" glide between the two "u" vowels (cf. the contrary phenomenon in יִשְׁתַּחֲוּוּ #396).

In some MSS, such as C, *dagesh* is used to mark *alef* as consonantal in other words, especially where its value might be in doubt, as Haggai 1:1 שְׁאַלְתִּיאֵל

Jer 38:12 בְּלוֹאֵי Is 51:19 קְרָאתַיִךְ

Non-consonantal *alef* is marked with *rafe* in nearly all MSS, but not consistently.

A few MSS, particularly C and S, frequently mark *rafe* on the *alef* in יִשְׂרָאֵל. This may reflect a pronunciation in which a glottal stop was not used in this situation.

396. (iii) *Waw* representing a consonant followed by *shureq* at the end of a word is often marked with a dot, possibly also indicating *shureq* , as וַיִּשְׁתַּחֲוּוּ (A, L, Dt 29:25), טָווּ (B, L, Ex 35:26), וְנִלְווּ (C, Jer 50:5). This appears to indicate that

this *waw* was assimilated to the following *shureq*, and pronounced as a long "u" vowel; i.e. - *wu* > - *uu* or *-u*. This phenomenon also appears within the word in קְוּצּוֹתָיו, קְוּצּוֹתַי (L, Song 5:2, 11).

In some other cases consonantal *waw* before *shureq* is marked not with a dot, but with the *rafe* sign, as וְתַשְׁוּוּ (C, Is 46:5) וְנִקְווּ (L[15], Jer 3:17, L וְנִקְוּוּ). It is not clear whether this was intended to mark consonantal or vocalic value.

Different ways of pronouncing consonantal *waw* are recorded in the Masorah also in וּפֻוָּה (L, Gen 46:13), where the *waw* follows a "u" vowel, and רִבְוָן (L, L[13], S[1], Dan 7:10). The Mp of L has רבבן ק בן אשר (as BHK), Mp of L[13] רוון ק.

The Marking of 'Rafe'

397. In most MSS, the *rafe* sign, a horizontal stroke, is used on the *begad-kefat* letters where they do not have *dagesh*. If two letters together both require *rafe*, the sign is generally only marked once, over the space between them. *Rafe* is also used to mark non-consonantal *he* and *alef*, as noted above. The *rafe* sign is not used consistently. It is used more frequently where there is some possibility of confusion, as with *begad-kefat* letters at the beginning of a word after a word ending with a vowel, but even there it is not marked consistently. Some MSS, such as B, mark *rafe* very rarely, and others, such as C and S, mark it frequently.

398. In the MSS, *rafe* is used on other letters besides *begad-kefat*, mainly in the following categories.

1) After *waw* with *shewa* at the beginning of a word, especially with verb forms, as וְיִשְׁמַע (A, Is 42:23), וְיָבֹא (A, 1S 4:3). This probably emphasizes the fact that *waw* consecutive is not used, but the same phenomenon occurs with nouns, as וְיָדִי (A, 1S 24:14), וְיִשְׁמָעֵאל (A, Jer 40:8). In MSS where *rafe* is often used, it may also be marked after other consonants with *shewa* at the beginning of a word, as מְנֻחָתוֹ (C, Is 11:10), מְלֵא (C, Jer 6:11), תְּמִימִם (S, Lev 14:10).

2) On a letter, particularly *yod*, which is pointed with *shewa* and has no *dagesh*, as וַיְבַקְשׁוּ (A, Jud 6:29) שִׁלְחוּ (A, Ps 74:7).

3) On *nun* in the first and third person pronominal suffixes, as

פְּדֵנִי (A, Ps 119:134), שַׁמְתַּנִי (A, Job 7:20), since the *nun* of the first person sometimes had *dagesh*. (See *Diqduqe ha-Ṭe^{c}amim*, Dotan, 1967, section 17). However MSS which mark *rafe* frequently, mark it on *nun* where there is no likelihood of confusion, as לָנוּ, אֲנִי, יִדְּעֹנִי (S, Lev 20:27).

4) On other letters where *dagesh* might be expected, as where *dagesh* "conjunctive" is not used: שִׂיחָה לִּי (A, Ps 119:99) מֹשְׁלָה לּוֹ (A, N, Is 40:10) יוֹרֶה שָׁם (C, Is 37:33).

Where *dagesh* is not marked following an accent

יִבְּלוּ	(A, 2S 22:46),	לָמָּה	(A, Job 7:20)
שַׁסּוּ	(A, L6, Ps 44:11),	מָטוּ	(A, Ps 46:7).

MSS which mark *rafe* frequently may also mark it on the letters נ, מ, ל, in other situations, as גְּמָלָנוּ (C, Is 63:7) חֵמְּצָתוֹ (C, Hos 7:4) וְלִשְׁנִינָה (S, Dt 28:37).

'Begad-Kefat' following י, ו, ה, א

399. If a word begins with one of the *begad-kefat* letters ב, ג, ד, כ, פ, or ת and follows a word ending with an open syllable which has a conjunctive accent or *maqqef*, then the *begad-kefat* letter has *rafe*. This rule is given in various masoretic sources (*Diqduqe ha-Ṭe^{c}amim*, Baer-Strack 1879, #29, *Horayat ha-Qore* p. 78, Dérenbourg, 1870, p. 386, and others). As a general rule, the vowel of the open syllable at the end of the first words of the pair is marked by a vowel letter, א, ה, ו, or י, so that the rule is referred to in the treatises as סימן אוי"ה ובג"ד כפ"ת. It should, however, be noted that not only is no vowel letter used in some cases, as נָחִיתָ בְחַסְדְּךָ (Ex 15:13), but, on the contrary, the final syllable of a word ending with א, ה, ו, or י, is sometimes closed, so that the *begad-kefat* letter has *dagesh*, as וַיַּרְא בָּלָק (Nu 22:2).

400. The Masorah mentions a number of מבטלים--phenomena which nullify the general rule, so that a *begad-kefat* letter after א, ה, ו, or י, has *dagesh*. These most commonly nullify the effect of the vowel at the end of the first word. They are:

1) *Mappiq*. If final ה, ו, or י, represents a consonant and not a vowel (if it is מַפִּיק "pronounced"), then a *begad-kefat* letter at the beginning of the next word has *dagesh*, as

Gen 6:16 בְּצִדָּהּ תָּשִׂים

Lev 7:30 יָדָיו תְּבִיאֶינָה

Gen 16:8 שָׂרַי גְּבִרְתִּי
and after יְהוָה (i.e. אֲדֹנָי) as Ps 2:11 יְהוָה בְּיִרְאָה
There are three exceptions where *dagesh* is not used after consonantal *waw* or *yod*:
Is 34:11 קַו־תֹהוּ
Ez 23:42 שָׁלֵו בָהּ
Ps 68:18 אֲדֹנָי בָם

In some versions of this rule it is stated that *dagesh* is used where final consonantal *yod* is preceded by *pataḥ* or *qameṣ*, but not where it is preceded by *ḥolem*, as in גּוֹי גָּדוֹל (Dt 4:8). This may possibly reflect a tradition in which *ḥireq* was pronounced after final consonantal *yod*, as is marked in some MSS with expanded Tiberian pointing, as גּוֹיִ.

2) *Paseq*. If the word which ends in an open syllable is followed by *paseq*, (#283), then the *begad-kefat* letter has *dagesh*, as
Dt 9:21 אֹתוֹ ׀ בָּאֵשׁ
1C 21:3 עַל־עַמּוֹ ׀ כָּהֵם
3) *Deḥiq* and *Ate Meraḥiq*, see #403.

401. Pairs of Similar Consonants at the beginning of the second word in this situation also nullify the rule. If the second word begins with one of the combinations בְּב, בְּפ, or כְּכ, the initial *bet* or *kaf* has *dagesh* even where the preceding word ends with a vowel and has a conjunctive accent, as
Gen 39:12 וַתִּתְפְּשֵׂהוּ בְּבִגְדוֹ
Is 10:9 הֲלֹא כְּכַרְכְּמִישׁ
Ex 14:4 וְאִכָּבְדָה בְּפַרְעֹה
However if the initial *bet* or *kaf* does not have *shewa*, it is *rafe*, as Lev 21:13 אִשָּׁה בִבְתוּלֶיהָ
Where other pairs of identical or similar letters occur at the beginning of a word in this situation, the initial letter usually has *rafe*, according to the general rule, as
Dt 23:8, 8 לֹא־תְתַעֵב
Gen 25:3 וּבְנֵי דְדָן
However in some combinations, such as בְּמ and כְּג, the first letter is marked with *dagesh* in some MSS where the preceding word ends with a vowel and has a conjunctive accent. For instance in Ez 17:10 bA has הֲלֹא כְגַעַת but bN has כְּגַעַת.

A *begad-kefat* letter at the beginning of a word following

ויהי with a conjunctive accent has *rafe*. However the *Sefer ha-Ḥillufim* notes seven cases where the word following וַיְהִי with a conjunctive accent begins with the preposition --כְּ and bN marks the *kaf* with *dagesh*. In three of these cases, the accent on וַיְהִי is *telisha qeṭannah*, as
Gen 19:17 וַיְהִי֩ כְּהוֹצִיאָם, but in the other cases it has other conjunctives, as Gen 39:15 וַיְהִ֣י כְשָׁמְע֔וֹ
Jos 9:1 וַיְהִ֣י כִשְׁמֹ֡עַ

402. Other Exceptions. Besides the categories noted in #400, 401, there is a small number of exceptional cases in which the general rule is not followed. In some of them similar consonants occur together, so possibly the exception is the result of dissimilation. There is general agreement on seven of these cases, which are listed in most of the sources:-
1, 2, Ex 15:1, 21 גָאֹ֣ה גָּאָ֔ה
3, Ex 15:11 מִ֥י כָּמֹ֖כָה
4, Ex 15:16 יִדְּמ֣וּ כָּאָ֑בֶן
5, Is 54:12 וְשַׂמְתִּ֤י כַּֽדְכֹד֙
6, Jer 20:9 וְנִלְאֵ֥יתִי כַּלְכֵ֖ל
7, Dan 5:11 וְחָכְמָ֥ה כְּחָכְמַת־
Ben Asher alone adds No. 8 זֽוּ־גָּאָ֑לְתָּ (Ex 15:13, for bN the *gimel* is *rafe*); bN alone adds five other cases:
9, 10, Dan 3:2 אֲדַרְגָּזְרַיָּא֩ גְדָבְרַיָּ֨א דְּתָבְרַיָּ֜א and similarly 3:3.
For bN the *gimel* of גְדָבְרַיָּא has *dagesh*, for bA *rafe*, but both agree that the *dalet* of דְּתָבְרַיָּא has *dagesh*, probably on account of the two similar consonants at the beginning of the word.
11, 1K 12:32 הַשְּׁמִינִ֣י בַּחֲמִשָּׁה־ (for bA the *bet* is *rafe*)
12, 13, Dan 3:5, 10 סַבְּכָ֣א פְּסַנְתֵּרִ֔ין (for bA the *pe* is *rafe*).

'Deḥiq' and 'Ate Meraḥiq' - אתי מרחיק, דחיק

403. If a word with a conjunctive accent ends with an open syllable pointed with *qameṣ* or *segol*, and the following word is stressed on its first syllable, (that is, on the first full vowel, whether or not it is preceded by *shewa*), then the first consonant of the second word may take "conjunctive *dagesh*". In the Masorah this phenomenon is called *deḥiq* or *ate meraḥiq*. In some sources these names are used for two different categories of this phenomenon, but it has recently been suggested by Dotan that the phenomenon itself was called *ate meraḥiq*, while the

dagesh used to mark it was called *deḥiq*. Rules governing this phenomenon were formulated by Baer, but the practice of the best Biblical MSS has not yet been studied in detail.

404. (i) Where the first word ends with *segol*. Conjunctive *dagesh* is used (1) when the first word has *maqqef*, as
Gen 43:15 וּמִשְׁנֶה־כֶּסֶף
Prov 24:6 תַּעֲשֶׂה־לְּךָ Gen 48:19 יִהְיֶה־לְּעָם
(for bN there is no *dagesh* in the *lamed*), Prov 26:27 כֹּרֶה־שַּׁחַת
2) Where the first word does not have *maqqef*, but has penultimate stress, either normally, as Gen 33:5 אֵלֶּה לָּךְ or as the result of retraction of the accent, as
Ez 17:8 שָׂדֶה טּוֹב Nu 23:15 אִקָּרֶה כֹּה
Prov 23:31 תֵּרֶא יָּיִן (the only example with a word ending in *alef*), Gen 1:11 עֹשֶׂה פְּרִי
There are a few exceptions to the rule, as Dt 5:3 אֵלֶּה פֹה

405. (ii) Where the first word ends with *qameṣ*. Conjunctive *dagesh* is used (1) where the first word characteristically has penultimate stress, as
Gen 38:29 עָלֶיךָ פָּרֶץ Gen 14:10 הֶרָה נָּסוּ
and with *dagesh* in *resh*, Hab 3:13 מָחַצְתָּ רֹּאשׁ
There are a few exceptions where *dagesh* is not used, as
Rut 1:20 תִּקְרֶאנָה לִי, קְרֶאןָ לִי Ps 119:14 עֵדְוֹתֶיךָ שַׂשְׂתִּי
Conjunctive *dagesh* is also used where the second word has *shewa* before the stressed vowel, as
Gen 12:5 אַרְצָה כְּנַעַן Is 5:14 הִרְחִיבָה שְּׁאוֹל
With an exception in Rut 4:17 וַתִּקְרֶאנָה שְׁמוֹ
However if the second word begins with prefixed --בְּ, --וְ, --כְּ, --לְ, *dagesh* is not used, as
Ex 33:12 יְדַעְתִּיךָ בְשֵׁם Is 42:6 קְרָאתִיךָ בְצֶדֶק
But *dagesh* is used in the word לְּךָ, as
Gen 18:25 חָלִלָה לְּךָ 2S 12:9 לָקַחְתָּ לְּךָ
and *dagesh* is used for phonetic reasons in
Ps 19:3 וְלַיְלָה לְּלַיְלָה
2) Where the first word has penultimate stress only through retraction of the accent, conjunctive *dagesh* is used only where the syllable so stressed could have *gaᶜya* on a long vowel before *shewa*, as Gen 19:38 יָלְדָה בֵּן
Jer 31:25 עָרְבָה לִּי Joel 4:13 מָלְאָה גַּת

There are a few exceptional cases in which *dagesh* is not used,

as Is 59:19 נֹסְסָה בוֹ Ps 84:4 מָצְאָה בַיִת

Prov 30:20 וּמָחֲתָה פִיהָ Job 21:16, 22:18 רָחֲקָה מֶנִּי

Is 40:10 מֹשְׁלָה לוֹ

If the first word could not have ga^{c}ya before *shewa*, conjunctive *dagesh* is not used, as Gen 4:6 חָרָה לָךְ

Nu 9:10 וְעָשָׂה פֶסַח Ps 119:99 שִׂיחָה לִי

Rut 1:21 עָנָה בִי

3) If the first word has *maqqef*, and the final *qameṣ* is preceded by vocal *shewa*, *dagesh* is usually used, as

Gen 27:26 גְּשָׁה־נָּא Rut 4:1 שְׁבָה־פֹּה

1S 28:7 וְאֶדְרְשָׁה־בָּהּ Job 34:4 נִבְחֲרָה־לָּנוּ

2K 25:30 נִתְּנָה־לּוֹ Ps 71:23 אֲזַמְּרָה־לָּךְ

This is also true where the *shewa* follows a long vowel, as

Gen 21:3 יָלְדָה־לּוֹ Gen 30:33 וְעָנְתָה־בִּי

Jer 5:5 אֵלְכָה־לִּי

and with *shewa* after phonetic ga^{c}ya, as

Gen 2:23 לֻקֳחָה־זֹּאת and also Rut 2:7 אֲלַקֳטָה־נָּא

In some exceptional cases, *dagesh* is not used, as

2K 7:1 סְאָה־סֹלֶת Prov 13:12 מַחֲלָה־לֵב

Prov 15:17 וְאַהֲבָה־שָׁם Prov 20:22 אֲשַׁלְּמָה־רָע

Dan 10:17 נִשְׁאֲרָה־בִי Job 5:23 הָשְׁלְמָה־לָךְ

If the *qameṣ* is not preceded by a vocal *shewa*, the *dagesh* is usually not marked, as Dt 11:22 וּלְדָבְקָה־בוֹ

Dt 33:4 צִוָּה־לָנוּ Ps 120:5 אוֹיָה־לִי

Mic 1:11 עֶרְיָה־בֹשֶׁת Gen 33:19 נָטָה־שָׁם

However there are a considerable number of exceptions in which the *dagesh* is used under these conditions, as

Ez 17:7 שִׁלְחָה־לּוֹ 2K 9:2 וּבָאתָ־שָּׁמָּה

Rut 1:10 וַתֹּאמַרְנָה־לָּהּ Gen 24:42 אִם־יֶשְׁךָ־נָּא

This is particularly common where the first word is a verb form in the long form of the imperfect or imperative, as

Job 32:10 שִׁמְעָה־לִּי Gen 27:26 וּשְׁקָה־לִּי

Gen 30:1 הָבָה־לִּי Nu 22:6 אָרָה־לִּי

Nu 22:11 קָבָה־לִּי Nu 22:17 וּלְכָה־נָּא

Is 5:5 אוֹדִיעָה־נָּא Gen 32:30 הַגִּידָה־נָּא

And cf. Ps 116:14, 18 נֶגְדָה־נָּא

In a few exceptional cases, *dagesh* is used even though there is no *maqqef*, as Ps 118:25 הוֹשִׁיעָה נָּא, הַצְלִיחָה נָּא

Where the second word of the pair begins with a *begad kefat* letter, conjunctive *dagesh* is used as on other consonants, so that this *dagesh* (*deḥiq* and *ate meraḥiq*) is regularly listed among the phenomena which nullify the rule that a *begad kefat* letter at the beginning of a word has *rafe* if it follows a word with a conjunctive accent which ends with an open syllable (#400).

406. Some scholars (Yequti'el ha-Naqdan, Heidenheim, Baer) state that conjunctive *dagesh* is used not only where the second word of the pair is stressed on its first syllable, but also where the first syllable of this word has *ga*^{c}*ya* on an open syllable or on a long vowel before *shewa*. In the early MSS, *dagesh* does appear in a few such situations, as

Lev 19:14, 32 וְיָרֵאתָ מֵּאֱלֹהֶיךָ   Ex 27:3 וְעָשִׂיתָ סִּירֹתָיו
Ps 31:20 צָפַנְתָּ לִּירֵאֶיךָ   Jos 8:2 עָשִׂיתָ לִּירִיחוֹ
Also Ex 25:29 וְעָשִׂיתָ קְּעָרֹתָיו

As a general rule, however, the *dagesh* is not used where the first syllable of the word could have *ga*^{c}*ya*, as

Gen 49:31 שָׁמָּה קָבְרוּ   Ex 15:1 אָשִׁירָה לַיהוָה
1S 1:6 וְכִעֲסַתָּה צָרָתָהּ   Ps 99:4 כּוֹנַנְתָּ מֵישָׁרִים

Literature. Baer 1880, Dotan, 1969.

Conjunctive 'Dagesh' in Other Situations

407. If a word with penultimate stress has a conjunctive accent, and ends with an open syllable, conjunctive *dagesh* is sometimes used under other circumstances than those listed above for *deḥiq*. These cases fall into several classes, but there are not many examples in any of them.

(i) After qameṣ. In a few cases, where the first word of the pair ends with *qameṣ*, *dagesh* is used in the first letter of the second word even where its second syllable is stressed. In most cases this first syllable is open, as

1S 1:13 שְׂפָתֶיהָ נָּעוֹת   Song 1:4 אַחֲרֶיךָ נָּרוּצָה
Dt 32:15 עָבִיתָ כָּשִׂיתָ   Dt 32:6 אָבִיךָ קָּנֶךָ
Is 34:14 הִרְגִּיעָה לִּילִית (*dagesh* used for phonetic reasons).

In a few cases the first syllable of the second word is closed, as Ps 77:16 גָּאַלְתָּ בִּזְרוֹעַ   Job 4:2 אֵלֶיךָ תִּלְאֶה

The *dagesh* may even be used when the third syllable of the word is stressed, as Jos 8:28 וַיְשִׂימֶהָ תֵּל־עוֹלָם

408. (ii) <u>After long vowels other than *qameṣ*</u>. Where the first word of the pair ends with a long vowel other than *qameṣ*, conjunctive *dagesh* is sometimes marked when the second word is stressed on its first syllable, as

Ps 20:9 וַאֲנַחְנוּ קַּמְנוּ Ps 118:18 יִסְּרַנִּי יָּהּ
Ps 118:5 קָרָאתִי יָּהּ

This occurs more commonly where the stressed vowel is preceded by *shewa*, as Gen 19:14 קוּמוּ צְּאוּ

Ex 12:15 תַּשְׁבִּיתוּ שְּׂאֹר Lam 3:14 הָיִיתִי שְּׂחֹק

(iii) <u>Other situations</u>. Conjunctive *dagesh* appears in a few cases which do not fit any of the rules given above, as

Jer 48:4 הִשְׁמִיעוּ זְּעָקָה Ps 17:10 חֶלְבָּמוֹ סָּגְרוּ
Ps 58:10 יָבִינוּ סִּירֹתֵיכֶם Gen 19:2 הִנֶּה נָּא־אֲדֹנַי

and the similar case in Jud 6:39.

'Dagesh' after מָה *and* זֶה

409. As a general rule, *dagesh* is used in the first letter of a word following מָה, unless this letter is *yod* pointed with *shewa*, as Jer 5:15 מַה־יְדַבֵּר Nu 9:8 מַה־יְצַוֶּה

Exceptions to this rule are Ps 84:2 מַה־יְּדִידוֹת where *dagesh* is used, and מַה־שְׁתֵּי (Zech 4:12) and מַה־לַתֶּבֶן (Jer 23:28) where *dagesh* is not used.

410. *Dagesh* is used in the first letter of the word following זֶה when the two words are joined by *maqqef*, and (for the most part) where the second word is stressed on its first syllable, as

Gen 31:41 זֶה־לִּי or where the first letter has *shewa*, as 1K 3:23 זֶה־בְּנִי Ex 3:12 וְזֶה־לְּךָ
Ex 3:15 זֶה־שְּׁמִי

Where the second word is not stressed in this way, *dagesh* is used in only two cases:-

Nu 13:27 וְזֶה־פִּרְיָהּ 1C 22:1 וְזֶה־מִּזְבֵּחַ

Elsewhere *dagesh* is not used, as

Jos 15:4 זֶה־יִהְיֶה Ps 56:10 זֶה־יָדַעְתִּי

'Dagesh' used to Divide or Distinguish

411. In the combination מֹשֶׁה לֵּאמֹר, *dagesh* is used in the *lamed* where the word מֹשֶׁה has a conjunctive accent. In some MSS, such as P, *dagesh* is used in the *lamed* of לֵּאמֹר even after a word ending with a closed syllable, as

Jer 1:4 אֵלַי לֵּאמֹר Jer 1:13 שֵׁנִית לֵּאמֹר

This *dagesh* appears to be used to emphasize the division between the two words.

412. In the combination וַיֹּאמְרוּ לֹּא (Gen 19:2, 1S 8:19) *dagesh* also appears to be used to emphasize the division between the words, in contrast to וַיֹּאמְרוּ לוֹ (Jud 18:19, Est 6:13) where the two words are connected and *dagesh* is not used.

In the combination וַיֹּאמֶר לֹא which occurs five times in the Bible, the division between the words (which contrasts with the connection in וַיֹּאמֶר לוֹ) is generally emphasized by the use of *ga^{c}ya* under the *mem*, and *paseq* between the words (#325). The Masorah records that ben Naftali uses *dagesh* in לֹּא in two cases, but in the other three agrees with bA in not using the *dagesh*. It is reported that bN similarly used *dagesh* in the *lamed* of פִּיו לֹּא (1S 16:7). The *dagesh* in all these cases presumably serves to emphasize the division between the words.

In four cases the *lamed* of לֹא in the combination לֹא לוֹ has *dagesh*, as Prov 26:17 רִיב לֹּא־לוֹ Gen 38:9 כִּי לֹּא לוֹ (after a disjunctive). This *dagesh* is presumably intended to distinguish לֹא from לוֹ. In the combination לוֹ לֹא no *dagesh* is used.

413. In cases where one word ends, and the next begins, with the same letter, *dagesh* is not generally used in early Tiberian MSS. However the Masorah records that ben Naftali used *dagesh* in the first letter of נוּן in the combination בִּן־נוּן, while bA did not. In a few MSS, such as L, *dagesh* is sometimes used on the first letter of the second word in combinations like וַיִּתֶּן־לּוֹ (Gen 24:36), where the first word ends with *nun*, and the second begins with *lamed*. So also וַיִּתֶּן־לּוֹ in JTS MS 226 in 1K 11:19. Redaq noted (*Miklol* 72b) on Gen 23:9 וְיִתֶּן־לִּי אֶת־מְעָרַת הַמַּכְפֵּלָה "The *nun* can be assimilated to the *lamed* of לִּי." It appears, then, that this

dagesh also serves to emphasize the division between the two words to avoid the assimilation of the *nun*.

414. In most early MSS, *dagesh* is not used after a guttural pointed with simple *shewa*. The *Sefer ha-Ḥillufim* reports that bN used *dagesh* in the *qof* יַעְקֹּב (Jer 9:3, *dagesh* is used here in C and L[15]). Some MSS occasionally show *dagesh* in this situation, as S, Gen 41:45 פַּעְנֵּחַ; N, Hos 10:2 יֶאְשָּׁמוּ; N, Ez 4:15 לַחְמְּךָ.
(Note the use of the term *dagesh* in #132 under דגש (3).)

(It is noteworthy that the *dagesh* sign is used quite commonly in some Palestinian MSS in the situations discussed in #413 and 414. See Revell, 1970, p. 77.)

The Value of Conjunctive 'Dagesh' and its Function

415. The function of *dagesh* in the uses discussed in #403 ff. seems to be indicated by the fact that these uses occur in situations similar to those in which *gaᶜya* and *paseq* may be used. These two signs indicate that words are separated and the reading slowed down. Thus both *dagesh* and *gaᶜya* may be used in the combination וַיֹּאמֶר לֹּא (#325). The use of *dagesh* in בִּן־נּוּן can be compared to the use of *paseq* after a word which ends with the letter with which the next begins. (#284). Certain forms of conjunctive *dagesh*, such as עָלֶיךָ פֶּרֶץ (#405) can be compared to the use of *gaᶜya* in an open syllable after the accent (#332), as 2K 1:13 עֲבָדֶיךָ אֵלֶּה--compare also the use of *mayela* (#216) in 2K 9:2 וּבָאתָ־שָּׁמָּה (where conjunctive *dagesh* is used) to the use of *gaᶜya* in L[18], Ez 11:18 וּבָאוּ־שָׁמָּה (where *gaᶜya* is used).

This comparison suggests that the *dagesh* is used, like *gaᶜya* and *paseq*, to mark separation. In cases where the need to emphasize separation became apparent, the Masoretes sometimes used *paseq* for this purpose, sometimes *dagesh*, and sometimes *gaᶜya* (particularly before gutturals). It can, then, be assumed that *dagesh* is intended to emphasize separation not only in cases like וַיֹּאמֶר לֹּא, but also where conjunctive *dagesh* is used after *qameṣ*, and possibly also after *segol*.

416. The value of conjunctive *dagesh* is uncertain. Is it simply a diacritic, or does it indicate some particular

pronunciation? *Dagesh* generally has the latter function, indicating that the *begad-kefat* letters represent stops, or that a consonant should be doubled, so it would seem likely that *dagesh* would have some phonetic value in the other cases of its use as well. Consequently, since conjunctive *dagesh* is not used only in *begad-kefat* letters, it can be argued that it represents "strong" *dagesh*, indicating the doubling of the consonant.

This is easy to see in cases where the *dagesh* is used after a short vowel, *pataḥ* or *segol*, as with מַה and זֶה, with conjunctive *dagesh* after *segol* as Ps 91:11 יְצַוֶּה־לָּךְ or even Ex 21:31 יֵעָשֶׂה לּוֹ. There is no problem in understanding *dagesh* here as indicating doubling: *maz-zɛh, yəṣawwɛl-lɔk.*

In some other cases, however, this view seems less acceptable. In וַיֹּאמֶר׀ לֹּא (Jos 5:14, where bN uses *dagesh*) the *dagesh* in the *lamed* cannot mark the preceding syllable as closed, since that syllable ends with *resh*, and the word has a disjunctive accent (*legarmeh*, see #278). The situation is similar in Hab 1:6 מִשְׁכָּנוֹת לֹּא־לוֹ for here the *dagesh* also stands in a letter following a word ending in a consonant. In the same way it is difficult to believe that conjunctive *dagesh* after a long vowel marks that the preceding syllable is closed, as

Gen 24:47	*yɔldɔl-ló*	יָלְדָה־לּוֹ
Ex 12:31	*qúmuṣ-ṣŭ'ú*	קוּמוּ צְּאוּ

A closed syllable with a long vowel normally only occurs as a word final stressed syllable.

Thus if it is assumed that the *dagesh* indicates the doubling of the consonant in these cases also, it seems necessary to suggest that it was not such that the doubling consonant closed one syllable and opened the next, as in קִטֵּל *qiṭ-ṭel*, but that the doubled consonant stood at the beginning of a syllable, as *wayyómɛr lló, yɔldɔ-lló, qúmu ṣṣŭ'ú,* etc. In this situation, presumably, the long vowel of the preceding syllable need not be shortened.

LIST OF WORKS CITED

The works cited in the text are listed in two sections. More recent works, cited in the text by the name of the author and the date of publication, are listed in the first section. Earlier works, cited in the text by the name of the author and the name of the work, or by the name of the work alone, are listed in the second section. The names of these earlier authors are given in the anglicized form used in the text, but, as this may differ from the form of the name used in Library catalogues and other works, a fuller Hebrew form is given to assist identification. Important works often appeared in many editions. As a rule only one (usually the first) is listed, but recent reprints are noted where known.

1. Recent Studies.

Ackermann, A.

1893 *Das hermeneutische Element der biblischen Accentuation*, Berlin.

Adler, E. N.

1897 גנזי מצרים - הלכות ספר תורה
An Eleventh Century Introduction to the Hebrew Bible, Oxford.

Albrecht, K.

1921 "Die sogennanten Sonderbarkeiten des masoretischen Textes", *Zeitschrift für die alttestamentliche Wissenschaft* 39 (1921), 160-169.

Allony, N. אלוני, נ.

1964 רשימת מונחים קראית מהמאה השמינית
כתבי החברה לחקר המקרא בישראל לזכר ד"ר י. פ.
קורנגרין ז"ל Tel Aviv, pp. 324-363.

Baer, S. I.

1852 *Torat Emet*, Rödelheim. See #186. תורת אמת
Tiqqun ha-Sofer weha-Qore, תקון הסופר והקורא
In an edition of the Torah, Rödelheim.

1880 *De primarum vocabulorum literarum dagessatione*, in S. Baer and F. Delitzsch, *Liber Proverbiorum* Lipsiae, 1880, pp. vii-xv. Translated as "The Dāghēsh in Initial Letters" in *Hebraica I* (1884-5), 142-152.

1896 "Die Metheg-Setzung", in *Archiv für wissenschaftliche Erforschung des A. T., Halle*, 1896, 55-67, 194-207.

Baer, S. and Delitzsch, F.

1869-1895 Edition of the Bible, (No general title, separate books titled in Latin), Lipsiae.

Baer, S. and Strack, H.

1879 *Die Dikduke ha-T^{e}amim des Ahron ben Moscheh ben Ascher*, Leipzig. Jerusalem^{2}, 1970.

Beit Arié, M.

1976 *Hebrew Codicology*, Paris.

Ben-David, A. בן-דוד, א.

1957 על מה נחלקו בן-אשר ובן-נפתלי
תרביץ *Tarbiz* 26 (1957), 384-409.

Ben-Ḥayyim, Z. בן-חיים, ז.

1957 מסורה ומסורת (בחינה משמעותית)
לשוננו *Leshonenu* 21 (1957), 283-292.

Ben-Ze'ev 1876 See under Ben-Ze'ev, Y. L. in section 2.

Ben-Yashar, M. בן-ישר, מ.

1976 חלוקת הסדרים בספרי הנ"ך
The Division into 'Sedarim' in the Prophets and Writings. Dissertation, Bar-Ilan, Ramat Gan.

Ben-Zvi, I.

1960 "The Codex of Ben Asher" *Textus I* (1960), 1-16.

Bergsträsser, G.

1918 *Hebräische Grammatik*, Leipzig. (Hildesheim^{2}, 1962).

Berliner, A.

1877 *Die Massorah zum Targum Onqelos*, Leipzig.

Birnbaum, S. A.

1971 *The Hebrew Scripts*, London (1954-1971).

Blau, L.

1902 *Studien zum althebräischen Buchwesen*, Strassburg.

Breuer, M. ברויאר, מ.

1957 Jerusalem פיסוק טעמים שבמקרא

1976 כתר ארם צובה והנוסח המקובל של המקרא *The Aleppo Codex and the Accepted Text of the Bible*, Jerusalem.

Butin, R.

1906 *The Ten Nequdot of the Torah*, Baltimore. (New York[2], 1969, with prolegomenon by S. Talmon).

Dérenbourg, J.

1870 "Manuel du lecteur d'un auteur inconnu" in *Journal Asiatique*, 6ème série, Tome xvi (1870), 309-550. Also issued separately with a title-page dated "Paris, 1871", and pagination in ink (p.1 = p.309 of the original).

Díaz Esteban, F.

1975 *Sefer Oklah we-Oklah*, Madrid.

Díez-Merino, L.

1975 *La biblia babilónica*, Madrid.

Dotan, A. See also Ginsburg 1880, Wickes 1881. דותן, א.

1967 ספר דקדוקי הטעמים לר' אהרן בן משה בן אשר Jerusalem.

1969 לבעיית דחיק ואתי מרחיק *Fourth World Congress of Jewish Studies, Papers* vol. II, Jerusalem, p.101-105, English summary, "The Problem of *deḥiq* and *atê mérahiq*", p.186.

1971 'סובאים' - עיונים בדרכי עבודתם של נקדני טבריה in המקרא ותולדות ישראל *Studies in Bible and Jewish History Dedicated to the Memory of Jacob Liver*, ed. B. Uffenheimer, Tel Aviv, pp.241-247.

1973a תורה נביאים וכתובים Bible edition (see #26), Tel Aviv.

(Dotan) 1974 Article "Masorah" in *Encyclopaedia Judaica* ed. 3, vol. 16, cols 1401-1482, Jerusalem.

1977 אוצר המסורה הטברנית
Thesaurus of the Tiberian Masorah, Tel Aviv.

Eldar, A. אלדר, א.

1976 שער נוח התיבות מתוך 'עין הקורא'
Leshonenu 40 (1976), 190-210; 41 (1977), לשוננו 205-215.

Faur, J. פאעור, י.

1967 רשימת מהאותיות הגדולות והקטנות שבמקרא מהגניזה הקאהירית
Proceedings of the American Academy for Jewish Research, 35 (1967) א-י.

Fitzmyer, J. A.

1975 *The Dead Sea Scrolls: Major Publications and Tools for Study*, Missoula. (Missoula[2] 1977).

Freedman, D. B. and Cohen, M. B.

1974 "The Masoretes as Exegetes: Selected Examples", *Masoretic Studies* I (1974) 35-46.

Frensdorff, S.

1864 *Ochlah W'ochlah*, Hannover. New York[2], 1972 .

1876 *Die Massora Magna*, Leipzig. New York[2], 1968, with prolegomenon by G. E. Weil .

Ginsburg, C. D.

1867 *The Massoreth ha-Massoreth of Elias Levita*, London. New York[2], 1968, with prolegomenon by N. H. Snaith .

1867a *Jacob ben Chajim ibn Adonijah's Introduction to the Rabbinic Bible*, London[2]. New York[3], 1968, with prolegomenon by N. H. Snaith .

1880 *The Massorah Compiled from Manuscripts*, London, 1880-1905. New York[2], 1968, with prolegomenon by A. Dotan .

1897 *Introduction to the Massoretico-Critical Edition of the Hebrew Bible*, London. New York[2] 1966, with prolegomenon by H. M. Orlinsky .

1897a *A Series of 15 Facsimiles of MSS of the Hebrew Bible*, London.

1899 "On the Relationship of the so-called Codex Babylonicus of A. D. 916 to the Eastern

(Ginsburg) Recension of the Hebrew Text" in *Receuil des travaux D. Chwolson*, Berlin, p. 149-188.

1908, 1926 Editions of the Hebrew Bible, London. The 1908 edition has no general title. The 1926 edition has the title in English *The Old Testament...with the Various Readings from MSS...*, and in Hebrew תורה נביאים וכתובים

Goldberg, D.

1866 *Sefer Taggin*, Paris. ספר תגין

1875 Frankfurt am Main. (ספר ה)זכרונות מכול מלות

Goldschmidt, L.

1950 *The Earliest Editions of the Hebrew Bible*, New York.

Gordis, R.

1937 *The Biblical Text in the Making*, Philadelphia. New York[2], 1971 .

Goshen-Gottstein, M. H.

1960 "The Authenticity of the Aleppo Codex", *Textus* I, 17-58.

1962 "Biblical Manuscripts in the United States" *Textus* 2, 28-59.

1963 "The Rise of the Tiberian Bible Text" in *Biblical and Other Studies*, ed. A. Altmann, Cambridge, Mass., 1963, pp. 79-122.

1972 מקראות גדולות
Biblia Rabbinica - a Reprint of the 1525 Venice Edition, Jerusalem. (Facsimile of V).

1975 *The Book of Isaiah*, parts 1 and 2, Jerusalem. (The Hebrew University Bible).

1976 כתר ארם צובא
The Aleppo Codex, Jerusalem. (Facsimile of A).

Gottheil, R.

1905 "Some Hebrew Manuscripts in Cairo", *Jewish Quarterly Review* 17 (1905), 609-655.

Greenspan, J. גרינשפן, י.

1961 בעיית נוסח בן אשר לאור תורת המתג
Sinai 49 (1961), 48-59. סיני

Gumpertz, F. גומפרץ, י. ג.

1958 שער המתיגות לר' יקותיאל הכהן בר יהודה
Leshonenu 22 (1958), 36-47, 137-146. לשוננו

Habermann, A. M. הברמן, א. מ.

1957 Article "Bible and Concordance" in *Thesaurus of the Language of the Bible* ed. S. E. Loewenstamm and J. Blau, Jerusalem, pp. xix-xxxviii.
המקרא והקונקורדנציה, באוצר לשון המקרא
כרך א' דף ג-מו

Hanau 1718 See under Hanau, Z. in section 2.

Harkavy, H. and Strack, H. L.

1875 *Catalog der hebräischen Bibelhandschriften der Kaiserlichen öffentlichen Bibliothek in St. Petersburg*, Petersburg - Leipzig.

Hartom, A. S.

1952 כללי המתג בכתב-היד של משה בן-אשר
Proceedings of the World Congress for Jewish Studies (1947), Jerusalem, pp. 190-194.

Heidenheim 1808, 1818, see under Heidenheim, W. in section 2.

Higger, M.

1936 מסכת סופרים ונלוו עליה מדרש מסכת סופרים ב
New York. Jerusalem^{2}, 1970 .

Höeg, C.

1935 *La notation ekphonētique*, Copenhagen.

Hyvernat, H.

1902 "Petite introduction à l'étude de la Massore" *Revue Biblique* 11 (1902), 551-563; 12 (1903), 529-542; 13 (1904), 521-546; 14 (1905), 203-234, 515-542. Divided into a preliminary chapter (1902), and "La langue et le langage de la Massore", A. Terminologie grammaticale (1903), B. Lexique massorétique (1904-1905).

Japhet, I. M.

1896 *Die Accente der heiligen Schrift*, מורה הקורא
Frankfurt.

Jellinek, A.

1876 *Jedidjah Salomo Norzi's Einleitung, Titelblatt, und Schlusswort zu seinem masoretischen Bibel-commentar*, Wien.

Joel, I.

1963 יכתרי משנת ה׳ אלפים ועשרים לבה"ע
"A Bible Manuscript Written in 1260"
Kirjath Sefer 38, 122-132. קרית ספר

Kahle, P. E.

1927 *Masoreten des Westens I*, Stuttgart.

1930 *Masoreten des Westens II*, Stuttgart.

1959 *The Cairo Geniza*, Oxford[2].

1961 *Der hebräische Bibeltext seit Franz Delitzsch*, Stuttgart.

Kennicott, B.

1776 *Vetus Testamentum hebraicum cum variis lectionibus*, Oxford, 1776-1780 (see #56).

Landauer, S.

1896 *Die Mâsôrâh zum Onkelos*, Amsterdam.
Jerusalem[2], 1970.

Levin, B. M. לוין ב. מ.

1911 מחכנת המסורה ומסורת רנב"י
Taḥkemoni 2 (1911), 19-30. תחכמני (מאסף)

Levy, K.

1936 *Zur masoretischen Grammatik*, Bonner Orientalistische Studien 15, Stuttgart.

Liebermann, S.

1962 *Hellenism in Jewish Palestine*, New York[2].

Lipschuetz, L.

1962 כתאב אלכ̇לף אלד̇י בין אלמעלמין בן אשר ובן נפתלי
"Mishael ben Uzziel's Treatise on the Differences between Ben Asher and Ben Naphtali" (The Arabic text of the *Sefer ha-Ḥillufim*)
Textus 2 (1962), א-נח.

1964 "Kitāb al-Khilaf, the Book of the Ḥillufim" (Introduction to Lipschuetz, 1962) *Textus 4* (1964), 1-29.

1965 Jerusalem. ספר החילופים - כתאב אלכ̇לף

Loewinger, D. S.

1960 "The Aleppo Codex and the Ben Asher Tradition"
Textus 1 (1960), 59-111.

1970 תורה נביאים וכתובים כתב יד לנינגרד B19[A]
Codex Leningrad B19[A] (Facsimile of L), Jerusalem.

(Loewinger)

1971 תורה נביאים וכתובים כתב יד קאהיר
Codex Cairo of the Bible (Facsimile of C), Jerusalem.

McKane, W.

1974 "Observations on the *Tiḳḳûnê Sôpᵉrîm*", in *On Language, Culture, and Religion: In Honour of Eugene A. Nida*, The Hague, 1974, pp.53-77.

Medan, M.

1968 Article טעמים
in אנציקלופדיה מקראית ג'
pp.394-406.

Melammed, E. Z. מלמד, ע. צ.

1970 טעמי המקרא בדברי פרשני המקרא
מחקרי המרכז לחקר הפולקלור Vol. 1, 1970, 195-199.

Morag, S. מורג, ש.

1963 העברית שבפי יהודי תימן Jerusalem.

Müller, J.

1878 מסכת סופרים *Massechet Soferim, der talmudische Tractat der Schrieber*, Leipzig.

Ne'eman, J. L. נאמן, י. ל.

1956 צלילי המקרא - יסודות המוסיקה של הטעמים
vol. 1, Tel Aviv, 1956, vol. 2, Jerusalem, 1971.

Neubauer, A.

1891 *Petite grammaire hébraique provenant du Yemen.* Leipzig.

Nutt, J. W.

1870 1870 *Two Treatises...by R. Jehuda Ḥayuġ of Fez*, London. Jerusalem[2] 1968.

Orlinsky, H. M. See also Ginsburg 1880.

1940 "Problems of Kethib-Qere", *Journal of the American Oriental Society* 60 (1940), 30-45.

1960 "The Origin of the Kethib-Qere System: a New Approach", in *Supplements to Vetus Testamentum* VII pp.184-192.

Perlman, M. פרלמן, מ.

1959 דפים ללימוד טעמי המקרא א-ז
Pages for the Study of the Biblical Accents I-VII, Jerusalem, 1959-1972.

Pérez-Castro, F.

1955 "Corregido y correcto", *Sefarad* 15 (1955), 3-30.

Pérez-Castro, F. and Azcárraga, M. J.

1968 "The Edition of the Kitāb al-Khilaf of Mišael Ben ᶜUzziel" in *In Memoriam Paul Kahle*, Berlin, pp.188-200.

Perrot, C.

1969 "*Petuḥot* et *Setumot*, Etude sur les alinéas du Pentateuque", *Revue Biblique* 76 (1969), 50-91.

Praetorius, F.

1897 *Über den rückweichenden Accent im Hebräischen*, Halle a/S.

1901 *Über die Herkunft der hebräischen Accente*. Berlin.

Qalman, J. יוסף קלמן בן שלמה (מקרלין)

1862, 1889, Warsaw. מבוא המסורה

1870 Wilna. שער המסורה

Rabin, C.

1968 Article מקרא: דפוסי המקרא
in אנציקלופדיה מקראית ה'
pp. 368-386.

Reach, J.

1895 *Die Sebirin der Masoreten von Tiberias*, Breslau.

Revell, E. J.

1970 *Hebrew Texts with Palestinian Vocalization*, Toronto.

1971 "The Oldest Evidence for the Hebrew Accent System" *Bulletin of the John Rylands Library* 54 (1971), 214-222.

1977 *Biblical Texts with Palestinian Pointing and their Accents*, Missoula.

1979 "Pausal Forms in Biblical Hebrew" to appear in *Journal of Semitic Studies* 25 (1980) or 26 (1981).

Rosenfeld, S. רוזנפלד, שמואל בן בנימן וולף

1883 Wilna. ספר משפחת סופרים

de Rossi, G. B.

1784 *Variae lectiones Veteris Testamenti*, Parma, 1784-1788 (see #56). Amsterdam², 1969-1970.

Segal, J.B.
1953 *The Diacritical Point and the Accents in Syriac*, Oxford.

Segal, M.Z. סגל, מ. צ.
1960 vol. IV, pp.5-46, Jerusalem. מבוא המקרא

Shereshevsky, E.
1972 "The Accents in Rashi's Commentary", *Jewish Quarterly Review* 62 (1971-72), 277-287.

Snaith, N.H. See Ginsburg 1867.

Spanier, A.
1927 *Die masoretischen Akzente*, Berlin.

Sperber, A.
1942 "Problems of the Masora", *Hebrew Union College Annual* 17 (1942-43), 293-394.

Talmon, S. see Butin 1906.

Weil, G.E. see also Frensdorff 1876.
1963 *Elie Lévita, humaniste et massorète*, Leiden.
1971 *Massorah Gedolah iuxta codicem Leningradensem B19a*, Rome.

Wickes, W.
1881 *A Treatise on the Accentuation of the Three so-called Poetical Books of the Old Testament* Oxford. New York[2], 1970 with prolegomenon by A. Dotan .
1887 *A Treatise on the Accentuation of the Twenty-One so-called Prose Books of the Old Testament*, Oxford. New York[2], 1970 with prolegomenon by A. Dotan .

Wijnkoop, I.J.
1881 *Darche Hannesigah* דרכי הנסיגה *sive leges de accentus hebraicae linguae ascensione*, Lugduni Batavorum.

Worms, A.A. ווירמש, אשר אנשיל
1892 Frankfurt am Main. סייג לתורה

Yalon, E. ילון, ח.
1971 Jerusalem. פרקי לשון

Yeivin, I.
1968 Jerusalem כתר ארם-צובה: ניקודו וטעמיו
1968a הניקוד הבבלי ומסורת-הלשון המשתקפת ממנו Jerusalem.

(Yeivin) 1968b Article מקרא: כתבי-יד של המקרא
in אנציקלופדיה מקראית ה'
pp. 418-437.

1968c Article מסורה
in אנציקלופדיה מקראית ה'
pp. 130-159.

1973 מסורת הלשון העברית המשתקפת בניקוד הבבלי
Jerusalem (Akademon).

2. Earlier Scholars and Sources.

Angel, M. אנג'יל, מ.

Mantua, 1622. ספר מסורת הברית הגדול

Archevolti, Shemu'el ארקיוולטי, שמואל בן אלחנן יעקב

Arugat ha-Bosem, Venice, 1602-6. ערוגת הבשם בדקדוק

Avot de-Rabbi Nathan אבות דר' נתן

Edition: מסכת אבות דר' נתן, בשתי נוסחאות

S. Schechter, New York, 1945.

Translation: see Talmud Babli, "Minor Tractates".

Ba^{c}al ha-Ṭurim בעל הטורים

A commentary which includes *Midrash ha-Masorah*, (see #168). Edition: see under Jacob ben R. Asher.

di Balmes, Abram אברהם בן מאיר די בלמש

Miqneh Abram, Venice, 1523. מקנה אברהם

Bemidbar Rabba - see *Midrash Rabba*

Ben-Ze'ev, Y. L. בן-זאב, י. ל.

ספר תלמוד לשון עברי

Various editions from 1796 to 1912. See #185.

Bereshit Rabba - see *Midrash Rabba*

Buxtorf, J. (pater)

Tiberias, Basle ^{1}1620, ^{2}1665. See #170.

Diqduqe ha-Ṭe^{c}amim - see #175. דקדוקי הטעמים

Editions, see Baer-Strack 1879, Dotan 1967.

Eliahu ha-Levi (Elias Levita) אליהו בחור בן אשר הלוי אשכנזי

Masoret ha-Masoret, Venice, 1538. מסורת המסורת

See #169. Edition: see Ginsburg 1867.

Sefer ha-Zikronot ספר הזכרונות מכל מלות...

Edition: D. Goldberg, Frankfurt, 1875.

Ṭuv Ṭa^{c}am, Venice, 1538. See #183. ספר טוב טעם

Ga'on (plural, *ge'onim*) גאון, גאונים

The title of the leader of the Babylonian Jewish community over the period 600-1040, which is sometimes times referred to as the period of the *ge'onim*.

Hanau, Z. ר' זלמן הענא

Sha^c are Zimrah, Hamburg, 1718. See #184. שערי זמרה

Heidenheim, W. היידנהים וולף

^c Eyn ha-Qore, Rödelheim, 1818-21. See #166 עין הקורא

^c Eyn ha-Sofer, Rödelheim, 1818-21. See #166 עין הסופר

Me'or ^c Eynayim, Rödelheim, 1818-21. מאור עינים

Mishpeṭe ha-Ṭe^c amim, ספר משפטי הטעמים

Rödelheim, 1808. New York², 1949. See #186.

Hidāyat al-Qāri - see #175, 182. הדאית אל-קאר

Hilkot Sefer Torah הלכות ספר תורה

See #74, and under Maimonides below.

Horayat ha-Qore - see #175, 182. הורית הקורא

This title is usually used for Hebrew translations of the *Hidāyat al-Qāri*, or works based on it, but here it indicates the separate issue of Dérenbourg 1870, which is usually referred to as the *Manuel du lecteur* or *Maḥberet ha-Tījān*.

Ibn Ezra אברהם אבן עזרא

A twelfth century grammarian and commentator.

Ibn Janāḥ יונה אבן ג'נאח

An eleventh century grammarian, author of

Sefer ha-Shorashim (a dictionary) ספר השורשים

Sefer ha-Riqmah (a grammar) ספר הרקמה

Jacob ben R. Asher ר' יעקוב בן ר' אשר

פירוש בעל הטורים על התורה

Edition: J. Q. Reinitz, Bene Beraq, 1971.

Jacob ben Ḥayyim יעקב בן חיים אבן אדוניה

Editor of the Venice 1524-5 edition of the Bible (V, see #60). For a facsimile of V, see Goshen-Gottstein 1972; for an edition of Jacob ben Ḥayyim's introduction, see Ginsburg 1867a.

Joseph ha-Kohen יוסף בן שניאור הכוהן

Minḥat Kohen, Qoro Gishmi, 1598. ספר מנחת כהן

Joseph ha-Qosṭandini יוסף הקוסטנדיני

^{c}Adat Devorim - see #175 . עדת דבורים

Judah ben Bal^{c}am יהודה אבן בלעם

Sefer Ṭa^{c}ame ha-Miqra, Paris, 1565. ספר טעמי המקרא

See #182.

Kitāb al-Khilaf - see #155-156. כתאב אל-כ̇לף

A treatise by Misha'el ben ^{c}Uzzi'el on the variants between ben Asher and ben Naftali and other scholars.

Edition: see Lipschuetz 1962, 1964, 1965.

Maḥberet ha-Tījān - see *Horayat ha-Qore*. מחברת התיג̇אן

Maimonides (Mosheh ben Maimon) משה בן מימון

A renowned twelfth century scholar, author of *Mishneh Torah*, a compendium of Jewish law arranged in 14 parts (from which it is known as יד החזקה, יד = 14). The second of these parts includes the *Hilkot Sefer Torah*, the laws concerning Torah Scrolls.

Manuel du Lecteur - see *Horayat ha-Qore*, and Dérenbourg 1870.

Masseket Sefer Torah - see #150 מסכת ספר תורה

Masseket Soferim - see #150 מסכת סופרים

Editions: see Müller 1878, Higger 1936.

Translation: see Talmud Babli "Minor Tractates".

Me'ir ha-Levi Abulafia מאיר בן טודרוס הלוי אבולעפיה

Masoret Siyag la-Torah - see #160 מסרת סיג לתורה

Venice, 1750, and later editions. Jerusalem, 1968.

Mekilta מכילתא דרבי ישמעאל

A midrash on Exodus.

Edition: H. S. Horovitz - I. A. Rabin, Frankfurt, 1931.

Mekilta de-R. Shim^{c}on ben Yoḥay מכילתא דרבי שמעון בן יוחי

A midrash on Exodus.

Edition: J.N. Epstein - E.Z. Melammed, Jerusalem 1955

Menaḥem di Lonzano מנחם בן יהודה די לונזאנו

Or Torah - see #162 אור תורה

First printed in his book *Shete Yadot*, Venice, 1618.

Menaḥem ha-Me'iri מנחם בן שלמה המאירי

Qiryat Sefer - see #161 ספר קרית ספר

Izmir, 1863-1881. Jerusalem^{2} 1969.

Midrash Ḥaserot wi-Yeterot - see #168 מדרש חסרות ויתרות

Edition: A. J. Wertheimer, Jerusalem, 1970.

Midrash Rabba

A Midrash on the Torah. The individual Books are referred to under their Hebrew titles:

Bereshit Rabba בראשית רבה

Shemot Rabba שמות רבה

Wayyiqra Rabba ויקרא רבה

Bemidbar Rabba במדבר רבה

Devarim Rabba דברים רבה

Many editions have been published. The best translation is *Midrash Rabbah translated into English* ...under the editorship of H. Freedman and M. Simon, Soncino Press, London, 1939.

Misha'el ben ᶜUzzi'el מישאל בן עוזיאל

Author of the *Kitāb al-Khilaf*, the best available list of *ḥillufim* between ben Asher and ben Naftali. (See #155)

Mishnah משנה

A collection of legal material which reached its received form about 200 CE. Divided into six *sedarim* ("Orders"), each of which contains a number of *massektot* ("Tractates"). The text is quoted by tractate, chapter, and paragraph, as Mishnah *Berakot* 2:3. Many editions have been published. The best translation is that of H. Danby, *The Mishnah*, London, 1933.

Mishneh Torah - see Maimonides.

Mosheh ha-Naqdan ר' משה הנקדן

Darke ha-Niqqud weha-Neginot דרכי הנקוד והנגינות

Edition: S. Loewinger, Budapest 1929.

Okhlah we-Okhlah - see #143-145. אכלה ואכלה

Editions: see Frensdorff, 1864, Díaz-Esteban, 1975.

Qimḥi, David ר' דויד קמחי

A thirteenth century grammarian and commentator. Author of a grammatical compendium containing a dictionary (ספר השורשים) and a grammar (ספר הדקדוק). *Miklol* (מכלול) originally the title of the whole work is now applied to the grammar alone. Also wrote *ᶜEṭ Sofer* (Lyck, 1864) - see #182 עט סופר

Quntrese ha-Masorah - see #175 קונטרסי המסורה

(Quntrese ha-Masorah) A source of the *Diqduqe ha-Ṭe^camim.*

Rashbam רשב"ם - ר' שמואל בן ר' מאיר

A twelfth century commentator.

Rashi רש"י - ר' שלמה יצחקי

An eleventh century commentator. Possibly the most famous of all.

Redaq - see Qimḥi, David. רד"ק - ר' דויד קמחי

Sefer ha-Ḥillufim - see #155 ספר החלופים

The Hebrew name of the *Kitāb al-Khilaf*, which lists the variants between ben Asher and ben Naftali.

Sefer Ṭa^came ha-Miqra - see Judah ben Bal^cam ספר טעמי המקרא

Sefer Taggin - see # 70. Edition: Goldberg 1866. ספר תגין

Shelomo Dubno שלמה בן יואל מדובנא

Tiqqun Soferim - see #165 תקון סופרים

Printed in a Bible edition, Fyorda 1803, and others.

Shelomo Yedidyah Norzi ידידיה שלמה רפאל בן אברהם מנורצי

Ma'amar ha-Ma'arik מאמר המאריך

Printed at the end of the Bible edition Mantua 1744.

Minḥat Shay - see #163 מנחת שי

Printed in Bibles, as the edition Mantua 1742-44, or as an independent work, Vienna 1813-15. See also Jellinek 1876.

Shemot Rabba - see *Midrash Rabba*

Sifra ספרא

A Halakic midrash on Leviticus, also called *Torat Kohanim*. Edition: L. Finkelstein, *Torat Kohanim* New York, 1956.

Sifre ספרי

A Halakic midrash on Numbers and Deuteronomy. Edition H. S. Horovitz, Lipsiae 1917 (Numbers), Berlin 1940 (Deuteronomy). New York^2, 1969.

Sifre Zuṭa ספרי זוטא

A small halakic midrash on Numbers. Edition: H. S. Horovitz, Lipsiae, 1917.

Talmud תלמוד

A collection of legal material based on the Mishna, and divided into the same orders and tractates. This material was collected, in the two scholarly centres, in slightly different forms, known as the *Talmud*

(Talmud) *Yerushalmi* (TY), from Eretz Israel, completed about 500, and the *Talmud Babli* (TB), from Babylonia, completed about 600, although additional material, known as the "Minor Tractates" was added later.

Talmud Babli (TB) תלמוד בבלי

Many editions have been published. The best translation is *The Babylonian Talmud*, ed. E. Epstein, Soncino Press, London 1935-52. The same press has issued a translation of *The Minor Tractates of the Talmud*, ed. A. Cohen, London, 1965.

The Babylonian Talmud is quoted by tractate and folio of the standard edition. The pages are identified as "a" (recto of the folio) or "b" (verso), as TB *Berakot* 21a.

Talmud Yerushalmi (TY) תלמוד ירושלמי

Editions: see *Encyclopaedia Judaica*.

Translation: M. Schwab, Paris, 1878-1890 (in French).

The Talmud Yerushalmi is quoted by tractate, chapter, and paragraph; generally the folio number of the Venice edition is added, with "a" or "b" (first or second column on recto), or "c" or "d" (first or second column on verso), as TY *Berakot* 3:6, fol. 6c.

Tanchuma תנחומא

A midrash on the Pentateuch, composed in the seventh or eighth century. Many editions.

Targum תרגום

The word means translation. It usually refers to an Aramaic translation of the Bible read after the Biblical passages in the Synagogue Service. The standard targum to the Pentateuch is known as Targum Onqelos, that to the Prophets as Targum Jonathan ben ^{c}Uzzi'el. Targums to the Pentateuch are known in several other forms: Targum Pseudo-Jonathan and Targum Neofiti complete, others fragmentary. These are given the general title "Palestinian" on a linguistic basis, as are a few fragments of other tarrums to the Prophets.

Token Ezra תוכן עזרא

A Hebrew adaptation of the *Hidāyat al-Qāri*.

Treatise on the *Shewa* מאמר השוא

An early masoretico-grammatical treatise which discusses the pronunciation of the *shewa* in great detail. Published (with a translation) in Levy 1936.

Viterbi, David ויטרבי, דוד

Em la-Masoret, Mantua, 1748. See #167 אם למסרת

Wayyiqra Rabba - see *Midrash Rabba*

Yaḥya Ṣāliḥ יחיא צאלח

Ḥeleq ha-Diqduq - see #164 ספר חלק הדקדוק

Printed in Ginsburg, 1880, vol. III, pp. 53-105.

Yequti'el ha-Naqdan יקותיאל בן יהודה הכהן הנקדן

ᶜEyn ha-Qore - see #159 עין הקורא

Editions: see under Heidenheim, W., also Gumpertz 1958, Eldar 1976.

INDEX

Reference is to paragraph numbers, save for references to the introduction, indicated by p(age). A line under one of several reference numbers indicates the main description of the subject. A hyphen between reference numbers indicates consecutive paragraphs dealing with the subject listed, but in most cases only the first paragraph of such a series is noted.

The listing of main entries is alphabetic, with *alef* and *ᶜayin* ignored in Hebrew words. The listing of sub-entries is alphabetic or topical.